PENGUIN BOOKS

The Irving Judgment

'History has had its day in court, and scored a crushing victory against Mr Irving's ideologically motivated abuse of the intellectual discipline of which he is a master. The case has indeed been a victory for free speech, and truth as well' *The Times*

'Mr Justice Gray put his finger on the essence – which is that all of Irving's arguments were designed to portray Hitler "in an unwarrantedly favourable light"' John Lukacs, *Newsweek*

'Much more than the fate of David Irving was decided yesterday. The High Court also drove a stake through the heart of "revisionism" – the right-wing credo which says the Jews have mounted a con-trick on the rest of humanity by inventing a tragedy. Gray has nailed that lie' Jonathan Freedland, *Guardian*

'Not since Oscar Wilde brought his case against the Marquess of Queensberry for calling him a "somdomite" (sic) has a libel action in this country so demolished its claimant' James Buchan, *New Statesman*

'His defeat in the High Court amounted to much more than a successful defence of academia against those who would corrupt it. It was a victory for a truth which must never be forgotten and a devastating blow against those who seek to employ that notorious fascist weapon, the big lie' *Scotsman*

'The hope now must be that although Mr Irving will go on talking and writing, fewer and fewer people will be listening and reading' *Economist*

'The judgment . . . is blunt and to the point. It is also entirely justified and much to be welcomed . . . This was a case about truth – the truth regarding the single greatest crime of the twentieth century' *Irish Times*

The Irving Judgment

David Irving v. Penguin Books and Professor Deborah Lipstadt

PENGUIN BOOKS

PENGUIN BOOKS

Published by the Penguin Group
Penguin Books Ltd, 27 Wrights Lane, London w8 5TZ, England
Penguin Putnam Inc., 375 Hudson Street, New York, New York 10014, USA
Penguin Books Australia Ltd, Ringwood, Victoria, Australia
Penguin Books Canada Ltd, 10 Alcorn Avenue, Toronto, Ontario, Canada M4V 3B2
Penguin Books India (P) Ltd, 11, Community Centre, Panchsheel Park, New Delhi – 110 017, India
Penguin Books (NZ) Ltd, Private Bag 102902, NSMC, Auckland, New Zealand
Penguin Books (South Africa) (Pty) Ltd, 5 Watkins Street, Denver Ext 4, Johannesburg 2094, South Africa

Penguin Books Ltd, Registered Offices: Harmondsworth, Middlesex, England

First published 2000
1

Set in 10/12.5pt Monotype Joanna
Typeset by Rowland Phototypesetting Ltd,
Bury St Edmunds, Suffolk
Printed in England by Clays Ltd, St Ives plc

In the High Court of Justice Queen's Bench Division

Before:
The Hon. Mr Justice Gray

BETWEEN:

David John Cawdell Irving (Claimant)

and

Penguin Books Limited (1st Defendant)
Deborah E. Lipstadt (2nd Defendant)

Mr David Irving (appeared in person).

Mr Richard Rampton QC (instructed by Messrs Davenport Lyons and Mishcon de Reya) appeared on behalf of the first and second Defendants.

Miss Heather Rogers (instructed by Messrs Davenport Lyons) appeared on behalf of the first Defendant, Penguin Books Limited.

Mr Anthony Julius (instructed by Messrs Mishcon de Reya) appeared on behalf of the second Defendant, Deborah Lipstadt.

Contents

Contents

Contents

Contents

Publisher's Note

Denying the Holocaust by Deborah Lipstadt was originally published in the US in 1993 by The Free Press. It was published in paperback in the UK by Penguin Books in 1994.

David Irving first complained about the references to him in *Denying the Holocaust* in a letter to Penguin Books during November 1995. He issued a writ claiming damages for libel in September 1996, naming Penguin, Professor Lipstadt and four individual Waterstones' booksellers as defendants. The writ was in due course served on each of the defendants, although the action against the four booksellers was later dropped.

The parties agreed that the action should be tried by a judge alone in view of the complexities of the evidence and Mr Justice Gray was assigned to the case. The trial opened in the High Court in London on Tuesday 11 January 2000 and closing speeches were heard on Wednesday 15 March 2000. Mr Justice Gray delivered his judgment in favour of the defendants on Tuesday 11 April 2000.

i. Introduction

A summary of the main issues

1.1 In this action the Claimant, David Irving, maintains that he has been libelled in a book entitled '*Denying the Holocaust – The Growing Assault on Truth and Memory*', which was published by Penguin Books Limited and written by Professor Deborah Lipstadt, who are respectively the First and Second Defendants in the action. (For the sake of brevity I shall refer to them, as in due course I shall refer to the expert witnesses, by their last names.)

1.2 The essential issues in the action can be summarized as follows: Irving complains that certain passages in the Defendants' book accuse him of being a Nazi apologist and an admirer of Hitler, who has resorted to the distortion of facts and to the manipulation of documents in support of his contention that the Holocaust did not take place. He contends that the Defendants' book is part of a concerted attempt to ruin his reputation as an historian and he seeks damages accordingly. The Defendants, whilst they do not accept the interpretation which Irving places on the passages complained of, assert that it is true that Irving is discredited as an historian by reason of his denial of the Holocaust and by reason of his persistent distortion of the historical record so as to depict Hitler in a favourable light. The Defendants maintain that the claim for damages for libel must in consequence fail.

1.3 Needless to say, the context in which these issues fall to be determined is one which arouses the strongest passions. On that account, it is important that I stress at the outset of this judgment that I do not regard it as being any part of my function as the trial judge to make findings of fact as to what did and what did not occur during the Nazi regime in Germany. It will be necessary for me to rehearse, at some length, certain historical data. The need for this arises because I must evaluate the criticisms of or

1

(as Irving would put it) the attack upon his conduct as an historian in the light of the available historical evidence. But it is not for me to form, still less to express, a judgement about what happened. That is a task for historians. It is important that those reading this judgment should bear well in mind the distinction between my judicial role in resolving the issues arising between these parties and the role of the historian seeking to provide an accurate narrative of past events.

The parties

1.4 David Irving, the Claimant, embarked on his career as an author in the early 1960s shortly after he left Imperial College London. He is the author of over 30 books, most of which are concerned with the events of and leading up to the Second World War (some of which were written and published in Germany). Amongst the better known titles are *The Destruction of Dresden, Hitler's War* (1977 and 1991 editions), *Goebbels – Mastermind of the Third Reich, Goering – a Biography* and *Nuremberg – The Last Battle*.

1.5 As these titles suggest, Irving has specialized in the history of the Third Reich. He describes himself as an expert in the principal Nazi leaders (although in his opening he was at pains to make clear that he does not regard himself as an historian of the Holocaust). Many of his works have been published by houses of the highest standing and have attracted favourable reviews. It is beyond dispute that over the years (Irving is now aged 62), he has devoted an enormous amount of time to researching and chronicling the history of the Third Reich. The books themselves are eloquent testimony to his industry and diligence.

1.6 Apart from his books Irving has written numerous articles and, particularly in recent years, lectured and spoken both in Europe and the Americas and participated in numerous radio and television broadcasts. He emphasizes that his reputation as an historian is founded upon his output of books.

1.7 As to his political beliefs, he describes himself as a Conservative with *laissez-faire* views. He mentions that he has not applauded the uncontrolled tide of Commonwealth immigration.

1.8 The 2nd Defendant, Deborah Lipstadt, lives and works in the United

States. She was raised in a traditional Jewish home (her parents having migrated from Germany and Poland). She attended City College of New York and spent a year at the Hebrew University in Jerusalem, where she took a series of courses on the history of the Holocaust, subsequently staying on for a further year. On her return to the United States she completed an M.A. and a Ph.D. in Jewish Studies.

1.9 Since then Lipstadt has pursued an academic career teaching modern Jewish history with an emphasis on the Holocaust. In 1993 she moved to Emory University, a research institution in Atlanta, Georgia, where she is Professor of Modern Jewish and Holocaust Studies. She has written two books about the responses to the Holocaust, *Beyond Belief: the American Press and the Coming of the Holocaust 1933–1945* and the book which has given rise to the present action, *Denying the Holocaust*. The latter was published by Penguin Books in an American edition and thereafter by Penguin Books Limited the first Defendants in an English paperback edition.

1.10 I should for the sake of completeness add that initially a number of individuals were joined as additional Defendants. The action is not pursued against them.

ii. The Words Complained of and their Meaning

The passages complained of

2.1 In *Denying the Holocaust* Lipstadt examines the origins and subsequent growth in the scope and intensity of what she describes as the phenomenon of Holocaust denial. She identifies several adherents of the revisionist movement and examines the basis for their beliefs, their methodology and the manner in which they deploy their arguments. She argues that 'the deniers' represent a clear and present danger that the lessons to be learned by future generations from the terrible events of the 1930s and 40s will be obfuscated.

2.2 Irving regards himself as being the victim of an orchestrated campaign of boycotting, hounding and persecution by organizations in the UK and elsewhere. He considers *Denying the Holocaust* to be one of the principal instruments deployed in the campaign to destroy him.

2.3 He has selected for complaint a number of passages from *Denying the Holocaust*. (I was told that the passages complained of represent in total no more than five pages from a book which runs to more than two hundred pages.) This is a course which he is entitled to take, providing of course that the removal of the passages from the context in which they appear in the book does not affect their interpretation. The Defendants are accordingly entitled to invite attention to the context in which the passages complained of appear in support of a submission that the context alters the meaning of the allegedly libellous passages. In the present case I do not understand the Defendants to be maintaining that the context materially affects the interpretation of any of the passages which Mr Irving has selected for complaint.

2.4 I shall therefore confine myself to setting out, with pagination, the passages which Irving contends are libellous of him (as well as highly damaging to his reputation as a serious historian):

Cover and title page:

'Denying the Holocaust

The Growing Assault on Truth and Memory'

Page 14:

The confluence between anti-Israel, anti-Semitic, and Holocaust denial forces was exemplified by a world anti-Zionist conference scheduled for Sweden in November 1992. Though cancelled at the last minute by the Swedish government, scheduled speakers included black Muslim leader Louis Farrakhan, Faurisson, Irving and Leuchter. Also scheduled to participate were representatives of a variety of anti-Semitic and anti-Israel organizations, including the Russian group Pamyat, the Iranian-backed Hezbollah, and the fundamentalist Islamic organization Hamas.[1]

1 *Jewish Telegraphic Agency*, 26 November 1992.

Page 111:

Nolte contended that Weizmann's official declaration at the outbreak of hostilities gave Hitler good reason 'to be convinced of his enemies' determination
to annihilate him much earlier than when the first information about Auschwitz
came to the knowledge of the world'[1] [. . .] When Nolte was criticized on
this point in light of prewar Nazi persecution of Jews, he said that he was only
quoting David Irving, the right-wing writer of historical works. How quoting
Irving justified using such a historically invalid point remains unexplained
[. . .][2] As we shall see in subsequent chapters, Irving [. . .] has become a
holocaust denier.

These works demonstrate how deniers misstate, misquote, falsify statistics and
falsely attribute conclusions to reliable sources. They rely on books that directly
contradict their arguments, quoting in a manner that completely distorts the
authors' objectives. Deniers count on the fact that the vast majority of readers
will not have access to the documentation or make the effort to determine how
they have falsified or misconstrued information.

Page 161:

At the second trial Christie and Faurisson were joined by David Irving, who
flew to Toronto in January 1988 to assist in the preparation of Zundel's second
defense and to testify on his behalf. Scholars have described Irving as a 'Hitler
partisan wearing blinkers' and have accused him of distorting evidence and
manipulating documents to serve his own purposes.[3] He is best known for his
thesis that Hitler did not know about the Final Solution, an idea that scholars
have dismissed.[4] The prominent British historian Hugh Trevor-Roper depicted
Irving as a man who 'seizes on a small and dubious particle of "evidence"'
using it to dismiss far-more substantial evidence that may not support his
thesis. His work has been described as 'closer to theology or mythology than

1 Ernst Nolte, 'Between Myth and Revisionism? The Third Reich in the Perspective of
the 1980's' in *Aspects of the Third Reich*, ed. H.W. Koch (London, 1985), pp. 36–7, Maier,
The Unmasterable Past, p. 29.
2 Maier, *The Unmasterable Past*, p. 179, n. 34.
3 Martin Broszat, *Vierteljahrshefte fuer Zeitgeschichte* (Oktober, 1977), pp. 742, 769, cited in
Patterns of Prejudice, no. 3–4 (1978), p. 8.
4 *Sunday Times*, 10 July 1977.

to history,' and he has been accused of skewing documents and misrepresenting data in order to reach historically untenable conclusions, particularly those that exonerate Hitler.[1] An ardent admirer of the Nazi leader, Irving placed a self-portrait of Hitler over his desk, described his visit to Hitler's mountaintop retreat as a spiritual experience,[2] and declared that Hitler repeatedly reached out to help the Jews.[3] In 1981 Irving, a self-described 'moderate fascist', established his own right-wing political party, founded on his belief that he was meant to be a future leader of Britain.[4] He is an ultra-nationalist who believes that Britain has been on a steady path of decline accelerated by its decision to launch a war against Nazi Germany. He has advocated that Rudolf Hess should have received the Nobel Prize for his efforts to try to stop war between Britain and Germany.[5] On some levels Irving seems to conceive himself as carrying on Hitler's legacy.

[. . .] Prior to participating in Zundel's trial, Irving had appeared at IHR conferences [. . .] but he had never denied the annihilation of the Jews.[6] That changed in 1988 as a result of the events in Toronto.

Both Irving and Faurisson advocated inviting an American prison warden who had performed gas executions to testify in Zundel's defense, arguing that this would be the best tactic for proving that the gas chambers were a fraud and too primitive to operate safely. They solicited help from Bill Armontrout, warden of the Missouri State Penitentiary, who agreed to testify and suggested they also contact Fred A. Leuchter, an 'engineer' residing in Boston who specialized in constructing and installing execution apparatus. Irving and Faurisson immediately flew off to meet Leuchter. Irving, who had long hovered on the edge of Holocaust denial, believed that Leuchter's testimony could provide the documentation he needed to prove the Holocaust a myth.[7] According to

1 Ibid., 12 June 1977; 10 July 1977.
2 Robert Harris, *Selling Hitler* (New York, 1986), p. 189.
3 *Canadian Jewish News*, 16 March 1989.
4 Ibid., *London Jewish Chronicle*, 27 May 1983.
5 *Spotlight*, June 1989.
6 'David Irving', Clipping Collection, Calgary Jewish Community Council, Alberta, Canada.
7 *Toronto Star*, 20 April 1988; Stephen Trombley, *The Execution Protocol: Inside America's Capital Punishment Industry* (New York, 1992), p. 85.

Faurisson, when he first met Leuchter, the Bostonian accepted the 'standard notion of the "Holocaust" '.[1] After spending two days with him, Faurisson declared that Leuchter was convinced that it was chemically and physically impossible for the Germans to have conducted gassings.[2] Having agreed to serve as an expert witness for the defense, Leuchter then went to Toronto to meet with Zundel and Christie and to examine the materials they had gathered for the trial.

Page 179:

David Irving, who during the Zundel trial declared himself converted by Leuchter's work to Holocaust denial and to the idea that the gas chambers were a myth, described himself as conducting a 'one man intifada' against the official history of the Holocaust.[3]

In his foreword to his publication of the Leuchter Report, Irving wrote that there was no doubt as to Leuchter's 'integrity' and 'scrupulous methods'. He made no mention of Leuchter's lack of technical expertise or of the many holes that had been poked in his findings. Most important, Irving wrote, 'Nobody likes to be swindled, still less where considerable sums of money are involved.' Irving identified Israel as the swindler, claiming that West Germany had given it more than ninety billion deutsche marks in voluntary reparations, 'essentially in atonement for the "gas chambers of Auschwitz" '. According to Irving the problem was that the latter was a myth that would 'not die easily'.[4] He subsequently set off to promulgate Holocaust denial notions in various countries. Fined for doing so in Germany, in his court room appeal against the fine he called on the court to 'fight a battle for the German people and put an end to the blood lie of the Holocaust which has been told against this country for fifty years.' He dismissed the memorial to the dead at Auschwitz as a 'tourist

---

1 Robert Faurisson, 'Foreword' *The Leuchter Report: The End of a Myth: An Engineering Report on the Alleged Execution Gas Chambers at Auschwitz, Birkenau, and Majdanek, Poland* (USA, 1988), p. 1 (hereafter cited as Leuchter Report).
2 Robert Faurisson, 'The Zundel Trials [1985 and 1988]', *Journal of Historical Review* (Winter, 1988–9), p. 429.
3 *Searchlight*, August 1989.
4 David Irving, 'Foreword', *Auschwitz: The End of the Line: The Leuchter Report* (London, 1989), p. 6.

attraction'.[1] He traced the origins of the myth to an 'ingenious plan' of the British Psychological Warfare Executive, which decided in 1942 to spread the propaganda story that Germans were 'using "gas chambers" to kill millions of Jews and other "undesirables" '.[2]

Branding Irving and Leuchter 'Hitler's heirs', the British House of Commons denounced the former as a 'Nazi propagandist and long time Hitler apologist' and the latter's report as a 'fascist publication'. One might have assumed that would have marked the end of Irving's reputation in England, but it did not. Condemned in the Times of London in 1989 as 'a man for whom Hitler is something of a hero and almost everything of an innocent and for whom Auschwitz is a Jewish deception', Irving may have had his reputation revived in 1992 by the London *Sunday Times*.[3] The paper hired Irving to translate the Goebbels diaries, which had been discovered in a Russian archive and, it was assumed, would shed light on the conduct of the Final Solution. The paper paid Irving a significant sum plus a percentage of the syndication fees.*

[Footnote] * The Russian archives granted Irving permission to copy two microfiche plates, each of which held about forty-five pages of the diaries. Irving immediately violated his agreement, took many plates, transported them abroad, and had them copied without archival permission. There is serious concern in archival circles that he may have significantly damaged the plates when he did so, rendering them of limited use to subsequent researchers.

Irving believes Jews are 'very foolish not to abandon the gas chamber theory while they still have time.' He 'foresees [a] new wave of anti-semitism' due to Jews' exploitation of the Holocaust 'myth', C.C. Aronsfeld, 'Holocaust revisionists are Busy in Britain,' Midstream, Jan. 1993, p.29.

Journalists and scholars alike were shocked that the Times chose such a discredited figure to do this work. Showered with criticism, the editor of the Sunday Times, Andrew Neil, denounced Irving's view as 'reprehensible' but defended engaging Irving because he was only being used as a 'transcribing technician'. Peter Pulzer, a professor of politics at Oxford and an expert on the

1 Times, London, 11 May 1992.
2 Irving, 'Foreword', Auschwitz: The End of the Line, p. 6.
3 Times, London, 14 May 1992.

Third Reich, observed that it was ludicrous for Neil to refer to Irving as a 'mere technician', arguing that when you hired someone to edit a 'set of documents others had not seen you took on the whole man'.[1]

However the matter is ultimately resolved, the Sunday Times had rescued Irving's reputation from the ignominy to which it had been consigned by the House of Commons. In the interest of a journalistic scoop, this British paper was willing to throw its task as a gatekeeper of the truth and of journalistic ethics to the winds. By resuscitating Irving's reputation, it also gave new life to the Leuchter Report.

Page 181:

A similar attitude is evident in the media reviews of David Irving's books: Most rarely address his neo-fascist or denial connections.[2]

Irving is one of the most dangerous spokespersons for Holocaust denial. Familiar with historical evidence, he bends it until it conforms with his ideological leanings and political agenda. A man who is convinced that Britain's great decline was accelerated by its decision to go to war with Germany, he is most facile at taking accurate information and shaping it to confirm his conclusions. A review of his recent book, Churchill's War, which appeared in New York Review of Books, accurately analyzed his practice of applying a double standard of evidence. He demands 'absolute documentary proof' when it comes to proving the Germans guilty, but he relies on highly circumstantial evidence to condemn the Allies.[3] This is an accurate description not only of Irving's tactics, but of those of deniers in general.

Page 213:

As we have seen above, Nolte echoing David Irving, argues that the Nazi 'internment' of Jews was justified because of Chaim Weizmann's September 1939 declaration that the Jews of the world would fight Nazism.

1 *Independent*, 11 July 1992.
2 Trombloy, *The Execution Protocol*, pp. 87–94; *New York Times Book Review*. 22 November 1992, p. 33.
3 *New York Review of Books*, 15 June 1989.

Page 221:

Another legal maneuver has been adopted by a growing number of countries. They have barred entry rights to known deniers. David Irving, for example, has been barred from Germany, Austria, Italy and Canada. Australia is apparently also considering barring him.[1]

2.5 These are the passages which (to quote Irving's opening) 'vandalized [his] legitimacy as an historian'.

The issue of identification

2.6 It is incumbent on Irving as Claimant to establish that these passages would have been understood by readers of *Denying the Holocaust* to refer to him. In their statement of case, the Defendants take issue with Irving's assertion that those passages refer to him.

2.7 To the extent that he is named in the passages cited above, readers would of course have taken them to be referring to Irving. With the exception of the title page, all the passages complained of do make mention of Irving by name. I am satisfied that readers would have understood all those passages to refer to Irving. The Defendants have not sought in the course of the trial to suggest otherwise.

2.8 I add the rider that the assertions, to be found principally at pages 111, 181 and 221, that Irving is a Holocaust 'denier' and a spokesperson for Holocaust denial will in my judgment cause readers to understand references to 'deniers' elsewhere in the passages complained of as importing a reference to Irving individually. Accordingly I am satisfied that readers of *Denying the Holocaust* would have understood Irving to be one of those who (to quote from page 111) 'misstate, misquote, falsify statistics and falsely attribute conclusions to reliable sources'.

1 *Toronto Sun*, 15 October 1992; *Jewish Telegraphic Agency*, 16 November 1992.

The issue of interpretation or meaning

Irving's case on meaning

2.9 Of greater substance is the question of what interpretation readers would have placed upon the references to Irving in Lipstadt's book. The burden rests on Irving to establish that, as a matter of probability, the passages of which he complains are defamatory of him, that is, that the ordinary reasonable reader of *Denying the Holocaust* would think the worse of him as a result of reading those passages. Irving is further required, as a matter of practice, to spell out what he contends are the specific defamatory meanings borne by those passages.

2.10 The contention of Irving is that the passages in question would in their natural and ordinary meaning (that is, without imputing any special extraneous knowledge to the reader) have been understood to bear the following defamatory meanings:

i   that the (Claimant) is a dangerous spokesman for Holocaust denial forces who deliberately and knowingly consorts and consorted with anti-Israel, anti-Semitic, and Holocaust denial forces and who contracted to attend a world anti-Zionist conference in Sweden in November 1992 thereby agreeing to appear in public in support of and alongside violent and extremist speakers including representatives of the violent and extremist anti-Semitic Russian group Pamyat and of the Iranian backed Hezbollah and of the fundamentalist Islamic organization Hamas and including the black Muslim minister Louis Farrakhan, born Louis Eugene Walcott, who is known as a Jew-baiting black agitator, as a leader of the U.S. Nation of Islam, as an admirer of Hitler and who is in the pay of Colonel Muammar Gaddafi;

ii   that the (Claimant) is an historian who has inexplicably misled academic historians like Ernst Nolte into quoting historically invalid points contained in his writings and who applauds the internment of Jews in Nazi concentration camps;

iii   that the (Claimant) routinely perversely and by way of his profession but essentially in order to serve his own reprehensible purposes ideological meanings and/or political agenda

- distorts accurate historical evidence and information
- misstates
- misconstrues
- misquotes
- falsifies statistics
- falsely attributes conclusions to reliable sources
- manipulates documents
- wrongfully quotes from books that directly contradict his arguments in such a manner as completely to distort their authors' objectives and while counting on the ignorance or indolence of the majority of readers not to realize this;

iv that the (Claimant) is an Adolf Hitler partisan who wears blinkers and skews documents and misrepresents data in order to reach historically untenable conclusions specifically those that exonerate Hitler;

v that the (Claimant) is an ardent admirer of the Nazi leader Adolf Hitler and conceives himself as carrying on Hitler's criminal legacy and had placed a self-portrait of Hitler over his desk and has described a visit to Hitler's mountain-top retreat as a spiritual experience and had described himself as a moderate fascist;

vi that before Zundel's trial began in 1988 in Toronto the (Claimant), compromising his integrity as an historian and in an attempt to pervert the course of justice, and with one Faurisson wrongfully and/or fraudulently conspired together to invite an American prison warden and thereafter one Fred A. Leuchter an engineer who is depicted by the Defendants as a charlatan to testify as a tactic for proving that the gas chambers were a myth;

vii that the (Claimant) after attending Zundel's trial in 1988 in Toronto having previously hovered on the brink now denies the murder by the Nazis of the Jews;

viii that the (Claimant) described the memorial to the dead at Auschwitz as a 'tourist attraction';

ix that the (Claimant) was branded by the British House of Commons as 'Hitler's heir' and denounced as a 'Nazi propagandist and long time Hitler apologist' and accused by them of publishing a 'fascist publication' and that this marked the end of the (Claimant's) reputation in England;

x   that some other person had discovered in a Russian archive in 1992 the Goebbels diaries and that it was assumed that these would shed light on the conduct of the Final Solution but that the (Claimant) was hired and paid a significant sum by the London *Sunday Times* to transcribe and translate them although he was a discredited and ignominious figure and although by hiring the (Claimant) the newspaper threw its task as a gatekeeper of the truth and of journalistic ethics to the winds and thereby increased the danger that the (Claimant) would in order to serve his own reprehensible purposes misstate, construe misquote falsify distort and/or manipulate these sets of documents which others had not seen in order to propagate his reprehensible views and that the (Claimant) was unfit to perform such a function for this newspaper;

xi that the (Claimant) violated an agreement with the Russian archives and took and copied many plates without permission causing significant damage to them and rendering them of limited use to subsequent researchers.

2.11 Irving contends in the alternative that the passages bear by innuendo, that is, by virtue of extrinsic facts which would have been known to readers or to some of them, the meaning that he is a person unfit to be allowed access to archival collections and that he is a person who should properly be banned from foreign countries. The extrinsic facts on which he relies in support of the innuendo meanings are in essence as follows:

i   that a Holocaust denier is someone who wilfully, perversely and in disregard of the evidence denies the mass murder by whatever means of the Jewish people;

ii   that Hezbollah is an international terrorist organization whose guerillas kill Israeli civilians and soldiers;

iii that Hamas is an Islamic fundamentalist terrorist organization.

In support of his argument that readers of the book would have known these extrinsic facts Irving produced a collection of press cuttings, which, I am satisfied, establish the extrinsic facts on which he relies.

The Defendants' case on meaning

2.12 The Defendants are also obliged to set out the defamatory meanings which they contend are borne by the passages in question (and which they seek to justify). These meanings are set out in paragraph 6 of their Defences in the following terms:

i   that the (Claimant) has on numerous occasions (in the manner hereinafter particularized) denied the Holocaust, the deliberate planned extermination of Europe's Jewish population by the Nazis, and denied that gas chambers were used by the Nazis as a means of carrying out that extermination;

ii that the (Claimant) holds extremist views, and has allied himself with others who do so, including individuals such as Dr. Robert Faurisson, and Ernst Zundel;

iii that the (Claimant), driven by his obsession with Hitler, distorts, manipulates and falsifies history in order to put Hitler in a more favourable light, thereby demonstrating a lack of the detachment, rationality and judgement necessary for an historian;

iv that there are grounds to suspect that the (Claimant) has removed certain microfiches of Goebbels' diaries contained in the Moscow archives, from the said archives without permission; and that the (Claimant) lied and/or exaggerated the position with regard to the unpublished diaries of Goebbels on microfiche contained in the Moscow archives, and used by him in the Goebbels book;

v   that in all the premises, the (Claimant) is discredited as an historian and user of source material, and that there was an increased risk that the (Claimant) would for his own purposes, distort, and manipulate the contents of the said microfiches in pursuance of his said obsession.

Approach to the issue of meaning

2.13 For the purpose of deciding this issue, it matters not what Lipstadt intended to convey to her readers; nor does it matter in what sense Irving understood them. I am not bound to accept the contentions of either party. My task is to arrive, without over-elaborate analysis, at the meaning or meanings which the notional typical reader of the publication in question, reading the book in ordinary circumstances, would have understood the words complained of, in their context, to bear. Such a reader is to be presumed to be fair-minded and not prone to jumping to conclusions but to be capable of a certain amount of loose thinking.[1]

Conclusion on meaning

2.14 I shall set out my findings as to the defamatory meanings borne by the passages complained of. In doing so, I will not allocate separate meanings to the individual passages selected for complaint because it is to be assumed that the reader's understanding as to what is being conveyed about Irving will be derived from his or her reading of the book as a whole including the passages to which objection is taken. I do not believe that it is necessary or desirable to set out the meanings in the order in which it may be said that they emerge in the book.

2.15 Adopting the approach set out earlier, my conclusion is that the passages complained of in their context and read collectively bear the following meanings all of which are defamatory of him:

i   that Irving is an apologist for and partisan of Hitler, who has resorted to the distortion of evidence; the manipulation and skewing of documents; the misrepresentation of data and the application of double standards to the evidence, in order to serve his own purpose of exonerating Hitler and portraying him as sympathetic towards the Jews;

ii   that Irving is one of the most dangerous spokespersons for Holocaust denial, who has on numerous occasions denied that the Nazis embarked upon the deliberate planned extermination of Jews and has alleged that it is a Jewish deception that gas chambers were used by the Nazis at Auschwitz as a means of carrying out such extermination;

iii that Irving, in denying that the Holocaust happened, has misstated evidence; misquoted sources; falsified statistics; misconstrued information and bent historical evidence so that it conforms to his neo-fascist political agenda and ideological beliefs;

1 *Skuse v Granada* (1996) EMLR 278.

iv   that Irving has allied himself with representatives of a variety of extremist and anti-semitic groups and individuals and on one occasion agreed to participate in a conference at which representatives of terrorist organizations were due to speak;

v   that Irving, in breach of an agreement which he had made and without permission, removed and transported abroad certain microfiches of Goebbels' diaries, thereby exposing them to a real risk of damage.

vi   that Irving is discredited as an historian.

2.16 I add two comments in relation to the meanings which I have found. The first is that I do not accept the contention of Irving that the passage at p. 14 of the book means that he supports violent groups. But I do consider that passage to be defamatory of him in suggesting that he agreed to take part in a meeting at which representatives of such groups would be present. My second comment is that I do not accept that the reference to Irving at p. 213 of the book, when read in the context of the other references to him, bears the meaning that he applauds the internment of Jews in Nazi concentration camps.

iii. The Nature of Irving's Claim for Damages

Relevant considerations
3.1 Where the publication of defamatory words is proved and no substantive defence has been established, English law presumes that damage will have been done to the reputation of the person defamed. The amount of the damages recoverable by a particular claimant, if successful on liability, will depend on a variety of factors including the nature and gravity of the libel; the extent of its dissemination; the standing of the claimant; the injury to his or her feelings; the extent of any additional injury inflicted by the conduct of the defendants; and so on. It is possible to claim pecuniary loss but no such claim arises here. Damages maybe reduced, perhaps even to vanishing point, to the

extent that the defendants succeed in partially justifying the defamatory imputations complained of.[1]

Irving's case on damages

3.2 Irving contends that Lipstadt in *Denying the Holocaust* makes an attack not only upon his competence as an historian but also upon his motivation. As I have already found, the book accuses Irving, amongst other things, of deliberate perversion of the historical evidence. I readily accept that, to any serious historian, his or her integrity is vital. That is no doubt why, in his evidence, Irving said that for him his reputation as a truth-seeking historian is more important than anything else. The other meanings which I have found the passages complained of to bear are also serious, although in my judgment less so. Irving is entitled to regard the passages in the book of which he complains as containing grave imputations against him in both his professional and personal capacity.

3.3 The Defendants admit that *Denying the Holocaust* has been published within the jurisdiction. Although not specifically so pleaded, I bear in mind the evidence of Irving that the book has been put on the Internet and widely circulated to libraries.

3.4 In relation to his own standing as an historian, Irving described his career as a writer and commentator on the Third Reich. He is the author of a great number of serious historical works, most of which have been favourably received. Irving referred to the favourable reviews accorded to his works by eminent historians such as Lord Dacre. He was understandably reluctant to sing his own praises. But he claimed credit for the amount of original research he has done and for the number of documents which he has discovered in the archives. Irving supplemented his own evidence with that of Professor Donald Watt (whom I describe in section iv below), who testified that, in those areas where his political convictions are not involved, he is most impressed by Irving's scholarship. Whilst he might not place Irving in the top class of military historians, his book *Hitler's War* was a work which deserved to be taken seriously. Watt also noted that Irving had stimulated debate

1 *Pamplin v Express Newspapers* (1988) 1 WLR 116.

and research into the Holocaust. Sir John Keegan (also described below) gave evidence that he adhered to a view which he had expressed some years ago that *Hitler's War* was one of two outstanding books on World War II.

3.5 On the other hand account must also be taken of the view expressed by one of the Defendants' experts, Professor Evans, that Irving has had 'a generally low reputation amongst professional historians since the end of the 1980s and at all times amongst those who have direct experience of researching in the areas with which he concerns himself'. Both Professor Watt and Sir John Keegan regarded as unacceptable the views expressed by Irving about the Holocaust and Hitler's knowledge of it.

3.6 It was abundantly plain from his conduct of the trial that the factor to which Irving attaches the greatest importance in connection with the issue of the damages is the conduct of the Defendants and the impact which that conduct has had on himself, both personally and professionally, as well as on his family. Irving made plain in his opening, on repeated occasions during the trial and in his written and closing submissions that he regards himself as the target of a well-funded and unscrupulous conspiracy on the part of 'our traditional enemies' aimed at preventing the dissemination of his books, ensuring that he is banned from as many countries as possible and stifling his right to freedom of expression. Although Irving at one stage disputed the point, it was reasonably clear that the 'traditional enemies' were the members of the Jewish community. His claim is that he is the victim of an international Jewish conspiracy determined to silence him. Irving's argument was supported, in general terms, by Professor Macdonald (whom I shall describe later) but the assistance which I derived from his evidence was limited.

3.7 The Defendants are critical of the latitude which I allowed Irving in developing this theme. They contend, correctly, that in the ordinary run of litigation, the rules of evidence would have prevented him advancing any such case. However, for a number of reasons, I thought it right not to take too strict a line. Irving has represented himself throughout (demonstrating, if I may say so, very considerable ability and showing commendable restraint). This has not been a trial where it has been possible or appropriate to observe strict rules of evidence. Furthermore Irving has been greatly hampered in presenting this aspect of his case by the unexpected decision of the Defendants, in full knowledge of the allegations which Irving was making about the conduct of Lipstadt, not to call her to give evidence and to be cross-examined by Irving. It goes without saying that the Defendants were perfectly entitled to adopt this tactic but it did place Irving, acting in person, at a disadvantage.

3.8 I explained to Irving that, in order to be able to obtain increased damages on this account, it would be necessary for him to prove on the balance of probability that both the Defendants were implicated in the alleged conspiracy.[1] Irving did not hesitate to accuse Lipstadt of having been a prime mover. He claimed that her book was part of a sinister international campaign to discredit him. He alleged that she was acting in league with the Anti Defamation League, the Board of Deputies of Jews and other organizations intent on targeting him. He called Professor Kevin Macdonald, a professor of psychology, to testify as to the machinations of the 'traditional enemies of free speech' (ie the Jews). Irving alleged that the passages to which he takes objection in Denying the Holocaust were inserted by Lipstadt at a late stage for the purpose of discrediting him. He complained that she made no attempt whatever to verify the allegations by contacting him or otherwise. He testified that it became apparent to him some three years after Denying the Holocaust was published that a concerted attempt was being made to persuade bookshops to cease stocking his work. According to Irving, Lipstadt was instrumental in procuring the decision of his American publishers not to go ahead with the publication of his most recent work, the biography of Goebbels, to which he had devoted no less than nine years work. He claimed, by implication at least, that she was also complicit in bringing pressure to bear on Irving's UK publishers to repudiate their contract to publish his Goebbels biography (at considerable cost to Irving). He claims that Lipstadt has been deeply involved in the campaign of intimidation against him and that she has actively sought to destroy him as an historian.

1 *Cassell v Broome* (1972) *AC* 1027.

3.9 In assessing these claims by Irving, whose suspicions and indignation are obviously genuine, I must act on evidence and not assertion. On the evidence of the contents of the book itself, I accept that it does indeed represent a deliberate attack on Irving, mounted in order to discredit him as an historian and so to undermine any credence which might otherwise be given to his denials of the Holocaust. That is a factor which is to be taken into account, if the issue of damages arises. Beyond that finding, however, I do not consider that Irving's claim to have been the victim of a conspiracy in which both Defendants were implicated is established by the evidence placed before me.

3.10 The question of damages will arise if, and only if, the substantive defence relied on by the Defendants fails. I therefore turn to that defence.

iv. The Defence of Justification: An Overview

The parties' statements of case

4.1 Irving having established, as I have found, that *Denying the Holocaust* contains passages which are defamatory of him, it is necessary for the Defendants, if they are to avoid liability, to establish a defence. The burden of doing so rests, under the English system of law, upon the Defendants.

4.2 The substantive defence relied on by both Defendants is justification, that is, that in their natural and ordinary meaning the passages of which Mr Irving complains are substantially true. I have already recited, in section II above, the so-called *Lucas-Box*[1] meanings or propositions the truth of which the Defendants seek to establish in order to make good their defences of justification.

4.3 As practice requires the Defendants also set out in their formal statement of case, served in February 1997, the detailed particulars on

1 *Lucas-Box v News Group Ltd* (1986) 1 WLR 147.

which they rely in support of their defence of justification. In November 1999 the Defendants served a revised document entitled *Defendants' Summary of Case*. This document comprehensively rearranges, supplements and in some cases abandons the particulars previously served. Irving has, in my view sensibly, raised no objection to this recasting of the Defendants' case of justification.

4.4 It is to be noted that in the particulars of their case of justification the Defendants do not confine themselves to the specific assertions made by Lipstadt in her book. To give but one example: no mention is made in *Denying the Holocaust* of the bombing of Dresden by the Allies in 1945. Yet section 5 of the *Defendants' Summary of Case* contains detailed particulars on that topic criticizing Irving's treatment of the subject in his book *Apocalypse 1945: the Destruction of Dresden*. No objection has been taken or, in my judgment, could be taken to this course since the Defendants are entitled[1] to rely on Irving's account of the bombing of Dresden in support of their contention that he falsifies data and misrepresents evidence. The same applies to other matters raised by the Defendants in their *Summary of Case* which are not mentioned in *Denying the Holocaust*.

4.5 For his part Irving has, in compliance with the rules, set out in summary form in his Replies to the Defences of the Defendants his answer to the allegations and criticisms advanced by the Defendants in justification of what was published. In October 1999 the Defendants sought from Irving answers to a series of detailed requests for further information about his case. Unfortunately most of those requests went unanswered. In the result much of Irving's case in rebuttal of the defence of justification emerged in the course of his evidence at trial and in the course of his cross-examination of the witnesses called by the Defendants. The Defendants, in my view rightly, felt themselves unable to object.

4.6 The Replies also include an allegation of malice against both Defendants, apparently introduced in the mistaken belief that they were relying also upon the defence of fair comment on a matter of public interest.

1 *Williams v Reason* (1988) 1 WLR 96.

Malice may nonetheless be relevant to the issue of damages, if that arises.

What has to be proved in order for the defence of justification to succeed

4.7 As I have already mentioned, the burden of proving the defence of justification rests upon the publishers. Defamatory words are presumed under English law to be untrue. It is not incumbent on defendants to prove the truth of every detail of the defamatory words published: what has to be proved is the *substantial* truth of the defamatory imputations published about the claimant. As it is sometimes expressed, what must be proved is the truth of the sting of the defamatory charges made.[1]

4.8 Section 5 of the Defamation Act, 1952 provides:

Justification. In an action for libel . . . in respect of words containing two or more distinct charges against the [claimant], a defence of justification shall not fail by reason only that the truth of every charge is not proved if the words not proved to be true do not materially injure the [claimant's] reputation having regard to the truth of the remaining charges.

It may accordingly be necessary, in a case like the present where a number of defamatory imputations are the subject of complaint, to consider whether such imputations (if any) as the Defendants have failed to prove to be true materially injure the reputation of the claimant in the light of those imputations against him which have been proved to be true.

4.9 The contention for the Defendants is that they have proved the substantial truth of what was published, so that the defence of justification succeeds without the need for resort to section 5. Irving, however, points out that there are imputations which the Defendants made in the book which they have not sought to prove to be true. The principal such imputation is that Irving agreed to participate in a conference at which representatives of violent and extremist groups such as Hezbollah were due to speak. Irving contends that this defamatory imputation is so serious that the Defendants' failure to prove it or even to attempt to

1 Edwards v Bell (1824) 1 *Bing* 403 at 409.

prove it is fatal to their plea of justification. The Defendants on the other hand argue that by virtue of section 5 of the 1952 Act their defence of justification should succeed notwithstanding their failure to prove the truth of this imputation because, relative to the other serious imputations which they maintain they have proved to be true, it has no significant deleterious effect on the reputation of Irving.

4.10 The standard of proof in civil cases is normally that parties must prove their claims or defences, as the case may be, on the balance of probabilities. In the present case Irving argued, however, that, since the imputations against him were so grave, a higher standard of proof should be applied to the case of the justification advanced by the Defendants. There is a line of authority which establishes that, whilst the standard of proof remains the civil standard, the more serious the allegation the less likely it is that the event occurred and hence the stronger should be the evidence before the court concludes that the allegation is established on the balance of probability.[1] I will adopt that approach when deciding if the truth of the defamatory imputations made against Irving has been established.

Pattern of the judgment on the issue of justification

4.11 It is convenient, in order that the pattern of the succeeding sections of this judgment is clear, that at this stage I explain how I propose to deal with the matters raised by the defence by way of justification. For the most part they relate to the period of the Third Reich. In geographical terms the events with which it is necessary to deal are centred on Berlin but they extend to most of the countries conquered by the Nazis. The Defendants rely in addition on the publications, utterances and conduct of Irving over the last thirty years. The number of documents involved is huge. The volume of evidence, mostly expert evidence, is massive. In these circumstances it has proved necessary, for purely practical reasons, to divide up the allegations made by the Defendants into a series of separate headings.

4.12 In the next eight sections of this judgment I shall attempt to summarize in some detail the arguments deployed by the parties in

1 Re H (minors) (1996) AC 563.

relation to the allegations made under those headings. I shall not attempt to rehearse each and every point taken in the reports submitted by the Defendants' experts. Some of the criticisms made of Irving's historiography appear rather pedantic. In any case both sides have agreed that I should confine myself to the issues which have been ventilated by one side or the other in cross-examination. Whilst I will deal with the Defendants' case on justification under the separate headings which I have mentioned, it is important to note that it is an essential feature of the Defendants' case that the allegations on which they rely overlap and (as the Defendants put it) converge, thus providing the foundation of their defence of justification.

4.13 Having summarized the parties' rival contentions, I shall then in a separate section of the judgement set out my conclusions on the central issue whether or not the defence of justification succeeds.

Evidence adduced in relation to the issue of justification

4.14 Before setting out the arguments and evidence, I will identify the witnesses whose evidence was tendered on each side in relation to the defence of justification.

4.15 I start with the evidence for the Defendants. As I have already said, Professor Lipstadt did not give evidence (although a witness statement from her had been served).

4.16 The only witness of fact for the Defendants was Ms Rebecca Guttman who is employed by the American Jewish Committee as an executive assistant. Her statement, admitted under the Civil Evidence Act, related to an event arranged by an allegedly right-wing organization in the US with which Irving is said to have connections.

4.17 The main corpus of evidence for the Defendants was provided by academic historians whose evidence was by consent admitted as expert evidence. Written and oral evidence was submitted by the following:

i   Professor Richard Evans, who is Professor of Modern History at the University of Cambridge and has written many historical works about Germany. He gave evidence principally about Irving's historiography, his exculpation of Hitler and his denial of the Holocaust.

ii Professor Robert Jan van Pelt, who is a Professor of Architecture in the School of Architecture, University of Waterloo in Canada. Professor van Pelt is an acknowledged authority on Auschwitz, about which he has written extensively, and this was the subject of his evidence.

iii Professor Christopher Browning, who is a Professor of History at Pacific Lutheran University, Tacoma, Washington. He gave evidence on the evidence about the implementation of the Final Solution, covering the shooting of Jews and others in the East and the gassing of Jews in death camps (apart from Auschwitz).

iv Dr Peter Longerich, who is Reader in the Department of German at the Royal Holloway College, University of London and a specialist in the Nazi era. He gave evidence of Hitler's role in the persecution of the Jews under the Nazi regime and of the systematic character of the Nazi policy for the extermination of the Jews.

v Professor Hajo Funke, who is Professor of Political Science at the Free University of Berlin. He gave evidence of Irving's alleged association with right-wing and neo-Nazi groups and individuals in Germany.

The reports submitted by these experts ran to a total of more than two thousand pages

4.18 Not unnaturally (since it is his views and his conduct as an historian which are being attacked by the Defendants) evidence in rebuttal of the case of the Defendants on justification came predominantly from Irving himself. The course which was taken with his evidence was as follows: he submitted a brief witness statement, which did not address the majority of the particulars relied on by the Defendants in support of their plea of justification. He provided some elaboration of his response to that plea in the course of his opening and in the course of answers to my questions. But it was mainly in the course of his answers in cross-examination and his cross-examination of the Defendants' witnesses that the detail of his case emerged.

4.19 In support of his denial of the allegation that he broke an agreement in relation to the microfiches in the Moscow archive containing the diaries of Goebbels, Irving called Peter Millar, a freelance journalist, who at the time of the discovery of those diaries in 1992 was acting for *The Sunday Times*.

4.20 Irving summoned to give evidence on his behalf two historians who were unwilling to testify voluntarily. Their evidence was directed primarily to the question of Irving's standing as an historian (in which connection I have already mentioned them) rather than to the plea of justification. The first was Professor Donald Watt, who is an Emeritus Professor at the London School of Economics and was described by Irving as 'the doyen of diplomatic historians'. Professor Watt was invited by Irving to give evidence about the evaluation of wartime documentation and about Irving's reputation and ability as an historian. The other witness summoned by Irving to give evidence on his behalf was Sir John Keegan, the Defence Editor for Telegraph Newspapers whose knighthood was for services to military history. He too dealt with Irving's standing as an historian. Another witness who gave evidence for Irving, in his case voluntarily, was Professor Kevin Macdonald, who is a Professor of Psychology at California State University-Long Beach. He gave evidence on what he termed 'Jewish-gentile interactions' from the perspective of evolutionary biology. There was no cross-examination by the Defendants' counsel of any of these witnesses.

4.21 In the course of my summary of the evidence and arguments on the issue of justification, I shall need to make frequent reference to the distinguished academic experts whom I have identified above. I hope that they will understand if, in referring to them, I dispense with their academic titles (as I have done with in the case of Professor Lipstadt). No disrespect is intended: it simply makes for easier reading.

v. Justification: The Defendants' Historiographical Criticisms of Irving's Portrayal of Hitler in Particular Regard to his Attitude Towards the Jewish Question

Introduction

5.1 A central tenet of Irving's historical writing about the Nazi era is that Hitler was not the vehement and ruthless persecutor of the Jews that he is usually portrayed to have been. Irving has on occasion gone so far as to say that Hitler was 'one of the best friends the Jews ever had in the Third Reich'. Even if that can be disregarded as hyperbole, Irving would not, I think, dispute that he has on many occasions put forward the contentious view that, at least from the date when he seized power in 1933, Hitler lost interest in his former anti-semitism and that his interventions thereafter in relation to the Jewish question were consistently designed to protect them from the murderous inclinations of other Nazis.

The general case for the Defendants

5.2 At p. 161 of *Denying the Holocaust* Lipstadt attributes to scholars the description of Irving as a 'Hitler partisan wearing blinkers'. That phrase, importing the suggestion that Irving deliberately ignores what is revealed by the historical record, encapsulates one of the main defamatory meanings of which Irving complains and which the Defendants seek to justify.

5.3 The way in which the Defendants summarize their plea of justification on this part of the case is as follows:

that the [Claimant], driven by his obsession with Hitler, distorts, manipulates and falsifies history in order to put Hitler in a more favourable light, thereby demonstrating a lack of the detachment, rationality and judgment necessary for an historian.

In their *Summary of Case* the Defendants highlight claims made by Irving as to Hitler's friendship for and leniency towards Jews, which claims they assert ignore a large and powerful body of contradictory evidence. The Defendants contend that Irving

misstates, misquotes, falsifies statistics, falsely attributes conclusions to reliable sources, relies on books and sources that directly contradict his arguments, quoting in a manner that completely distorts the author's objectives, manipulates documents to serve his own purposes, skews documents and misrepresents data in order to reach historically untenable conclusions, bends historical evidence until it conforms to his ideological leanings and political agenda, takes accurate information and shapes it to confirm his conclusion and constantly suppresses or deliberately overlooks sources with which he is familiar because they contradict the line of argument which he wishes to advance.

5.4 The Defendants advance a similar case against Irving in relation to his account of the Nazi persecution of the Jews, culminating in the genocide which they assert took place in the gas chambers, and his claims as to the extent of Hitler's involvement in that persecution. I shall deal with that part of the defendants' plea of justification in sections vi. to viii. below. The present section is confined to certain specific instances where the Defendants attack Irving's historiography.
5.5 The principal protagonist amongst the Defendants' witnesses of the view that Irving persistently and deliberately falsifies history is Evans. In seeking to make good this full-blooded assault on Irving's historiographical approach, Evans included in his lengthy written report multiple examples of the way in which in his opinion Irving portrays Hitler in a manner which is utterly at odds with the available evidence. He cited numerous occasions when, so he alleged, Irving distorted the historical record by one means or another; suppressed evidence; made uncritical use of unreliable sources and arrived at perverse irrational conclusions about events and documents. Evans also drew attention to

occasions when Irving has written in inappropriately flattering terms about him. One example is Irving's description of the *Fuhrer* in *Hitler's War* as 'a friend of the arts, benefactor of the impoverished, defender of the innocent, persecutor of the delinquent'. Evans considers that the consistent bias in favour of Hitler which is manifested in Irving's works may stem in part from Irving's identification with Hitler and from his professed intention to write *Hitler's War* from Hitler's perspective. Irving has himself written that he sees himself as having acted as Hitler's 'ambassador to the afterlife' when he was engaged upon writing his biography of Hitler. On the evidence of what Irving has written and what he has said in his talks and speeches, Evans concludes that Irving remains an ardent admirer of Hitler despite the overwhelming evidence which condemns him.

5.6 Evans does not stand alone in making these harsh criticisms of Irving's historical method. In the narrower fields covered by their evidence van Pelt, Browning and Longerich level similar criticisms at him.

5.7 The Defendants based their attack on Irving's historiography upon a number of selected episodes. They contend that a detailed analysis of the evidence which was available to Irving supports their case that in his account of those episodes Irving has persistently and deliberately falsified, manipulated and suppressed documents so as to present a picture which is skewed and misleading. The Defendants focus their attention on a 'chain of documents' upon which Irving has relied, initially on BBC television in June 1977 and on several later occasions, in support of his view that Hitler opposed the persecution of the Jews and sought to protect them from the excesses advocated by other Nazis. I shall consider the parties' arguments in relation to each of the incidents to which the chain of documents relates.

5.8 Evans's detailed examination of those documents reveals, so he alleged, consistent falsification of the historical record on the part of Irving. Evans expressed the opinion that what he described as Irving's 'egregious errors' were calculated and deliberate. He accepted that anyone can make mistakes but pointed out (as did Browning) that, where all the so-called mistakes are exculpatory of Hitler, the natural inference is that the falsification of the record is intentional. Evans did not resile in his oral evidence from the view expressed in his written report that Irving does not deserve to be called an historian.

Irving's general response

5.9 As I have already observed, Irving regards the imputation that he has deliberately falsified the historical record as one of the most serious which can be levelled against an historian. He testified that he had never knowingly or wilfully misrepresented a document or misquoted or suppressed any document which would run counter to his case. He repudiated each and every one of the Defendants' allegations of misquoting, misconstruing, mistranslating, distorting or manipulating the evidence.

5.10 Irving denied any obsession with Hitler, as he denied any falsification of history so as to portray Hitler in a more favourable light. Irving argued that he has every right to praise Hitler where praise is merited. Other historians, such as AJP Taylor, have taken a similar line. Irving also resents the claim made by Lipstadt that he has placed above his desk a self-portrait of Hitler. In fact it is nothing more than a postcard-sized sketch which is not on display, although he occasionally shows it to visitors.

5.11 Irving drew attention to the fact that in Hitler's War, as well as in his other published works, he frequently includes material to the discredit of Hitler and other senior Nazis and makes criticism of them. He pointed out that he has expressly drawn his readers' attention to crimes committed by Hitler. In his closing submission he included a list of derogatory references which has made about Hitler. He refuted the notion that these critical references were inserted for tactical purposes, that is, to enable him to point to them in the event of commentators accusing him of being a Hitler partisan. He has made no attempt to conceal from his readers the rabid anti-semitism displayed by Hitler in the early days. In his use of material obtained in his interviews with Hitler's former adjutants or their widows, he has included information provided by them which reflects adversely on Hitler.

5.12 As Evans acknowledged, Irving has uncovered much new material

about the Third Reich. He has researched documents not previously
visited by historians, for example the Himmler papers in Washington
and the Goebbels diaries in Moscow. He has tracked down and interviewed individuals (such as Hitler's adjutants or their widows) who
participated in or observed some of the events which took place during
Hitler's regime. Irving pointed out that, when he uncovers new documents or sources, he habitually makes them publicly available by
placing them on his website or by some other means. Irving argues
that no duplicitous historian would behave in this way, for he would
be providing the evidence of his own duplicity to other historians.
Irving advances a similar general argument in rebuttal of the claim
that he has deliberately misrepresented or skewed or mistranslated
documents. Irving said that he invariably indicates in a footnote where
the document is to be found and often quotes the document in the
original German. Irving contended that a historian intent on misleading
his readers would not be so forthcoming with the evidence of his own
disreputable conduct.

5.13 Irving rejected the attack upon his historiography mounted by
Evans: the criticisms are sweeping but the instances cited in support of
them are, he claimed, relatively insignificant. Evans takes no account,
Irving complained, of the quality of the historical work displayed in
his many published works many of which have been favourably
reviewed by fellow historians. Irving was critical of frequency with
which Evans resorted to 'the consensus amongst historians' by way of
support for his attack on Irving. He suggested that many of the criticisms
advanced by Evans were derived by him from the work of Professor
Broszat, who had personal reasons for writing corrosively about him.
Irving stressed that he should be judged by the use which he made of
the evidence which was available to him at the time of writing and not
by reference to evidence which has come to light more recently.

5.14 Irving was, understandably, indignant that Evans included in his
report a reference to his having been required by the British Museum
to read *Hitler's War* in the section of the library reserved for pornographic
material. By way of rejoinder he stated that the librarian of the Widener
Library in Harvard apparently thinks well enough of him to stock
forty-seven of his books.

5.15 Irving's general response to this part of the Defendants' case of justification is that, when the pertinent documentary evidence is subjected to 'rigid historical criteria' (i.e. when due account is taken of the authenticity and the reliability of the evidence, the reason for its existence and the vantage point of the source or author), a relatively slim dossier of evidence emerges which does indeed show Hitler intervening in every instance to mitigate or lessen the wrongdoing against the Jews. Few, if any, documents point in the opposite direction.

The specific criticisms made by the Defendants of Irving's historiography

5.16 In dealing with the Defendants' examples of Irving's alleged distortions of the historical record, I shall adopt the approach taken by the Defendants in their *Summary of Case* and deal with them one by one and, so far as practicable, in a chronological order. In each case I shall start with a brief account of the relevant historical background. Then I shall be setting out in summary the criticisms made by the Defendants of the use made by Irving of the evidence available to him in relation to the particular episode and thereafter I will summarize Irving's response to those criticisms.

(i) Hitler's trial in 1924

Introduction
5.17 In 1924 Hitler was tried and, following his conviction, imprisoned for his role in the Nazi uprising in Munich in November 1923.

5.18 At p. 18 of the 1991 edition of *Hitler's War* Irving makes a passing reference to Hitler's attempted *putsch*, on which occasion, according to Irving, Hitler 'disciplined a Nazi squad for having looted a Jewish delicatessen'.

5.19 A more detailed account of Hitler's role in the *putsch* is given at p. 59 of *Goering*, where Irving writes:

Meanwhile Hitler acted to maintain order. Learning that one Nazi squad had ransacked a kosher grocery store during the night, he sent for the ex-Army lieutenant who led the raid. 'We took off our Nazi insignia first!' expostulated the officer – to no avail, as Hitler dismissed him from the party on the spot. 'I shall see that no other nationalist unit allows you to join either!' Goring goggled at this exchange, as did a police sergeant who testified to it at the Hitler trial a few weeks later.

Case for the Defendants

5.20 Evans noted that, whereas in *Hitler's War* it is claimed by Irving that the whole squad which was involved in the looting was disciplined by Hitler, in *Goering* it is just the ex-army lieutenant. The reader who seeks to resolve the inconsistency is not assisted by any footnote identifying either the police sergeant who is said by Irving to have witnessed the dismissal or the occasion when he gave his evidence (as would be conventional practice for a reputable historian). Irving says at p. 518 that his account is knitted together from eye-witness evidence at the trial.

5.21 Evans managed to track down the identity of the police officer, who was called Hofmann. The Defendants criticize Irving for his failure to inform the reader that Hofmann was a loyal member of the Nazi party who participated in the *putsch* and who was on that account likely, when testifying on his behalf at his criminal trial, to give a favourable account of the conduct of his *Fuhrer* in his testimony and to depict him as a law-abiding citizen.

5.22 According to Evans, examination of the transcript of Hofmann's testimony reveals several inaccuracies in Irving's account. There is no support for the claim that Hitler summoned or 'sent for' the former lieutenant or that either the police sergeant officer or Goering 'goggled' when Hitler admonished him for raiding the Jewish shop. The admonition took place before the *putsch* and so cannot have formed any part of an attempt by Hitler to maintain order during it.

5.23 Irving's account is also criticized for misrepresenting the nature of Hitler's concern about the raid on the Jewish shop. The record of the evidence given at the trial demonstrates that Hitler's concern was not to punish the officer for victimizing a Jewish shopkeeper but rather that the incident might convey a bad impression of his new party.

5.24 Evans maintained that, far from acting to protect Jewish property during the *putsch*, there is reliable evidence that Hitler (as he himself admitted at his trial) ordered a raid on a Jewish printing house by armed Storm Division troops, who under threat of violence stole 14.5 billion marks. This robbery is presented by Irving at p. 59 of *Goering* as a 'requisition' of 'funds'.

5.25 The Defendants maintain that in the respects which I have summarized, in his account of Hitler's reaction to the raid on the Jewish delicatessen and the evidence given at his trial, Irving persistently twists and embroiders the facts so as to exculpate Hitler and portray him as having acted sympathetically towards the Jews. Evans emphasized that it is essential for any historian to pay close attention to the background of any source he intends to quote so as to ensure that he is a reliable witness. He concluded that Irving deliberately suppressed the information as to Hofmann's background, preferring instead to present him to the reader as an objective and trustworthy source, when to Irving's knowledge he was nothing of the kind.

Irving's response

5.26 In the course of his own evidence and his cross-examination of Evans Irving made a number of claims about his treatment of Hofmann's evidence. He repudiated the suggestion that he had deliberately provided a footnote for Hofmann's evidence which would make it difficult for anyone so minded to track it down. By way of explanation, he explained that his publisher had called for cuts to be made in the text, so he had abbreviated the footnotes with the result that they are not as helpful as they might otherwise have been.

5.27 Irving initially excused his version of events by saying that what he wrote was based on the microfiches of Hofmann's testimony rather than the verbatim transcript of the evidence given at the trial. But Evans pointed out that the contents of both were the same. Irving next claimed that he had no way of knowing that Hofmann was a longstanding member of the Nazi party and so likely to present Hitler in a favourable light. Evans responded that this would have been apparent on the face of Hofmann's testimony, which Irving read on microfiches and which recounted his close relationship with Hitler and his involvement in the *putsch*. Moreover the Judge is recorded on the transcript as having congratulated Hofmann for speaking out on behalf of his *Fuhrer*. Irving responded that he had not had the transcript of Hofmann's evidence when he wrote *Goering* or, if he had, he had not read that section of the testimony which related to Hofmann's membership of the Nazi party. When it was then pointed out to Irving that, in the course of his own cross-examination, he had said that he had read the whole transcript of Hofmann's evidence (which was only five pages long), Irving explained that, whilst it was true that he had read Hofmann's evidence, he had not 'paid attention' to what he had said about his background. He added that readers of *Hitler's War* and *Goering* would be able to work out for themselves that Hofmann was not an objective witness without that fact being spelled out.

5.28 Irving accepted that there is no evidence that Goering 'goggled' when Hitler disciplined the former lieutenant but regards that as permissible 'author's licence'. Irving defended his description of the robbery of the bank as 'requisitioning' the bank's funds by saying that the robbery was an obvious prank: he was seeking to write with a 'light touch'.

(ii) Crime statistics for Berlin in 1932

Introduction

5.29 During the Weimar Republic statistics were maintained for the numbers of crimes committed year on year. The crimes were broken down into types of offences.

5.30 In the context of describing in his book *Goebbels* how Goebbels turned anti-semitic when he realized the dominant position occupied by the Jews in Berlin in the 1930s, Irving wrote that Goebbels was unfortunately 'not always wrong' to highlight every malfeasance of the criminal *demi-monde* and identify it as Jewish. He added at pp. 46–7:

In 1930 no fewer than 31,000 cases of fraud, mainly insurance swindles, would be committed by Jews.

Irving cited in the supporting footnote various references including Interpol figures which are said to be quoted in the *Deutsche Nachrichten Buro* (DNB), 20 July 1935 and Kurt Daluege '*Judenfrage als Grundsatz*' in *Angriff*, 3 August 1935. Two other sources are also given, namely Kiaulehn and Wieglin.

Case for the Defendants

5.31 The Defendants assert that the claim about offences of fraud committed by Jews, espoused by Irving in *Goebbels*, is factually incorrect and that the references cited by him in the footnote do not bear out his claim.

5.32 Indeed, say the Defendants, Interpol did not exist in 1932. The DNB, according to Evans, was a news agency which acted as the mouthpiece of the Nazi regime. In any case the DNB article cited by Irving did not contain any Interpol statistics but quoted remarks made by Daluege at a press conference which was nothing more than a propaganda exercise designed to justify the brutal persecution of the Jews.

5.33 As for Daluege, he was an enthusiastic member of the Nazi party who later emerged as a mass murderer on the Eastern front. His article in *Angriff*, relied on by Irving, was an attempt to justify the remarks made at the press conference in July 1932. The transcript of those remarks does not bear out the figure which appears in Irving's text. Nor, claimed Evans, do the other two references given by Irving in the footnote.

5.34 The Defendants argue that, if (as a reputable historian would and should do) Irving had checked the official statistics, it would have been obvious that no more than 74 Jews were convicted of insurance frauds. Irving has greatly exaggerated Daleuge's already suspect claim as to the number of such offences committed by Jews. No evidence is cited by Irving, or has been subsequently produced by him, for the claim that Jews committed 31,000 offences of fraud that year or anywhere near that many.

Response of Irving

5.35 The 'conditional response', as Irving put it, to this criticism is that due to an error on his part the footnote cites the wrong sources. He was, however, unable to identify the correct sources because, since he was banned from entering Germany in 1993, he no longer has access to the material documents.

5.36 Irving was unwilling to accept that the figure which he quoted was wrong. He claims that it was not unreasonable to rely on Daluege, who was admittedly 'a dodgy source' but was at the time the head of the German police system making it necessary to rely on him. Irving said that everyone would know that Daleuge was an active Nazi, so there was no reason to include in the text or in the footnote a cautionary note warning readers about placing reliance on Daluege as an objective and trustworthy source. Irving added that the two other sources cited by him do confirm the figure he quoted but, as already explained, Irving cannot gain access to them.

(iii) The events of Kristallnacht in November 1938

Introduction

5.37 The next example of alleged historical distortion by Irving relied on by the Defendants is his account of the events in Munich and elsewhere on the night of 9/10 November 1938 known as *Kristallnacht* (the night of broken glass). This is the second link in the chain which Irving regards as proving that Hitler defended the Jews.

5.38 9 November 1938, being the anniversary of the failed *putsch* of 1923, was marked by various parades and a celebratory dinner at Munich Old Town Hall attended by Hitler. After Hitler's departure, Goebbels made a speech in the course of which he informed his audience of anti-Jewish demonstrations which had been taking place in Hesse and Magdeburg-Anhalt and which had resulted in the destruction of Jewish businesses and synagogues. These demonstrations had apparently been prompted by the murder in Paris of a German diplomat named von Rath by a young Pole (described by Irving as 'a crazed Jew').

5.39 Goebbels said in his speech at the Old Town Hall:

On his briefing the Fuhrer had decided that such demonstrations were neither to be prepared nor organized by the party, but insofar as they are spontaneous in origin, they should likewise not be quelled.

Those present understood Goebbels to mean that the party should organize anti-Jewish actions without being seen to do so. Accordingly during the night of 9/10 November, 76 synagogues were destroyed and a further 191 set on fire, 7500 Jewish shops and businesses were destroyed; widespread looting occurred and 20,000 Jews were arrested and sent to concentration camps where they were severely mistreated. Such incidents were not confined to Munich: it was a nationwide pogrom.

The Defendants' case

5.40 The principal account of *Kristallnacht* by Irving is to be found at pp. 273–7 of his biography *Goebbels* but other references are to be found at pp. 196, 281 and 612–4. There are also accounts of the events of *Kristallnacht* in *Hitler's War* and in other articles published by Irving. All these accounts were subjected to detailed and severe criticism by Evans and by Longerich.

5.41 The first and main point on which the Defendants' experts take issue with Irving's account is his claim that the nationwide pogrom was conceived and initiated by Goebbels and that Hitler did not approve or even know about the pogrom until it was well under way and, when informed, was livid and tried to stop it. In order to make this claim, the Defendants allege that Irving has resorted to systematic distortion and suppression of data.

5.42 According to Goebbels's diary

Big demonstrations against the Jews in Kassell and Dessau, synagogues set on fire and businesses demolished . . .I go to the party reception in the Old Town Hall. Colossal activity. I brief the Fuhrer. He orders: let the demonstrations go on. Withdraw the police. The Jews must for once feel the people's fury. That is right.

This passage is rendered as follows by Mr Irving at pp. 273–4 of *Goebbels*:

. . . [Goebbels and Hitler] . . . learned that the police were intervening against anti-Jewish demonstrators in Munich. Hitler remarked that the police should not crack down too harshly under the circumstances. 'Colossal activity', the Goebbels diary entry reports, then claims: 'I brief the Fuhrer on the affair. He decides: allow the demonstrations to continue. Hold back the police. The Jews must be given a taste of the public anger for a change

5.43 Evans claims that the cumulative effect of the mistranslations and omissions in Irving's account give the false impression that Hitler merely ordered the police not to intervene against some unspecified anti-Jewish demonstrators in Munich, when in truth he had given positive orders that the demonstrations should continue not just in Munich but also elsewhere. These orders had been given by Hitler after he had been briefed by Goebbels about the burning of synagogues and demolition of businesses in Kassell and Magdeburg-Anhalt. Evans alleged that Irving has mistranslated *zuruckziehen* as meaning 'hold back' when it actually means 'withdraw'. What Hitler had actually wanted was that the police should be removed from the scenes of violence altogether. The reason, according to Goebbels's diary, was that the Jews might feel the people's fury (not, as Irving translates the German, be 'given a taste of the public anger').

5.44 Evans criticizes as being contrary to the evidence Irving's suggestion that it was not until after Hitler had left the Old Town Hall that Goebbels learned of widespread anti-Jewish violence and decided off his own bat to unleash the pogrom. This suggestion distances Hitler from responsibility for the violence which occurred later that night and the following day. The Defendants contend that, in making that suggestion, Irving ignores or suppresses the evidence that it was Hitler who authorized the continuation of the widespread violence of which he had been informed by Goebbels before he (Hitler) left the Old Town Hall.

5.45 Longerich expressed the view that the course of the pogrom clearly demonstrates Hitler's personal initiative. Goebbels' diary entry for 9 November, already quoted, refers to big demonstrations against the Jews in Kassell and Magdeburg, which had in any case been reported in the Nazi press that morning. So the suggestion that Hitler did not know about them when he left the Old Town Hall is unsustainable, as is the further suggestion that Goebbels first learned of the scale of the violence of them after Hitler had departed.

5.46 At pp. 275 and 281 of *Goebbels*, Irving refers to 'Goebbels's sole personal guilt' and to his 'folly' respectively. In the following passages Irving claims that Hitler, Himmler and Heydrich were all opposed to the pogrom. Another person presented by Irving as an opponent of the burning of synagogues and violence towards the Jews is the SA leader Victor Lutze. Irving also claims that SA *Gruppenfuhrer* Fust (wrongly called Lust by Irving) explicitly ordered that no synagogues were to be burned. These claims buttress the contention advanced by Irving that Goebbels was solely responsible for the orgy of violence which marked *Kristallnacht*.

5.47 Evans dismissed these claims as being the product of a manipulation of the evidence by Irving. According to Evans, the evidence tends to suggest that the SA group leaders generally played an active role in starting the violence. Evans argues that Juttner, who was the source for Irving's claim that Lutze opposed the pogrom, is wholly unreliable: he was himself a senior SA leader and his role in the events of that evening make it very improbable that he disapproved the violence. As for Irving's claim that Fust took action to prevent the burning of synagogues, Evans concluded that it was simply invented by Irving.

5.48 On this aspect of *Kristallnacht*, Evans was also critical of the omission of any reference in Irving's account of the night's events to the report of the internal enquiry subsequently held by the Nazi Party in February 1939. According to that report, Goebbels in his speech at the Old Town Hall told party members that Hitler, having been briefed by him about the burning of Jewish shops and synagogues, had decided that in so far as they occurred spontaneously they were not to be stopped. Evans pointed out that it would have been foolhardy in the extreme for Goebbels to have lied to old party comrades in the context of the party enquiry about what Hitler had said and decided about the anti-Jewish demonstrations.

5.49 The Defendants further contend that Irving's account of events during the night of 9/10 November seriously distorts the role played by Hitler. In the first place the Defendants criticize Irving for his omission to refer to a telegram sent from Berlin at 23.55 on 9 November by Muller, head of the Security Police, to officers warning them of the forthcoming outbreak of anti-Jewish demonstrations and ordering that they were not to be interrupted. The Defendants contend that this is an important document which reflects precisely what Hitler had ordered earlier that evening. They argue that it is obvious that Muller (who was answerable to Heydrich, who in turn was answerable through Himmler to Hitler) was acting on instructions from the highest level. Yet no mention of Muller's telegram is made in the text of Irving's writing about *Kristallnacht*.

5.50 Evans canvassed the question whether Hitler was consulted before the telegram from Muller was dispatched. He pointed to evidence, consisting in the testimony at Nuremberg of one SS officer (Schallerme-ier) and the witness statement of another (Wolff) and confirmed by a contemporaneous report to the Foreign Office, which suggests that it is very likely that Hitler and Himmler met before Muller sent the telegram. Himmler and Hitler were seen together in conversation earlier that evening before the dinner at the Old Town Hall. If Hitler and Himmler did meet, argued Evans, it is inconceivable that Muller's telegram would have been sent out in those terms without Hitler's approval. According to Evans, it is therefore to be inferred that, far from ordering that action against Jews be halted, Hitler in truth ordered it to continue. The evidence relied on by Evans in support of this inference is ignored or dismissed by Irving, unwarrantably so in the opinion of Evans.

5.51 Criticism of Irving was made by the Defendants for his omission to make reference to an instruction issued by the leader of SA group *Nordsee*, Bohmcker, which alluded to the wish of Hitler that the police should not interfere with the anti-Jewish demonstrations. The reason why Irving omits this message, suggested the Defendants, is that it runs counter to his thesis that Hitler was throughout concerned to protect the Jews.

5.52 At pp. 276–7 of *Goebbels* Irving writes that, when Hitler learned of the pogrom at about 1am on 10m November, he was 'livid with rage' and snapped to Goebbels by telephone to find out what was going on. Hitler is said to have made a 'terrible scene with Goebbels' who did not anticipate Hitler's 'fury'. Hitler's alleged reaction supports the thesis advanced by Irving that Hitler did not instigate the violence of that night.

5.53 In this portrayal of Hitler's reaction, Evans accused Mr Irving of further invention, manipulation and suppression. Irving's account of the events of the night of 9/10 November, including in particular his account of Hitler's reaction when apprised of the violence, depends heavily on the interviews which he conducted long after the war with Hitler's adjutants, that is, officers closely attached to Hitler. Evans claimed that Irving adopted a deplorably uncritical attitude towards the adjutants' version of events. Not only were they trying to call to mind events which took place long ago, they were also highly likely to slant their accounts in favour of Hitler. Another reason for scepticism about their accounts is their wish to exculpate themselves. Moreover, argued Evans, it is essential for an objective historian to weigh the testimony of such witnesses against the totality of the available evidence in order to test its reliability. The contemporaneous documents created during the night of violence are likely to prove a far more reliable guide than the self-serving and untested accounts of Hitler's staff. Irving, he contended, failed lamentably to weigh that evidence in the balance.

5.54 The principal source for the claim that Hitler was observed by Eberstein, Chief of Police in Munich, to be 'livid with rage' is said by Irving to be Hitler's chief former personal adjutant, Wilhelm Bruckner. Irving obtained Bruckner's papers from his son and donated them to the Institute of History in Munich to which Irving no longer has access. He was therefore unable to produce documentary verification of Bruckner's account. He was able to produce a *Deckblatt* (cover sheet) which includes a summary of the contents of the relevant file in Munich but that does not indicate the presence in the file of any *Kristallnacht* material. Evans's assistant searched the relevant file in Munich but was unable to find any document there which related to *Kristallnacht*. So the evidential position is unsatisfactory. Another reason put forward by Evans for doubting Irving's account is that contemporaneous documents establish that later that night at 2.10am Eberstein telephoned to the *Gestapo* in various towns repeating the order that police were not to interfere with actions against Jews. Eberstein would have done no such thing, argued Evans, if indeed he had seen Hitler livid with rage about the actions against the Jews. Irving makes no mention of Eberstein's instruction in his book about Hitler.

5.55 Be that as it may, Bruckner was a close associate of Hitler, so that, according to Evans his evidence needs to be treated with caution. In any case, according to a second-hand summary made by a German historian of a statement made by Bruckner, he was able to say no more than that Eberstein 'probably' went to see Hitler. In his evidence at Nuremberg, Eberstein did not mention having had this meeting with Hitler. So, according to Evans, the evidence for Hitler's reaction having been one of anger is very thin and difficult to reconcile with other events that evening. The violence continued virtually unabated throughout the night; this is unlikely to have occurred if indeed Hitler had at any stage wanted to bring it to a halt.

5.56 Another witness relied on by Irving for Hitler's reaction to the mayhem which broke out is Julius Schaub, a long-standing Nazi party member and senior SS officer (who after the war described Hitler as a peace-loving man). In his papers Schaub claimed that Goebbels 'ordained Kristallnacht Sunday (sic)' and that Hitler was furious when he learned of the outrages. Evans argued that Schaub too was close to Hitler and his evidence on that account should be treated with scepticism. Schaub's evidence, like that of the other witnesses relied on by Irving, is impossible to reconcile with Hitler's attitude towards the violence in the early evening of 9 November or with the orders (to which I shall shortly come) which went out in the early hours of 10 November permitting the excesses to continue.

5.57 The third witness relied on by Irving for Hitler's reaction on hearing of the anti-Jewish outrages is von Below, who was a Colonel in the Luftwaffe. Irving interviewed him some thirty years after the event. He was present in the hotel where Hitler was based at the time. He claimed to recall that Hitler's reaction, when hearing of the violence from von Eberstein, was to ask what was going on. He said that Hitler became angry and demanded that order in Munich be restored at once. Evans noted that in his memoirs (as opposed to his interview by Irving) von Below made clear that he was not present when, on learning of the pogrom, Hitler spoke to Goebbels by phone and so could not have overheard any part of their conversation. Evans argued that Irving's note of his interview with von Below makes clear that, contrary to Irving's claim in Goebbels, Hitler asked Eberstein (not Goebbels) to find out what was going on. There is no evidence, said Evans, for Irving's claim that Hitler 'snapped' orders at Goebbels. Evans regarded von Below as a variable witness whose account of *Kristallnacht* is wholly unreliable.

5.58 Another source for Irving's contention that Hitler condemned the pogrom is Hederich, a longstanding senior Nazi. Evans criticized Irving for his reliance on him. Hederich based his assessment of Hitler's attitude towards the violence upon his impression of a speech which he claimed Hitler made at the Old Town Hall before Goebbels spoke. But the evidence is clear, according to Evans, that Hitler made no speech at the Old Town Hall that evening.

5.59 At p. 276 of *Goebbels* Irving gives the following account of the message sent shortly after 1 am by Heydrich (Head of German Security Police):

What of Himmler and Hitler? Both were totally unaware of what Goebbels had done until the synagogue next to Munich's Four Seasons Hotel set on fire around 1 am. Heydrich, Himmler's national chief of police, was relaxing down in the hotel bar; he hurried up to Himmler's room, then telexed instructions to all police authorities to restore law and order, protect Jews and Jewish property and halt any ongoing incidents.

According to Evans this is a blatant manipulation of the historical record. Heydrich's telex sent to police chiefs and security service officers at 1.20 am on 10 November, which emanated from Himmler, instructed them that the demonstrations against the Jews expected during that night were 'not to be obstructed' subject to the following restrictions:

a only such measures may be taken as do not involve any endangering of German life or property (eg synagogue fires only if there is no danger of the fire spreading to surrounding buildings),

b the shops and dwellings of Jews may only be destroyed not looted. The police are instructed to supervise the implementation of this order and to arrest looters,

c care is to be taken that non-Jewish shops in shopping streets are unconditionally secured against damage, d   foreign nationals may not be assaulted, even if they are Jews.

Evans maintained that the meaning is clear: apart from those specific, narrow circumstances, the police were ordered *not* to intervene. The Defendants contend that Heydrich's order confirms and repeats the instruction of Himmler (which Irving accepts would have originated from Hitler) that the demonstrations were not to be interrupted. The restrictions only applied in identified and limited circumstances (eg where there was risk of damage to non-Jewish property). So it is alleged that Heydrich's telex ordered the exact opposite of what Irving claimed in *Goebbels*.

5.60 Evans advanced a similar criticism of Irving's treatment at p. 277 of *Goebbels* of a telex sent at 2.56am from the office of Rudolf Hess. Irving writes that

Hess's staff began cabling, telephoning and radioing instructions to *Gauleiters* and police authorities around the nation to halt the madness.

In fact, according to Evans, the order read:

On express orders from the very highest level, acts of arson against Jewish shops and the like are under no circumstances and under no conditions whatsoever to take place.

It is common ground that the message is referring to an order from Hitler ('the very highest level'). That order, according to Evans, had the limited effect of preventing fire-raising in Jewish shops and the like ('*Geschaften oder dergleichen*') and was not aimed at preventing attacks on Jews and their property generally. The concern for shops arose, said Evans, because they were in most cases owned by Germans. The order did not purport to proscribe attacks on Jewish homes or on synagogues. It referred only to arson and not to other forms of violence. Its tenor is consistent with the telegrams sent out by Muller and by Heydrich earlier that evening. There is, asserted Evans, no warrant for the claim which was made by Irving in an article published in 1983 that this order shows that Hitler ordered 'the outrage' to stop forthwith. If he had so ordered, why, asked Evans, did the violence continue. Far from ordering the outrage to cease, Hitler was by necessary inference authorizing the continuation of most of the lawlessness.

5.61 Evans alleged that Irving is guilty of further manipulation of evidence in relation to the account given by Hitler's adjutant, Wiedemann, which Irving uses to support his thesis that Hitler ordered Goebbels to stop the attacks when he heard about them. In *Goebbels* Irving writes:

Fritz Wiedemann, another of Hitler's adjutants, saw Goebbels spending much of that night, $9^{th}/10^{th}$, telephoning . . . to halt the most violent excesses.

Evans claimed that there are good reasons to doubt the reliability of Wiedemann and that in any event Irving has distorted or at least exaggerated his evidence. What in fact Wiedemann wrote was that 'it is reliably reported that' Goebbels had been seen making these telephone calls. There was therefore no justification for Irving's claim that Wiedemann 'saw' Goebbels making these calls. It was mere hearsay. In any event, said Evans, the picture conveyed by Irving is wholly inconsistent with other evidence of what Goebbels was doing that night.

5.62 Irving is further criticized by the Defendants for ignoring evidence, which according to Evans is inherently more reliable, namely the evidence contained in the report of the Supreme Party Tribunal report of 13 February 1939. That report includes a finding that when, at about 2am on 10 November, Goebbels was informed of the first death of a Jew in the progrom, he reacted by saying it would be the first of many. This reaction accords, say the Defendants, with the diary entry made by Goebbels that morning rejoicing in the violence ('Bravo!').

5.63 Lastly in relation to the events of *Kristallnacht*, Irving at p. 281 of *Goebbels* quotes from the diary of a diplomat named van Hassell recording the reaction of Rudolf Hess to the violent actions directed at the Jews. It reads:

[Hess] had left [the Bruckmanns] in no doubt that he completely disapproved the action against the Jews; he had also reported his views in an energetic manner to the *Fuhrer* and begged him to drop the matter, but unfortunately completely in vain. Hess pointed to Goebbels as the actual 'originator'.

In *Goebbels* Irving refers only to Hess's view that Goebbels was the originator of *Kristallnacht*. Whilst no objection was taken by him to the use of that part of the quotation, Evans did criticize Irving for his failure to refer to what Evans regarded as the far more significant aspect of

Hess's account, namely that Hitler had ignored his plea to halt the pogrom. That omission amounts, according to Evans, to a blatant misrepresentation of the diary entry. Evans also criticized Irving for his failure to mention the immediately following passage from the same diary which recounts a conversation Hassell had with the Prussian Finance Minister, Popitz, who is recorded as having said that Goering considered Hitler responsible for the events of *Kristallnacht*.

5.64 Evans concluded that Irving's claim that during the night of 9/10 November Hitler did everything he could to prevent violence towards the Jews and their property is based upon a tissue of inventions, manipulations, suppressions and omissions.

Irving's response

5.65 Irving denied that in his account of the events of *Kristallnacht* he had misrepresented the attitude Hitler adopted towards the violence directed at the Jews and their property. He maintained that the violence was initiated and promoted by Goebbels, who was acting without the authority of Hitler. He argued that, once Hitler became aware of the scale of the anti-Jewish rioting, he did his best to limit the violence.

5.66 Irving justified his translation of the account given by Goebbels in his diary of the remarks made by Hitler when he was told about the demonstrations as an attempt on his part to convey to his readers in the vernacular the flavour of Goebbels' style of writing in his diary. He denied that his version contains any mistranslation of the entry. As to the significance of what Hitler ordered at that early stage of the evening's events, Irving at one stage in his evidence suggested that what Goebbels had reported to Hitler was the death of van Rath rather than that demonstrations against Jews had broken out. But he later conceded that Hitler would have been told about the demonstrations against Jews. He emphasized that, at the point when Hitler gave his order for the police to be pulled back, the scale of the anti-Jewish demonstrations was modest. So it could not be said, claimed Irving, that Hitler was sanctioning excessive violence. It was not until later that night, towards midnight, that the demonstrations got out of hand and turned into a full-scale pogrom against the Jews.

5.67 Irving accepted that his account of Hitler's reaction on hearing in the early hours of the morning of 10 November about the outrages which were taking place is heavily reliant on the testimony of Hitler's adjutants provided many years after the event. Irving said that he was scrupulously careful not to put words into the mouths of those whom he interviewed. Irving testified that he spoke to von Below on no less than ten occasions. He claimed that what von Below then said is more worthy of belief than what he wrote in his memoirs. Irving pointed out there is no evidence which directly contradicts the accounts of the adjutants on which he has placed reliance. Their accounts converge and so may be said to corroborate one another. Irving did not accept that, in accepting the evidence of the adjutants about Kristallnacht but rejecting for example the evidence of survivors about events at Auschwitz, he has been guilty of applying double standards.

5.68 As to Muller's telegram, Irving agreed that he was aware of it but made no mention of it in Goebbels. He testified that he did not regard it as adding much. Moreover Irving did not accept that the evidence shows that Hitler authorized or even knew of Muller's order. Muller was in Berlin whereas Hitler was in Munich. Nor, said Irving, does Bohmcker's message add anything to what is already known from other sources. He pointed out that he did refer to Bohmcker in a footnote.

5.69 Irving denied having misrepresented Heydrich's telex of 1.26am. The reference given in the footnote in Goebbels for this message is ND:3052-PS. In cross-examination the message with reference number ND:3051-PS, which the Defendants claim is Heydrich's 1.20am message, was put to Irving. He said that he was quoting from a different message sent by Heydrich, namely ND:3052-PS, which is the reference given in Goebbels. He disagreed with the suggestion that it was unlikely that Heydrich would have sent another telex at about the same time. His answer to the Defendants' accusation of misrepresentation was therefore that he was summarizing the content of a different message sent by Heydrich at about the same time (which he was unfortunately unable to produce). However, when confronted with the text of message ND:3052-PS which the Defendants had obtained overnight, Irving accepted that it cannot have been the source for what he wrote. When reminded that on his own website he had admitted muddling 3051 and 3052, Irving conceded that there had been no other source for what he wrote about Heydrich's telex. In the end, as I understood him, Irving answered the criticism made by the Defendants of his account in *Goebbels* of Heydrich's telex by saying that, if he misinterpreted it, it was an innocent error or glitch which occurred in the redrafting process. He maintained that the error is in the context of the book as a whole a trivial one. In any event Irving reiterated that at this stage in the evening (1.20am), the full-scale pogrom had still not developed.

5.70 As regards Eberstein's telephone message at 2.10am, Irving gave various reasons why he attached no importance to it. He claimed that the original message would have gone out earlier. It is, he argued, a mere repetition of the instruction to the police not to interfere. Irving put to Evans various suggestions about the message: that Eberstein might not have been present when it was sent; that Eberstein might have been with Hitler when it went out; that it was an 'igniting' document. In any event, said Irving, the message was overtaken by events. For these reasons Irving said that he saw no need to refer to it in *Hitler's War*. Evans accepted none of these suggestions. Whether or not it is likely that Eberstein would have sent that message after seeing Hitler's reaction to the news of the night's events, Irving stated that two eye-witnesses, namely adjutants von Below and Futkammer, had confirmed Hitler's angry reaction to the news. In regard to Hederich, Irving justified his reliance upon his evidence. He contended that there was no reason for doubting what Hederich was quoted as having said. Despite having written in *Goebbels* that what Goebbels said 'conflicted with the tenor of Hitler's speech', Irving denied that Hederich had meant that Hitler made a speech at the Old Town Hall: he was referring to what he understood Hitler to have been saying about the violence. Irving did not accept the criticisms advanced by Evans of his reliance on these witnesses (summarized above).

5.71 Irving disagreed totally with the interpretation placed by the Defendants upon Rudolf Hess's message sent at 2.56am. He pointed out that it was he who had discovered the message and first brought it to the notice of historians. Whilst he accepted that there might have been reasons for singling out Jewish businesses for protection, such as the danger of damage being done to adjacent non-Jewish property or the likelihood that the Jewish property was insured with non-Jewish insurance companies, he was adamant that the order was intended to confer blanket protection on all Jewish property. He read the words *und dergleichen* as qualifying acts of arson, so that his interpretation of the message is that it covers acts of arson and all other forms of violence. He did not accept that the order of words in the message indicates that *und dergleichen* qualifies shops, so extending the order to shops and the like. It was Irving's case that the order sent at 2.56am emanated from Hitler and it was a direction that all actions against the Jews must stop forthwith. Accordingly his description of the message as conveying an order from Hitler 'to halt the madness' was appropriate and justified. Furthermore, in his response to the Defendants' closing submission, Irving also drew attention to a telegram sent out at 3.45am by *Gestapo* Section II signed 'p.p. Bartz' which required the immediate execution of Heydrich's order that all kinds of arson were to be hindered.

5.72 Given the passage of time since he had tried to decipher the handwriting of Wiedemann, Irving felt unable to respond to the criticism that he had misrepresented his account. He did agree that he may have made a mistake. Irving agreed that at the time when he was writing *Goebbels* he was aware of the diary entry of Hassell recording the comments made about *Kristallnacht* by Rudolf Hess. Irving argued that, when Hess said he had reported his views in an energetic manner to Hitler and begged him to drop 'the matter', Hess was obviously referring to the action subsequently taken by the Nazi party to fine the Jews. Hess was not begging Hitler to drop the anti-Jewish actions when they were in progress that night. Evans dismissed that as a blatant misconstruction of the diary entry which was plainly referring to the violence. Irving commented that he did not in any event consider that the entry adds much to what is already known.

(iv) The aftermath of Kristallnacht

Introduction

5.73 Once the killing, rape and wholesale destruction of property which marked *Kristallnacht* came to an end, questions arose how these actions against the Jews had come about and what should be done with the perpetrators. Discussions took place between Hitler and Goebbels. In due course the *Oberste Parteigericht*, a party court which formed no part of the criminal justice system, conducted an investigation and compiled a report about the affair.

The Defendants' case

5.74 In relation to Irving's portrayal of the events immediately following *Kristallnacht*, Evans again made criticisms of the manner in which he manipulated, misquoted and discounted reliable evidence. Evans contended that, contrary to the impression conveyed by passages in *Goebbels* at pp. 277–8, the diary entries made by Goebbels, as well as statements made by him at the time, provide convincing proof that Hitler wholeheartedly approved the pogrom and himself afterwards proposed economic measures to be taken against Jews.

5.75 Page 277 of *Goebbels* includes the following paraphrase of Goebbels' diary entry:

As more ugly bulletins rained down on him the next morning, 10 November 1938, Goebbels went to see Hitler to discuss 'what to do next' – there is surely an involuntary hint of apprehension in the phrase.

The vice which the Defendants perceive is that Irving's account suggests that Goebbels knew he was to blame for the pogrom and was apprehensive that Hitler would be angry with him. The Defendants contend that Irving had no basis whatever for adding the gloss that Goebbels was apprehensive since there is no such indication to be found in the diary. Far from being apprehensive, Goebbels's diary entry for 11 November shows how delighted he was at the success of the pogrom. Irving claimed that this entry is mendacious.

5.76 Goebbels's diary entry continues:

I report to the *Fuhrer* in the Osteria. He agrees with everything. His views are totally radical and aggressive. The action itself has taken place without any problems. 17 dead. But no German property damaged. The *Fuhrer* approves my decree concerning the ending of the actions with small amendments. I announce it via the press and radio. The *Fuhrer* wants to take very sharp measures against the Jews. They must themselves put their businesses in order again. The insurance will not pay them a thing. Then the Fuhrer wants a gradual expropriation of Jewish businesses.

The Defendants contend that this passage from Goebbels's diary makes crystal clear that, far from condemning Goebbels for what had occurred during Kristallnacht, Hitler in fact approved what had happened. The Defendants add that this is borne out by the fact that Goebbels that same afternoon told the local party chief that the Fuhrer had sanctioned the measures taken thus far and had declared that he did not disapprove of them.

5.77 Yet at page 278 of Goebbels Irving described the meeting at the Osteria in the following terms:

[Goebbels] made his report [on 'what to do next'] to Hitler in the Osteria . . . and was careful to record this – perhaps slanted – note in his diary which stands alone, and in direct contradiction to the evidence of Hitler's entire immediate entourage. 'He is in agreement with everything. His views are quite aggressive and radical. The action itself went off without a hitch. 100 dead. But no German property damaged. Each of these five sentences was untrue as will be seen.

The Defendants cite this as an instance of Irving perverting what Goebbels recorded in his diary and distorting what actually happened in order to exculpate Hitler.

5.78 Evans deduced that the probable sequence of events was that during the morning of 10 November Hitler and Goebbels discussed what to do next. Hitler told Goebbels to draft an order calling a halt to the violence because, in effect, the objective had by that stage been achieved. They then met for lunch at the Osteria and Hitler approved the order Goebbels had drafted. The terms of the order were broadcast at some stage during the afternoon and the order was formally promulgated at 4pm. The significance of the timing, according to Evans, is that the violence was in effect permitted to continue for most of 10 November. (In Vienna the violence against the Jews did not begin until 10 o'clock that morning.)

5.78 At a meeting held on 12 November, attended by amongst others Goering and Goebbels, the decision was taken that the Jews should, irrespective of any insurance cover, bear the cost of the pogrom;

that Jewish property should be 'aryanized' and that Jews should be forbidden to run shops or businesses. Evans criticized Irving for omitting to mention, in his account of this meeting at p. 281 of *Goebbels*, that these decisions reflected the wishes expressed by Hitler on 10 November and, according to Goering, were taken in response to Hitler's express request. Nor does Irving mention that, according again to Goering and to an official of the Four Year Plan named Kehrl, Hitler had expressly endorsed the action taken against the Jews.

5.79 At p. 281 of *Goebbels*, Irving writes:

Hess ordered the Gestapo and the party's courts to delve into the origins of the night's violence and turn the culprits over to the public prosecutors.

The Defendants assert that, since the court in question was a party and not a criminal court, there was no warrant for Irving to write that the culprits were to be handed over to the public prosecutors. Further Evans pointed out that the document cited in support of this passage, an order of 19 December 1938, made clear that referrals to the prosecution service were to take place only in cases arising out of 'personal and base motives'. The Ministry of Justice had already ordained that no action was to be taken in those cases where Jewish property was set on fire or blown up. None of this is mentioned by Irving. On the Defendants' case, the intent and effect of Hess's order is thus completely misrepresented by Irving, whose wording suggested to his readers that the Nazis determined to take firm disciplinary action against party members who had been guilty of unlawful violence during *Kristallnacht* and that anyone guilty of any misdemeanour would be handed over to be dealt with in the criminal courts.

5.80 In the event, according to the Defendants, the proceedings of the Party Court were a farce. According to its report of 13 February 1939, it investigated only sixteen cases of alleged unlawful activity. In only two of those cases were the suspects handed over to the criminal courts. Those two cases involved sexual offences against Jewish women: the reason for their referral was that the offences involved 'racial defilement'. In the other fourteen cases (which included allegations that twenty-one Jews had been murdered), the punishments were trivial, apparently because the Party Court took the view that the culprits were carrying out Hitler's orders. Hitler was asked to quash the proceedings against those fourteen. The criticism of Irving is that he makes no reference to what the Defendants describe as a scandalous manipulation of the justice system. The disciplinary action instituted by the Nazi party was virtually non-existent.

5.81 Irving suggested in *Goebbels* that following *Kristallnacht* Hitler distanced himself from Goebbels because he disapproved what he had done. But Evans contended that the record, including Goebbels' diary, suggests otherwise. For instance Goebbels reported in his diary that, when Hitler visited him on 15 November , Hitler 'was in a good mood. Sharply against the Jews. Approves my and our policy totally'. Evans asserted that there is no justification whatever for supposing, as Irving implies at p. 282 of his book, that that was an invention on the part of Goebbels.

5.82 Evans also disputed Irving's claim that the memoirs of Ribbentrop are further evidence that of Hitler's disapprobation of Goebbels. According to Evans, the documents cited by Irving do not upon examination support his claim that Goebbels was a pariah in Berlin and even less popular than Ribbentrop and Himmler. Evans noted Irving makes several references to an author named I Weckert, without giving the reader any indication that she is a well-known anti-semitic Nazi sympathizer, who in Evans's opinion is discredited as an historian.

5.83 The final criticism made by Evans is that at p. 276 of *Goebbels* and elsewhere Irving seriously understates the suffering inflicted upon the Jews in the pogrom. The number of synagogues destroyed far exceeded Irving's figure of 191. The extent of the damage to Jewish shops is also downplayed by Irving. The number of Jews killed was many more than the thirty-six claimed by Irving, even if those who died en route to concentration camps are left out of account.

Irving's response

5.84 By way of explanation of his reference to Goebbels having felt apprehensive when he went to see Hitler on 10 November 1938, Irving stressed that his paraphrase 'what to do next' is an accurate rendition of the German:

Ich uberlege mit dem Fuhrer unsere nunmehrigen Massnahmen.

According to Irving, those words mean that Goebbels discussed with Hitler the measures which need to be taken 'now more than ever'. The reason why he wrote that Goebbels was apprehensive was that he had been summoned to see Hitler at a time when Germany was going up in flames. Goebbels had believed that he had acted in accordance with Hitler's wishes but to his consternation he had discovered that he had been doing the exact opposite of what Hitler wished. Irving did, however, agree that Goebbels' diary entry indicates that he was discussing with Hitler whether to let the actions against the Jews continue or to call a halt. He claimed (and Evans agreed) that the probability is that in the course of a telephone conversation on the morning of 10 November Hitler instructed Goebbels to draw up an order calling a halt to the violence.

5.85 But Irving did not accept the rest of Evans's reconstruction of the sequence of events on 10 November. In regard to Goebbels' account in his diary of his meeting with Hitler at the Osteria restaurant, Irving argued that the claim that Hitler endorsed what Goebbels had done was false, that is, Goebbels was lying in that diary entry. Goebbels was prone, said Irving, to claiming that Hitler had approved his actions when in truth he had done nothing of the kind. Goebbels was being denounced on all sides so he needed to claim he had the approval of Hitler. Irving did, however, agree that Hitler did express the intention that Jewish businesses should be expropriated. Irving suggested, on the basis of information said to have been uncovered by Ingrid Wechert (to whom I have already referred), that an instruction to halt the demonstrations and actions was broadcast as early as 10am on 10 November. Evans doubted the timing claimed by Wechert and Irving: the only record of the content of the broadcast gives the time of transmission as the afternoon. It is accepted that the order calling a halt to the violence was issued at 4pm. Evans considered it to be unlikely that there would have been a delay of six hours between the broadcast and the promulgation of the order.

5.86 Irving justified the doubt which he cast in *Goebbels* on the diary entry in which Goebbels recorded Hitler's visit on 15 November and claimed that Hitler had indicated that he approved totally 'my and our policy'. According to Irving, it was obvious from the handwritten diary entry that 'my' was inserted by accident and Goebbels then added 'and our' as an afterthought because it would have been, as Irving put it, a bit of a giveaway if he had crossed out 'my'. Evans refused to accept that interpretation of the entry.

5.87 Similarly in relation to the message sent by Goebbels to the Nazi party chief in Munich-Upper Bavaria that 'the *Fuhrer* sanctions the measures taken so far and declares that he does not disapprove of them', Irving argued that it cannot be taken at face value. The reason, according to Irving, is the double negative in the second part of the sentence, which indicates that Goebbels was providing an alibi for himself by claiming that he had Hitler's authority when in fact he did not.

5.88 Irving did not accept that in his account in *Goebbels* he had falsely given the impression that firm action was taken against those involved in the violence on *Kristallnacht*. He defended his reference in *Goebbels* to 'turning the culprits over to the public prosecutors' by claiming that there were a large number of prosecutions and that many were sent to gaol. He did, however, accept that it was inappropriate to refer to the party court as the public prosecutor. He also agreed that there would have been many who had committed grave crimes against the Jews who were let off. Irving sought to justify this lenient treatment on the basis that their acts of violence had been authorized by the state. Irving made reference to a passage in the report of the Party Court which was in the following terms:

The individual perpetrators [of the acts of violence etc] had put into action, not merely the supposed will of the leadership, but the to be sure vaguely expressed but correctly recognized view of the leadership.

Irving took this to be saying by implication that the perpetrators knew they were *not* acting on the order of Hitler. Evans claimed in reply that that is the exact opposite of what the report says: the perpetrators were acting in accordance with the wishes of the leadership. That is the basis on which those who compiled the report concluded that the perpetrators should not be punished.

5.89 Whilst Irving accepted that only two of the sixteen suspects referred to in the report of the Party Court were handed over to the criminal courts, he claimed that many others were prosecuted. Space reasons prevented him from telling his readers how many escaped virtually scot-free. He did not accept that it was the intention of the Nazi party that all but a tiny minority should get off.

(v) Expulsion of Jews from Berlin in 1941

Introduction

5.90 In the autumn of 1941 there remained living in Germany, albeit under increasingly restrictive conditions, some 146,000 Jews of which 76,000 or so resided in Berlin. In October 1941, following the invasion of the Soviet Union, which was accompanied by the mass murder of Soviet Jews by *Einsatzgruppen*, the compulsory deportation of Jews from Berlin to the East and principally to Poland commenced.

5.91 At 1.30pm on 30 November 1941 Himmler had a telephone conversation with Heydrich. The relevant part of Himmler's note of that conversation reads:

Judentransport aus Berlin. (Jew-transport from Berlin.)

Keine liquidierung. (No liquidation.)

Despite that instruction a trainload of Jews who arrived in Riga that day were massacred on arrival.

The Defendants' case

5.92 The Defendants advance numerous criticisms of the manner in which Irving has written about the deportation of the German Jews from Berlin and in particular the role of Hitler in the affair. The Defendants are also critical of the account given by Irving of the circumstances surrounding the execution of the Berlin Jews on arrival in Riga (with which I shall deal later).

5.93 The starting point for the Defendants' criticisms is the claim made by Irving that, unlike Goebbels, Hitler was not at this time driven by anti-semitism. In *Goebbels* Irving quotes from an article by Goebbels published in *Das Reich* to show that he was more violently anti-semitic than Hitler. But Evans observed that Irving omits to mention that Goebbels started his article by quoting Hitler's celebrated 1939 prediction of the annihilation of the Jews. In his report Evans quoted numerous utterances by Hitler at this time to show that Hitler was expressing similar views to those of Goebbels about the Jews. A comprehensive list of Hitler's statements about the Jews, covering the period 1919 to 1945 has been collated by the Defendants and is include at tab 5(i) of their written closing submissions. I shall revert to the list hereafter.

5.94 Irving claimed in *Goebbels* that it was Goebbels's article in *Das Reich* which inspired the killing of thousands of the Berlin Jews in Riga in November 1941. This claim is based on the testimony of Wisliceny (one of Eichmann's top officials who was responsible for the Final Solution in Slovakia and elsewhere). At p. 379 of *Goebbels*, Irving wrote that Wisliceny described the *Das Reich* article as 'the watershed'. Wisliceny did indeed refer to that article but he also reported that 'In this period of time, after the beginning of the war with the USA, I am convinced must fall the decision of Hitler which ordered the biological annihilation of European Jewry'. The Defendants contend that, not only was Irving wrong to attribute to Wisliceny the view that the article in *Das Reich* was in truth the watershed, but that he also deliberately suppressed the crucial passage referring to Hitler's order for the biological annihilation of the Jews.

5.95 At p. 377 of *Goebbels* Irving claims that Hitler was neither consulted nor informed about the deportation of Jews from Berlin in 1941. Evans contended that this claim is another manipulation of the historical record. Goebbels in his diary on 19 August 1941 states that the *Fuhrer* gave him his approval for the transports of the Jews out of Berlin. A corroborative entry is to be found in entries in Goebbels' diary for 19 and 24 September 1941. Greiser, who was stationed in the Warethegau and was answerable to Hitler, was similarly told by Himmler that the *Fuhrer* wanted the Old Reich and the Protectorate to be cleared of Jews. The evidence of Hitler's involvement is clear, say the Defendants.

5.96 Irving based his assertion of Hitler's non-involvement upon his Table Talk of 25 October 1941. (I interpolate that the Table Talk is a record in note form, compiled by adjutants of Bormann named Heim and Picker, of remarks made by Hitler at informal gatherings). But, said Evans, Irving misconstrues and mistranslates the record of what Hitler then said, which properly understood was that he was no longer remaining 'inactive' against the Jews and had started to deal with them.

5.97 The Defendants contend that the claim made by Irving that Hitler personally intervened in an attempt (unsuccessful as it turned out) to prevent the Berlin Jews being liquidated is wholly unwarranted by the evidence. In the 1977 edition of *Hitler's War* Irving wrote at p. 332 that Himmler was 'summoned' to the Wolf's Lair (Hitler's Headquarters) and 'obliged' to telephone an order to Heydrich that there was to be no liquidation of Jews. The reader is given to understand that Hitler procured an order which applied to all Jews. Moreover in the introduction to *Hitler's War* Irving describes that note as 'incontrovertible evidence' that Hitler issued a general order prohibiting the liquidation of Jews generally. He attaches sufficient importance to the note to reproduce a photograph of it in the book.

5.98 The Defendants assert that Irving's interpretation of Himmler's note (cited above in the Introduction to this section) is perverse and a clear falsification of the document. Evans alleged, firstly, that it is clear on the face of the note that it is referring to a single transport of Jews out of Berlin which departed on 27 November: the German word *transport* is in the singular, the plural would be *transporte*. Both the language and the context make it plain that what is being referred to is a single transport of Jews. What is more it is clear that the note is talking only of Berliner Jews because it includes the words *aus Berlin*. Moreover, say the Defendants, there is no evidence for the claim that any order was issued by Hitler or indeed that he was involved at all. True it is that the telephone call was made by Himmler from Hitler's bunker. But it was made at 1.30pm and Himmler's appointment diary suggests that Hitler and Himmler did not meet for lunch until later that afternoon.

5.99 From about the mid-1980s Irving accepted that the note does indeed refer to the single transport out of Berlin and not to Jews generally. Nevertheless the error was not corrected in the 1991 edition of *Hitler's War*. Irving explained this by saying that the 1991 edition went to press in the mid-80s. It is, however, right to note that in *Goebbels* Irving no longer claims that the order applied to Jews generally.

However, he continued to assert that the order emanated from Hitler. Thus at p. 379 of *Goebbels* Irving writes that, even as the Jews were being shot in Riga, 'Hitler . . . was instructing Himmler that these Berlin Jews were not to be liquidated'. In May 1998 Irving accepted through his website that his theory that Hitler told Himmler to tell Heydrich to stop the shooting had been wrong. Despite this on 31 August 1998 Irving posted another document in which he asserted that Hitler had demonstrably originated the order not to kill the Jews in Riga. Evans apostrophized this behaviour on the part of Irving as egregious and disreputable. The Defendants cite this as an example of Irving continuing to twist the evidence in order to portray Hitler favourably even after the error of his ways had been pointed out to him.

5.100 Nor, according to Evans, is there any basis for Irving's claim in the 1977 edition of *Hitler's War* that on 1 December 1941 Himmler telephoned Pohl, an SS General, to tell him that Jews were to 'stay where they are' (that is, out of harm's way). Irving based this claim on Himmler's phone log, which contained this entry:

Verwaltungsfuhrer der SS (Administrative leaders of the SS)

haben zu bleiben (have to stay)

Irving now accepts that he misread '*haben*' as '*Juden*' and that the order was stating that administrative leaders of the SS had to stay where they were. The Defendants do not accept that the mistranscription was due to an innocent misreading of Himmler's manuscript. They point to other manuscript words in the same document which should have alerted Irving (and on the Defendants' case did alert him) to the fact that the word Himmler actually wrote was '*haben*'. Irving ignored the fact that there is no full stop after SS and before *haben*. He also ignored the fact that *haben zu bleiben* is indented, suggesting that it is linked to the previous line. Irving agreed in cross-examination that to read that entry as 'Administrative officers of the SS Jews to remain' would be meaningless because it would be saying nothing in relation to the administrative officers. Evans considered this to be deliberately a perverse misreading by Irving borne of his overwhelming desire to portray Hitler as a friend of the Jews.

Irving's response

5.101 Irving argued that there is what he describes as another 'chain of documents' which impels one to the conclusion that Hitler was intent upon protecting the Berlin Jews.

5.102 In regard to his claim in *Goebbels* that Hitler was neither consulted nor informed about the expulsion of Jews from Berlin, Irving accepted on the basis of the evidence now available that the initiative for the expulsions came from Hitler. He denies having suppressed any relevant material of which he was aware at the time. Irving discounted the Wisliceny report with its reference to an order by Hitler for the biological annihilation of the Jews because it was made in 1946 when Wisliceny was facing the gallows. In any case Irving dismissed the report as speculative and made by a man 'at janitorial level'. Irving did not accept that in this context *'vernichtung'* connotes extermination. He denied having applied double standards in his reliance on Wisliceny, adopting those parts which suited his case and discarding the rest.

5.103 In support of his argument that Hitler was protective towards the Jews, Irving pointed to an entry in Himmler's telephone log for 17 November 1941, which he said imports that Himmler has had his knuckles rapped by Hitler for wanting to get rid of the Jews in the General Government. He also relied, as a 'tiny dent' in the public perception that the Jews were transported in cattle trucks in atrocious conditions, on messages which indicate that the trains taking Jews from Berlin to the East were amply provisioned and that Jews were permitted to take with them the tools of their trade. Irving claimed that this is inconsistent with the existence of a policy of systematic extermination.

5.104 In relation to the entry in Himmler's log for 30 November 1941 (quoted in in the introduction to this section) which included the phrase *'Judentransport aus Berlin – keine liquidierung'*, Irving accepted that he has no direct evidence that Himmler was 'summoned' to see Hitler or that he was 'obliged' to issue the order. But he pointed out that Himmler had spent that morning working at Hitler's headquarters and suggested that the probability is that Himmler would have spoken on the telephone to Hitler before the two of them met for lunch at 2.30pm. Irving argued that the likelihood of such a conversation having taken place before Himmler spoke to Heydrich of the telephone, together with the fact that Himmler was at Hitler's headquarters when the call was made, suggest that it was Hitler who originated the order that the Jews were not to be liquidated. He agreed that there is no evidence that Himmler and Hitler met before the call was made to Heydrich at 1.30pm on 30 November 1941. However, he suggested that the reasonable inference 'with very strong evidence' is that they spoke on the phone before that time. He maintained this position despite the entry on his own website accepting that his original theory that Himmler had discussed the matter with Hitler before phoning Heydrich had been wrong. Evans replied that there is no evidence that Himmler spoke to Hitler that morning. There were several bunkers at Hitler's headquarters and there was no reason for Himmler to communicate either face to face or by telephone with Hitler before they met for lunch.

5.105 Another reason advanced by Irving to justify his contention that the instruction *Keine Liquidierung* emanated from Hitler is that it was Himmler who telephoned Heydrich and not *vice versa*. This is not apparent from Himmler's note of the call. But Irving pointed to another instruction issued by Himmler to Heydrich made from Hitler's headquarters months afterwards on 20 April 1942 that there was to be no annihilation of gypsies. Irving inferred that that instruction emanated from Hitler and argued that the same inference is to be drawn in relation to the instruction on 30 November 1941. Evans's response was that there is no reason whatever to suppose that there was any connection between Hitler and either of these instructions issued by Himmler.

5.106 In relation to the entry in Himmler's log for 1 December 1941, Irving said that he misread Himmler's spidery *Sutterlin* handwriting: he thought he had written *Judentransporte* in the plural. It was, he said, a 'silly misreading'. He firmly denied any deliberate manipulation. He denied that he was lying when he claimed to have made an innocent slip. He was, however, constrained to admit that in a letter to Dr Kabermann written in 1974 he had correctly transcribed the word in the singular. On reflection he claimed that his original explanation that he though the note referred to transports in the plural was a slip of the memory. He explained that he believes he understood *transport* to mean transportation in the generic sense. He pointed out that no definite article comes before the noun (which Evans says is rare in the case of

Himmler's notes). He argued that dictionary definitions of the meaning of that word bear him out but he was unable to produce a contemporaneous (ie 1930s) dictionary which gave the meaning 'transportation'. He rejected the claim made by Evans that this explanation is equally unconvincing, not least because it omits to take account of the words *aus Berlin*.

5.107 Despite his eventual acceptance that the conversation between Himmler and Heydrich on 30 November related to a single trainload of Jews, Irving continued to suggest in his cross-examination of Evans that the instruction *Keine Liquidierung* had a wider significance and applied to all European Jews. He relied on a message sent on 1 December 1941 to the local SS commander in Riga, named Jeckeln, summoning him to a meeting with Himmler in Berlin on 4 December. Irving pointed out that this summons had followed rapidly upon a request made from Riga to Berlin by the murderous Jeckeln for ten military pistols for *Sonderactionen* (special measures). Irving interpreted Himmler's appointments diary for 4 December 1941 as showing that he gave Jeckeln a rap over the knuckles.

5.108 Irving relied also on the contents of a telegram sent on the same day to Jeckeln by Himmler, which reads:

The Jews being outplaced to Ostland are to be dealt with only in accordance with the guidelines laid down by myself or the *Reichssicherheitshauptamt* on my orders. I would punish arbitrary and disobedient acts.

Irving described this as an incredibly important message because it shows that at headquarters the shooting of the Jews was disapproved. He further asserted that the absence of any reference to Hitler in the message indicates that Hitler had nothing to do with the promulgation of guidelines as to circumstances in which European Jews were to be killed. Irving claims that the consequence of this sequence of events was that the shooting of German Jews stopped for many months. Evans accepted the killing of German Jews was halted for some months after December 1941 but pointed out that the surviving Jews in the ghetto in Riga were murdered on 8 December presumably with the concurrence of Himmler. The massacre of non-German Jews in the *Ostland* continued unabated.

5.109 Irving argued that the inference to be drawn from the communications referred to at paragraphs 5.107–8 indicate that there were in existence at the time guidelines which prohibited the killing of European Jews and that the shooting of the Berlin Jews in Riga was a transgression of those guidelines.

5.110 In reference to Himmler's telephone log for 1 December 1941 Irving testified that he innocently misread 'haben' for 'Juden' because the two words appear similar in the Gothic manuscript. He said that Himmler's handwriting at this point is very indistinct. He did not spot that there was no full stop after *Verwaltungsfuhrer SS*. It was a reasonable mistake to make and certainly not a deliberate misreading. In any event Irving dismissed this entry in the log as totally immaterial. The failure to correct the 1991 edition of *Hitler's War* was an oversight. Evans disagreed that the misreading of the note was an innocent mistake. He argued that no historian who was not biased could read the words as saying anything other than *haben zu bleiben*.

(vi) Shooting of Jews in Riga

Introduction

5.111 It is common ground between the Defendants and Irving that, from about the summer of 1941 onwards until the end of 1942, a large number of Jews in the area of the General Government (as a large part of occupied Poland was called) were shot and killed by Nazi *Einsatzgruppen*. There are issues between the parties as to the scale of the executions which took place and as to whether Hitler approved or knew of the executions. I shall revert to these issues when I come to deal later in the judgment with the extent of Hitler's knowledge of and responsibility for the mass extermination of the Jews.

5.112 The immediate issue relates to the manner in which Irving deals in his published works with the circumstances under which the Berlin Jews who, as I have just described, were deported to Riga came to be executed by Jeckeln and his henchmen.

Case for the Defendants

5.113 The Defendants also cite Irving's treatment of the shooting of these Jews as another instance of his misrepresentation of events and his determination to exculpate Hitler from responsibility for their fate. In particular the Defendants criticize Irving for his omission to record what Bruns had to say about the shooting of Berlin Jews. In 1941 Bruns had been a colonel stationed in Riga. Later in 1945, when in captivity, he spoke about the shooting to fellow prisoners. His words were surreptitiously recorded so (say the Defendants) there is no reason to suppose he was not telling the truth. The transcript records him as saying that a junior officer named Altemeyer had told him that the Berlin Jews were to be shot 'in accordance with the Fuhrer's orders'. According to the same transcript, after Hitler had been informed of the shooting Altemeyer showed Bruns another order and said:

Here is an order just issued, prohibiting mass-shootings on that scale from taking place in future. They are to be carried out more discreetly.

The Defendants contend that Bruns's words represent important and credible evidence from a reliable witness, firstly, that Hitler personally ordered the Riga executions and, secondly, that once informed of the shooting Hitler, far from prohibiting such conduct in the future, ordered that shootings of this kind should continue but on a more discreet basis.

5.114 Despite the crucial importance of Bruns's evidence, of which Irving was aware, there is no reference in any of Irving's books to his claim as to the apparent role of Hitler in regard to the deaths of the Berlin Jews in Riga. Reference is made to Bruns in the introduction to the American edition of *Hitler's War*, where Irving refers to Hitler's 'renewed orders that such mass murders were to stop forthwith'. The Defendants contend that this reference wholly perverts the sense of Bruns's account.

5.115 In the text of *Goebbels* at p. 645 Irving writes that 1000 Berlin Jews and 4000 Riga Jews were shot on 30 November. According to Evans and Browning, the true figure was found in later reports to be at least twice that number and higher estimates of 13–15,000 were given in post-war trials. The Defendants are critical of Irving for minimizing the number of those killed. They accept that he refers, albeit tucked away in a footnote, to a claim that 27,800 Jews were murdered but he there describes that claim as exaggerated. Evans testified that the figure of 27,800, which was reported by Einsatzgruppe A was probably justified.

5.116 In relation to Hitler's attitude towards the shooting of the German Jews in Riga, the Defendants also criticize Irving for making no mention whatever of the evidence of Schultz-Dubois. This young Nazi officer was entrusted with the task of conveying to Admiral Canaris a report prepared by another officer based in Riga protesting at the shooting. The intention was that Canaris should raise the matter with Hitler. According to a letter from the widow of Schultz-Dubois, which is quoted in a book by Professor Gerald Fleming, Canaris did so but was met with the response:

You want to show weakness, do you *mein Herr*! I have to do that, for after me there will not be another one to do it.

This, say the Defendants, is clear evidence that Hitler approved the shooting the Jews yet Irving suppressed it.

Case for Mr Irving

5.117 Irving in his evidence adopted an equivocal attitude towards the covertly recorded words of General Bruns about events in Riga. He accepted that in general Bruns is reliable and credible, partly because he did not know his words were being recorded. Nevertheless, noting that Bruns at his trial had denied even having been present at the Riga shootings, there were parts of Bruns's recorded account which Irving discounted. In relation to Bruns's account of Altemeyer having said to him:

Here's an order that's come, saying that mass shootings of this kind may no longer take place in future. That is to be done more cautiously now.

Irving claimed that the first part means that Hitler had ordered that the mass killings had got to stop. But Irving dismissed the second part, that is, the instruction that the shooting should be done more cautiously in future as nothing more than a sneering aside by Altemeyer.

5.118 Irving's reason for discounting these words is that Altemeyer was at the time a young officer in his early 20s and so likely to have fobbed off criticism by a senior officer of what he was doing by referring to 'the *Fuhrer*'s orders'. It was, according to Irving 'a throwaway line'. Irving argued that his interpretation of Altemeyer's words is consistent with the intercepted message from Himmler to Jeckeln of 1 December 1941 requiring him to comply with the guidelines for dealing with deported German Jews.

5.119 In contrast to his initial assessment of Bruns's reliability, Irving went so far in his cross-examination of Evans as to suggest that his account was third hand and, having been provided four years after the event, could not be treated as hard evidence.

5.120 As to the number of casualties in Riga on 30 November 1941, Irving sought to justify the figure he gave in the text of *Goebbels*, namely 5,000, by a calculation of the number of corpses which could have been fitted into the pits which General Bruns described in his account of the shootings. If those pits measured 25 metres long by 3 metres wide and 2 metres deep, Irving worked out that, assuming 10 bodies per cubic metre, the pits would have accommodated in the region of 7,000 bodies. Evans expressed the view that such a calculation was meaningless because it contained so many assumptions, not least the assumption that the pits were only 2 metres deep. Irving added that he had not concealed the claim that there were over 28,000 deaths: the claim was in the footnote to which readers could refer.

5.121 Irving rejected the Defendants' criticism of him for ignoring altogether in his writing about the Riga shootings the evidence of the widow of Schultz-Dubois, who had been responsible for transmitting a report by a young army officer protesting about the shootings to Admiral Canaris in order that the Admiral might bring it to the attention of Hitler. I understood Irving to say that, although the letter of Mrs Schultz-Dubois which contains this information is to be found on his website, he had not at the material time read it. Irving testified that, whilst he had in 1982 looked at parts of the book by Professor Fleming in which the letter of *Frau* Schultz-Dubois is quoted, he had not read that passage which at page 98 contains the quotation from her letter. It was put to Irving in cross-examination that the markings in his copy of Fleming's book indicate that he read as far as page 104 and so would have read the contents of the letter at page 98. Irving denied that allegation.

5.122 Irving did, however, agree that Hitler's reaction as recounted in the letter of Frau Schultz-Dubois is some evidence that Hitler considered it to be his task to kill the Jews. That, Irving agreed, must be what was meant by Hitler's phrase 'after me there will not be another one to do it [carry out the shootings]'. But Canaris was known to be anti-Nazi and so, argued Irving, his report of Hitler's reaction to the report has to be discounted.

(vii) Hitler's views on the Jewish question

Introduction

5.123 This is another topic to which I shall need to revert at greater length when I come to deal with the criticisms levelled by the Defendants against Irving for his denial that Hitler was complicit in the genocidal policy of deporting and subsequently killing by the use of gas vast numbers of Jews from all over Europe. At this point I shall confine myself to a summary of the criticisms advanced by the Defendants of Irving's portrayal, in selected passages from his books, of Hitler's stance on the Jewish question, together with Irving's answers to those criticisms.

The Defendants' case

5.124 The case for the Defendants is that at every opportunity Irving portrays Hitler as adopting a non-confrontational posture towards the Jews and being kept in ignorance, at least until the autumn of 1943, of the wholesale liquidation which was under way. This picture is a wholly false one, say the Defendants. It will suffice if I give a selection of the statements made by Hitler on the subject of the Jews on which the Defendants place reliance.

5.125 The Defendants accuse Irving of perverse and selective quotation and deliberate mistranslation in a passage at p. 377 of *Goebbels* which purports to give an account of an occasion described in Hitler's Table Talk for 25 October 1941. Irving describes how Hitler soliloquized to Himmler and Heydrich in the following terms:

Hitler was neither consulted nor informed [about the mass deportation of Jews from Berlin]. Ten days after the forced exodus began, he referred, soliloquizing over supper to Himmler and Heydrich, to the way the Jews had started the war. 'Let nobody tell me', Hitler added, 'that despite that we can't park them in the marshier parts of Russia! By the way', he added, 'it's not a bad thing that public rumour attributes to us a plan to exterminate the Jews'. He pointed out, however, that he had no intention of starting anything at present. 'There's no point in adding to our difficulties at a time like this'.

Evans asserted that the claim that Hitler was neither consulted nor informed about the deportations is pure invention. He contended that a true translation of that extract from the Table Talk is as follows:

Nobody can tell me: but we can't send them into the morass! For who bothers about our people? Its good if the terror (*schrecken*) that we are exterminating Jewry goes before us . . . I'm forced to pile up an enormous amount of things myself; but that doesn't mean that what I take cognisance of without reacting to it immediately, just disappears. It goes into an account; one day the book is taken out. I had to remain inactive for a long time against the Jews too. There's no sense in artificially making extra difficulties for one's self; the more cleverly one operates, the better . . .

5.126 A series of cumulative criticisms are made of Irving's version of this extract from Hitler's Table Talk. The original text does not refer to 'parking' nor to Russia. By rendering *schrecken* as 'rumour' Irving waters down the original. Besides there is no reference in the original to 'attributing': the extermination is presented as a fact. The German original makes clear that Hitler regarded the period of inaction vis-à-vis the Jews to be over. The moment has come to strike. The Defendants argue that the net result of Irving's version of Hitler's remarks is wholly to misrepresent the thrust of Hitler's remarks.

5.127 In his diary Goebbels recorded a meeting with Hitler on 21 November 1941 in terms which included the following:

The *Fuhrer* also completely agrees with my views with reference to the Jewish question. He wants an energetic policy against the Jews, which, however, does not cause us unnecessary difficulties.

Yet at p. 379 of *Goebbels* Irving writes that Goebbels displayed a far more uncompromising face than Hitler's towards the Jews. That is followed by a passage quoting the extract from Goebbels's diary just cited in the following terms:

. . . [Hitler] again instructed Goebbels to pursue a policy against the Jews that does not cause us endless difficulties . . .

The Defendants claim that Irving distorts the sense of the diary entry by omitting the reference to Hitler wanting an energetic policy towards the Jews and by omitting the first sentence recording Hitler's agreement with his (Goebbels') views about the Jewish question.

5.128 The Defendants rely also upon Irving's account of a speech made by Hitler to the Gauleiter on 12 December 1941, when, according to Goebbels' diary (in Longerich's translation):

As concerns the Jewish question, the *Fuhrer* is determined to make a clean sweep. He had prophesied to the Jews that if they once again brought about a world war they would experience their own extermination (*vernichtung*). This was not just an empty phrase. The World War is there, the extermination of Jewry (*Judentum*) must be the necessary consequence. This question must be seen without sentimentality. We are not here in order to have sympathy with the Jews, rather we sympathize with our own German people. If the German people have now once again sacrificed as many as 16,000 dead in the Eastern campaign, then the authors of this bloody conflict must pay with their lives.

The Defendants' case is that, according to Goebbels' account, Hitler was expressly contemplating the extermination of Jews generally. The Defendants argue that this passage, which followed one day after the outbreak of war between Nazi Germany and the Unites States, echoes what Goebbels had earlier written in an article in *Das Reich* and that it demonstrates that Hitler was determined to act no less brutally towards the Jews than was Goebbels. It marks, say the Defendants, the reaction of Hitler to the outbreak of world war, which was that the Jews must be annihilated.

5.129 According to the Defendants, confirmation for this proposition is to be found in the account of General Governor Hans Frank (who Irving accepts was in Berlin when Hitler spoke to the *Gauleiter*), which states:

In Berlin we were told 'why all this trouble? We cannot use them in the *Ostland* or the *Reichscommissariat* either. Liquidate them yourselves!' We must destroy the Jews wherever we encounter them and wherever it is possible in order to preserve the entire structure of the Third Reich.

Frank's diary contains the following further passage:

. . . we cannot shoot these 3.5 million Jews. We can't poison them. But we will, however, be able to undertake interventions which in some way lead to a successful annihilation, and indeed in connection with the large scale measures to be undertaken from the Reich and to be discussed. The General Government must become just as free of Jews as the Reich is. Where and how that happens is a matter for the institutions which we must put into action and create here and the effectiveness I will report on to you in good time.

The Defendants contend that Frank was there recording what had in effect been a direction to the General Government from Berlin to liquidate the Jews. The Defendants assert that the latter passage is 'an evolutionary document', presaging the extermination of Jews by gassing.

Criticism was levelled at Irving for his claim at p. 428 of the 1991 edition of *Hitler's War* that Hitler was in East Prussia when the instruction to liquidate the Jews was issued. The probability is that Hitler was in Berlin at the material time, since he did not leave Berlin for the East until 16 December. This, according to the Defendants, is an instance of Irving manipulating the record and telling 'a fib' in order to distance Hitler from the instruction to liquidate the Jews.

5.130 Next the Defendants rely on a manuscript note made by Himmler of a conversation he had with Hitler on 16 December 1941 which includes the words:

Jewish question / to be extirpated (*auszurotten*) as partisans.

Longerich regarded this note as confirmation of Hitler's intention to continue and intensify the mass murders of Soviet Jews. It is consistent with the way in which the killing of 363,211 Jews was treated in a report by the *Einsatzgruppen* of 26 December 1942 (to which I shall refer again later): in that report the number of Jews killed was included as a separate category under the heading of partisan accomplices. This report is endorsed in manuscript 'laid before [*vorgelegt*] Hitler'.

5.131 The Defendants criticize the account given by Irving at p. 465 of *Hitler's War* (1991 edition) of Hitler's attitude towards the Jews in March 1942. The reader is given to understand that the concern of Hitler was to procure the deportation of Jews out of Europe. Irving refers to Hitler's wish, repeatedly stated, to postpone dealing with the Jewish problem until after the war is over. He claims that Goebbels never discussed with Hitler the realities of what was happening to the Jews in the General Government.

That account, say the Defendants, takes no account of the statements repeatedly made by Hitler from 1941 onwards that the Jews must be eliminated and that they were a 'bacillus' which needed to be eliminated. Examples are to be found in the entries made by Goebbels in his diary on 15 February and 20 March 1942 and in Hitler's Table Talk on 22 February 1942.

Also omitted by Irving is the reference made by Goebbels to Hitler as a protagonist for and champion of the radical solution to the Jewish question necessitated by the 'way things are'. There is, according to the Defendants, no justification for Irving's claim that Goebbels discussed with Hitler 'the realities' of the situation. What Irving is unwarrantably seeking to do, say the Defendants, is to distance Hitler from the policy of killing the Jews.

5.132 Next the Defendants accuse Irving of suppressing several references made by Hitler in January and February 1942 to the extermination (*ausrottung*) of Jews, for example in his Table Talk on 25 January 1942. Hitler is there recorded as having said on that occasion:

The Jew has to get out of Europe . . . If he collapses in the course of it, I can't help there. I can see only one thing: absolute extermination, if they don't go of their own accord . . .

The latter sentence is omitted at p. 464 of *Hitler's War* (1991 edition) in order, so the Defendants say, to exculpate Hitler.

5.133 Similarly the Defendants point to the omission by Irving of any reference to Hitler's statements in the Table Talk for 22 February 1942: 'We will get well when we eliminate the Jew'. They rely also on the omission of a similar remark by Hitler to NSDAP party members on 24 February 1942 when Hitler again talked of extermination and removing parasites.

5.134 Evans in his report criticizes the omission from Irving's account of Goebbels' diary entry for 30 May 1942 but the Defendants no longer rely on this criticism. Similarly the Defendants no longer pursue Evans's criticism of Irving for not recognizing that the reference in the Hitler Table Talk of July 1942 to Jews emigrating to Madagascar was euphemistic.

5.135 However the Defendants rely further in this connection on the following: the reaction of Hitler to the shooting of the Jews in Riga in November 1941, as reported by the widow of Schultz-Dubois (referred to at (vii) above); Himmler's minute of 22 September 1942; Himmler's note of 10 December 1942; Hitler's meetings with Antonescu and Horthy in April 1943 and Ribbentrop's statements made at Nuremberg (all of which will be referred to later in this section).

5.136 The Defendants contend that, individually and collectively, the misinterpretations, partial quotations and omissions which I have summarized amount to a serious misrepresentation of Hitler's attitude towards the Jewish question. As further evidence of the uncompromisingly harsh and active role in the persecution of the Jews the Defendants rely also on his role in such events as the expulsion and shooting of the Berlin Jews in Riga (with which I have already dealt); his role in the deportation of European Jews to the East; his attitude towards the Jews in France; his determination to procure the extermination of the Hungarian Jews and Ribbentrop's assessment of Hitler's responsibility for the fate which befell the Jews (to all of which issues I will shortly come).

Irving's response

5.137 In the course of his cross-examination, Irving produced another 'chain of documents' by way of positive rebuttal of the contention of the Defendants, that his portrayal of the attitude of Hitler to the Jewish question was fundamentally false. It consisted of a selection of documents which, he said, support his contention that Hitler was a friend of the Jews. Included amongst those documents were, firstly, an order dating back to 1935 that isolated actions against Jews were not to take place and would be severely punished; a directive issued in 1936 that there were to be no excesses against the Jews following the assassination of a Swiss named Gustlov; another directive of July 1937 by which Hitler permitted selected non-Aryans to remain in the Nazi party and a 1939 document in which the Czech Foreign Minister reports Hitler saying the Jews were being economically annihilated and talking of deporting them to Madagascar.

5.138 Later documents in Irving's 'chain' include a note made by the Nazi ambassador to France in August 1940 recording Hitler's wish to include in peace treaties with nations defeated by the Nazis a condition that they should deport their Jews out of Europe. Another document relied on by Irving is a query raised in November 1941 by the *Reichskommissar* for the *Ostland* asking whether all Jews in his area are to be liquidated since he can find no directive to that effect. Irving claimed that this indicates that there was no such directive. Irving also relied on the instruction given by Himmler in November 1941 (which is considered above) that there is to be no liquidation of Jews from Berlin. Next in the 'chain' relied on by Irving is a note by Rosenberg of a conversation he had with Hitler in December 1941 (shortly after war was declared on America) which records Hitler as having approved Rosenberg's policy of not talking about the extirpation of Jewry. According to the note, Hitler had said that Jews had brought about the war and had thereby brought about their own destruction. Rosenberg did not record Hitler as favouring a policy of exterminating the Jews.

5.139 As to Himmler's note of his discussion with Hitler on 18 December 1941 about the Jewish question, which records that the decision that Jews were to be extirpated as partisans (*auszurotten als Partisane*), Irving interpreted this note as meaning that the Jews were to be executed as partisans because that is what they were. Irving made reference to the recollection over twenty years afterwards of one of the authors of Hitler's Table Talk that Hitler had in December 1941 said that all he was asking of the Jews was that they should perform hard labour somewhere. In the same vein Irving referred to a document dated 6 July 1942 recording Hitler's decision that Jews in specific occupations should be protected from persecution. Then Irving cited

Hitler's Table Talk for 24 July 1942 for Hitler's comment about getting rid of the Jews to Madagascar.

5.140 The last documents in Irving's 'chain' is the letter from Himmler to General Berger dated 28 July 1942 in which he writes that the Fuhrer has placed on his shoulders the burdensome task of rendering the eastern territories free of Jews. Irving interpreted this to mean that Hitler has ordered Himmler to remove the Jews from those territories (whereas Evans said it plainly means they were to be killed).

5.141 Irving relies also upon extracts from the agenda for two discussions between Hitler and Himmler on 17 or 22 July and 10 December 1942 respectively. The former includes the words '*Judenauswanderung* (Jewish emigration) – how to proceed further'. The latter has the word *abschaffen* (abolished) written beside a reference to 600–700,00 Jews supposedly in France. It is followed by a memorandum from Himmler that these Jews are to be *abtransportiert* (deported). Irving maintains that the terms used in these documents all suggest that deportation was the policy towards Jews. Irving's chain ends there because, with effect from October 1943, he accepts Hitler knew of the policy of exterminating the Jews.

5.142 Evans's response to the series of documents was that they do not amount to much. He did not accept that they justified or excused the way Irving portrays Hitler's position on the Jewish question. Evans agreed that Hitler undoubtedly in specific occasions did intervene on behalf of identified Jews or groups of Jews. He accepted that until the latter part of 1941 Hitler's preferred solution to the Jewish problem was deportation. Thereafter Evans contended that Hitler approved their extermination even though he did not say so in terms. That is the interpretation which he puts on Rosenberg's note of December 1941. The reference to deportation to Madagascar in Hitler's Table Talk for 24 July 1942 is camouflage, according to Evans, since the Madagascar plan had been abandoned in February 1942. Bearing in mind what was going on in mid-July 1942 Evans takes the view that *Judenauswanderung* and *abtransportiert* are plainly euphemisms for extermination. Evans asserted that Irving's selection of documents ignores the vastly greater number of documents which evidence Hitler's murderous intentions towards Jews of all nationalities.

5.143 Dealing with the specific passages in his books which the Defendants highlighted, Irving excused the inaccuracies in his version of Hitler's reported comments made in October 1941 about parking Jews in the marshier parts of Russia by saying, correctly, that at the time in the 1970s when he wrote the first edition of *Hitler's War* the only version which was available to him was the English translation of those comments made for Weidenfeld & Nicolson in 1953. Irving followed that translation. Irving conceded, however, that even after the German original became available to him, he repeated the translation errors in the second edition of *Hitler's War* and retained some of them in *Goebbels*. This he excused on the basis that the Weidenfeld's translation is not a serious deviation from the original and has the virtue that it is not a 'wooden' version. Irving totally disagreed with the suggestion put to him that he was deliberately using a mistranslation in order to exculpate Hitler.

5.144 Irving rejected the criticism of his account of Goebbels' diary entry for 22 November 1991 which gives an account of his meeting with Hitler the previous day. He admitted that he omitted the word 'energetic' but contended that it was legitimate to leave the matter 'neutral' because the account had been filtered through the evil brain of Goebbels who was given to claiming falsely to have the *Fuhrer's* authority for what he had done.

5.145 In regard to Hitler's speech to the *Gauleiter* on 12 December 1941, Irving claimed that the account given by Goebbels of what Hitler said was mendacious. He argued that the extermination (*vernichtung*) of Jews was not a quotation of what Hitler had said (although Hitler had used that word in relation to the Jews in his famous speech to the *Reichstag* in 1939) but rather Goebbels expressing his own view and intention. If he had been quoting Hitler, said Irving, Goebbels would have used the subjunctive tense. He did, however, agree that it is impossible to say which part of the diary is recording Goebbels' own thoughts and which parts are recording what Hitler said. Irving was reluctant to accept the translation of *vernichtung* as extermination. He claimed that what the reference was to the annihilation of Judaism as opposed to the extermination of Jewry.

5.146 Irving agreed that there is no reference in his biography *Goebbels* to this part of Hitler's speech to the *Gauleiter* on 12 December 1941. The reason, according to Irving, is that at the time of publication he had not seen the microfiche containing those words. Irving offered the explanation that, when he went to Moscow to inspect the microfiches of the Goebbels diaries there, he was looking for entries relating to Pearl Harbour. He claimed that, when he came to the entry for 13 December 1941 (in which entry Hitler's remarks of the previous day are recorded) he did not read as far as the passage relating to what Hitler said to the *Gauleiter* about the Jews. The Defendants do not accept the veracity of Irving's answer: they assert that Irving, when in Moscow, started reading the entry for 13 December. The Defendants refuse to accept that Irving would have stopped reading the entry mid-way through and before the highly significant passage relating to the Jews which is contained in Goebbels' account of Hitler's speech to the *Gauleiter*. Irving responded that he was under pressure of time when in Moscow. He firmly denied having read that passage, adding that, even if he had read it, he would not have regarded Hitler's remarks as significant since it is 'the old Adolph Hitler gramophone record'.

5.147 As to General Governor Frank's account on 16 December 1941 of what he had been told in Berlin, Irving claimed in cross-examination that the logical interpretation was that he (Frank) had told the authorities in Berlin to liquidate the Jews themselves and not the other way round. It was put to Irving that this was not how he had interpreted Frank's words at p. 427 of *Hitler's War* (1991 edition). Irving refused to accept that the 'large scale measures' of which Frank spoke in his diary meant that Jews were to be exterminated. Asked why, in that passage in *Hitler's War*, he had taken pains to claim that Hitler was not in Berlin at the time, Irving conceded that he was indicating to readers that Hitler had not been in Berlin when Heydrich's agencies were giving the instruction to liquidate the Jews. Irving accepted that there was no indication in Goebbels' diary or in Frank's account that it was Heydrich or his agencies which had issued that instruction.

5.148 Irving gave evidence that he did not see the note of Hitler's conversation with Himmler on 16 December 1941 until the summer of 1999 and so could not be criticized for not referring to it in the 1991 edition of *Hitler's War*. But he accepted, with some reluctance, that it does establish that Hitler authorized the liquidation of Jews in the East as if they were partisans.

5.149 In answer to the criticism that he omitted from his account of Hitler's Table Talk for 25 January 1942 Hitler's reference to exterminating the Jews, Irving responds that he gave the reader 'the meat' of what Hitler said by recording that he repeated the prophecy made in the *Reichstag* in 1939. Irving dismissed the criticism of his account of Hitler's attitude towards the Jewish problem in March 1942. Nowhere is there any sheet of paper recording Hitler as having said 'liquidate the Jews'. Irving asserted that he has faithfully reflected what Goebbels reported. Hitler was still talking of deportation. Even in the reports of Hitler's Table Talk (when Hitler was amongst friends and so, according to Irving likely to be candid and unlikely to resort to camouflage), he is recorded as speaking of the plan to deport the Jews to Madagascar at the end of the war. Irving repudiated the suggestion that this was a euphemism. When asked how he reconciled the notion that Hitler was thinking in terms of deportation with his acceptance that Hitler knew about and approved the mass shootings of Jews on the Eastern front, Irving responded that he believed Hitler drew a distinction between European Jews (for whom he planned deportation) and the Jews in the East (whom he regarded as vermin fit only to be shot).

5.150 Irving regarded Goebbels' diary entry for 30 May 1942 as constituting 'acres of sludge' not worth including in his book. He maintained that he is right to treat the reference to Madagascar in Hitler's Table Talk of 24 July 1942 as Hitler talking of resuming the Madagascar plan after the war. Irving insisted that his portrayal of Hitler's views about the Jews over this period was fair, objective and warranted by the available evidence.

(viii) The timing of the 'final solution' to the Jewish problem: the 'Schlegelberger note'

Introduction

5.151 One central document cited by Irving in support of his case that Hitler consistently intervened to mitigate the harm sought to be done to the Jews is a note said to have been dictated by an official in the Reich Ministry of Justice, namely Schlegelberger, which is undated but which is claimed to have come into existence in the spring of 1942, which records what he has been told by Lammers, a senior civil servant at the *Reichskanzlerei*:

Reichsminister informed me that the *Fuhrer* has repeatedly declared to him that he wants to hear that the solution to the Jewish question has been postponed until after the war is over.

That note, says Irving, is incompatible with the notion that Hitler authorized or condoned the wholesale extermination of Jewry during the war.

The Defendants' case

5.152 Evans identified several curious features about this note and its provenance: it is undated; it bears no signature; the addressees are not listed in the conventional manner; it appears to come from a file containing miscellaneous documents about Jews which was put together after 1945 by the prosecutors at Nuremberg. Not all the documents in the file deal with the same subject-matter. Despite these unsatisfactory features Evans accepted that the memorandum is authentic. He does, however, add that it is no more than speculation that Schlegelberger is the author of the memorandum.

5.153 Evans canvassed the possibility that the note dates back to 1941, in which case the view attributed to Hitler would be consistent with the attitude towards the Jewish question which he was advocating at that time, namely to postpone dealing with it until after the war was over. In support of this theory Evans drew attention to figures appearing on the document '17.7'. If the document is dated 17 July 1941, that would be the day after an important meeting at which arrangements were set in place for the administration of the Eastern territories.

5.154 Another possibility recognized by Evans is that the document did come into existence in early 1942 in the wake of the Wannsee conference, at which the Defendants (basing themselves largely on the admissions which were made by Eichmann in the course of his interrogation by the Israelis) contend the extermination of the Jews was discussed and the means of achieving that end were in broad terms agreed upon. Evans accepted that on balance it is more likely that the date of the memorandum is 1942 rather than 1941.

5.155 He expressed the opinion that the subject matter of the note was probably not the Jewish question generally but rather the narrower issue of mixed marriages between Jews and gentiles and the children of such marriages (mischlinge). This contentious question had been discussed at the Wannsee conference in January 1942, at which time no decision was arrived at how mischlinge should be treated, although the policy of deportation of 'full Jews' to the East had already been agreed upon. There is, according to Evans, evidence that active discussions thereafter took place within the Ministry of Justice as to what policy and classification should adopted in relation to the mischlinge. A further conference was called for 6 March 1942 with a view to hammering out a solution. It is an important component of the Defendants' argument that, as the minute of the meeting on 6 March shows and as Schlegelberger testified at his trial, it was devoted exclusively to a discussion of the mischlinge problem.

5.156 Various proposals were canvassed, including suggestions that sterilization should be undertaken and that mixed marriages should be annulled by law. But the meeting was inconclusive. At the meeting on 6 March it was decided that the issue should be referred to Hitler for his decision. Evans stressed that, odd though it may seem with the Nazi army in dire straits in Russia, the problem of mischlinge was taken extremely seriously. Contemporaneous documents reveal Shlegelberger to have been seriously concerned at the ramifications of one of the proposed courses of action, namely deciding on a case by case basis what should be done with individual mischlinge Jews. Suggestions such as sterilization and the annulment of mixed marriages were also a cause for concern within the Ministry which would have the responsibility for the supervision of whatever policy was decided upon.

5.157 Accordingly Schlegelberger wanted to raise the matter with Lammers and did so on 10 March 1942. It is not clear whether Lammers did in fact consult Hitler on the issue. The language of the memorandum does not suggest that Lammers went to Hitler and obtained a fresh ruling from him on the specific question of the mischlinge. In any case the likely reaction of Hitler to the complex issues raised by the many problems surrounding the question of half and quarter Jews would have been to postpone their consideration. Whether or not Hitler was consulted, the natural inference, according to Evans, is that the memorandum is confined to the question of *mischlinge*. The description in the memorandum of the discussions as 'theoretical' is also suggestive of the fact that the subject matter is confined to *Mischlinge*. Hitler would not have agreed to the postponement of the Jewish question in its entirety, argued Evans, so soon after the Wannsee conference. Moreover, added Evans, it was Hitler who had set in train the policy of deporting the Jews to the Eastern territories. That policy had been implemented over the previous months. In those circumstances Hitler is unlikely to have ordered that the whole Jewish question be postponed until the end of the war.

5.158 Evans concluded that it is very likely that the Schlegelberger note should be interpreted as addressing the limited question of the solution to the problem of half Jews. Longerich concurred with this opinion.

5.159 Evans was critical of Irving for the way in which he describes the memorandum in *Goebbels*:

Hitler wearily told Lammers that he wanted the solution of the Jewish problem postponed until after the war was over, a ruling that remarkably few historians now seem disposed to quote.

Evans regarded that passage as a complete misrepresentation of the memorandum. There was no ruling by Hitler. In any case the deportations and killings continued unabated, which would scarcely have happened if Hitler had ordered their suspension.

5.160 But Evans reserved the main thrust of his criticism for the account of the memorandum in *Hitler's War*, where the reader is clearly given to understand by the passage at p. 464 that the note is 'highly significant' because it shows Hitler to be wanting to put off the entire Jewish question until the end of the war. Irving regards the note as so important that he includes the following reference to it in the introduction:

Whatever way one looks at it, this document is incompatible with the notion that Hitler had ordered an urgent liquidation programme.

Evans maintained that evidence of actions taken within the Ministry of Justice and elsewhere belie Irving's claim. Moreover, if Hitler had indeed given an instruction to postpone the final solution of the Jewish question until after the war, how is it, asked Evans, that the extermination programme pressed ahead in the remaining months of 1942 and thereafter.

5.161 The Defendants argue that no reputable and objective historian would nail his colours to the mast in the way that Irving has done by admitting only one possible interpretation of the note. The nub of their criticism is that Irving treats the Schlegelberger memorandum as if it permitted of only construction, namely that it evidences Hitler ordaining the postponement of the Jewish question until the end of the war. Irving glosses over the many doubts which exist about the document. He ignores the alternative construction of which the memorandum is equally susceptible (to put it no higher), namely that it is confined to the problem of the *mischlinge*. An unbiassed historian would have placed squarely before his readers the problems and doubts about the document. It is, say the Defendants, another instance of deliberate distortion.

Irving's response

5.162 Irving acknowledged that the Schlegelberger memorandum is an unsatisfactory document. But he is satisfied that it is authentic. He pointed out reference was made to a complete copy of the memorandum (typed out in full with initials) as early as 1945 in a list compiled by the British Foreign Office of documents found in the files of the Nazi Ministry of Justice. That copy subsequently went missing. Irving has attempted, without success, to obtain the top copy from the US National Archives. He speculated that the copy in the file which was assembled by the prosecutors at Nuremberg may have been removed by them because they did not want Lammers to be able to use it to exculpate himself. At all events Irving has no doubts about the genuineness of the memorandum. (Evans agreed that the Abschrift is a record of an authentic memorandum, adding the rider that Irving's eagerness to treat this document as genuine contrasts starkly with his scepticism about the integrity of documents which do not fit in with his thesis.)

5.163 Regardless of its unsatisfactory features, Irving remained firm in his view that the Schlegelberger note is a vital document which provides a clear indication of Hitler's wish expressed in the spring of 1942 to postpone a decision on the Jewish question generally until after the end of the war. During the evidence Irving made reference time and again to the memorandum, which he regards as the linchpin of his case for saying that Hitler sought to protect the Jews.

5.164 Irving dismissed the notion that the note dates back to 1941 as a 'vanishingly small probability'. In support of this conclusion Irving referred to a Staff Evidence Analysis sheet, apparently prepared by the prosecutors at Nuremberg who assembled the file which contained the memorandum. Irving points out that, with one exception, the documents in the file come from the period March to April 1942. So the 1942 date tallies with the dates of most of the documents in the file.

5.165 In support of his contention that Schlegelberger was referring to the Jewish question generally, Irving argued firstly that the discussion at the continuation of the Wannsee conference on 6 March 1942 was not confined to the mischlinge problem (although he agreed that the minute of the meeting suggests otherwise). Irving cited in support of this contention the post-war evidence of Ficker and Boley who were both present. (Evans dismissed their evidence as self-exculpatory.) Irving went on to point out that the file in which the memorandum was contained is broadly entitled 'Treatment of the Jews'. Another document in the file is 'Overall solution of the Jewish problem'. Irving maintained that the immediately preceding document in the file supports his interpretation of the note that it is dealing with the question of Jews generally, not just mischlinge. In that document dated 12 March 1942 Schlegelberger referred to the meeting which had been held on 6 March as having been concerned with the treatment of Jews and mixed races. He expressed the wish that Lammers should consult Hitler about the decisions which would need to be taken which he considered to be completely impossible. Irving argues that this letter also indicates that both the Jews generally and the mixed race issue were under discussion. Following his receipt of that message, it appears that Lammers offered to meet Schlegelberger on the return of the former to

Berlin at the end of March. As Evans agreed, the pair probably met in early April. Irving argued that this chronology suggests that the date of the memorandum would be early April by which time Lammers had spoken to Hitler.

5.166 Irving relied on the terms of the Schlegelberger memorandum itself. He pointed out that it refers conjunctively to Jews and mixed marriages as if both (separate) topics were under consideration. It is headed 'The solution of the Jewish question', which suggests a broad not a narrow subject-matter. (Were it not so headed he would have considered Evans's interpretation a viable alternative theory). Irving argued that there is nothing in the terms of the memorandum itself to justify the narrow interpretation put on it by the Defendants. Irving argued that in the spring of 1942 Hitler was preoccupied with events on the Eastern front. In that situation his likely reaction, upon being asked about the Jewish question, was that it should be put off until the end of the war. Evans considered that this argument ignores Hitler's obsessive anti-semitism which continued to dominate Hitler's thinking, even at times of military crisis.

5.167 Irving produced what he described as an extract from the evidence which Lammers gave at his trial when he testified that Hitler had told him that he had given Himmler an order for the evacuation of the Jews and that he (Hitler) did not want to hear any more about the problem until the end of the war. Evans took the view that Lammers was seeking to avoid incriminating himself when he claimed that Hitler wanted no more than the deportation of the Jews.

5.168 Irving defended his treatment of the note at p. 464 of the 1991 edition of *Hitler's War* by pointing out that he did make mention of the problem of the mischlinge. He explained that pressure of space prevented him from making clear to the reader of the text of *Goebbels* that the 6 March 1942 conference was confined to the mischlinge issue. There was, he said, no question of his having distorted the evidence.

5.169 Irving maintained that the Defendants are trying to devalue what is a 'high level diamond document' when they argue that it bears only on the problem of the mischlinge.

(ix) Goebbels' diary entry for 27 March 1942

Introduction

5.170 After the successful Nazi invasion of Poland in 1939, part of the newly acquired territory was absorbed into the Reich. In order to make way for ethnic Germans from other parts of Eastern Europe, the Poles from that area were deported eastwards into central Poland, which constituted the western sector of the General Government. The Jews and gypsies were deported into the eastern sector of the General Government in the region of Lublin.

5.171 Initially the Jews were concentrated in ghettoes where living conditions were atrocious. But, following the Nazi invasion of Russia in June 1941, there was a change of policy. As I will describe in greater detail hereafter, task forces called *Einsatzgruppen* set about the systematic killing of Soviet Jews. In about the autumn of 1941 the extermination policy was extended to Jews in the area of the General Government. The gassing of Jews commenced in December 1941 at an extermination centre called Chelmno in the Warthegau; the latter being an area containing territory incorporated into the Reich after the conquest of Poland. In November 1941 construction of another death camp started in the General Government at Belzec which is situated south-east of Lublin. Jews were murdered in gas chambers at this camp. Two further camps were established the following year at Sobibor and Treblinka.

5.172 So much is common ground between the parties. What is in issue is the manner in which Irving deals with the question of whether Hitler was aware of the policy of exterminating Jews.

The case for the Defendants

5.173 In *Hitler's War* (1977 edition) Irving claims that Hitler was kept in the dark about the policy of exterminating Jews in the East. He wrote at p. 392:

The ghastly secrets of Auschwitz and Treblinka were well kept. Goebbels wrote a frank summary of them in his diary on March 27 1942, but evidently held his tongue when he met Hitler two days later, for he quotes only Hitler's remark: 'The Jews must get out of Europe. If need be, we must resort to the most brutal methods'.

Irving wrote in similar terms in the 1991 edition. After quoting the references in Goebbels's diary to the brutal methods being employed against the Jews, he continued:

'The Jews have nothing to laugh about now', commented Goebbels. But he evidently never discussed these realities with Hitler. Thus this two-faced Minister dictated, after a further visit to Hitler on April 26, 'I have once again talked over the Jewish question with the Fuhrer. His position on this problem is merciless. He wants to force the Jews right out of Europe . . .'

5.174 The Defendants' case is that Irving's claim that Goebbels deceived Hitler when (according to Irving) they met on 29 March is wrong: they accuse Irving of manipulating the diary entry for 27 March and ignoring other documents and sources which demonstrate that Hitler was well aware what was happening to the Jews in the East. The full diary entry (quoted at p. 400 of Evans's report) included the following passages:

The Jews are now being pushed out of the General Government, beginning near Lublin, to the East. A pretty barbaric procedure is being applied here, and it is not to be described in any more detail, and not much is left of the Jews themselves. In general one may conclude that 60% of them must be liquidated, while only 40% can be put to work. The former *Gauleiter* of Vienna [Globocnik], who is carrying out this action, is doing it pretty prudently and with a procedure that doesn't work too conspicuously. The Jews are being punished barbarically, to be sure, but they have fully deserved it. The prophesy that the *Fuhrer* issued to them on the way, for the eventuality that they started a new world war, is beginning to realize itself in the most terrible manner. One must not allow any sentimentalities to rule in these matters. If we did not defend ourselves against them, the Jews would annihilate us. It is a struggle for life and death between the Aryan race and the Jewish bacillus. No other government and no other regime could muster the strength for a general solution of the question. Here too the *Fuhrer* is the persistent pioneer and spokesman of a radical solution, which is demanded by the way things are and thus appears to be unavoidable. Thank God during the war we have a whole lot of possibilities which were barred to us in peacetime. We must exploit them. The ghettos which are becoming available in the General Government are now being filled with the Jews who are being pushed out of the *Reich*, and after a certain time the process is then to renew itself here. Jewry has nothing to laugh about . . .

5.175 Evans argued that the references to Globocnik and to killings to the east of Lublin make clear that Goebbels was writing about Belzec and not about Auschwitz or Treblinka, as Irving claimed in his text. But the key omission in *Hitler's War*, according to Evans, is Goebbels' description of Hitler as 'the persistent pioneer and spokesman of a radical solution'. The radical solution cannot in the context be taken to refer to the policy of deporting Jews to the East. It must indicate that Hitler was aware what was going on in the extermination camps in the East. By deliberately omitting of that reference, Evans alleges that Irving perverts the true significance of the entry. There is absolutely no evidence that Goebbels 'held his tongue'. The overwhelming likelihood is that the pair of them would have discussed enthusiastically what treatment was being meted out to the Jews in the General Government. **5.176** The Defendants claim that, when Hitler is recorded as having spoken at this time of the annihilation (*vernichtung*) or extirpation (*ausrottung*) of the Jews he was indeed using the terms in a genocidal sense. Moreover the stance attributed to Hitler by Goebbels accords with sentiments previously expressed by Hitler, notably in his speech to the *Gauleiter* on 12 December 1941 (to which I have already referred) when Hitler spoke of the Jews 'experiencing their own annihilation' if they should once more bring about a world war. It also accords with two of Goebbels's diary entries from this period. The entry for 20 March 1942 records Hitler as having remarked:

We speak in conclusion about the Jewish question. Here the *Fuhrer* remains now as before unrelenting. The Jews must get out of Europe, if necessary, with the application of the most brutal means.

The entry for 30 March 1942 includes the following passage:

Thus I plead once again for a more radical Jewish policy, whereby I am just pushing at an open door with the *Fuhrer*.

5.177 In both editions of *Hitler's War*, Irving asserts that Hitler was speaking of deporting the Jews from Europe and so must be taken to have been ignorant of the programme of extermination. But Evans, having analysed the quotations given by Irving together with other reports of statements made by Hitler on the topic, concluded that they show that, when Hitler talked of pushing the Jews out of Europe to the East, he was well aware of the genocidal fate which awaited them. Evans expressed the opinion that this was the radical solution which Hitler was advocating, in full knowledge of what it entailed. Hitler knew that Jews were being systematically killed in the East. Hitler spoke frequently of the murderous fate awaiting the Jews, using such terms as 'annihilation' and 'extermination' although he took care not to go into the detail of the programmes. Irving, so it is alleged, was at pains to suppress this body of evidence.

5.178 Evans on behalf of the Defendants concluded that Irving's treatment of Goebbels' diary entry for 27 March 1942 wholly misrepresents Hitler's state of knowledge.

Irving's response

5.179 Irving suggested (and Evans agreed) that it is apparent from Goebbels' diary entry for 27 March 1942 that he is there summarizing information which has been provided to him. There is no evidence that Hitler was provided with that information. Irving advanced the somewhat technical argument that Goebbels' diary entry might be evidence against him as to his state of knowledge but could not be evidence of the state of knowledge of Hitler because as against him it is hearsay. As Evans pointed out, historians, including Irving, perforce use hearsay evidence all the time. But Irving persisted in his assertion that the entry is at worst evidence of Goebbels' knowledge of the gassing and does not touch upon the question of Hitler's knowledge. Irving claimed that Hitler and Goebbels did not see each other in private more than about ten times in 1942.

5.180 Moreover, according to Irving, the entry does not establish that even Goebbels knew what was happening in the death camps: he is just speculating when he writes that 60% of the Jews must be liquidated. Evans pointed out that this contention is difficult to reconcile with

Irving's claim that on 27 March 1942 Goebbels was summarizing in his diary 'the ghastly secrets of Auschwitz and Treblinka'. Irving criticized Evans's translation of 'Im grossen kann man wohl feststellen . . .' as 'In general one may conclude that . . .' because it omits the word wohl which is indicative of the speculative nature of this part of the diary entry.

5.181 A further argument advanced by Irving is that, in several of the diary entries relied on by the Defendants, Goebbels falsely claims to be acting with the knowledge and authority of Hitler so as to provide himself with an alibi or excuse in case of later blame or criticism.

5.182 Irving claimed that there are many other contemporaneous documents which show Hitler displaying an attitude towards the Jews which is anything but homicidal. One example which Irving cites is Goebbels's diary entry for 30 May 1942 on which Evans also placed reliance. Irving drew particular attention to the following:

Therefore the Fuhrer does also not wish at all for the Jews to be evacuated to Siberia. There, under the harshest living conditions, they would undoubtedly form an element of vitality once more. His preferred solution would be to settle them in central Africa. There they live in a climate which would surely not render them strong and capable of resistance. In any case it is the Fuhrer's wish to make west Europe completely Jew-free. Here they will not be allowed to have any home anymore.

Irving argued that this passage demonstrates that Hitler was still thinking in terms of deportation and resettlement. Hitler was 'talking tough' about the loss of life which the Jews might suffer in the course of deportation but he was not contemplating genocide. Irving argued that, when Hitler uses such terms as ausrotten in relation to the Jews, he is talking of them being uprooted and transported elsewhere not of their being liquidated. Irving cited other instances where Hitler is recorded as having used at about this time such terms as Auswanderung and Evakuierung. Hitler talked also of resettling the Jews in Siberia or Lapland or even Madagascar. Evans rejected that argument. Hitler's references to resettlement of the Jews at this time are euphemistic. It would have been impractical, Evans suggested, to carry out a programme of extermination by the use of coded language. Hitler's reference to deporting the Jews to Madgascar must be camouflage because Hitler himself had earlier in the year called a halt to that plan and ordered that the Jews be sent to the East.

5.183 As to the entry in Goebbels' diary for 30 March 1942, it is, according to Evans, clear from the earlier section that, in his confidential meeting with Goebbels, Hitler told him he favoured a radical solution of the Jewish problem. The latter part of the entry, relied on by Irving, corresponds very closely with Hitler's Table Talk on 29 May 1942. Evans considered that Goebbels in the latter part of the entry was recording in his diary what he had heard Hitler say in the course of a general discussion on 29 May rather than continuing with his account of their private meeting. That, according to Evans, explains why camouflage language is to be found in the latter part of the diary entry. Evans contended that Hitler habitually resorted to camouflage when others were present. According to Picker (one of those who recorded Hitler's Table Talk) Hitler never spoke over the table of the concentration camps. Evans concluded that the reference in the diary entry to sending the Jews to central Africa is therefore not to be taken seriously.

5.184 Similarly the record of Hitler's reference on 24 July 1942 to the emigration of Jews to Madagascar cannot, according to the Defendants, sensibly be taken at face value: the 'Madagascar plan' had, on Hitler's own orders, been abandoned long since. Hitler was pretending to be ignorant about the killing of Jews.

5.185 Another reason relied on by Irving for his contention that Hitler was unaware of deliberate extermination of Jews being carried out on a massive scale in 1942 is that none of his adjutants or stenographers recalls any mention being made by Hitler of anything of the kind. Irving described the time and trouble he has devoted to tracking down and interviewing those who remain alive and to obtain the papers of those who have not survived. Irving claimed that none of them had any recollection of Hitler discussing concentration camps either generally or individually. The Holocaust was not mentioned.

5.186 Evans does not accept that the evidence of the adjutants and secretaries is of any real value. In the first place, Hitler when in company deliberately refrained from talking of the concentration camps and used euphemistic language when talking of the Jews. Moreover Hitler's personal staff had good reason to be cautious in making public statements about what Hitler said in their presence. Moreover, claimed Evans, several of them expressed the view that Hitler was aware of the genocide which was being perpetrated. He named Major (later Lieutenant General) Engel, who recorded in his diaries that Himmler reported to Hitler about the shooting of Jews in Riga and Minsk; von Puttkamer, who impliedly suggested that Hitler kept from his press spokesman the fact that Jews were being exterminated; von Bruckner, who suggested that discussion about the extermination of the Jews was kept by Hitler within a limited circle; Krieger, one of Hitler's stenographers, who was undecided whether Hitler issued orders to exterminate the Jews or gave general orders to others to that effect and Buchholz, who considered that it was possible Hitler had issued such an order and was convinced that the matter was discussed between Himmler and Hitler. Others mentioned by Evans as coming within this category were Linge; Brautigam; Sonnleithner and Schroeder. Evans readily accepted that many of these former Hitler aides are unreliable for one reason or another. The point he sought to make was that, whatever weight is to be attached to the evidence of the adjutants and stenographers, they do not support Irving's claim that Hitler was ignorant of the extermination programme.

(x) Himmler minute of 22 September 1942

Introduction
5.187 Himmler prepared a handwritten agenda for a meeting he was to have with Hitler on 22 September 1942. Its format and wording were as follows:

1. Emigration of Jews
       How to proceed further

2.	Settlement Lublin	Circumstances
	Lorrainers	Gen Gouv.
	Germans from Bosnia	Globus
	Bessarabia	

The Defendants' case

5.188 The Defendants' case is that this note, despite its camouflaged language, raises the strong suspicion that Himmler proposed to discuss with Hitler at their meeting the mass annihilation of Jews. The background to the note is that the killing of Jews had (on the Defendants' case) commenced in November 1941 at Chelmno and some months later at Belzec, Sobibor and Treblinka. During the summer of 1942 there was a wish to accelerate the extermination process but it met with resistance. Himmler, who was in overall charge of the programme, needed the support of Hitler.

5.189 Evans interpreted the agenda note made by Himmler as meaning that he intended to discuss with Hitler the extermination of Jews (for which *auswanderung* or 'emigration' was a euphemism). Evans interpreted the note in the following way: 'Globus' was the nickname of Globocnik, the Lublin Chief of Police to whom, according to the Defendants, was delegated the executive responsibility for both deportation and extermination in the General Government area. Two months earlier, just before the mass killings started at Treblinka, Globocnik had welcomed the order recently issued by Himmler saying that with it 'all our most secret wishes are to be fulfilled'. Evans interpreted Himmler's agenda note as contemplating the repopulation of Lublin with Lorrainers, Germans and Bessarabians. The Jews were to be deported to make way for them and then executed. That was Globocnik's 'most secret wish'. The significance of Himmler's note, so the Defendants contend, is that it implicates Hitler in the extermination policy.

5.190 The Defendants allege that Irving glosses over this significant note and perverts its true sense. Indeed at p. 467 of the 1991 edition of *Hitler's War* Irving uses it to support his thesis that Himmler did not enlighten Hitler about the true fate of the Jews. He prefaced his reference to Himmler's note of 17 September with these words: 'Himmler meanwhile continued to pull the wool over Hitler's eyes'. According to the Defendants, there is no evidence that Himmler did any such thing. Evans argued that the euphemistic reference in the note to 'emigration of Jews' is not indicative of a wish to keep Hitler in the dark but rather a reflection of the common Nazi practice of camouflaging references to the policy of exterminating Jews. The Defendants contend that it is inconceivable that

Himmler should have prepared an agenda for a discussion with Hitler about these matters in the knowledge that Hitler knew nothing about them and with the intention of concealing them from him.

Irving's response

5.191 In his evidence Irving accepted that there was possibly something sinister under discussion between Himmler and Hitler. But he argued that there is no reason to suppose that Himmler went into any detail about it. Irving maintained that in *Hitler's War* he quoted what Himmler's note said and let the readers draw their own conclusions.

5.192 However, when cross-examining Evans, Irving advanced the contention that what Himmler was discussing with Hitler was the resettlement of Lublin with ethnic Germans and the removal of the Jews then in Lublin to make way for them. Irving claimed that resettlement of those Jews, rather than their extermination, was the topic under discussion. He contended that Evans's interpretation of the note is speculative and over-adventurous. He agreed that the note proposed the evacuation and repopulation of Lublin. But he maintained that there is no warrant for reading into it that any discussion was intended by Himmler to take place with Hitler about killing the displaced Jewish Lubliners. Indeed, he argued, it was the resettlement of Lublin which was Globocnik's 'most secret wish'. Evans responded that the deportation of the Lubliner Jews and their execution are so intimately connected that it is impossible to draw a distinction between them.

5.193 Irving defended the use of the phrase 'pulling the wool over Hitler's eyes' by pointing out that there is no reference on the face of Himmler's note to any of the sinister things which (as Irving agreed) were by then in train.

(xi) Himmler's note for his meeting with Hitler on 10 December 1942

Introduction

5.194 In accordance with his usual practice, Himmler listed in manuscript the points which he proposed to raise with Hitler at their meeting on 10 December 1942. One of them reads: 'Jews in France 600–700,000'. Alongside those words there appears a tick. Himmler has also added in manuscript the word '*abschaffen*'. Longerich translated this as 'to liquidate'. After his meeting with Hitler, Himmler sent a note to Muller, the head of the *Gestapo*, to the effect that the French Jews should be arrested and deported to a special camp (*Sonderlager*). At the same time Himmler secured the agreement of Hitler that a camp should be set up for 10,000 well-to-do Jews from France, Hungary and Romania, in conditions 'whereby they remain healthy and alive'.

Case for the Defendants

5.195 The significance of Himmler's agenda, according to the Defendants, when considered in the light of the note to Muller and the setting up of a camp for well-to-do Jews, is that it reveals him discussing with Hitler the liquidation or extermination of large numbers of French Jews. The contrast between the fate of the French Jews who are to kept healthy and alive and the remainder is obvious, say the Defendants.

5.196 The Defendants criticize Irving for his treatment of the note in *Hitler's War* (1977 edition) where Irving translates *abschaffen* as 'to remove', which the Defendants allege misrepresents the true significance of the note. In the 1991 edition *abschaffen* is translated as 'to extract' and the reference to setting up a camp for well-to-do French Jews has disappeared in order, claim the Defendants, to remove the highly significant contrast between their treatment and that awaiting the deported French Jews.

Irving's response

5.197 Irving asserted that there were nowhere near 600,000 Jews in France. He argued that his translation of *abschaffen* is correct and is consistent with the word *abtransportieren* which is to be found in the typed version of the note. Irving did not accept the suggestion put to him that *abtransportieren* was euphemistic language adopted for the official record of the meeting. He argued that his interpretation of the note is borne out by what in the event happened to the French Jews: they were transported to camps in Germany, where large numbers of them were put to work in the armaments industry.

5.198 Irving claimed that his account in the 1977 edition of *Hitler's War* is accurate. He explained that the reference to the note was deleted from the 1991 edition because it was an abridged edition and part of the text had to be deleted.

(xii) Hitler's meetings with Antonescu and Horthy in April 1943

Introduction

5.199 On 12/13 April 1943, Hitler met the military dictator of Romania, Antonescu in order to discuss Romania's position in the war. In the course of their discussion the question of the Jews in Romania was raised.

5.200 In 1943 there were in Hungary some 750,000 Jews if not more. The Hungarian government, under the leadership of Admiral Horthy, deported many non-Hungarian Jews over the border into Nazi-controlled territory where most of them were murdered. The Nazis brought pressure to bear on the Hungarians to identify and deport in a similar manner the very considerable number of Jews who remained in Hungary. But the Hungarians were reluctant to comply, preferring to solve their own Jewish question in their own way. A meeting was arranged between Hitler and Horthy: it took place on two separate days, namely 16 and 17 April 1943, shortly after Hitler's meeting with Antonescu. The object was to resolve the impasse.

5.201 In the result the Hungarian refused to hand over Hungary's Jews. Hungary was subsequently invaded and occupied by the Nazis. Eichmann thereupon organized the forcible deportation of the Jews from Hungary to the General Government. According to the Defendants in June 1944, 450,000 Hungarian Jews were murdered at Auschwitz. Irving alleges that the number killed is smaller.

Case for the Defendants

5.202 In relation to Hitler's meeting with Antonescu, the Defendants reproach Irving for his omission to mention in either edition of *Hitler's War* the uncompromizing and anti-semitic words used by Hitler on 13

April in reference to the Jews. The minutes record him as having said:

Therefore, in contrast to Marshal Antonescu, the Fuhrer took the view that one must proceed against the Jews, the more radically the better. He . . . would rather burn all his bridges behind him because the Jewish hatred is so enormously great anyway. In Germany, as a consequence of the clearing up of the Jewish question, one had a united people without opposition at one's disposal . . . however, once the way had been embarked on, there was no turning back.

This, say the Defendants, evidences Hitler placing pressure on Antonescu to effect a radical 'removal' of Romania's Jews. Yet Irving ignores it altogether in his account of the meeting.

5.203 As to the meeting which started three days later between Hitler and Horthy, the Defendants' contention is that the evidence indicates that at the first session, which took place on 16 April and which was attended by amongst others Hitler and Ribbentrop as well as Horthy, Hitler sought to persuade Horthy to agree to the expulsion of the Hungarian Jews. He reassured Horthy that there would be no need to kill them. But Horthy remained unpersuaded.

5.204 Accordingly, say the Defendants, at the next session on 17 April Hitler and Ribbentrop expressed themselves more explicitly. The Defendants contend that the language used by Hitler on the second day points unequivocally to Hitler's knowledge of the extermination of Jews in Poland, as does the language used by Ribbentrop in Hitler's presence on that occasion. Minutes of the meeting on 17 April were taken by Dr Paul-Otto Schmidt. They record Ribbentrop saying in the presence of Hitler:

On Horthy's retort, what should he do with the Jews then, after he had taken pretty well all means of living from them – he surely couldn't beat them to death – the Reich Foreign Minister replied that the Jews must either be annihilated or taken to concentration camps. There was no other way.

Shortly afterwards Hitler himself is recorded as having said:

If the Jews [in Poland] didn't want to work, they were shot. If they couldn't work, they had to perish. They had to be treated like tuberculosis bacilli, from which a healthy body can be infected. That was not cruel; if one remembered that even innocent natural creatures like hares and deer had to be killed so that no harm was caused. Why should one spare the beasts who wanted to bring us bolshevism? Nations who did not rid themselves of Jews perished.

The Defendants' case is that these passages are significant in that they afford powerful evidence that Hitler knew of and approved the extermination of Jews. The flavour of Hitler's remarks points towards an intention to exterminate the Hungarian Jews. It is difficult, say the Defendants, to visualize any other reason why the Nazis were so insistent to get their hands on the Hungarian Jews.

5.205 The Defendants contend that Irving in Hitler's War uses a variety of discreditable devices to obscure the significance of the minutes and to twist their meaning. They allege that the passage at p. 509–10 of the 1977 edition of Hitler's War is a 'shocking manipulation' of Schmidt's note of the meeting. In the first place, Irving gives as the pretext for the pressure being brought to bear on Horthy by Hitler and Ribbentrop the Warsaw ghetto uprising. But there is no mention of that uprising in the note of the meeting, which, say the Defendants, is unsurprising because it did not take place until three days later (19 April). Irving marginalizes the significance of Ribbentrop's remarks in the presence of Hitler by tucking away what he said in a footnote (where Irving seeks to cast doubt on the accuracy of Schmidt's note by quoting Horthy's later draft letter to Hitler of May 7 which refers to the 'stamping out' (Ausrottung) of Jewry). Further Irving depicts Hitler as having used the devastation wreaked by Allied bombing to justify a harsher policy towards the Jews, whereas the contemporaneous evidence shows that Hitler regarded the bombing as 'irritating but wholly trivial'.

5.206 But the major criticism directed by the Defendants at Irving's account arises out of the transposition by Irving to the 17 April of a remark made by Hitler in the course of the meeting on 16 April. The Defendants allege that in a similar manner Irving minimizes the significance of what Hitler said. After quoting the statement made by Hitler on 17 April which is set out above, Irving adds the following words:

'But they can hardly be murdered or otherwise eliminated', [Horthy] protested. Hitler reassured him: 'There is no need for that.'

Hitler had indeed used those words but not on 17 April. He spoke those words at the earlier session on 16 April. By the following day the Nazi attitude had hardened. By transposing to 17 April remarks which Hitler had in fact made on 16 April, so the Defendants say, Irving diluted the uncompromising and brutal language Hitler used on 17 April when exhorting Horthy to kill all Hungary's Jews. Irving was, as he accepted, warned in 1977 that he had made an error about the date when Hitler made this remark. But took no action to correct the error in the 1991 edition.

5.207 The Defendants are further critical of Irving for watering down what Hitler did say on 17 April when it came to the 1991 edition of *Hitler's War*. Irving omitted Hitler's statement about having to kill hares and deer; he omitted the question why the 'beasts' (ie the Jews) should be spared and he omitted his reference to nations who did not get rid of the Jews perishing. According to the Defendants Irving was guilty of atrocious manipulation of what Hitler said.

Irving's reponse

5.208 Irving agreed that in his account in *Hitler's War* of the meeting which took place between Hitler and Antonescu, he omitted to refer to Hitler's anti-semitic outburst which included the remark that 'one must proceed against the Jews, the more radically the better'. Irving justified the omission by saying that it adds not one iota to what is already known.

5.209 In this connection Irving, in order to rebut the claim that Hitler displayed a vindictive attitude towards the Jews on this (or any other) occasion, drew attention to the willingness of Hitler on occasion to approve some merciful disposal for individual Jews or groups of Jews. Irving instanced the permission given by Hitler for 70,000 Jewish children to leave Romania and travel to Palestine. Longerich agreed that there were times when Hitler exempted certain Jews from deportation or extermination.

5.210 In regard to the meeting between Hitler and Horthy, Irving in his response laid stress on what Hitler said at the first session on 16 April, namely that the Jews would not need to be killed. He argued that it was throughout Hitler's position that there was no need to murder the

Hungarian Jews, since they could be accommodated in concentration camps as had happened in the case of the Slovakian Jews. Irving argued that, when Hitler is recorded in the minutes of the meeting taken by Hilgruber as having referred to Jews having 'vanished' to the East, he was referring to their deportation. Evans's answer to this was that on 16 April Hitler was setting up a smoke-screen and seeking to conceal from Horthy what his true intentions were. Longerich concurred, adding that Hitler's reference to the Slovakian Jews is significant because (as Hitler must by this time have known) they had been put to death in extermination camps.

5.211 Irving did not in his evidence dispute the accuracy of the record made by Schmidt of the meeting on 17 April. Irving argued that the reason why Ribbentrop said what he did is that the Hungarian Jews were posing a security threat: what Ribbentrop was proposing was that, on that account, they should be sent to concentration camps; if they refused (but not otherwise) they would be shot. Evans replied that Irving is perverting and distorting the clear sense of what Ribbentrop said. Irving persisted in his claim that the use of the term '*Ausrottung*' in Horthy's draft letter to Hitler of 7 May is significant because it contemplates the Jews being forcibly deported rather than killed.

5.212 Irving agreed that he wrongly reported Hitler as saying on 17 April what he had in fact said on 16 April. He also agreed that his error had been pointed out to him as long ago as 1977 by the historian Martin Broszat. But he contended that his error as to the date is a matter of no consequence. That, he claimed, is why he did not correct the reference in the 1991 edition of *Hitler's War*. There was no deliberate misrepresentation or deliberate suppression. Irving asserted that he included in the 1977 edition the substance of what Hitler said about the Jews on 17 April. His explanation for the removal in the 1991 edition of part of what Hitler said is that it was an abridged edition. In any case he considered that the omitted words do not add much.

5.213 As regards Hitler's language, Irving drew attention to the fact that the internal record of the meeting kept by the Hungarians (as opposed to the official Nazi minute) made no mention of the deported Hungarian Jews being killed. There would have been no reason for the Hungarians to conceal the fact that they were to be killed, if that had indeed been stated at the meeting to be the intention. If Hitler had said that the Nazis were proposing to kill the Hungarian Jews, one would expect, suggested Irving, the Hungarians' internal record to include a protest at such barbarism.

5.214 Irving explained that Hitler was distressed and angry about the recent Allied bombing raids of cities in Germany. That was the reason for Hitler's outburst to Horthy. Evans pointed out that in the 1977 edition of *Hitler's War* Irving gave a different explanation for Hitler's menacing words, namely the Warsaw uprising. Another explanation offered by Irving for the words used by Hitler is that he was full of resentment about the massacre at Katyn. All these explanations and excuses are bogus, according to Evans.

(xiii) Deportation and murder of the Roman Jews in October 1943

Introduction

5.215 Although this episode is one of those deployed by Evans in his report to substantiate the attack upon Irving's historiography, I will take it shortly because the Defendants did at one stage indicate that they were not intending to rely on it. Irving nevertheless chose to cross-examine Evans about it.

5.216 The position in Italy in October 1943 was that Mussolini had been overthrown three months earlier to be replaced by a new Italian government which promptly surrendered to the Allies. The Nazis thereupon invaded Italy. Rome fell to the advancing Nazis. The country in general and Rome is particular were in a state of some administrative confusion. The position in the north of Italy was unstable.

5.217 Both the 1977 and 1991 editions of *Hitler's War* recount how on 6 October 1943 the SS chief in Rome received an order to transfer 12,000 Roman Jews to northern Italy where they would be liquidated. According to Irving's account, the matter was then referred to Hitler's headquarters and the order came back that these Jews were to be taken to a concentration camp in upper Italy named Mauthausen to be held there as hostages, rather than be liquidated as had been ordered by

Himmler. Irving argued that this episode reveals Hitler again showing concern for the Jews and striving to ensure that they would be kept alive.

The case for the Defendants

5.218 The Defendants' case is that in his account Irving has again manipulated the historical record and misrepresented the effect of Hitler's intervention. According to Evans, Irving achieves this by, firstly, suppressing documents which demonstrate that the background to Hitler's intervention was a dispute whether (as Field Marsahll Kesselring was urging) the Jews should be kept in Rome on fortification work or whether (as Himmler had ordered) they should be sent to the Reich and liquidated. There was strong local feeling in Rome that the Jews should stay there. Evans agreed that the documents show that Hitler directed via Ribbentrop that the Roman Jews were to be taken to Mauthausen as hostages. But their fate was then to be left in the hands of the SS, that is, effectively in the hands of *Reichsfuhrer-SS* Himmler. So, Evans contended, far from interceding on behalf of the Jews, the effect of Hitler's intervention was to place these Jews in the murderous hands of the SS. The dispute was thus resolved by Hitler against those like Kesselring who were trying in Rome to save the Jews and in favour of the SS who had already made clear that they intended to kill the Jews when they got their hands on them.

5.219 The Roman Jews were transported northwards, not to Mauthausen, but to Auschwitz where they were in due course murdered. According to Evans, the claim that the Jews were to be held at Mauthausen 'as hostages' was intended to disguise the fate which the SS had in mind for the Jews in the hope that it would appease the anxious officials in Rome. Hitler knew perfectly well what was going to happen to them. It was in reality no part of Hitler's intention that the Roman Jews should be kept alive. Mauthausen was a notorious concentration camp, where the inmates were systematically worked to death.

5.220 Irving, say the Defendants, having unjustifiably praised Hitler for his intercession on behalf of the Jews, compounds the error by suppressing the fact that the Roman Jews were murdered.

Irving's response

5.221 The nub of Irving's response is that the order handed down by Hitler meant what it said, namely that the Jews were not to be liquidated as the SS had apparently been intending, but rather that they should be kept alive in Mauthausen for later use as hostages should the need arise. Irving claimed that Hitler did indeed intercede in a manner which was intended by him to preserve the lives of the Roman Jews. He did not accept that Hitler foresaw, still less that he intended, that the SS would send them to their deaths. That the Roman Jews were in the event murdered was a violation of Hitler's express order and contrary to his intention. Irving denied any manipulation of the evidence or suppression in his account of this episode.

(xiv) Himmler's speeches on 6 October 1943, and 5 and 24 May 1944

Introduction

5.222 On 6 October 1943 Himmler spoke to a gathering of Reichsleiter and Gauleiter. He said:

I do ask you to keep secret, to listen to what I am saying and never to speak about it, what I am saying in these circles. We came up against the question, what about the women and children, and I took the decision here too for a clear solution. I did not consider myself justified in liquidating just the men to leave alive the children to act as the avengers against our sons and grandchildren. There had to be taken the grave decision to have this people disappear from the face of the earth.

5.223 The following year, on 5 May 1944, Himmler spoke to the generals of the *Wehrmacht*. According to the transcript of his speech he said:

The Jewish question has been solved within Germany itself and in general within the countries occupied by Germany. It was solved in an uncompromising fashion in accordance with the life and death struggle of our nation in which the existence of our blood is at stake. You can understand how difficult it was for me to carry out this soldierly order (*soldatische Befehl*) and which I carried out from obedience and from a sense of complete conviction.

5.224 Next on 24 May 1944 Himmler spoke to the generals again, saying:

Another question which was decisive for the inner security of the *Reich* in Europe was the Jewish question. It was uncompromisingly solved after orders and rational recognition. I believe gentlemen that you know me well enough to know that I am not a bloodthirsty person. I am not a man who takes pleasure or joy when something rough must be done. However, on the other hand I have such good nerves and such a developed sense of duty I could say that much for myself. When I recognize something as necessary, I can implement it without compromise. I have not considered myself entitled, this concerns especially the Jewish women and children, to allow the children to grow into the avengers who will murder our fathers and grandchildren. That would have been cowardly. Consequently, the question was uncompromizingly resolved.

Defendants' case

5.225 The Defendants contend that in all three speeches Himmler is speaking in brutal terms of the murder of the Jews. Irving did not dissent from this. But for present purposes, the primary significance of this trilogy of speeches is that they shed light on the question whether Hitler knew of the killing. As to the first of these speeches the Defendants say that Himmler would not have spoken in such explicit terms if Hitler was unaware of the killings. Himmler would have realized that members of his audience would or might raise the matter with Hitler. In relation to the speech on 5 May 1944 the Defendants contend that the reference to a 'soldierly order' must signify that Himmler had taken his order as to the solution to the Jewish problem from Hitler since he is only person in a position to give orders to Himmler. Similarly, in relation to the speech of 24 May, the Defendants assert that the 'orders' must connote orders from Hitler. Read together, the Defendants maintain that the terminology of the speeches by Himmler in May 1944 demonstrate Hitler's knowledge of and responsibility for the murders of Jews including women and children.

5.227 The Defendants direct particular criticism at Irving for the way in which he deals at p. 630 of *Hitler's War* (1977 edition) with the speech of 5 May. He there paraphrases what Himmler said in such a way as to conceal the uncompromizingly brutal language used by Himmler. After the reference to Himmler's speech, Irving adds:

Never before, and never after, did Himmler hint at a Fuhrer order, but there is reason to doubt that he showed this passage to his Fuhrer.

The Defendants reply that it is pure surmise on Irving's part that the relevant passage was not shown to Hitler but it is presented by him to the reader as established fact. They point out that in the 1991 edition the reference to Himmler's speech of 5 May has been omitted altogether. The Defendants maintain that it is an important part of the narrative because it casts light on Hitler's role in the extermination of the Jews. The inescapable inference is that Irving was determined to avoid compromizing Hitler.

5.228 The reader is directed to a footnote in which Irving claims that the page containing the key sentence referring to a military order was 'manifestly' retyped and inserted in the transcript at a later date. Irving suggested that this indicates that the version of the speech which was shown to Hitler was sanitized so as to exclude any reference to Himmler having been ordered by Hitler to carry out a bloody solution to the Jewish problem. It is Irving's argument that Himmler did this because he knew very well that Hitler had given him no such order.

Irving's response

5.229 Irving accepted that with effect from October 1943 it has to be conceded that Hitler cannot have been ignorant of the extermination programme. But he emphasized that in his speech on 6 October 1943. Himmler spoke of a decision which he, rather than Hitler, had taken. He disputed the contention that the speech of 5 May points towards the existence of a Hitler order. From the facts that the transcript of the relevant page of the speech has evidently been typed on a different typewriter and the pagination has been altered, Irving deduced that the document has been tampered with and is accordingly unreliable. He rejected the mundane explanation that Himmler was simply revising what he proposed to say in his speech. Irving further argued that it is to be inferred that the transcript was sanitized before it was submitted to Hitler because Himmler did not want Hitler to know that he (Himmler) was claiming falsely to have been acting on the order of Hitler. As to the speech of 24 May (which Irving suspects has also been tampered with) he argued that the orders referred to could just as well be taken to mean orders given by Himmler to his subordinates.

5.230 Irving defended the treatment of these speeches in *Hitler's War* by saying that he quoted them and left the reader to draw his or her own conclusions. He pointed out that at the meetings between Hitler and Himmler which took place during the summer of 1944 Hitler is reported to be referring still to the expulsion (rather than the extermination) of the Jews. These statements cannot be airily dismissed as camouflage since Hitler had no need to use euphemisms when speaking to Himmler.

(xv) Hitler's speech on 26 May 1944

Introduction

5.231 Hitler addressed senior officers of the Wehrmacht on 26 May 1944 in the following terms:

By removing the Jew, I abolished in Germany the possibility to build up a revolutionary core or nucleus. One could naturally say to me: Yes, couldn't you have solved this more simply – or not simply since all other means would have been more complicated – but more humanely? My dear officers, we are engaged in a life or death struggle. If our opponents win in this struggle, then the German people would be extirpated.

The case for the Defendants

5.232 The Defendants maintain that this amounts to an admission by Hitler that had used inhumane means to remove (that is, to kill) the Jews. They contend that Irving obfuscates the true sense of what Hitler was saying at p. 631 of *Hitler's War* (1977 edition). Irving there prefaces his quotation from Hitler's speech with the comment that Hitler was speaking 'in terms that were both philosophical and less ambiguous'. He writes that Hitler was speaking of the reasons why he had 'expelled' the Jews. The Defendants argue that by these devices Irving sought to blunt the significance of the reference by Hitler to the 'extirpation' of the Jews.

Irving's response

5.234 Irving pointed out that it was he who first discovered the text of this speech. He claimed that he quoted it accurately. He agreed that the less humane method of which Hitler spoke may well have been killing. But again he said that he left it to his readers to draw their own conclusions.

(xvi) Ribbentrop's testimony from his cell at Nuremberg

Introduction

5.235 In a footnote at p. 851 of the 1977 edition of *Hitler's War* Irving quoted a passage extracted from notes made by Ribbentrop when incarcerated in the prison at Nuremberg:

. . . that [Hitler] ordered [the destruction of the Jews] I refuse to believe, because such an act would be wholly incompatible with the picture I always had of him.

The case for the Defendants

5.236 The Defendants make no complaint of what Irving did quote from Ribbentrop's notes. But they do criticize him severely for his omission to quote the immediately following passage which reads:

On the other hand, judging from [Hitler's] Last Will, one must suppose that he at least knew about it, if, in his fanaticism against the Jews, he didn't also order [it].

The Defendants say that this editing of Ribbentrop's notes is indefensible. They further criticize Irving for not questioning the reliability of Ribbentrop as a source, given his unwavering loyalty to Hitler and his own demonstrably false claim to have been unaware of the fate awaiting the Jews after their deportation.

5.237 Further the Defendants allege that Irving has unjustifiably ignored the account by the prison psychologist at Nuremberg, Dr Gilbert, of his conversation with Ribbentrop in which the latter appears to concede that Hitler may have ordered the extermination of the Jews in 1941. Evans asserted that Irving has also ignored the transcript of a conversation in which Ribbentrop tells a British officer how in 1944 he discussed with Hitler the atrocities taking place in the camps.

5.238 The consequence of Irving's carefully selected quotation together with his omission of other quotations is that the reader is given a wholly distorted impression of Ribbentrop's view of the knowledge of the Holocaust possessed by Hitler.

Irving's response

5.239 Irving agreed that he left out from his citation of Ribbentrop's prison notes the passage which is cited above. He did so because writers have to be selective and avoid writing 'pages of sludge'. The omitted passage cried out to be cut. It was mere supposition on Ribbentrop's part. Irving disagreed with the suggestion that his account gave a false and unbalanced picture of Ribbentrop's assessment of Hitler's responsibility for the extermination of the Jews. Irving justified his omission of the other statements made by Ribbentrop about Hitler's knowledge of the extermination of the Jews by saying that none of them is reliable.

(xvii) Marie Vaillant-Couturier

Introduction

5.240 Marie Vaillant-Couturier, a gentile and member of the resistance in France, was a prisoner in the womens' camp at Auschwitz from 1942 until the end of the war. In 1946 she gave vivid and detailed evidence to the International Military Tribunal at Nuremberg about the atrocious conditions in the camp, the sterilization of women, the killing of babies born to women who arrived pregnant and so on. One of the presiding judges was an American, Judge Biddle.

Case for the Defendants

5.241 In relation to Mme Vaillant-Couturier the criticism directed at Irving by van Pelt relates, not to his published work, but to his claim, made on occasions, including a press conference in 1989 to celebrate the English publication of the Leuchter report (with which I shall deal in the section vii. relating to Auschwitz), that:

> she gave a heart-breaking testimony about what she had survived and in his diary at the end of the day, Judge Biddle privately wrote 'I don't believe a word of what she is saying, I think she is a bloody liar'

Irving made a similar statement earlier, on 13 August 1988, at Toronto, when he claimed that the Judge had written '*All* this I doubt' (emphasis added).

5.242 The Defendants contend that these statements wholly misrepresent the view which the Judge took of Vaillant-Couturier's evidence. The Judge's contemporaneous note of her evidence reveal that he inserted in parentheses the words 'This I doubt' at the end of a paragraph in which he noted her claim that all camps had a system of selecting prostitutes for SS officers. That does not appear to have been a claim that she made of her own knowledge. There is no reason whatever, say the Defendants, for supposing that Judge Biddle disbelieved any other aspect of her testimony. The statement made by Irving at the press conference was a disreputable attempt by him to discredit the witness on a basis which, as he must have appreciated, was utterly untenable. The addition of the word 'all' in the Toronto speech was, say the Defendants, deliberate distortion.

Irving's response

5.243 Irving did not accept that Judge Biddle's note was referring merely to the passage which I summarized above. He asserted in his closing submission that, when cross-examining her, defence counsel had suggested that she had not even been in Auschwitz. This was not a proposition which Irving put to Evans in cross-examination (and he directed no questions on this topic to van Pelt). Irving argued that Mme Vaillant-Couturier had made some absurd claims in her testimony (for example that there was a man-beating machine at the camp). Irving persisted in his claim that, from what he had read of the Judge's private papers on the testimony given by the various witnesses, he was able to assert that Judge Biddle was making a general comment on her evidence. Irving did not produce whatever papers he was basing this claim upon. **5.244** In his evidence he asserted that Judge Biddle 'became so fed up with this woman's testimony that he can finally stand it no longer and he dictates in parenthesis into his report – he says "this I doubt"'. But he did agree that what he had said at the launch of the Leuchter report was a 'gloss' on the Judge's comment. He excused it by saying, incorrectly, that it was years since he had read the Judge's notes. By way of explanation for the fact that he had quoted the Judge as saying 'All this I doubt' when he spoke in Toronto, Irving claimed, firstly, that he added the word 'all' to make it more literate for his audience and later that the Judge had altered the words 'This I doubt' to 'All this I doubt'. He produced no evidence for the latter claim.

(xviii) Kurt Aumeier

Introduction
5.245 Kurt Aumeier was for a while Hoss's deputy at Auschwitz. Shortly after the war he was captured and interned by the British. Whilst in captivity he wrote two hundred pages of hand written memoirs about his experiences at the camp. He went into great detail about the manner in which the gas chambers were operated. He described the gassing procedures and referred to the construction of crematorium 3. He was subsequently extradited to Poland, where he was tried, found guilty and hanged. His memoirs did not become available to historians until 1992, when they were read by Irving shortly after their release by the Public Record Office in London.

The Defendants' case
5.245 The Defendants contend that, despite the existence of a number of inaccuracies in his account, Aumeier is an important and credible witness whose detailed description of Bunkers I and II and the way the gas chambers in crematoria 2 and 4 were operated powerfully supports

their case for saying that gas chambers were used on a massive scale at Auschwitz. Through van Pelt and Evans the Defendants allege that Irving recognized the problem Aumeier's memoirs posed for revisionists in relation to the existence of gas chambers at Auschwitz. He wrote to Marcellus of the Institute for Historical Research ('the IHR') on 4 June 1942 that 'these MSS are going to be a problem for revisionists, and need analysing now in advance of our enemies and answering'.

5.246 In order to meet the 'problem' posed by Aumeier's account, Irving first surmised, without any evidential basis for doing so, that his account had been extracted by brute force on the part of his interrogators. Thereafter, Defendants allege that Irving suppressed the Aumeier material because it powerfully undermined his thesis that there were no gas chambers at Auschwitz. He continued to make speeches denying the Holocaust without mentioning Aumeier's account. Although Irving had read the memoirs in 1992, it was not until May 1996 that Irving informed van Pelt by writing to tell him of their existence. Van Pelt observed that the private disclosure of the memoirs to him is a far cry from placing them in the public domain, which is what a reputable and objective historian should and would have done.

Irving's response

5.247 Irving agreed that he wrote to Marcellus of the IHR saying that the Aumeier manuscripts were going to be a problem for revisionists and that they needed to be analysed in advance of 'our enemies' and answered. What Irving claimed he meant by this was that the memoirs were damaging to the revisionist position. He said that the 'enemies' referred to were irresponsible historians who will leap onto any document and inflate it.

5.248 Despite what he wrote to the IHR, Irving argued that Aumeier is an unreliable witness. Amongst the errors in his account to which Irving pointed was his claim that during his tenure of office at Auschwitz (which lasted for most of 1942) 15,000 people were killed by gas at Auschwitz. That estimate does not accord with other evidence. In addition many of his dates are confused. Irving maintained his claim that Auemier had been subjected to maltreatment by his British captors. He identified a British officer who, he claimed, used brute force to compel Aumeier to provide a more detailed and exaggerated account of what he had seen. These were the reasons why Irving confined his reference to Aumeier's evidence in his writings about Auschwitz to a footnote in his book *Nuremberg*. When it was pointed out to him that he had there referred to Aumeier's testimony as 'compelling', Irving explained that he meant it was compelling evidence which needed to be examined. Irving pointed out that the footnote did also make reference to the pressure brought to bear upon Aumeier during his interrogation.

5.249 Irving denied the charge of suppression. He said that he drew the attention of various historians to Aumeier's account. In May 1997 he wrote to van Pelt, the acknowledged world expert, telling him of the memoirs but received no reply. (Van Pelt gave evidence that he had not received the letter) He agreed that it was not until the publication of *Nuremberg* in the same year that he first made public the memoirs. Irving (correctly) dismissed the suggestion made at one stage by the Defendants that this disclosure was made only because their legal advisers had been alerted to the existence of the memoirs because Irving disclosed them in this action.

vi. Justification: Evidence of the Attitude of Hitler Towards the Jews and of the Extent, if any, of his Knowledge of and Responsibility for the Evolving Policy of Extermination

Preamble

6.1 Apart from the specific criticisms made by the Defendants of Irving's historiography, with which I have dealt in the preceding section v. of this judgment, the Defendants make the broader criticism of him that he persistently and seriously misrepresents what the evidence, obectively analysed, shows to have been the attitude adopted by Hitler towards the Jews in general and his involvement in the evolving policy to exterminate them. The Defendants' case is that, in order to arrive at any conclusion about the extent of Hitler's knowledge of the persecution which culminated in the genocide which took place in the gas chambers, it is necessary to take account of his conduct (including his public statements) throughout his political life. If this approach is adopted, the Defendants maintain that it becomes apparent that the proposition that Hitler did not know about or authorize the genesis of the gassing programme is unsustainable.

6.2 In this section I shall set out the parties' respective arguments in relation to this issue. I shall start with the issue whether and, if so, over what period the evidence shows Hitler to have been anti-semitic. I shall then rehearse the arguments as to the extent, if any, of his knowledge of and responsibility for the policies of shooting, deporting and exterminating Jews by means including gassing. For the sake of clarity I shall deal with each of those policies in separate sections, recognizing that there is a degree of artificiality in such an approach. The policy of exterminating the Jews was not introduced in phases. I recognize also that there is an overlap between the questions with which this section is concerned and the issues addressed in section v. (especially at (vi)). Inevitably there will be some duplication.

Hitler's anti-semitism

The issue between the parties

6.3 Irving does not dispute that Hitler was deeply anti-semitic from at least the end of World War I. But he claimed that, once Hitler came to power, he lost interest in anti-semitism. Hitler had espoused anti-semitism in the first place for reasons which were essentially political, according to Irving. The Defendants case is that Hitler was rabidly anti-semitic throughout and continued to play an active part in overseeing and controlling anti-Jewish policy up to and including the war years.

The case for the Defendants

6.4 Longerich examined in his report the genealogy of Hitler's role in the persecution of the Jews. He began with the emergence of Hitler's anti-Semitism after the First World War. In correspondence in 1919 Hitler outlined the differences between what he called emotional and rational forms of anti-semitism. The latter form ultimately led Hitler to call for the removal of the Jews altogether. By 1920 he was already using terms such as extirpation, annihilation and extermination in relation to the Jews. He referred to the Jews as a plague, an epidemic, germ carriers, a harmful bacillus, a cancer and as maggots. In his writings and speeches Hitler blamed the situation of Germany at the end of the First World War on an international Jewish conspiracy. His basic wish throughout had been by one means or another to remove the Jews from German soil. As is evident from the Goebbels diaries, Hitler and Goebbels devoted much time to the prosecution of anti-semitic policy.

6.5 In *Mein Kampf*, which was published in 1926, Hitler developed his anti-semitism by placing his desire to remove the Jews in the context of a wider theory of the struggle between races for living space. In Hitler's view the Jews, lacking a state of their own, were parasites trying to destroy those states which had been established by superior races. This idea was developed in his 'Second Book' which was written in 1927 although not published in his lifetime. In his speeches in the late 1920s Hitler stated that Jews were not able to work productively because they lacked a proper relationship with the soil. As a consequence they were parasites and spongers. This did not prevent Hitler from claiming that the Jews had achieved economic dominance and the ability to control and manipulate the media to their own advantage. He spoke of the need to eliminate the economic ascendancy of the Jews, if necessary by means of their physical removal. Longerich asserted that anti-semitism was an integral part of Hitler's *Weltanshauung*.

6.6 According to Longerich, when the Nazi party began to attract mass support in the early 1930s, the anti-semitic element was played down for political reasons. Even so, Hitler continued to refer to the Germans as being poisoned by another people. From 1935 onwards Hitler's attitude towards the Jews was reflected in the anti-semitic policies pursued by the Nazi government. Longerich cited, by way of illustration of these policies, Hitler's role in organizing the boycott of Jewish businesses on 1 April 1933 and the enactment between 1935 and 1937 of various discriminatory laws. Jews were excluded from holding public office and the practice of law. Quotas for Jewish pupils and students were brought in. Longerich notes that after coming to power in 1933 there are examples of Hitler exercizing a moderate influence on Jewish policy but in his view this was dictated by tactical considerations.

6.7 Hitler's anti-semitism is evident in his public statements in the 1930s. In his speech to the Reich Party Congress in 1937 Hitler talked of Jewish-Bolshevist subversion. The pogrom of 9 November 1938, *Reichskristallnacht*, marks the first occasion when Jews and their property were subjected to serious and widespread violence and destruction. I have already set out in section v.(iii) and (iv) above the reasons why the Defendants contend that Hitler approved and promoted the pogrom. Hitler addressed the *Reichstag* on 30 January 1939 on the topic of the Jewish question. He said:

In my life I have often been a prophet and was generally laughed at. During my struggle for power it was mostly the Jewish people who laughed at my prophecies that I would some day assume the leadership of the state and thereby of the entire *Volk* and them, among many other things, achieve a solution of the Jewish problem. I believe that in the meantime the then resounding laughter of Jewry in Germany is now choking in their throats.

Today I will be a prophet again; if international Jewry within Europe and abroad should succeed once more in plunging the peoples into a world war, then the consequence will be not the Bolshevization of the world and therewith a victory of Jewry, but on the contrary, the annihilation of the Jewish race in Europe.

On the Defendants' case, this was a theme to which Hitler reverted on numerous occasions during the war as the Nazi line against the Jews hardened. I have already referred in section v.(viii) to Hitler's pronouncements on the Jewish question and I will not repeat them here.

Irving's response

6.8 As I have already indicated, Irving conceded, inevitably, that in the early years Hitler was a profound anti-semite, although he claimed that Goebbels's hatred for the Jews was more intense than that of Hitler. He also accepted that anti-semitism was from the outset one of the major planks of Nazi policy. However, he suggested that Hitler's anti-semitism was cynical in the sense that he adopted it as a means of getting power. Once he came to power, Hitler's anti-semitism receded. Irving pointed to occasions when Hitler had interceded on behalf of individual Jews. He even had a Jew on his staff. He retained General Milsch, a half-Jew.

6.9 In relation to the public statements on which the Defendants rely as evidence of Hitler's continuing anti-semitism after the establishment of the Third Reich, Irving's stance can be summarized as follows: he accepts that on occasion Hitler used harsh language in relation to the Jews. But Hitler's concern and objective in relation to the Jewish problem was that it should be solved by their deportation and resettlement outside the *Reich*. I have set out in some detail at section v.(viii) and elsewhere the reasons advanced by Irving for saying that the Defendants have misinterpreted the public statements made by Hitler in relation to the Jewish question. Irving argued that his description of Hitler as 'the best friend' the Jews had in the Third Reich was justified.

The policy of shooting of Jews

Introduction

Evidence of system and the scale of the shootings

6.10 It is common ground between the parties that over a period which started in the summer of 1941 and ran on throughout 1942, vast numbers of Jews within the area of the General Government (as occupied Poland was now called) were killed by shooting. The Defendants contend, principally through the reports and evidence of Browning and Longerich, that large numbers of Jews were executed in this manner and that the executions were carried out pursuant to a systematic programme which Hitler knew about and approved.

6.11 Irving accepts that the number of Jews who were executed was large but disputes that it occurred on the scale alleged by the Defendants. He accepts that the killing was systematic. After some hesitation he conceded that the evidence which he has now seen indicates that Hitler knew and approved what was going on.

6.12 Much of the material and documentary evidence relating to he shooting in the East was destroyed. What remains suffices to establish that (as Irving accepted) four mobile SS units called *Einsatzgruppen* were established by Himmler's deputy, Heydrich, who was Chief of the Security Police and Security Services. The *Einsatzgruppen* provided information relating, amongst other things, to the number of Jews and others who had been shot. The information was collated into reports which were sent to Berlin where Heydrich's staff processed the information into event reports (*Ereignismeldungen*). Activity reports were also prepared. These documents represent the primary source of knowledge about the shootings on the Eastern front up to the spring of 1942. In addition to the *Einsatzgruppen*, there were other units who were also carrying out killings. For instance a police unit, presided over by Jeckeln, who was a Higher SS and Police Leader, killed 44,125 persons in August 1941. Other units carried out mass killings on a similar, if not greater, scale.

6.13 On numerous occasions prior to the commencement of this trial, and in the early stages of the present hearing, Irving claimed that the shooting of the Jews in the East was random, unauthorized and carried out by individual groups or commanders. Irving compared the shooting to the tragic events at Mi-Lai during the Vietnam war. However, in the course of the trial Irving radically modified his position: he accepted that the killing by shooting had been on a massive scale of between 500,000 and 1,500,000 and that the programme of executions had been carried out in a systematic way and in accordance with orders from Berlin. On the vital question whether Hitler knew and approved the shooting of the Jews in the East, Irving was equivocal. In the end I understood it to be his position that he now accepts that Hitler did know and approve what was going on. But that at the time when he was writing about the treatment of the Jews in the East (which, as he rightly stresses is the material time for the purpose of evaluating the

Defendants' case against him) the available evidence did not implicate Hitler. I shall therefore concentrate on the arguments advanced by the parties on that aspect.

Case for the Defendants

6.13 According to the Defendants, the sequence of events was broadly as follows: on 19 May 1941 *Wehrmacht* guidelines were issued calling for 'ruthless, energetic and drastic measures' to be taken against amongst others Jews generally. There was no explicit authorization for executions to take place. However, by his order of 2 July 1941, Heydrich identified the categories of Jews to be killed. The instructions which he issued to the *Einsatzgruppen* in a section of the order headed 'Executions' included the following categories who were to be shot:

To be executed are all
functionaries of the Comintern (as well as all professional Communists)
the higher middle and radical lower functionaries of the Party, the Central Committee, the district and regional committees
people's commissars
Jews in party and state functions
other radical elements (saboteurs, propagandists, snipers, assassins and agitators etc)

At the same time Heydrich gave instructions for the surreptitious promotion of pogroms in the Jewish ghettoes. The *Einsatzgruppen* were instructed to foment local anti-Jewish elements to promote such pogroms but without leaving any trace of Nazi involvement. Longerich pointed out that, once pogroms have started, there is no way control can be exercised over those who will be killed.

6.14 Browning gave evidence that in the initial stages the Jews who were targeted were males in leadership positions and in selected professions (excluding doctors, who were spared, although not, according to Browning, for military reasons). Longerich testified that in a state-run economy there would have been a large number of Jews occupying positions in the party or the state, perhaps hundreds of thousands. He stressed the width of the last of the categories in Heydrich's order which concludes with the potentially wide-ranging catch-all 'etc'. In effect, according to Longerich, it permitted men in the field to carry out executions at will.

6.15 In the event Heydrich's instructions were interpreted broadly: the *Einsatzgruppen* reports show that large numbers of adult Jews were straightaway put to death whether or not they held state or party positions. Browning notes that professionals and other community leaders were targeted. He cites as an example the report in July 1941 by *Einsatzgruppe* C that 'leaders of Jewish intelligentsia (in particular, teachers, lawyers, Soviet officials) liquidated'. A pointer towards the escalation in the scale of shootings is to be found in a footnote to a report by the leader of an *Einsatzkommando*, Jager, dated 2 August 1941. Jager had advocated the ghettoization of the Jews in the *Ostland* but his superior, Stahlecker, informed him of the receipt of 'general orders from above which cannot be discussed in writing'. Thereafter Jager's *Kommando* shot Jews, including women and children, in sharply increased numbers. So it would appear, say the Defendants, that such restrictions as had been imposed on the Jews who were to be shot had been relaxed.

6.16 In August 1941 the killing campaign had escalated further to include Jewish women and children. On 1 August 1941 an 'explicit order' was issued to SS units who were preparing to sweep the Pripet marshes by Himmler:

All Jews must be shot. Drive the female Jews into the swamp.

Browning argued that the reply to those instructions by *Obersturm-bannfuhrer* Magill demonstrates that he well understood the intention which lay behind them, namely that the Jews in question should be killed:

Driving women and children into the swamps did not have the intended success because the swamps were not so deep that a sinking under could occur.

Longerich too interpreted the instructions as ordering the death of the Jews in question including the women. But he agreed that they were not of general application but rather were confined to the operation to clear the Pripet marshes. Even so, Longerich estimated the number killed at about 14,000.

6.17 The Defendants say that the total numbers killed can be derived or extrapolated from the reports based on information supplied by the *Einsatzgruppen*. Those reports, if taken at face value, indicate that each of the four groups reported having killed tens of thousands of Jews in the latter months of 1941. Not all of the reports distinguish between Jews and non-Jews but some do. Browning cites as a typical example the so-called Jager report. That report gives as the number of non-Jews killed by a single *Kommando*, *Einsatzkommando* 3 in Lithuania in the period to December 1941 at 2,042, that is, barely 1.5% of the total number of 134,000 odd reported to have been killed. Other reports provide broadly similar proportions. Browning concluded that there is compelling evidence to conclude that the overwhelming majority of the people reported as executed were Jews. The Defendants rely, in support of their contention that the shooting was carried out systematically, upon the fact that reports of the shootings were sent regularly to Berlin.

6.18 According to Browning, there was a further escalation in the killing campaign from late September onwards, when *Grossaktionen* (large scale actions) commenced in which whole Jewish communities were wiped out. For instance 33,000 Jews in Kiev were killed on 29–30 September 1941. Not only were the Jewish inhabitants of the ghettos in large cities exterminated, smaller towns and rural areas were also rendered *Judenfrei* (free of Jews). Longerich testified that in the autumn of 1941 the programme of killing Jews moved into a second phase. Until then the targets had been Soviet Jews, focussing initially on the intelligentsia but then spreading to other Jews. He said that the evidence shows that from the autumn of 1941 the killing was extended to Jews in parts of Poland and in Serbia. In the spring and summer of 1942 the killing extended even further afield. Stahlecker, reporting on 15 October 1941, admitted that it had been realized from the start that ghettos would not solve the Jewish problem and that 'basic orders' had therefore called for the most complete means possible of the Jews.

6.19 The Defendants rely on an exchange of correspondence which took place in November and December 1941 as indicating what was the policy towards the execution of Jews at this period. On 15 November 1941 Lohse, *Reichskomissar* for the Eastern Territores, wrote to Rosenberg, *Reichsminister* for those territories, informing him that he had forbidden the 'uncontrolled' execution of Jews in a town in Latvia because they had not been carried out in a manner which was justified. Lohse enquired whether there was a directive to liquidate all Jews in the East irrespective of the economic interests of the *Wehrmacht*. The response from Rosenberg's office on 18 December 1941 stated that 'clarification of the Jewish question has most likely been achieved by now through verbal discussions'. The letter continued that economic considerations must be disregarded and that any question arising should be settled directly with higher SS and police officers. Longerich interpreted this exchange as an instruction to Lohse that in future the SS were to have *carte blanche* to carry out executions of the Jews. No instructions were given that mass shootings should not take place in future. To the contrary Rosenberg was confirming that mass-shootings were to continue but in future they were to be carried out in a better organized manner under the supervision of the SS. According to Longerich this broadly tallies with the order referred to by Bruns in his account of events following the shooting of the Jews in Riga on 1 December 1941. I have set out in the section v.(vii) of this judgment the account given by Bruns of the order which he was told about, namely that shooting shall be done more discreetly in future.

6.20 During the winter of 1941–2 there was a temporary lull in the shootings in the areas outside the Baltic states, due in part to the frozen ground preventing the digging of pits for burying the murdered Jews and in part to the need to utilize Jewish labour. But elsewhere, according to a situation report by Himmler in February 1942:

While the Jewish question in the *Ostland* can be seen as practically solved and cleansed, progress continues to be made on the clarification of this problem on other occupied territories in the east.

In the spring of 1942 the intensive campaign of killing was resumed. Its scale can be judged by reference to a report dated 26 December 1942 (to which I shall refer in more detail later) which stated that in the Ukraine and Bialystok 363,211 Jews were exterminated over the four months from August to November. By this time even Jewish labourers who might have made a contribution to the Nazi war effort were not spared.

6.21 Further evidence for the existence of a systematic programme for the mass killing of Jews is to be derived, according to the Defendants, from what Longerich, on their behalf described as an extraordinary speech by Himmler to SS officers at Posnan on 4 October 1943. He said:

I also want to talk to you quite frankly about a very grave matter. We can talk about it quite openly among ourselves, but nevertheless we can never speak of it publicly. Just as we did not hesitate on 30 June 1934 to do our duty as we were bidden, and to stand comrades who had lapsed up against the wall and shoot them, so we have never spoken about it and will never speak of it. It was a natural assumption of tact – an assumption which, thank God, is inherent in us – that we never discussed it among ourselves, never spoke of it . . . Most of you will know what it means to have a hundred or five hundred corpses lying together before you. To have been through this and – disregarding exceptional cases of human weakness – to have remained decent, that is what has made us tough. This is a glorious page in our history, one that has never been written and can never be written.

Longerich accepted the suggestion put to him by Irving that Himmler may have been trying to make his SS officers into accomplices after the fact. But in the speech Himmler expressly acknowedged the widespread killing operations in which the SS had been engaged.

6.22 Browning and Longerich conclude that there is in the Nazi documents (some of which I have reviewed above) clearly visible evidence of a programme for the systematic mass-murder of Jews in occupied Soviet territory and in the General Government by shooting them. The explicit goal of this policy was to cleanse the area, that is, to rid these territories of Jews. The scale of the killing, say the Defendants was awesome.

Hitler's knowledge

6.23 Was Hitler aware what was going on and did he approve of it? Although (as I have already indicated) Irving was prepared at one stage of the trial to agree that in broad terms the answer to this question is in the affirmative, he later shifted his ground. In these circumstances it is necessary for me to rehearse the rival arguments on this issue.

6.24 The Defendants' answer to this question is, firstly, that the scale of the killing was so immense and its effect on the war effort so great, that it is difficult to conceive that Hitler was not consulted and his authority sought. The Defendants adopted the evidence of Sir John Keegan, summoned to give evidence by Irving, that it was perverse to suggest that Hitler was unaware until October 1943 what was happening to the Jewish population: it defies common sense. But the Defendants assert that there was what Browning described as incremental decision-making process. Browning gave evidence that in his view Hitler had made clear to Himmler and to Heydrich what he wanted done in terms of ethnic cleansing and then left it to his subordinates to carry out his wishes. I shall summarize the stages by which on the Defendants' case the programme was set in place.

6.25 According to Himmler, Hitler commented that a memorandum which Himmler had presented to him on 25 May 1940 was 'very good and correct'. The memorandum had expressed the hope that by means of a large emigration of all Jews to an African colony, 'the concept of the Jew will be fully extinguished'. Although the memorandum described the physical extirpation of the Jews as 'un-German and impossible', Browning pointed out that this exchange took place at a time when the ethnic cleansing of the Jews (as he described it) had slowed down markedly at the instigation of Goering and Frank, who were concerned to give priority to the war effort. Browning asserted that, with a Nazi victory in France apparently assured, the memorandum indicates that Himmler approached Hitler to obtain his approval for the revalidation of the programme of ethnic cleansing. He needed Hitler's approval in order to counter any moves by Goering or Frank to block the programme.

6.26 In the spring of 1941, whilst preparations were under way for Barbarossa (the invasion of Russia), Hitler made clear his view that a war of destruction was about to start and called for the destruction of the Judaeo-Bolshevik intelligentsia. This sentiment generated proposals for the establishment of the *Einsatzgruppen* and the programme of mass shootings as I have already described. That programme was not, as Browning put it, 'micro-managed' by Hitler. But he claimed that it was Hitler whose vision and expectation created a genocidal atmosphere which brought forth concrete proposals for its implementation. Browning argued that Hitler wanted his generals to see the war against Russia as embracing a very strong ideological dimension and not just a conventional war. Having been effectively invited to do so by Hitler, the SS together with the military planners produced concrete plans to turn Hitler's vision into reality.

6.27 The Defendants recognize that the documentary evidence for implicating Hitler in any policy for the systematic shooting of Jews is sparse. There is no 'smoking gun'. A large number of documents were destroyed, many of them on the orders of Heydrich, so the documentary picture is a partial one. However, the Defendants do highlight a number of documents which, they contend, point, albeit not unambiguously, to Hitler's complicity.

6.28 The starting point for the documentary pointers towards Hitler's complicity is the record of the instructions given by Hitler to General Jodl, Chief of the Army Leadership Staff, on 3 March 1941 in relation to revised guidelines to be followed in the areas of Russia expected to be conquered. Hitler ordained:

This coming campaign is more than a struggle of arms; it will also lead to the confrontation of two world views. In order to end this war it will not suffice merely to defeat the enemy army . . . The Jewish-Bolshevik intelligentsia, the hitherto oppressor of the people must be eliminated (*beseitigt*)'

These instructions, together with other similar utterances by Hitler at this time, evidence of the central role which, according to the Defendants, Hitler played when it came to converting Nazi ideological thought into concrete action. According to Browning, it is discernible that Hitler was talking not only of military, but also ideological, necessity. As Longerich put it, Hitler was laying the ground for a racist war of extermination.

6.29 There followed what Longerich described as a package of measures, with which Hitler was intimately involved, for the implementation of that war. Following on the heels of Hitler's instructions to Jodl, on 13 March 1941 Jodl issued a directive which stated:

In the operation area of the Army, the *Reichsführer SS* is granted special responsibilities by order of the *Führer* for the preparation of the political administration;

these special responsibilities arise from the ultimate decisive struggle between two opposing political systems. In the context of these responsibilities, the *Reichsfuhrer SS* will act independently and at his own risk.

Longerich infers that the reason why Himmler was being given these undefined special responsibilities was that the Army was not willing to be radical enough in carrying out the policing and security operations. **6.30** Hitler made a similar statement, albeit one not explicitly directed at the Jews, to senior army officers on 17 March 1941 when he said:

The intelligentsia installed by Stalin must be destroyed (*vernichtet*). The leadership machine of the Russian empire must be defeated. In the Greater Russian area the use of the most brutal force is necessary

He spoke in similar vein to a meeting of generals on 30 March 1941, when, according to the abbreviated record of General Halder, Hitler said:

Communism unbelievable danger for the future . . . The Communist is not a comrade, neither before nor after. We are talking about a war of extermination . . . We are not waging war in order to conserve the enemy . . . war against Russia: extermination of the Bolshevik Commissars and the Communist intelligentsia.

6.31 On 16 July 1941 a conference took place which was attended by amongst others Hitler and Rosenberg. According to a memorandum by Bormann, Hitler said:

The giant area must naturally be pacified as quickly as possible; this will happen at best if anyone who just looks funny (or in an alternative translation preferred by Irving 'anyone who looks askance at us') should be shot.

Longerich asserted that Hitler was thereby demonstratively endorsing the brutal massacres which were taking place and in effect authorizing execution on suspicion alone. As Browning put it, it was an open shooting licence.
6.32 The Defendants attach considerable importance, in connection with the issue of Hitler's knowledge of the shootings, to an instruction issued on 1 August 1941 to the *Einsatzgruppen* by Muller, the head of the Gestapo within Heydrich's Security Police, in which he stipulated:

The *Fuhrer* is to be kept informed continually from here about the work of the *Einsatzgruppen* in the East

The Defendants' case is that this document (to which I have already made refernce in the preceding section) shows that the reports from the *Einsatzgruppen* providing information about the executions carried out by them would at least be available on a continuous basis to Hitler. The distribution lists demonstrate how widely these reports were circulated. Copies went to the *Reich* Chancellery. According to Longerich, there is evidence that a copy of at least one such report went to Bormann. He concluded that it is inconceivable that Hitler did not see the reports. Muller's instruction coincided with the escalation of the shootings from selected groups to indiscriminate killing of Jews including women and children. The Defendants contend that Hitler's apparent wish to be kept informed will have meant that he would have received regular reports of the shooting of the Jews over the following months.

6.33 As I have already mentioned in section v.(viii), on 25 October 1941, according to his Table Talk Hitler said:

This criminal race [the Jews] has the two million dead from the World War on its conscience, now again hundreds of thousands. No one can say to me: we cannot send them in the morass! Who then cares about our people? It is good if the terror (*Schrecken*) we are exterminating Jewry goes before us.

The Defendants say it is to be inferred from these words that Hitler was indeed receiving reports from the *Einsatzgruppen* as contemplated in Muller's instruction of 1 August.

6.34 On 30 November 1941 Himmler visited the Wolf's Lair. At 13.30, before meeting Hitler for lunch, he telephoned Heydrich in Prague about a transport of Jews from Berlin. Himmler's note contains the entry '*Keine Liquidierung*' that is in contention between the parties. I have set out the rival arguments in section v.(vi) above. On the Defendants' interpretation of that note, the likelihood is that Himmler discussed with Hitler the particular transport from Berlin to Riga. Although Himmler ordered that there should be no killing of the Jews aboard that transport, it is reasonable to infer that Hitler knew about and approved the shooting of other Jews in the East.

6.35 At paragraphs 5.127 to 131 above I have made reference to Goebbels's diary entry relating to his meeting with Hitler on 21 November 1941; the speech made by Hitler to the *Gauleiter* on 12 December 1941 and Frank's report of that speech on 16 December 1941. I shall not repeat myself, save to say that these are relied on by the Defendants in support of their contention that Hitler was aware of and approved the policy of executing Jews and others in the East by shooting.

6.36 An entry in Himmler's appointment book for 18 December 1941 recorded that one of the proposed topics for discussion between himself and Hitler at their forthcoming meeting was the *Judenfrage* (the Jewish question). Against that entry, apparently (say the Defendants) following the discussion with Hitler, Himmler has noted '*als Partisanane auszurotten*' (to be annihilated as if partisans). According to the Defendants this shows that Hitler, expressly consulted, approved the killing of the Jews under cover of killing partisans as the solution to the Jewish question.

6.37 The Defendants argue that this interpretation of Himmler's note is confirmed by and consistent with a report no. 51 dated 26 December 1942 on the campaign against partisans in the Ukraine, Southern Russia and Bialystok, which was retyped three days later in larger type, in order, so the Defendants say, that Hitler with his poor eyesight could read it. In its retyped form it is headed: 'Reports to the *Fuhrer* on combating partisans'. It is endorsed on the front page '*vorgelegt* (laid before or submitted) 31.12.42'. It reports the numbers killed over the preceding four months. The number of Jews executed is given as 363,211. Browning infers that this is but one of a series of reports which Hitler received in accordance with the instruction issued by Muller on 12 August 1941 that Hitler was to be kept well informed of the shootings being carried out by the *Einsatzgruppen*.

6.38 Longerich was clear in his conclusion that, if one takes account of the scale of policy of extermination and what it entailed in terms of logistics and expense, it is wholly inconceivable that Hitler was unaware not only of the fact of the shootings but also of their scale. Such contemporaneous evidence as has survived confirms, according to the Defendants, that Hitler knew and approved. Browning rejected as being absurd the notion that Himmler, who was always anxious to do his master's bidding, would not have discussed regularly with Hitler the wholesale executions of Jews and others by SS units.

Irving's response

Evidence of system and the scale of the shootings

6.39 I have already drawn attention to the number of those who, as Irving eventually admitted, were killed in the East. Irving acknowledged that the evidence shows that there was an appalling massacre of Jews on the Eastern front but he argued that, at least in their initial stages, the shootings were selective, confined to the intelligentsia and served a military purpose. He disputed that the shootings took place on the massive scale alleged by the Defendants. He suggested that many of the figures cited by the Defendants' experts and in the documents on which they relied were 'fantasy figures'.

6.40 Irving argued that the 'ruthless, energetic and drastic measures' against the Jews ordained in the guidelines issued on 19 May 1941 did not mean that they should be shot but rather than they should be arrested and imprisoned. If the guidelines had meant that the Jews were to be killed, they would have said so. Longerich rejected this contention.

6.41 Irving pointed out that Heydrich's instructions of 2 July 1941 strictly limited the Jews who were to be executed to those in state or party positions. He did not accept that it was legitimate to infer that the instructions were intended to be construed more widely simply because the executions thereafter carried out extended far beyond these limited categories. Irving submitted that no evidence has come to light of any order which authorizes the execution of broader categories of Jews.

6.42 Irving devoted a considerable amount of time in his cross-examination of Longerich to the details of the killings by Einsatzgruppen A, B, C and D which he derived for the most part from the reports submitted by them. Irving suggested, for example, that some of those reports were compiled by those who, like General Bach-Zelewski, were mass murderers and whose reporting is on that account unreliable. Irving did not accept that the reports of the Einsatzgruppen should be taken at face value. He argued that the leaders of the Einsatzkommandos, which made up the Einsatzgruppen, would have been anxious to impress their superiors with the numbers killed and so would have exaggerated the figures. Browning and Longerich both accepted that some *kommandos* may have been anxious to avoid appearing to lack zeal and so may have exaggerated their achievements. But Browning considered the figures to be accurate as 'ballpark figures'. He added (and Irving agreed) that the numbers, even if not precisely accurate, are on any view huge. Longerich concurred. He added that the numbers do not derive solely from the reports of the *Einsatzgruppen*: there are other sources.

6.43 Irving expressed doubts about the logistical feasibility of the *Einsatzgruppen* having been able to carry out executions on the reported scale, given their limited numbers and equipment and the other tasks which they were charged with carrying out. The *Einsatzgruppen* consisted of only 3,000 men. But Browning pointed out that the army was called on to provide support. Longerich calculated that, if allowance is made for the auxiliary manpower available, the total number of those involved in the shootings would have been around 30,000.

6.44 Another argument canvassed by Irving is that the reports may have been inaccurate in their statements of the numbers of Jews shot because the SS auxiliaries would not always have known whether or not those they were executing were Jews. He suggested that this must have been the reaction of British intelligence when they intercepted reports of the numbers killed. Browning responded that the Jager report is illustrative of the care taken to classify Jewish men, women and children. He explained the passive British response to the intercepts probably reflected an inability on their part to comprehend the notion that the Nazis would devote resources sorely required for their war effort to killing vast numbers of Jewish men, women and children whilst there was a war on.

6.45 Irving also argued that there will have been many who, becoming aware of the wholesale murders taking place at the hands of the SS, will have fled eastwards into Russia (there to be met, no doubt, with the same fate). A report dated 12 September 1941 refers to the 'gratuitous evacuation' of hundreds of thousands of Jews by inference across the Urals representing an indirect success for the security forces. According to Irving, in calculating the scale of the shootings, allowance should be made for the Jews who fled eastwards to avoid being shot.

Irving also suggested that many of the murdered Jews died at the hands of local anti-Jewish populations as opposed being executed by the *Einsatzgruppen*. Browning's evidence was that such pogroms did occur but for a limited period only in the opening days of the war.

Hitler's knowledge

6.46 As I have already said, Irving's stance on this issue fluctuated as the trial proceeded. In course of his own evidence, having advanced a number of reasons for doubting Hitler's knowledge of any systematic programme for the killing of Jews in Russia or elsewhere in the eastern territories, Irving conceded under cross-examination that it was a legitimate conclusion that the shootings in the east were carried out with the knowledge and approval not only of Heydrich but also of Himmler and Hitler himself. He accepted that the reports of numbers killed were sent by the *Einsatzgruppen* to Berlin on a regular basis. Irving said that he had been unaware until the summer of 1999 of the Muller document of August 1941, according to which Hitler asked for reports from the *Einsatzgruppen* to be supplied to him. But he conceded that the evidence now available points to there having been a coordinated and systematic direction by Berlin of the killings on the eastern front. In particular Irving accepted in the light of the note in Himmler's appointment book for 18 December 1941 that the massacre of Jews in the *Ostland* was carried out on the authority of Hitler. He also accepted that there had been a systematic programme for the shooting of Jews and others of which Hitler was aware and which he approved.

6.47 But in the course of his cross-examination of Longerich, Irving put to him a large number of questions which appeared to suggest that it was his case Hitler had no such knowledge and that he did not authorize any such programme or policy. He pointed out that no document has come to light indicating that Hitler expressly authorized the shootings. In the course of his cross-examination Irving advanced various arguments why it would be wrong to suppose that Hitler was complicit in the shooting of Jews and others in the period 1941–2. Irving contended (and Longerich agreed) that prior to the middle of 1941 there is no directive emanating from Hitler that Jews are to be exterminated. Thus there is no indication in the instructions or guidelines issued by Hitler to General Jodl and to the High Command Operations staff on 3 March 1941 that Jews are to be executed when the Russian campaign begins. Irving argued that these instructions, as well as the guidelines issued in October 1941, should be seen as purely military measures. Hitler was addressing the issue of military discipline and not authorizing or condoning ideological extermination. He was in effect saying that the Reich was facing a Judaeo-Bolshevik enemy which must be destroyed as a matter of military necessity. No order was issued by Hitler which explicitly said that the Jews must be killed systematically. Moreover, contended Irving, the initiative for the orders came from the Nazi High Command rather than from Hitler.

6.48 As to the 'special responsibilites' which Jodl directed, were, in accordance with Hitler's order, to be given to Himmler, Irving suggested that this flowed from Himmler's wish to enlarge his area of responsibility. He claimed that Hitler's attitude was to give Himmler *carte blanche* without any requirement to let him (Hitler) know what he was doing. In any event, argued Irving, Hitler was concerned for military as opposed to ideological reasons to ensure the security of the area to the rear of the Nazi army as it advanced into Russia. Longerich disagreed: the military and the ideological goals cannot be differentiated.

6.49 In relation to Hitler's various statements in the spring of 1941 to the forthcoming 'war of destruction' and the 'extermination of the Jews', Irving pointed out that the Nazis were about to embark on Barbarossa, so that these utterances must be seen in a military, rather than an ideological, light. Moreover Hitler was well aware of the ruthlessness of which the Red Army was capable and was issuing a warning what the war would entail. The response of Browning to this proposition is that the campaign had both a military and an ideological objective.

6.50 Irving cast doubt on the Defendants' contention that the *Einstaz-gruppen* were set up as a consequence of the preparations laid down by Hitler. Their existence came about, he suggested, 'like an act of spontaneous combustion'.

6.51 Irving devoted a considerable amount of time to casting doubt on the authenticity of the document dated 1 August 1941 claimed to evidence an instruction by Muller to furnish Hitler with reports of shootings. He pointed out that the document before the Court is no more than an *Abschrift*: the original is missing. It bears the modest security classification *geheim* (secret) which is inappropriate for a document related to the Final Solution. Irving produced a letter from the German Federal archives that the document is not to be found in the file from which it purports to come. The Defendants countered this claim by pointing out that the document has been known about and accepted as authentic for twenty years. Copies of the *Abschrift* are to be found in the Moscow archive as well as in the Ludswigsberg archive. They were also able to point to several documents of a similar sensitivity which were also classified *geheim*. The reason why no copy of the Muller document was found in the file referred to in the letter from the German archivist is that the wrong file number was quoted. Longerich is in no doubt that the document is an authentic copy of the original. Ultimately Irving accepted its authenticity, although he continued to express considerable misgivings about it.

6.52 In the end Irving took the position that he did not challenge the authenticity of the Muller document. He submitted, however, that since its existence was unknown to him until he was presented with the document in the course of cross-examination, no criticism could fairly be made of him for not taking it into account. The Defendants were unable to accept this evidence. The reasons are, firstly, that the Muller document is set out at page 86 of Fleming's work *Hitler und die Endlosung*. Irving's marked copy of that book appears to show that he has read the passage at page 86 (although Irving denied it). The second reason is that Fleming gives a reference to the archive where the document can be found in Munich. The third reason is that, when asked about Fleming's book in 1983, Irving answered that it was 'a lie'. In his evidence Irving claimed that he was basing what he said on reviews of Fleming's book.

6.53 Irving argued that the Muller document does not in any event have the significance for which the Defendants contend. It did not require the *Einstazgruppen* to report shootings to Hitler. As its heading and text indicate, it related solely to the procuring of visual materials such as placards and photographs as part of the groups' intelligence-gathering operations. Despite this both Browning and Longerich persisted in their contention that the reporting requirement embraced all the activities of the Einsatzgruppen including shooting. But they agreed that this document is the only one to which he can point as evidence for the proposition that Hitler was kept informed of the shootings. Irving stressed that, apart from Event Report no 51, no report has come to light which has been retyped in the large type which Hitler's eyesight required.

6.54 Further evidence relied on by Irving for Hitler's unawareness of any systematic programme of extermination is the entry in Himmler's telephone log for 30 November 1941 relating to a telephone call made by him from Hitler's bunker to Heydrich in Prague. I have already referred at paragraphs 5.97–8 and 5.104 above to the argument which Irving bases on this entry.

6.55 Irving advanced a similar argument in relation to the message sent on 1 December 1941 by Himmler to Jeckeln, the SS chief stationed in Riga, following the shooting of the trainloads of German Jews on arrival in Kovno. This is dealt with at paragraph 5.107–8 above. Browning and Longerich place an opposite interpretation on the Himmler's message to Jeckeln: it was reprimanding Jeckeln for the shooting of the Jews who had arrived in Minsk the previous day from Berlin. Longerich agreed that the message indicates that Jeckeln had exceeded his authority but suggests that so modest a punishment indicates that Himmler was not unduly concerned by the murder of so large a number of Jews. Longerich agreed that the killing of German Jews ceased for some time afterwards. He did not, however, accept that the fact that Jews took provisions with them on the train indicates that there was no intention to kill them. The Jewish Commission paid for the provisions and no doubt the Jews were deceived into believing that they were being taken to a new life in the East. Browning argued that the message, relating as it does to killings in Riga, indicates that the shooting of the Jews in Kovno had been authorized (which is why Jeckeln was not disciplined). Browning claimed that there had been a change of policy afterwards because of the concern felt about German Jews being killed. The guidelines enunciated the new policy.

6.56 In relation to Himmler's appointment book entry for 18 December 1941, Irving accepted that in this context *ausrotten* means 'annihilate' but he quarrelled with the translation of *als Partisanen* as 'to be annihilated as partisans', contending that it really means 'as partisans', that is, annihilated because and to the extent that they are partisans. Browning retorted that the primary meaning of *als* is 'as' and that the policy was clearly not to shoot only Jewish partisans because the records show that thousands of women and children were also shot. In relation to that note Irving in the course of his cross-examination of Longerich made for the first time the further suggestion that Himmler may have made the notation *als Partisanen auszurotten*, not because that was something that he and Hitler had discussed and agreed upon, but rather because it had for some time been Himmler's standard attitude that Jews should be exterminated as partisans. Himmler had expressed that view on previous occasions. So, Irving argued, the note expresses no more than Himmler's own view and does not implicate Hitler. On reflection Irving did not pursue this suggestion. Later in the cross-examination Irving fell back upon the suggestion that the issue was discussed between Himmler and Hitler but that the initiative for shooting the Jews as partisans came from Himmler and not from Hitler. He argued that this is consistent with the passive attitude which Hitler adopted towards the Jewish question.

6.57 Irving pointed out that in a number of their reports the *Einsatzgruppen* give pretexts for killing Jews. This, argued Irving, is inconsistent with a policy of killing Jews indiscriminately. But Longerich met this suggestion by referring to the so-called Jager report of *Einsatzkommando* 3 of 1 August 1941 that large numbers of Jews (including many women and children) had been executed without any excuse or pretext being given.

6.58 Irving did not initially accept that the endorsement *vorgelegt* on report no. 51 of 26 December 1941 meant that Hitler read the document. The Stalingrad crisis was at its height at this time. But later he agreed that it was highly likely to have been shown to him. Irving conceded that it followed that Hitler was to that extent implicated in the murder of 363,000 mentioned in that report.

6.59 When objection was taken on behalf of the Defendants to this sustained line of questioning on the ground that Irving was resiling from admissions he had previously made in cross-examination as to the state of Hitler's knowledge of the shooting, Irving agreed to set out his case in writing. Irving thereupon took the position that, in regard to Eastern European and Russian Jews, Hitler had authorized the summary execution of unspecified numbers of Jewish/Bolshevik intelligentsia and leaders; that Hitler was probably informed of 'anti-partisan' operations, though not on a regular basis; that there is evidence that no secret was made of the inclusion of large numbers of (non-German) Jews in the resulting body counts of 'partisans'. As regards Western European and German Jews, Irving's restated case is that there is no clear or unambiguous evidence that Hitler was aware of any mass murders.

The policy of deporting the Jews

Introduction

6.60 Whilst it would not be right to say that there is no issue between the parties in relation to the existence of a policy of deporting Jews eastwards, the differences in the parties' respective case appear to me to be comparatively unimportant. The topic can therefore be taken quite shortly.

6.61 According to Longerich, the Nazi policy towards the Jews evolved over the years. In the 1920s and 30s various legal and economic sanctions were applied to Jews in Germany with a view to compelling them to emigrate. Longerich draws attention to various statements made by Hitler at this time which foreshadow a more radical solution to the Jewish question. Towards the end of the 1930s pressure for the emigration and even expulsion of the Jews intensified. The term *Endlosung* (final solution) came into use, carrying with it the implication that all Jews would be removed from Nazi Germany.

6.62 Hitler's attitude at this time is reflected in an entry in Goebbels' diary for 24 August 1938:

We discuss the Jewish question. The *Fuhrer* approves my procedures in Berlin. What the foreign press writes is insignificant. The main thing is that the Jews be pushed out. In 10 years they must be removed from Germany. But in the interim we still want to keep the Jews here as pawns.

6.63 From the outbreak of war in September 1939 the policy towards the European Jews in those countries invaded by the Nazis was to find for them a 'territorial solution', that is, to find an area at the periphery of the Nazi empire to which the Jews might be deported and where they might very well perish. At this stage, Longerich agrees, the policy was not a homicidal one, although he adds the rider that there already existed what he called the 'perspective' of mass murder. His argument is that this is discernible from the comments made at the time which suggest that it was recognized that it was unlikely that the Jews would survive for long after their deportation. They would perish through disease or starvation.
6.64 It is the Defendants' case, largely although not entirely accepted by Irving, that the hard-line policy towards the Jews manifested itself when the Nazis invaded and conquered Poland in September 1939. There were two aspects: the first was the establishment of a reservation in Poland between the Vistula and the Bug into which all Jews under Nazi domination would be deported. The second was a programme to execute selected Jews in Poland as a means among others of rendering the country leaderless and destroying it as a nation. According to Longerich, the first aspect commenced with the deportation from about the autumn of 1941 of Jews from the Central Europe into the ghettoes in Eastern Europe. The intention was to deport them further east later, probably in the spring of 1942, when they would perish.
6.65 On 18 September Himmler wrote to the Gauleiter in Warthegau, Greiser, informing him:

The *Fuhrer* wishes that the Old *Reich* and the Protectorate be emptied and freed of Jews from west to east as quickly as possible. I am therefore striving to transport the Jews of the *Altreich* and the *Protektorat* in the Eastern territories that became part of the *Reich* two years ago. It is desirable that this be accomplished by the end of this year, as a first and initial step in deporting them even further to the East next spring.

I intend to remove a full 60,000 Jews of the *Altreich* and the *Protektorat* to the Litzmannstadt ghetto for the winter. This has, I have heard, the space to accommodate them.

Himmler forewarned Greiser of the arrival of Jewish transports from the *Reich*. Hitler appears therefore to have initiated the programme of deportation some time before mid-September 1941.

6.66 The deportations, which were initially to ghettoes in Lodz, Riga and Misk, began in early to mid-October 1941. Although six trainloads of Jews were summarily executed on their arrival at Kovno and in Riga, Longerich agreed that the policy at this time in relation to European Jews was to deport them and not to kill them or at least not to kill them on the spot. The Defendants say that vast numbers of Jews were deported from the *Altreich*, the *Protektorat*, Austria, France, Slovakia, Croatia and Romania to the East. Many of these European Jews may have been led to believe that they were going to a new life in the East. That explains why they travelled with food and in some cases with the tools of their trade (although Longerich points out that the food was provided by the Jewish Commission and not by the Nazis). Irving put it to Browning (and Browning accepted) that the extant records relating to deportations, consisting mainly of transport documents, are incomplete. In consequence, suggested Irving, the estimates of the numbers deported vary enormously. Irving maintains that the scale of the intended deportation was nowhere near as comprehensive as the Defendants maintain. In France for example estimates of the number of deportees range from 25,000 to 200,000. (Browning asserted that the consensus now is 75,000 French Jews were deported.)

6.67 Irving recognized the emergence of a policy of wholesale deportation of European Jews. He accepted that Hitler was an advocate of this policy. Indeed Irving's case is that the deportation of the Jews continued to be Hitler's preferred solution to the Jewish question until 1942. The so-called 'Madagascar plan', whereby the Jews were to be deported from the *Reich* to the island off the east coast of Africa, was not abandoned until then. Thereafter it is Irving's case that Hitler wanted the entire Jewish question put off until after the end of the war (see section v.(ix) above under the heading 'The Schlegelberger note'). Whether or not Irving is right about that, he firmly rejected the contention for the Defendants that the evidence shows that there was to the knowledge of Hitler a genocidal implication underlying the policy of deportation.

Genesis of gassing programme

The origins of the use of gas by the Nazi regime

6.68 In order to pinpoint the origins of the Nazi practice of killing by the administration of poison gas, it is necessary to go back some years. There was a measure of agreement between the parties that the Nazis moved from the gassing of the disabled to the gassing of able-bodied Jews in the period from 1939 to early 1942.

6.69 As Irving accepted, the so-called 'euthanasia programme' was authorized by Hitler in September 1939. It permitted specified doctors to put to death those suffering from grave mental or physical disabilities. Thousands were killed, mostly by the administration of carbon monoxide gas kept in bottles. In addition, however, many were killed using gas vans which the victims of the programme were induced to enter, whereupon the exhaust of the vans was pumped inside killing those inside within 20 minutes or so. The euthanasia programme was discontinued on Hitler's order in August 1941 because it was causing public disquiet.

The use of the gas vans to kill healthy Jews

6.70 As Irving also accepted, the gas vans and associated personnel were then moved to the East and placed at the disposal of Globocnik, the SS officer in charge of police in Lublin, where they arrived in late 1941 and early 1942. In September 1941 there is evidence that experimental gassing of Soviet POWs and others took place in Auschwitz. On 25 October 1941 Himmler met Globocnik at Mogilev, where an extermination camp was planned. On the same day Wetzel of the Ostministerium in Berlin met, firstly, Brack, a senior official of the *Reich* Chancellery who had been involved in the euthanasia programme, and later Eichmann. Wetzel drafted a letter to Rosenberg (*Reichsminister* for the Occupied Eastern Territories) and Lohse (*Reichskomissar* for the *Ostland*) that Brack was prepared to help set up gassing apparatuses in Riga and that there were no objections if Jews who were not fit for work were 'removed' by these apparatuses. On the same evening Hitler met Himmler and Heydrich.

6.71 The experimental use of the gas vans continued. In November 1941

30 prisoners were killed by exhaust fumes from a van at Sachsenhausen. There was debate in the course of the evidence about the number of vans employed and their killing capacity. Longerich maintained that a minimum of six vans were used. Irving suggested only three were ever built. The Defendants adduced in evidence a report from a sergeant in the motor pool dated 5 June 1942, which records that 97,000 had been killed by means of the use of three vans over the preceding six months. Irving made a number of observations about the document designed, as he put it, to plant suspicion about it. For instance he queried how 97,000 could have been killed over that period, when according to court records only 700 were killed in gas vans in an action 'lasting several days' at the end of November 1991. The figure of 97,000 struck Browning as perfectly feasible. He testified that the carrying capacity of the vans ranged from 30 to 80 people and that the arithmetic indicates that the three vans would have been capable of putting 97,000 to death in a period of 172 days. As to the 700 killed over several days at the end of November 1941, Longerich explained that after a period of experimentation, the Nazis improved their technique. In the end Irving accepted the authenticity of the sergeant's report.

6.72 Whilst Irving does not dispute that homicidal use was made of gas by the Nazis during the euthanasia programme and that thereafter the vans were put to use in the East to kill Jews in increasing numbers, he does quarrel with the Defendants' estimates as to the numbers killed. What is more important, Irving disputes the claim advanced by the Defendants that Hitler was kept informed of the killing of Jews by gas and approved it. I shall therefore summarize the parties' respective arguments on these contentious issues.

The Defendants' case as to the scale on which Jews were gassed to death at camps excluding Auschwitz and the extent, if any, of Hitler's knowledge of and complicity in the killing

6.73 The Defendants accept that initially Hitler's attitude towards the problem of finding a solution to the problem of the Jewish 'bacillus' was that the Jews should be deported from the Reich. They contend, however, that there is circumstantial and documentary evidence that, from about the autumn of 1941, this policy was reversed and that, with the knowledge of Hitler and at his instigation, the policy was adopted of deporting Jews *en masse* from Europe and killing them in death camps on the eastern borders of the Reich. It was the contention of Longerich that, as the killings of Soviet Jews by shooting spread in the period from autumn 1941 to spring 1942 from the Soviet union to other regions, in particular to the Warthegau, Lublin, Riga, Minsk and Serbia, so in these same areas plans were made for the construction of gas killing facilities. In so far as it related to the area of the General Government this operation was code-named Operation Reinhard.

6.74 There is little mention of Operation Reinhard or *Aktion Reinhard* in the surviving contemporaneous documents. Browning referred in his report to a document dated 18 July 1942 mentioning 'Einsatz Reinhard'. There are several other documents marked 'AR'. According to the Defendants little documentary evidence survives because the records relating to it were ordered to be destroyed in January 1944. Nonetheless, say the Defendants, the evidence does establish that deportation of European Jews to ghettoes and thence to camps at Chelmno, Semlin, Belzec, Sobibor and Treblinka took place on a massive scale. The Defendants contend that the assignment to construct the death camp at Belzec was entrusted by Himmler to Globocnik at a meeting between them on 13 October 1941. Although the document recording the proposal for their meeting referred to taking 'security-political steps' against the Jews and to 'limiting their influence', Longerich contended that it is legitimate to infer that the plan to build the Belzec death camp originated at this meeting. Globocnik was looking for more radical solutions for the Jewish question and the building work started at Belzec soon afterwards.

6.75 A start was made on the construction of Belzec in October 1941. Another huge complex of gas chambers was planned (but not proceeded with) at Mogilev. Similar facilities were commissioned at Chelmno, Sobibor and Treblinka. Browning testified that the use of the gas vans at camps, starting at Chelmno and Semlin, was an intermediate phase, coming between the shootings by the *Einsatzgruppen* and the use of primitive gas chambers at those camps and elsewhere. The custom-built gas chambers at Auschwitz came later. On arrival at the camps the great majority of these Jews were killed in gas chambers or by other means. Of these camps Chelmno was situated to the north-west of Lublin; Semlin was outside Belgrade; Belzec and Sobibor were in what was then south-eastern Poland not far from Lublin and Treblinka is north-east of Warsaw close to the frontier at that time with Russia. Longerich testified that it might in broad terms be said that the policy of exterminating the Jews evolved out of the policy of deporting them. Indeed it is, he claimed, impossible to draw a demarcation line between the two policies. The Nazis were well aware that the policy of deportation to the East resulted in the death from starvation or disease of many of those who were deported. Longerich termed this *Vernichtung durch Arbeit* (annihilation through work). There was some debate whether that term had been used at the time. But in the end it was common ground that it mattered little whether such a label was used. Longerich was clear in his opinion that such a policy was effectively equivalent to a policy of outright killing.

6.76 Other aspects of Operation Reinhard were the collection and use of materials belonging to the Jews (watches and the like) and the selective use of Jewish labour. It was an SS operation under the direction of Globocnik, who was answerable to Kruger, chief of police in the General Government, who in turn was answerable to Himmler. According to Browning, there is evidence that Globocnik on occasion dealt directly with Himmler.

6.77 Longerich contended that it appeared from the evidence that the Jews who were sent to the death camps were in the first instance local Jews from local villages and ghettos in the region. This phase commenced at Chelmno on 8 December 1941, from which date about 140,000 Jews from the Warthegau were gassed there. The same occurred at Belzec (where the gassing, mainly of Jews from the area of Lublin, started in March 1942), Sobibor (where gassing started in May 1942) and Treblinka (where the gassing started in July 1942). The extermination of these local Jews made way in the ghettos for the European Jews to replace them.

6.78 Gassing commenced at Auschwitz between September and

December 1941, when 600 Soviet prisoners of war were killed by the administration probably by means of bottles of Zyklon-B gas in the basement of Block II. Irving, by reference to a passage from a book by van Pelt referring to the death of Soviet Jews because the lack of hygiene at the camp, suggested that the deaths were not due to poisoning by gas.

6.79 At the same time as the local Jews were being put to death in these camps, the programme of deporting German Jews (that is, Jews from those parts of Europe in Nazi control) to the East was being implemented. These Jews (or those of them who were judged unfit for labour) were initially sent to ghettos but they were ultimately transported onwards to the camps where they were killed in the gas chambers, principally at Belzec. The liquidation of the German Jews ran from the spring of 1942 onwards. This was the second phase of the extermination programme. It was, said Longerich, a systematic programme of extermination, albeit one that gradually emerged.

6.80 What is the evidence for mass extermination of Jews at those camps? The consequence of the absence of any overt documentary evidence of gas chambers at these camps, coupled with the lack of archeological evidence, means that reliance has to be placed on eye witness and circumstantial evidence, which I shall shortly summarize. In giving an account of the Defendants' case as to the scale of the exterminations, I shall also summarize their argument that Hitler was complicit in the mass murder. The starting point is the evidence, such as it is, which is contained in contemporaneous documents.

6.81 I have referred at paragraph 6.70 above to the meeting which took place between Hitler and Himmler and Heydrich on 25 October 1941. Although the plan to construct gas chambers at Riga was not implemented, it is further evidence, say the Defendants, of the genesis of a policy, agreed at a high level, to use gas as a method of extermination.

6.82 From about that date, according to the Defendants, Hitler made repeated references to the extermination of the Jews and to doing away with them. On 16 November 1941 Rosenberg met Hitler and Himmler, who the next day (according to his *Dienstkalendar*) told Heydrich by telephone that he had discussed the *Beseitigung* (doing away with) of the Jews. Two days later Rosenberg gave a confidential briefing to the press in which he spoke of the biological eradication of the whole of Jewry in Europe. From this date onwards, according to the Defendants, Hitler's pronouncements on the Jewish question, become more frequent and increasingly blunt.

6.83 The Defendants attach significance to Hitler's speech to the *Gauleiter* on 12 December 1941 (already referred to in section v.) when, according to Goebbels's diary, he said:

. . . Concerning the Jewish question the *Fuhrer* is determined to make a clean sweep. He prophesied that, if they were once again to cause a world war, the result would be their own destruction. That was no figure of speech. The world war is here, the destruction (*Vernichtung*) of the Jews must be the inevitable consequence. The question must be seen without sentimentality. We are not here in order to have sympathy with the Jews, rather we sympathize with our own German people. If the German people have now once again sacrificed as many as 160,000 dead in the Eastern campaign, then the authors of this bloody conflict must pay with their lives.

According to Browning, this speech stemmed from the recognition that an early end to war was no longer on the cards. It made clear that the Nazis would nonetheless proceed with the extermination of Jews generally and not just the Jews in the occupied eastern regions.

6.84 As already stated in section v. above, Hans Frank, General Governor of the General Government, attended the meeting on 12 December 1941 (and, according to Browning, may well have had a meeting with Hitler). Four days later he passed on what he had learned in Berlin to his subordinates, telling them what Hitler had said and adding:

But what is to happen to the Jews? Do you believe that they will be lodged in the settlements in the *Ostland*? In Berlin we were told: why all this trouble, we cannot use them in the *Ostland* or the *Reichskommissariat* either; liquidate them yourselves! Gentlemen, I must ask you: arm yourselves against any thoughts of compassion. We must destroy the Jews, wherever we encounter them and wherever it is possible, in order to preserve the entire structure of the Reich . . . [for the omitted words see below] . . .nonetheless we will take some kind of action that will lead to a successful destruction, and indeed in conjunction with the important measures to be discussed in the *Reich*.

The Defendants rely on what Frank said as further evidence of the emerging policy of destroying the Jews by killing them.

6.85 As noted above, on 18 December 1941 Himmler met Hitler, who, according to Himmler's note, agreed that the Jews were to be annihilated as if partisans. The Defendants accept that Hitler expressed that sentiment in the context of the programme of shooting Jews in the East, but it is, according to them, indicative of his murderous intentions towards the Jews at this time. In January 1942 Hitler again confirmed in his New Year's address that it would be the Jews rather than the Aryan peoples of Europe would be *ausgerottet* (exterminated). He spoke in similar terms at the *Reichstag* on 30 January 1942 and thereafter on 14, 22 and 24 February 1942.

6.86 As Frank had told his audience it would be, a meeting was convened in Berlin and took place in Berlin on 20 January 1942 under the chairmanship of Heydrich. It is known as the Wannsee conference. The invitations to the conference were accompanied by an authorization, signed by Goering, to prepare a European-wide Final Solution to the Jewish problem. State Secretaries, ranking just below Cabinet ministers, attended, as did amongst others Muller, Hofmann and Eichmann. According to the Defendants, it marks an important milestone in the evolution of the policy of extermination. Irving totally rejected the significance which the Defendants attach to this conference.

6.87 Heydrich told those present:

A further possible solution [of the Jewish question] instead of emigration has come up. After appropriate approval by the *Fuhrer*, the evacuation of the Jews to the East has stepped into its place. These actions, however, must be regarded as only as an alternative solution. But already the practical experience (*praktischen Ehrfahrungen*) is being gathered which is of great importance to the coming Final Solution of the Jewish question. Under the appropriate direction the Jews shall now be put to work in the course of the Final Solution. Organized into large work gangs and segregated according to sex, those Jews fit for work will be led into these areas as road builders, whereby no doubt a large part will fall out by natural elimination. The remainder who will survive – and they will certainly be those who have the greatest power of endurance – will have to be dealt with accordingly. For, if released, they would, according to the natural selection of the fittest, form the seed of a new Jewish regeneration.

Longerich noted the reference made by Heydrich to the approval of the Fuhrer. He asserted that 'to be dealt with accordingly' is a typical SS expression for liquidation. So the Jews who survived the labour regime (if any did) were to be liquidated. Moreover the Defendants draw attention to what they regard as a notable and sinister omission from those words: what was to happen to those Jews who were already unable to work (as most were)? The answer, according to the Defendants, is that, having been judged unfit for work, they were condemned to be killed. The Defendants give, as a further reason for saying that Wannsee had the significance for which they contend, the fact that shortly after Wannsee the construction of the death camps at Sobibor and Treblinka started and gas chambers were built at Auschwitz. The enormous task of killing the Jews then began in earnest, say the Defendants.

The Defendants' case is that Wannsee was what Browning described as an 'implementation conference' at which the participants were concerned to set up a ministerial bureaucracy, under the leadership of Heydrich, for the extermination of the Jews. It was not a theoretical discussion.

6.88 It is the Defendants' case that the scale of the gassing programme escalated in March 1942. On 3 March 1942 the Prime Minister of Slovakia announced that agreement had been reached with the Nazis for the deportation to Auschwitz of the 70,000 remaining Slovakian Jews.

6.89 Himmler's Dienstkalendar reveals that, following dinner with Hitler on 10 March 1942, Himmler spoke by telephone to Heydrich on 11 March when they discussed the Judenfrage (Jewish question). On 13 March Himmler travelled to Cracow (where he met Frank and Kruger) and thence on 14 March to Lublin (where he met Kruger and Globocnik). On his return to Berlin, Himmler on 17 March had lunch and dinner with Hitler at the Wolfschanze (Wolf's Lair). Goebbels's diary entry for 20 March records that on the previous day Hitler had displayed a merciless attitude towards the Jews and had stated that the Jews must be got out of Europe, if necessary by the most brutal means.

6.90 Browning referred to evidence that in mid-March 1942 it was agreed that deported Jews arriving at Lublin should be divided into those capable of work and those not so capable. The latter were to be sent to Belzec, where gassing commenced on 17 March. Large-scale gassing continued at Belzec in the following months. In the same month construction of Sobibor began and bunker 1 at Auschwitz started operation as a gas chamber. Gassing had started at Sobibor by May 1942. Construction of the death camp at Treblikna commenced at about this time. In the first six months of 1942 some 10,000 Jews had been gassed at Chelmno. Vast numbers of Jews in the General Government and in the Warthegau were, according to the Defendants, killed by the use of gas.

6.91 The Defendants also rely on a letter dated 11 April 1942 which Dr Turner, whose rank was equivalent to that of a Privy Councillor, wrote from Serbia to Karl Wolff, Himmler's adjutant and sometime liaison officer to Hitler. The letter was marked 'AR' for Action Reinhard. It referred in rather unsubtle code to the use of gassing trucks at Semlin on a scale which Irving agreed could not be described as limited or experimental. Irving conceded that the document is a sinister one.

6.92 On 1 May 1942 Greiser wrote to Himmler, following a meeting with Globocnik in May 1942, that 'the special treatment' (*Sonderbehandlung*) of around 100,000 Jews in his district, which had been authorized by Himmler in agreement with Heydrich, could be completed in the next 2–3 months. Irving accepted that, in the light of what subsequently emerged (although not, he said, on the face of this document) 'special treatment' meant killing. He was critical of Longerich for, as he put it, 'extrapolating backwards' from what subsequently happened at the camps, that it had throughout been the plan that the killings should occur. Longerich answered this criticism by saying that, in the nature of things, historians must frequently have resort to this method, which is in any event wholly unobjectionable. The document did not spell out where the special treatment was being meted out but in the opinion of Browning it is a reasonable inference that it was at Chelmno, which was operating at the time. Irving makes the point that this letter does not say that it was written on the instructions of the *Fuhrer*.

6.93 Browning gave evidence that contemporaneous documents show that from the summer of 1942 trainloads of Jews were being transported westwards from the occupied eastern territories to Belzec and to Treblinka. The significance of this westward movement of Jews, according to both Browning and Longerich, is that it demonstrates that the policy was no longer to keep deporting the Jews further and further to the East but rather to exterminate them.

6.94 On 17 and 18 July 1942 Himmler visited Auschwitz. He had met Hitler over a meal on two occasions in the preceding ten days. At Auschwitz he met the Commandant, Hoss. He then travelled to Lublin, where he met Kruger, Globocnik and Pohl. On 19 July Himmler, according to the evidence of Browning who was basing himself on contemporaneous documents, laid down a schedule for the extermination of the entire Jewish population of the General Government by the end of the year (save only for certain Jews employed in ghettos on war work). The Defendants assert that with effect from 22 July 1942 there were massive deportations from Warsaw and northern Lublin district to Treblinka and from Przemsyl to Belzec. On 23 July 1942 gassing started at Treblinka. On 24 and 27 July 1942 Himmler lunched with Hitler. Three days later Himmler wrote to Berger, a senior officer at the SS Headquarters, a letter which on the Defendants' case is highly revealing. He wrote that the occupied Eastern territories were to be free of Jews by the end of the year. Himmler added that the 'carrying out of this very hard order had been placed on his shoulders by the *Fuhrer*'. The extermination of Jews on a massive scale in the death camps commenced at this time.

6.95 Browning relied also on the protocol of a meeting in Berlin on September 26–8 1942 as showing that train transports to the death camps had been proposed by Brunner, whose immediate superior was Himmler. Browning pointed out that on 28 July 1942 Ganzenmuller, a senior official in the Ministry of Transport, reported to Wolff, an SS officer who Irving accepted was close to Hitler, that trains were regularly transporting Jews in large numbers to both Treblinka and Belzec. On 13 August Wolff, writing from Hitler's headquarters, wrote to Ganzenmuller expressing his joy at the assurance that for the next two weeks there would be a daily train carrying 5,000 of the 'chosen people' to Treblinka.

6.96 The Defendants rely in addition on what they claim to be an explicit mention of the policy of extermination which is contained in the so-called Kinna report, written by an SS corporal dated 16 December

1942 from Zamosk in Poland about the transport of 644 Poles to Auschwitz. This report records SS *Hauptsturmfuhrer* Aumeier as having explained that only Poles fit for labour should be delivered to Auschwitz and that, in order to relieve the camp, 'limited people, idiots, cripples and sick people must be removed from the same by liquidation'. The report continues that 'in contrast to the measures applied to the Jews, the Poles must die a natural death'. This, say the Defendants, points unequivocally to a policy of exterminating the Jews being in place at Auschwitz and inferentially elsewhere.

6.97 Apart from these sparse documentary references, the Defendants rely upon what might be described as circumstantial evidence that extermination on a massive scale took place. In relation to the fact and scale of the extermination, they commend as accurate the figures given in the report of Dr Korherr, who was the statistician working for Himmler. He gave as the number of those deported from the Warthegau for *Sonderbehandlung* (special treatment) a total of 1,419,467.

6.98 Browning advanced what is in effect a demographic argument in support of the Defendants' contention that Jews were exterminated in the gas chambers at the death camps in vast numbers. He calculated the approximate number who were deported from western European countries and removed from the ghettos of Poland; he asserted that contemporanous evidence proves that many of them were transported to Belzec, Sobibor and Treblinka; since they were never heard of again, Browning considers it reasonable to infer that they were put to death in the camps. It is the Defendants' case that between 750,000 and 950,000 Jews were killed by gas at Treblinka; 550,000 at Belzec; 200,000 at Sobibor and 150–200,000 at Chelmno. Those were the estimates based on expert German witnesses and accepted in the German criminal prosecutions in the 1960s.

6.99 Longerich supported Browning's estimate for the number killed at Belzec. Basing himself on the evidence given at the trial of those involved in the camp, he put the figure at between 500,000 and 600,000. He agreed that estimates given by the historian, Michael Tregenza, were unreliable but said that he had not relied on him in that connection. Longerich testified that Belzec was initially employed in gassing Jews from the areas of Lublin and Galicia.

6.100 In addition to the circumstantial evidence, the Defendants rely on the evidence of eye-witnesses in support of their case that gas chambers were used at Belzec, Sobibor and Treblinka to kill hundreds of thousands of Jews. Browning divided these witnesses into five categories: (i) German visitors to these camps; (ii) German personnel stationed there; (iii) Ukrainian guards assigned to the camps; (iv) Poles living in the vicinity of the camps and (v) Jews who escaped. In view of the position adopted by Irving on the question of gassing at these camps (to which I shall refer in due course), it is unnecessary for me to set out at length who all of these witnesses were or what they were able to describe. According to Browning, there are over one hundred of them.

6.101 Within category (i) comes Eichmann, who is regarded by Browning as being in general a credible witness. His testimony takes various forms: an interview with a journalist in South America before his apprehension; memoirs and evidence at his trial. (During the course of the present trial evidence was released by the Israeli government of what Eichmann said under interrrogation by Israeli prosecutors. Since, however, this evidence was not available to Irving at any material time, no reliance was placed on it by the Defendants in support of their plea of justification). Eichmann stated that he was sent by Heydrich to discuss with Globocnik the implementation of what he was told was Hitler's order to kill the Jews. In the autumn of 1941 he was shown a building under construction at Belzec, which he was told would be used as a gas chamber to kill Jews with carbon monoxide gas. The following summer he saw Jews about to enter the gas chamber at Treblinka. He also witnessed the gassing of Jews at Chelmno.

6.102 Another German visitor was Kurt Gerstein. He described how he was deputed to take 100 kilos of prussic acid to Lublin in August 1942. Accompanied by a chemistry professor named Pfannenstiel, he travelled to Belzec where he claimed that he witnessed about 750 Jews being driven naked into four gas chambers. After a delay because the motor would not start, the Jews were gassed. The process took 32 minutes. The bodies were then thrown into trenches. The next day Gerstein went to Treblinka, where he saw mounds of clothing. On his return to Berlin, he told a Swedish diplomat what he had seen. His account was written in about April 1945. He died shortly afterwards. Browning accepted that many aspects of Gerstein's testimony are problematic and that he was prone to exaggeration but concluded that on vital matters of which he was able to speak from his own knowledge he is reliable. His evidence is largely corroborated by that of Pfannenstiel.

6.103 Category (ii) consists of twenty-nine German camp officials all of whom confirm that the camps were equipped with gas chambers in which thousands of Jews were put to death. This category includes witnesses who provided signed and sworn statements, which gave detailed and gruesome evidence of the procedures followed at each of the camps in administering the gas and disposing of the corpses afterwards. Category (iii) included the Poles who lived in the neighbourhood of the camps and so witnessed the endless flow of transports to the camps, smelled the deathly smells from the camps and heard rumours what was going on there. Category (iv) consisted of those Jews who were able to make their escape. There were breakouts from Sobibor and Treblika. Some of the fifty survivors of these camps gave evidence of their experiences. In relation to Belzec, a Jew named Reder provided a detailed account of the gas chambers, even though it did not in all respects accord with other testimony.

6.104 Finally the Defendants rely in support of their case that Hitler knew of the Holocaust upon a letter written in 1977 to a journalist named Gita Sereny by Christa Schroeder, formerly personal secretary to Hitler and, say the Defendants, well placed to know the state of his knowledge. *Frau* Schroeder wrote:

As far as the *Judenfrage*, I consider it improbable that Hitler knew nothing. He had frequent conversations with Himmler which took place *tete-a-tete*.

What Irving disputed, however, is the Defendants' contention that the extermination of the Jews in the death camps was carried out pursuant to some official Nazi policy sanctioned by Hitler.

6.105 The Defendants, on the basis of the evidence which I have summarized above, contend that from October 1941 Himmler was embarked upon a gigantic homicidal gassing programme, first of the Jews of the Warthegau and Poland and, from late spring 1942, of the Jews from the rest of Europe, at camps specially designed for the purpose. The Defendants accept that there is no explicit evidence that

Himmler discussed with Hitler the extermination of the Jews by gassing. But in the light of the evidence recited above, including the scale of the programme; the fact that it was overseen by Himmler; the frequency with which Himmler and Hitler met and spoke together at this time and the evidence of Hitler's thoughts and public statements about the Jews, the Defendants argue it is inconceivable that Hitler did not know and authorize the mass extermination of Jews by gassing.

Irving's response: the scale of the killings by gassing

6.106 As I have already pointed out, Irving accepted that the object of Operation Reinhard was broadly that contended for by the Defendants. What he disputed are the Defendants' contentions as to scale of the operation and Hitler's knowledge and approval of it. As to the scale of the extermination programme, Irving's stance in regard to the question whether gas chambers were employed at the Reinhard camps for the killing of Jews and, if so, on what scale appeared to evolve during the course of the hearing. He produced documents which show that various poisonous gasses were employed by the Nazis for non-lethal purposes, in particular for the fumigation of clothing. Indeed the Nazis trained people in the use of gas for fumigation purposes. He spent some time in his own evidence and during the course of his cross-examination of Browning stressing the marked absence of documentary evidence of the gassing in contrast with the ample documentation which has survived of the execution of Jews by shooting. He pointed out that, of the many thousands of messages intercepted by the British at Bletchley and elsewhere, none mentions gassing. Browning accepted that, with the exception of a few documents referring to the use of gas vans by the Einsatzgruppen and their use at Chelmno, documents do not now exist. His explanation was that Operation Reinhard was centralized and so required little communication, whereas the shooting was carried out by means of numerous local operations. He added that most of the Reinhard documents had in any event been systematically destroyed.

6.107 Irving was critical of the reliance placed by the Defendants on such documents as are said by them to cast light on the allegedly genocidal use to which the camps were put. Much time was spent in evidence and argument on discussing the meaning and true significance of a number of German words to be found in the speeches of Hitler and others and in contemporaneous documents generally. There was prolonged cross-examination of Longerich by Irving as to the meaning of certain German words which he listed in a glossary prepared for the purpose of these proceedings. Those words include *ausrotten, vernichten, liquidieren, evakuieren, umsiedeln* and *abschieben*. A considerable number of documents were scrutinized in an attempt to ascertain whether the words in question were being used or understood in a genocidal sense. Irving contended that most of these words are properly to be understood in a non-genocidal sense. Longerich agreed that most, if not all, of these words are capable of being used in a non-genocidal sense. For example *ausrotten* can bear such anodyne meanings as 'get rid of' or 'wipe out' without connoting physical extermination. But he asserted that its usual and primary meaning is 'exterminate' or 'kill off', especially when applied to people or to a group of people as opposed to, for example a religion. He contended that all depends on the context in which the words are used. Another example is *Umsiedlung*, which can mean no more than resettlement in a ghetto but more often embraces a homicidal meaning as well. Whilst Longerich was prepared to concede that some of the words in question may be used in a non-genocidal sense in the years leading up to 1941, he argued that from about that date onwards the words are invariably used in a sinister sense to connote killing on a major scale. For instance he contends that when, in a document dated 20 February 1942 the *Reichsicherheitshauptamt* (RHSA) use the term *Evakuierung* in connection with the issuing of guidelines for the implementation of the evacuation of Jews to Auschwitz, the word is being used in a genocidal sense.

6.108 Irving was also critical of the Defendants' experts for their readiness, as he saw it, to dismiss as 'euphemistic' German words which on their face are anodyne or imprecise in their connotation. Examples of such words include *Sonderbehandlung* (special treatment), *Evakuierung* (evacuation) and *Umsiedlung* (resettlement). According to the Defendants, such words were often employed where the writer or speaker wished either to be evasive or to speak in a coded language calculated to mislead outsiders. Browning used Event report 21 of 13 July 1941 together with a number of other similar reports to demonstrate that *Sonderbehandlung* was used to mean liquidation or shooting or execution. He also cited a document which refers to the *Umsiedlung* (resettlement) in the *Kreisgebiet* Brest-Litovsk of 20,000 Jews who can be shown to have been killed. Browning and Irving were in agreement that in the case of camouflage documents such as these it is necessary to take careful account of the context when deciding what these terms really signified. According to both of them, it is legitimate and indeed necessary for an historian to have regard not only to the circumstances as they existed at the time when the document came into existence but also to what happened later.

6.109 As regards the mass extermination of Jews, Irving accepted that gas vans were employed to kill Jews at camps in the east. When asked whether he accepted that at Treblinka, Sobibor and Belzec Jews were killed with gas, Irving answered that, on the basis of evidence contained in Eichmann's private papers, he accepts that there was gassing in vans at Chelmno. He said, however, that he has not seen evidence of the use of gas vans at the other camps. He maintained the position that this was a very inefficient method of killing. He also pointed out that there was some disagreement as to the way in which the poison was administered and whether it was carbon monoxide or some other form of poison. Irving also queried whether it would have been feasible to have buried so many corpses.

6.110 But in the end Irving's doubts were no more than academic. For, despite his original claim that gassing occurred on a limited basis involving the use of no more that six to eight vans, Irving, in the light of documents he had seen in the past six months, made a number of concessions. He did not quarrel with the assertion of Browning that in a period of about five weeks in 1942 97,000 were killed at Chelmno by the use of gas vans. Irving suggested that figure may be an exaggeration but he agreed that was not limited or experimental but systematic. He further agreed that the evidence established that Jewish women and children were gassed to death in vans in Semlin, near Belgrade, in 1942.

6.111 However, despite his acceptance at an earlier stage of the trial that the gassing at the *Reinhard* camps had been systematic and on a considerable scale, Irving cross-examined Evans on the basis that the gas vans had been used to kill Jews on a basis which was no more than experimental. Evans's evidence was that, whilst the vans were used in a transitional stage only, they were nevertheless used on a large scale.

6.112 As to the specific documents relied on by the Defendants, Irving agreed that Wetzel's letter of 25 October 1941 was concerned with liquidating Jews but stressed that, as the Defendants accept, no gas chambers were in the event constructed in Riga. Irving also noted that Wetzel was never prosecuted. Browning's explanation is that there is no evidence he did anything more than propose the construction of gas chambers.

6.113 In reliance on the remarks made by Rosenberg at a press conference on 18 November 1941 about six million Jews being 'brought across the Urals', Irving argued that the primary Nazi intention was to transport them yet further to the East rather than to exterminate them. Rosenberg specifically referred to the option of expelling them to the eastern side of the Urals, so he should not be taken to have had in mind that the Jews would be killed. Longerich in reply pointed out that Rosenberg had spoken of 'the biological eradication of the entirety of Jewry' at a time when 500,000 odd Soviet Jews had already been exterminated. Rosenberg was intent on exterminating the Jews by one means or another, according to Longerich, for he said:

For this it is necessary to push them over the Urals *or otherwise* (my italics) eradicate them.

Irving's response: Hitler's knowledge of the gassing at the Reinhard Camps

6.114 In regard to Hitler's speech to the *Gauleiter* on 12 December 1941, Irving denied that it constitutes evidence of Hitler's knowledge of a policy of exterminating the Jews. He dismissed it as 'the old familiar Adolf Hitler gramophone record' harking back to his 1939 prophecy as to the fate awaiting the Jews. Browning considered that its terms indicate that a decision had been taken what to do about the Jews ('the

Fuhrer has decided . . .'). Irving was reluctant to accept that Goebbels was accurately recording what Hitler had said and argued that he may have been interpolating his own aspirations in regard to the Jews.

6.115 Irving is critical of Browning for the tendentious omission from his account of Frank's speech of 16 December 1941 of Frank's statement:

We cannot shoot [the Germans in the General Government]. We cannot poison them.

According to Irving, those words make clear that Frank was ruling out extermination as a solution, which makes nonsense of the Defendants' argument that the speech is evidence of a policy of extermination. Browning drew attention to the immediately following words, 'We will find a way to bring about a successful destruction', which he argued demonstrate that what Frank was saying was that alternative means must be found of getting rid of the Jews. Irving's riposte is that gassing is no less objectionable than poisoning.

6.116 Irving argued that a similar inference that the policy continued to be one of deportation further east could be drawn from Hitler's statement on 27 January 1942, as recorded in his Table Talk. Irving relied also on Hitler's reported reference on 30 January 1942 to the Jews 'disappearing from Europe' to be resettled in central Africa. But Longerich countered that these remarks, made at the time of the Wannsee conference, must be regarded as camouflage for public consumption. To take these statements by Hitler at their face value would, according to Longerich, be wholly irreconcilable with the mass exterminations which were already under way at Chelmno and Belzec. Longerich asserted that Hitler and Goebbels were constantly talking about the Jews; that Hitler was well aware of the mass gassings but they were guarded in what they said or wrote about them.

6.117 Irving refused to accept the claim of Longerich that there is evidence that there was a systematic expulsion of the eastern Jews from the ghettos in order to send them to the death camps so as to make way for the German and European Jews who, having arrived in large numbers in the east in trainloads from the rest of Europe, were kept for a while in the ghettos before themselves being sent to the gas chambers. If this occurred, argued Irving, orders and plans would surely have been found. Irving maintained that the evidence for saying that there was a systematic policy of extermination is inferential or secondary. Longerich's explanation for the lack of documentation is that, for reasons of secrecy, much of the planning was discussed verbally between Hitler and Himmler; that the Nazis tried systematically to destroy documents and files on this subject with the result that such documents as have survived are spread round European archives and that the death camps were systematically destroyed by the Nazis at the end of the war.

6.118 Irving pointed out, correctly, that the protocol issued following the Wannsee conference on 20 January 1942 did not discuss methods of killing but rather talked in terms of finding solutions. Irving argued that the minute of the conference makes reference to 'the evacuation of the Jews' having stepped into the place of emigration as a solution to the Jewish question. Why, asked Irving, should 'evacuation' not be given its natural meaning. Longerich answered this question by pointing to the immediately following paragraph of the minute, which he regards as the central passage, where Heydrich explains what is to be the Final Solution. Heydrich talks of those Jews who survive the work gangs being 'dealt with accordingly' for, if released, they would form the seed of a new Jewish regeneration. But Irving put a different construction on the paragraph: he contended that Heydrich was speaking of what should happen after the release (*bei Freilassung*) of the Jews. Heydrich was proposing the Jews should upon their release be free to regenerate themselves somewhere outside the *Reich*. Longerich countered by saying that regeneration of the Jews was precisely what Heydrich was concernd to ensure did not happen. If Heydrich had been contemplating what would happen *after* the Jews were released, he would have used the term *nach Freilassung*.

6.119 What is more, argued Irving, there are clear indications in the minute of the conference that the Final Solution was not to be embarked upon until after the war, when mass extermination of the Jews would have been out of the question. Longerich doubted the impracticability of carrying out the Nazi Final Solution if the Nazis had won the war. But he added that Heydrich clearly intended the Jewish work gangs to be put to work forthwith (nun). Longerich did, however, agree that the implementation of the programme of killing all the Jews would not be capable of being completed until after the war was over.

6.120 Next Irving relied, in support of his argument that the topic of killing Jews was not discussed at Wannsee, on the statements to that effect made after the war by most of the participants. Longerich and Browning both answered that there is nothing surprising or convincing about those denials: they were made during the Nuremberg trials and were plainly self-exculpatory. Irving also relied on an extract from a speech made by Heydrich a week or so later in Prague, which is quoted in part in a book by the historian Gotz Aly. Himmler referred in that speech to the option of deporting the Jews to the White Sea (in northern Russia), which he describes as an ideal homeland for them. Irving suggested that Himmler's words should be taken at face value. But Longerich disagreed: he pointed out that Gotz Aly, the author of the book which quoted the speech, is himself of the opinion that the policy of extermination was decided upon in October 1941. Moreover, added Longerich, there is no evidence that any Jew was in fact sent to the White Sea nor is there any evidence that any camp was constructed for them there.

6.121 Irving further relied on a letter written in June 1942 by Walter Furl, the officer stationed in Krokow who was responsible for resettlement in the General Government, to his SS officers in which he described how trainloads of Jews arrived at Krakow and were given first aid and provisional accommodation, before being deported towards the White Sea where many of them would assuredly not survive. This, said Irving, is further evidence that the policy continued to be deportation not extermination. What, according to Irving, is significant is that the Jews in question were not sent to Auschwitz. Longerich dismissed this as camouflage, as did Aly Gotz who first quoted the document and who undertook considerable research in the area. There is no evidence that any camps were constructed in the area or that trains ran from the Polish towns to the White Sea or that roads leading in that direction were ever built. The Defendants say that Furl was concerned to conceal the fact that the Jews in question were going to be shot, probably in Minsk. Irving replied that there was no reason why Furl would want to pull the wool over the eyes of his comrades. If that had been Furl's intention, why should he have referred openly to many of the Jews assuredly not surviving. Irving complained that, on every occasion when a document appears which does not fit in with the Defendants' thesis, they dismiss it as camouflage or euphemism.

6.122 Irving claimed to find support for his contention that the policy towards European Jews was not genocidal in a letter from Himmler to the Minister of Finance dated 17 August 1942. He argued that it proposed, on grounds of cost, that the French Jews should be housed in a camp to be built on the western boundary of France rather than have them transported across the *Reich* to Auschwitz. Longerich replied that this letter is pure deception.

6.123 Irving next relied on a report by Horst Ahnert of a meeting on 1 September 1942 at which Eichmann, who chaired the meeting, informed participants that the current programme for the evacuation of Jews from France was to be completed by the end of the year. The report referred to the commandant of Auschwitz having requested that deportees should take with them blankets, shoes and feeding utensils. Irving argued that such a request would not have been made if the Jews were going to be executed on arrival. Longerich responded that the request was no doubt made because not all Jews were executed on arrival: those who were fit enough were sent to the labour camp, where they would need food and clothing. Irving relied on another section of the report of this meeting which stated that the purchase of barracks, requested by the chief of security policy in The Hague, for the construction of a camp in Russia should be put in hand. Irving deployed this part of the report as further evidence that the Dutch Jews were not going to be deported to a death camp. Longerich had no knowledge of any such camp having been constructed in Russia. He did, however, concede that there are odd references in documents which date from this period to the construction of camps to house Jews. Longerich was not prepared to accept the suggestion put to him by Irving that such documents evidenced a non-genocidal intention towards the Jews. The evidence that Jews were at this time being massacred in large numbers is, he contends, overwhelming. His argument was that Eichmann and others were camouflaging what was going on.

6.124 Irving relied on another letter written on 28 December 1942 by Furl to Pohl about the measures to be undertaken by the doctors at certain camps to ensure that the mortality rate was reduced. This letter, suggested Irving, is inconsistent with the existence of a policy to exterminate all Jews. Longerich disagreed: Pohl was in charge of the labour concentration camps and had no responsibility for the Operation Reinhard death camps. It follows, say the Defendants, that the letter does not touch upon the question what was happening in the death camps

6.125 In relation to the Kinna report of 16 December 1942, Irving accepted that it is an important document in that it does indeed indicate that Jews at Auschwitz could be killed at will. But he pointed out that the author of the report was a junior SS officer, who may have been imprecise in his use of language.

6.126 Irving also placed reliance on the fact that no archaeological evidence has been uncovered which confirms the existence of gas chambers at any of these camps; indeed the only camp where excavation has been carried out is Belzec and that has only just started.

6.127 Irving made clear that he regards eye witness evidence as deeply suspect. As in the case of Auschwitz, to which I will turn shortly, Irving is inclined to dismiss all such evidence on the ground that it is either the product of duress or bribery or some other inducement or is otherwise unreliable. When I come to deal with Auschwitz I shall recite the various reasons advanced by Irving for dismissing or at least treating with extreme scepticism the evidence of eye-witnesses. Irving was critical of the reliance placed by the Defendants' experts on this body of evidence in its entirety. But he selected, by way of example of his general attack on their credibility, individual witnesses for specific criticism.

6.128 He suggested that Eichmann said what he did out of a desire to please or perhaps was subject to some psychological impulse to incriminate himself. He suggested further that Eichmann may have been suffering from sleep deprivation when he gave evidence at this trial. He pointed out that Eichmann claimed wrongly that he was acting pursuant to a Hitler order (having been told so by Heydrich). He suggested that the journalist may have invented Eichmann's confession to spice up the report of the interview he had with him whilst he was still at liberty.

6.129 As to Gerstein, Irving doubted his claim to have been a covert anti-Nazi. He suggested that it was most unlikely that he and Pfannenstiel would have been permitted to observe events which were treated as top secret. Irving suggested that it would have been 'no skin off [Pfannenstiel's] nose' to admit having watched the gassing when asked about it. He drew attention to the many fantastic claims made by Gerstein in his various accounts, for example his claim that Globocnik told him that between 10,000 and 25,000 Jews were being killed per day at each of the camps and his claim to have seen piles of shoes 25 metres high. Browning conceded that Gerstein was prone to extraordinary exaggerations but he would not accept that he has been wholly discredited. Besides, said Browning, Gerstein is corroborated by others.

6.130 Despite the arguments which he advanced and which I have summarized, Irving, after being repeatedly pressed, did finally concede that one of the proposed methods of liquidation was by the use of carbon monoxide in gas chambers. He further accepted that on the balance of probabilities from the spring of 1942 (and earlier in the case of Chelmno) hundreds of thousands of Jews were deliberately killed at those camps. What he does not accept, however, is that any of these camps were purpose-built death camps. To take Treblinka as an example, Irving asserted that forensic tests and aerial photographs indicate that there was no purpose-built extermination facility there.

6.131 As regards the scale of the exterminations at these camps, Irving did accept that hundreds of thousands of Jews were intentionally killed, by some means or another, at Belzec, Sobibor and Treblinka. He agreed that the contemporaneous evidence discloses daily trains transporting Jews in large numbers (perhaps as many as 5000 per train) eastwards from various departure points to Treblinka, Sobibor and Belzec. Although he queried at one point how the corpses had been disposed of, he did not resile from his acceptance that Jews were killed in huge numbers in the camps at these three villages.

6.132 In connection with the scale of the extermination whch took place in the death camps, Irving relied on two documents, one bearing the initials of Himmler, which reported the amount of property taken from Jews in the period to 30 April 1943, evidently in the execution of Operation Reinhard, for distribution amongst Nazi units. The figure for wrist and pocket watches, totalling about 120,000, indicates, according to Irving, that a relatively small number of Jews were dispossessed and a correspondingly lower figure deported and killed. Browning did not accept that the list of property was a complete list of all property removed. He did not consider that the documents assist in determining the likely number of deportees.

Irving's response: Hitler's knowledge of and complicity in the gassing programme

6.133 Turning to the issue of Hitler's knowledge of and complicity in the gassing programme, Irving argued that there is no evidence that Hitler was personally involved in the decision to transfer the gas vans which had been used in connection with the euthanasia programme to the East to assist in liquidating Jews there. Longerich replied that Hitler was intimately involved with the euthanasia programme, so it is logical to assume that he would have been similarly involved in the transfer of the equipment and personnel to the eastern front once the euthanasia programme was halted. The documents show that the *Fuhrerkanzlerei* was involved in the transfer and the Chancellery reported to Hitler.

6.134 Irving argued that, at least until October 1943, it remained Hitler's preferred solution to the Jewish problem that the Jews should ultimately be deported but not until the war was over. Whilst he accepted that, at least in general terms, Hitler was aware that Jews were being shot in large numbers by the *Einsatzgruppen*, he contended that the evidence does not establish Hitler's involvement in or his knowledge of Operation Reinhard, that is, the operation involving the killing of hundreds of thousands of Jews in gas chambers at the Reinhard death camps. Irving's stance was that, whilst Hitler had no excuse for not knowing about the extermination programme from October 1943 onwards, the documents are unhelpful as to his state of knowledge over the previous 18 months or so. In this context Irving again emphasized that there is no 'Hitler Befehl' (Hitler order). The eminent German historian Hilfberg originally claimed that there had been but in later editions he took out all references to there having been such an order. Irving criticized Browning's claim that Hitler gave signals and set expectations as 'frightfully vague'. But he did recognize that, if Hitler had been informed of the killings prior to October 1943, he would have raised no objection.

6.135 As to the Wannsee conference, said Irving, Hitler was not present and there is no evidence that he was apprised of the discussions which took place there. Heydrich's claim to have the authority of Hitler was either *pro forma* or a false claim designed to provide reassurance to those present.

6.136 Irving underlined the fact that from 1938 right through to 24 July 1942, as evidenced by his Table Talk for that day, Hitler continued to talk of the Madagascar plan. Browning agreed that until about 1940 that was a concrete plan on which the Nazis' people were working which they might have attempted to implement but he asserted that after 1940 it became an anti-semitic fantasy. Irving maintained that Hitler's preferred solution to the Jewish question was deportation and not genocide.

6.137 Irving accepted that SS General Wolff, one of whose roles was to act as a conduit between Himmler and Hitler, would have told Hitler about the transports of Jews to the death camps. But he relied on the post-war recollection of Wolff (dismissed by Longerich as self-serving) that he was certain that Hitler did not know what was going on. Irving produced an extract made in manuscript from a document contained in the Munich archive in which Wolff is recorded as having said in 1952 that only 70 odd people ranging from Himmler to Hess (whose association went back to the 1920s) were involved in the extermination of the Jews. When the complete document was obtained, it became apparent that Wolff had said that 'probably' (*wohl*) only those 70 had been involved. Wolff is also recorded as having said that Bormann and Himmler were the real culprits; they had taken the view that the Jewish problem had to be dealt with without Hitler 'getting his fingers dirty'. Himmler is said by Wolff to have taken the whole burden on his own shoulders for the sake of the German people and their *Fuhrer*. Irving relied heavily on this document, emanating from someone close to both Himmler and Hitler, as convincing evidence that Hitler was not implicated in or even aware of the killing in the death camps.

6.138 Dealing with the Wolff document, Longerich described it as 'interesting' in that it refers to millions of Jews having been killed and to 'the gassing idea' probably having emerged when an epidemic broke out. He observed parenthetically that in his translation Irving translated *Ausrottung* as 'extermination'. But Longerich was distinctly unimpressed by the record of the interview as a whole: Wolff was plainly concerned to distance himself from the events of the Holocaust. Unless he placed on record his denial that Hitler had any knowledge of the murders, it might be inferred, since he was the conduit between Himmler and Hitler, that he was himself implicated. Moreoever Wolff was and remained an admirer of Hitler anxious to portray him in the best light. Longerich was unable to accept that Himmler was acting unilaterally, not least because he had himself referred to the burden of carrying out this very hard order placed on his shoulders by Hitler, when writing to Berger on 28 July 1942. In any event Longerich considered that the figure of seventy for those involved in the 'ghastly secret' was too low. Wolff in the interview himself described Himmler as subservient. Longerich observed that this description ill accorded with the notion that Himmler was acting on his own initiative. The interview of Wolff is in his opinion worth little and should be discounted.

6.139 Irving rejected the criticism levelled at him that, in his use of Wolff's recollections, he picked that part which fitted with his thesis about Hitler's ignorance about the mass extermination policy and ignored or suppressed the rest, in particular Wolff's references to gassing and to millions of Jews having been murdered. Irving surmised that Wolff referred to the gassing idea because he had read about it in the newspapers since the war.

6.140 Irving argued that, whilst there may be documents which at least arguably incriminate Himmler, they do not implicate Hitler. Moreover he argued that, when Himmler stated on 28 July 1942 that Hitler had placed on his shoulders the implementation of this very difficult order, what he meant was that Hitler had left it entirely to Himmler to decide by what means to empty the *Ostland* of Jews. In other words Hitler was not involved. Similarly Irving relied on Himmler's remark of 4 October 1943 that 'we do not talk about this between ourselves' as indicating that the exterminations were kept from Hitler. Irving notes that in his speech on 6 October 1942 Himmler claims that it was he, rather than Hitler, who took the decision to extend the shooting to women and children.

6.141 Irving rejected Longerich's claim that it is inconceivable that Himmler did not discuss with Hitler the extermination of Jews by gassing. He dismissed that claim as mere speculation based on little more than the fact that they met and spoke regularly. At the time there were many other more pressing matters to attend to. Longerich answered that it is absurd to argue, as does Irving, that Himmler could have carried out the vast, expensive and logistically complex enterprise behind Hitler's back. Browning likewise argued that, from his understanding of the relationship between the two of them, Himmler was not a man to act without the authority of the *Fuhrer*. Both Browning and Longerich contend that it was a Hitler order which initiated the executions, which were carried out with the full knowledge and approval of Hitler.

6.142 Irving pointed to the absence from *Gauleiter* Greiser's letter to Himmler of 1 May 1942, concerning the 'special treatment' of 100,0000 Jews in his area, of any reference to Hitler having authorized their being killed. The letter talks entirely of authority having been given by Himmler and Heydrich. Greiser, argued Irving, would have wanted to be sure that Hitler approved the 'special action'. Longerich agrees that there is no reference to Hitler having given such authority but claims that it is clear that Greiser was only too keen to conduct the operation and did not feel any need for Hitler's go-ahead.

6.143 Irving referred to the evidence given at Nuremburg by Frank, General Governor of the General Government, who recalled having asked Hitler on 2 July 1944 about rumours of Jews being exterminated. According to Frank, Hitler in reply acknowledged that executions were going on but apart from that claimed to know nothing. When Frank persisted, Hitler suggested Frank should ask Himmler.

6.144 In answer to the criticism made of him that he omitted to mention that *Frau* Schroeder had written to the journalist Gita Sereny that Hitler knew what was being done about the Jewish question by virtue of his private conversations with Himmler, Irving testified in the course of the present trial on 21 February 2000 that he had not done so because

Ms Sereny had produced no record or notes or anything of any such interview, so he had concluded that she was making the whole thing up. It was then put to him that in a parallel action he had written to solicitors acting for Ms Sereny seeking specific disclosure of notes of that and other interviews. In their reply dated 10 February 2000 Ms Sereny's solicitors had informed Irving that there were no notes because *Frau* Schroeder had imparted her information about Hitler by means of a letter which had already been disclosed. The solicitors gave Irving the disclosure number. Irving repudiated the suggestion put to him later that his early answer on 21 February had to his knowledge been false. He claimed that he had not had time to look out the letter to which Ms Sereny's solicitors had referred him. He refused to withdraw the allegation that Ms Sereny had made the whole thing up.

vii. Auschwitz

Description of the camp and overview of the principal issue

7.1 Auschwitz is a small town in the region of Upper Silesia in Poland, which was annexed by the Third Reich when Poland fell in 1940. Hitler entrusted *Reichsfuhrer-SS* Himmler with the task of 'Germanizing' the annexed territories. His original plan to repopulate with Germans places such as Auschwitz, deporting Poles and Jews to the eastern sector of the General Government to make way for the Germans, proved not to be feasible. So the decision was taken to set up a concentration camp in a suburb of the town.

7.2 The Auschwitz camp area was located in a fork between the River Vistula in the west and the River Sola in the east. Part of the camp area also extended across the River Sola on its eastern bank. Surrounding the camp was an agricultural area which was originally designated to be worked by ethnic German farmers. Within the fork between the two rivers was a zone which extended to some fifteen square miles. All civilians had been deported from this area which was now controlled by the SS. This zone and its surrounding area served many purposes and forms of activity, including an experimental farm, a forced labour pool for the chemical company plant which IG Farben was planning to construct nearby at Monowitz and other industrial concerns. The town of Auschwitz was outside the concentration camp area. It is located on the eastern side of the River Sola. To the east of the town was the IG Farben Buna Factory beside which was the labour camp. The whole area and system of camps is collectively referred to as 'Auschwitz'.

7.3 Within the overall camp was a smaller security area which was surrounded by guard posts. This area contained the two main camps that formed part of Auschwitz. To the eastern side of the River Vistula there was Birkenau (also known as Auschwitz II). This was the principal camp where most of the extermination occurred. Approximately two kilometres to the east of Birkenau, separated from it by a railway corridor, was the smaller camp known variously as Auschwitz, Auschwitz I or the *Stammlager*. The headquarters of the camp were situated here. Located at a point along the railway line between Auschwitz and Birkenau was the ramp at which trains transporting Jews would halted. Later a spur was built, linking Birkenau to the railway and providing a further terminus.

7.4 Auschwitz fell within the jurisdiction of Himmler, who was in overall charge of the establishment and running of concentration camps. Heydrich, Chief of the Security Police and the SD and Head of the RSHA, reported directly to Himmler. Eichmann, who worked within the RSHA, also reported to Himmler, was entrusted in 1941 with responsibility for the carrying out and co-ordinating of the Final Solution. *SS Obergruppenfuhrer* Oswald Pohl was Head of the Economic and Administrative Office of the SS which had executive responsibility for the running of the labour camps. *SS Hauptsturmbannfuhrer* Rudolf Hoss was installed as Camp Commandant of Auschwitz in May 1941 and continued in a leading capacity throughout the period when, on the Defendants' case most of the gassings took place (with the exception of a period in 1943–4 when he was posted to Berlin to work in the Concentration Camp Inspectorate). The camp was manned by the SS. But the assistance of Jewish inmates was enlisted to perform some of the more grisly tasks in the crematoria. They were called *Sonderkommando*.

About 200 worked in each crematorium. They were housed either in the crematoria where they worked or in special barracks. At periodic intervals, many of the *Sonderkommando* were themselves gassed and replaced by other inmates.

7.5 It is common ground that from the autumn of 1941 large numbers of Jews were deported to Auschwitz from Germany and from the eleven other countries which had been occupied or formed part of Nazi controlled Europe. The overall question which I have to decide is whether the available evidence, considered in its totality, would convince any objective and reasonable historian that Auschwitz was not merely one of the many concentration or labour camps established by the Nazi regime but that it also served as a death or extermination camp, where hundreds of thousands of Jews were systematically put to death in gas chambers over the period from late 1941 until 1944.

The case for the Defendants in summary

7.6 Auschwitz was not, on the Defendants' case, either the first or by any means the only extermination camp where gas chambers were employed to kill Jews. However, according to the Defendants, the evidence establishes that more deaths occurred at Auschwitz than in all the other extermination camps put together. The case advanced by the Defendants can by simply summarized: they contend that there is a substantial body of evidence, from a variety of different sources, which should demonstrate to any fair-minded objective commentator that gas chambers were constructed at Auschwitz and that they were used to exterminate Jews on a massive scale. This case rests upon what the Defendants contend is abundant evidence, both contemporaneous and more recent, which amounts to convincing proof that Auschwitz played a pivotal role in the Nazi scheme to exterminate European Jewry. It is the Defendants' case that in the period from late 1941 to 1944, when the gas chambers were dismantled, approximately one million Jews were murdered by the use of gas at the camp.

7.7 The Defendants allege that, if Irving had approached the evidence in a detached and objective manner, he could not have failed to appreciate that the evidence is overwhelming that the gas chambers at Auschwitz were systematically used to kill Jews. In arriving at an answer to this question, the Defendants submit that it is relevant to bear in mind the concessions that Irving has already made as to the fact, scale and systematic nature of, firstly, the killing of the Jews in the East by shooting and, secondly, the gassing of Jews from Poland and from Europe in the Reinhard death camps. The Defendants maintain that Irving's denial of the genocidal use of the gas chambers, often expressed in the most intemperate language, flies in the face of the evidence and is explicable only on the basis that Irving is driven by his own extremist ideological views. Moreover the Defendants point out that Irving's denial appears to have been prompted, almost overnight, by his reading the Leuchter report, which, say the Defendants, is deeply flawed from both a scientific and an historical point of view.

Irving's case in summary

7.8 As it was originally formulated, the case advanced by Irving was that no convincing evidence exists that gas chambers were at the material time in existence at Auschwitz and that there is no evidence that such chambers were commissioned. Further, said Irving, there is no convincing evidence that any Jew at Auschwitz lost his or her life as a result of being gassed (though he conceded from the outset that many died as a result of the epidemics which, due to the appalling lack of hygiene, regularly swept the camp).

7.9 The reason why Irving originally adopted that stance was that he was enormously impressed by a report compiled in 1988 by a Mr Fred Leuchter, described by Irving as a professional consultant who routinely advised penitentiaries on electric chair and gas-chamber execution procedures. His report entitled '*An Engineering Report on the Alleged Execution Gas Chambers at Auschwitz, Birkenau and Majdanek Poland*' concluded that no gas chambers operated at Auschwitz. Irving regarded that report as an important historical document and he adopted its major conclusions. He contended that subsequent tests had replicated the results obtained by Leuchter.

7.10 At this trial Irving appeared to place less reliance on the Leuchter report than he had done in his written statement of case. He advanced a variety of arguments for discrediting the evidence relied on by the Defendants. He relied heavily on the argument that the roof of morgue I at crematorium 2 (which is where on the Defendants' case in excess of 500,000 Jews were gassed to death) shows no sign of the wire-mesh columns through which the Defendants maintain that the gas was introduced into the chamber below.

7.11 In the course of the trial Irving modified his position: he was prepared to concede that gassing of human beings had taken place at Auschwitz but on a limited scale. However, he continued to assert that it was not a death factory (totesfabrik). He maintained that there is certainly no question of 500,000 Jews having perished in morgue I of crematorium 2 as the Defendants contend.

7.12 In support of his modified denial that Jews were put to death in the gas chambers on any significant scale, Irving relied on the fact that in all the surviving contemporaneous archival and other documentary records of the Third Reich, there is no reference to the commissioning, construction or operation of the gas chambers. He emphasized that amongst the voluminous documentary material relating to Auschwitz, there is only one document which contains what might be regarded as a reference to the genocidal use of the crematoria. Irving argues that the lack of (as he put it) incriminating documents is extraordinary, if indeed gas chambers were in operation on the scale alleged by the Defendants.

7.13 Amongst the arguments advanced by Irving in support of his case that killing by gas took place at the camp on no more than a limited scale was the fact that the top-secret daily reports sent from the camp to Berlin in cypher, which purport to record the numbers of inmates, arrivals and 'departures by any means', including deaths, make no mention of any inmate having been gassed, although they contain many references to deaths from illness, by shootings and hangings. The number of deaths recorded in these reports is far smaller than the number of those who, on the Defendants' case, lost their lives in the gas chambers. Moreover, asked Irving, if so many were led to their deaths in the gas chambers, what has become of the cadavers. Why,

Irving continued, should Eichmann, whose diaries were remarkably frank in regard to the killing of Jews, omit to mention gas chambers when recording his visit to Auschwitz in early 1942.

7.14 According to Irving the evidence simply fails to establish that Jews were killed in gas chambers at Auschwitz on anything approaching the scale claimed by the Defendants.

The evidence relied on by the Defendants as demonstrating that gas chambers were constructed at Auschwitz and operated there to kill a vast number of Jews

7.15 It is therefore necessary to consider with care what is the nature of the evidence relied on by the Defendants. It is contained principally in the expert report prepared by van Pelt. Longerich and Evans also deal in their reports with certain aspects of this topic. The evidence comes, as I have said, from a variety of sources. Since it is the case for the Defendants that it is the totality of that evidence which amounts to convincing proof of the mass extermination of Jews by gas, it is necessary for me to attempt to summarize it by category.

Early reports

7.16 As early as November 1941 reports had begun to emerge of a violent camp at Oswiecim (that is, Auschwitz) and another camp nearby where poison gas was being used on an experimental basis. But for the most part the early reports mentioned Belzec, Treblinka and Sobibor rather than Auschwitz. However, in March 1943 a radio message to London from Polish resistance sources reported the gassing of more than 500,000 at Oswiecim. There were other reports in the course of 1944 to similar effect. But none of them attracted much attention at the time. Other reports mentioned Birkenau but its connection with Auschwitz does not appear to have been appreciated. Cypher reports from Auschwitz (and other camps) to Berlin were being intercepted by British intelligence at Bletchley but (as will be seen) these made no mention of deaths by gassing.

7.17 In mid-1944 two young Slovak Jews, named Rudolf Vrba and

Alfred Wetzlar, who had escaped from Auschwitz, gave accounts of the systematic extermination of Jews at Birkenau (ie Auschwitz II), commencing in the summer of 1942 and involving the use of specially-constructed gas chambers and crematoria. This account was circulated to London and Washington. Another corroborative account, from a Polish gentile, Jerzy Tabeau, who had also escaped from the camp, also appeared. In June and July 1944 there was publicity in the *New York Times* about the mass killing of Jews by gassing at Auschwitz.

Evidence gathered by the investigation under the aegis of the Soviet State Extraordinary Commission

7.18 The early reports referred to above tallied with the findings of a joint Polish-Soviet commission set up to investigate events at Majdanek, another extermination camp at Lublin in the General Government which had fallen into Russian hands in July 1944. Auschwitz itself was liberated on 27th January 1945 by the advancing Russian army. The Russians found a total of 7,500 inmates. Some 60,000 inmates had been forced to march west a week earlier. Large quantities of shoes, suits, clothes, toothbrushes, glasses, false teeth, hair and other personal effects were found in storage barracks.

7.19 A Soviet State Extraordinary Commission was set up to investigate what had occurred at the camp. On 6 May 1945 it issued its findings. It concluded, on the basis of evidence from inmates, Nazi documents found at the camp and an inspection of the remains of the crematoria, that more than four million people had been annihilated at the camp. The Commission concluded that gas chambers had been used to kill people at the camp and their remains had been incinerated in crematoria. The Commission also reported that the zinc covers used in connection with the ventilation system had been tested in a forensic laboratory. Hydrocyanide was found to be present.

7.20 Although the archive of the camp *Kommandantur* had been destroyed by the Nazis, the archive of the Central Construction Office survived, apparently by an oversight, and was recovered by the Russians. Basing himself on the blueprints for the construction and adaptation of the crematoria and morgues and on visits made to the site, a Polish specialist in combustion technology named Davidowski compiled a report on the technology of mass extermination employed at Auschwitz. He noted that terms such as *Spezialeinrichtungen* (special installations) were used in the documents to describe the crematoria and that there was a reference to a *Vergasungskeller* (gassing cellar).

7.21 In his evidence van Pelt did, however, concede that the evidential value of the Russian report is limited.

Evidence gathered by the Polish Central Commission for Investigation of German Crimes in Poland 1945–7

7.22 In 1945 the forensic laboratory in Cracow carried out an analysis of, firstly, zinc covers removed from the alleged gas chambers at Birkenau and, secondly, 25.5kg of human hair recovered from the camp. Both were found to contain traces of cyanide. The Defendants point to this as further evidence of the use of the chambers to kill Jews.

The Olere drawings

7.23 David Olere was a painter, who was born in Warsaw and later moved to Paris, where he was arrested and deported to Auschwitz in March 1943. He worked in the Sonderkommando for Crematorium 3. He lived in the attic of Crematorium 3 and observed the building and related activity. After his liberation he returned to Paris where he began to draw and record his memories. He produced over fifty sketches in 1945–46.

7.24 Among the sketches Olere produced were architectural drawings of Crematorium 3 which show the basement level with the underground dressing room and the gas chamber, and the ground floor with the incineration room the ovens and the chimney. Arrows indicate the functional relationship of the rooms. They show how people were directed to the gas chamber; how bodies were moved to the corpse elevator; how they were taken to the incineration room and how coke was brought to the ovens in the incineration room.

7.25 In his drawings of Crematorium 3 and its environs Olere depicted people filing into the compound from the road and moving into the dressing room. A sketch from 1946 shows the dressing room, the benches and the hooks for clothes. Another sketch shows the *Sonderkommandos* collecting gold teeth and hair from the women. One of the wire mesh columns is visible in the background. Van Pelt commented that the information in these drawings is corroborated by the testimony of Tauber (see below). He also pointed out that none of the drawings could have been made on the basis of published material as there was not any available at the time.

7.26 Other sketches by Olere show Bunker 2, which was a peasant cottage converted into a gas chamber. Van Pelt noted that the undressing barrack is correctly positioned vis-à-vis the cottage. He pointed out the small window with the heavy wooden shutter through which Zyklon-B was introduced. Another sketch portrays the murder of women and children with Crematorium 5 in the background. Van Pelt claimed the representation of the crematorium to be architecturally correct save for minor inaccuracies which can be ascribed to the fact it was drawn from memory.

7.27 Van Pelt noted that Olere's sketches are corroborated by plans that the Russians found in the Central Construction Office, save that Olere depicts vertical wire mesh columns in the gas chamber (through which the Defendants allege that Zyklon-B was inserted) which are not to be found in the original architectural plans for the site. Olere's arrangement has the mesh columns attached to the west side of the first and fifth structural columns and on the east side of the third and seventh structural columns in the gas chamber.

Eye-witness evidence from camp officials and employees

7.28 In his report van Pelt identified a number of those employed at Auschwitz in various capacities who have given accounts of the use of gas at the camp.

7.29 The principal of these Rudolf Hoss, the Auschwitz Kommandant, was captured by the British on 11 March 1946. In the course of his interrogation at Nuremberg Hoss produced a detailed list of the numbers of people transported to Auschwitz from various countries in Europe. The list totalled well over one million. When asked how so large a number could be accommodated at the camp, given that Hoss had said that there were facilities for only 130,000 at the camp, Hoss answered that most of those transported to the camp were taken there to be exterminated. Hoss later swore an affidavit in which he admitted that he had overseen the extermination, by gassing and burning, of at least two and a half million people. He stated that Zyklon-B was dropped into the death chamber through a small opening. It took from 3 to 15 minutes to kill those in the chamber. After half an hour the bodies were removed. *Sonderkommandos* or Special commandos removed their rings and extracted the gold from their teeth. Hoss described the process by which those to be gassed were selected. He stated that attempts were made to deceive the victims that they were going to be deloused. He said that the gas chambers were capable of accommodating 2,000 people at one time. Dr Gustav Gilbert, the Nuremberg prison psychologist, recorded in his diary an account of a conversation with Hoss in which he confirmed that two and a half million people had been exterminated under his direction.

7.30 Dr Johann Paul Kremer worked as a physician at Auschwitz from August to November 1942. He kept a diary in which he recorded evidence of activities of what had taken place at Auschwitz. He recorded being present at a 'special action' by comparison with which 'Dante's inferno seems almost a comedy'. The diary contains an entry that Auschwitz is justly called an extermination camp. Prior to his trial before the Supreme National Tribunal in Cracow in November and December 1947 Kremer was interrogated. He admitted that he had taken part in gassing people on several occasions in September and October 1942. He too described the selection process, after which the selected victims were required to undress before being led into the gas chamber. He described how an SS man threw the contents of a Zyklon tin through a side opening. He mentioned an occasion when about 1,600 Dutch people were gassed.

7.31 Pery Broad was an officer in the Auschwitz Political Department. He voluntarily wrote a report of his activities whilst working for the British as a translator in a prisoner-of-war camp after the war. Broad's report corroborates Dragon's account of the extermination installations and of the burning of the corpses. He described how the area surrounding the crematorium was kept closed. The Jews arrived in columns. They were told they were going to be disinfected. After they entered the chamber, the door was bolted. The contents of tins of Zyklon-B were thrown into the chamber through six holes in the roof. The screaming of the victims quickly ceased and was followed by complete silence. Broad gave evidence of how bodies were removed and burnt after they had been gassed. In addition Broad reported that the reason for building the four new crematoria in Birkenau was that the Nazis were finding it difficult to keep the killings at Bunkers 1 and 2 a secret. In the two underground gas chambers 4,000 people could be killed at a time. He described the layout of the new installation, including the ovens, each of which he said was equipped to hold four or five corpses.

7.32 SS-*Hauptsturmfuhrer* (Captain) Hans Aumeier became the *Lagerfuhrer* (Camp Leader) of Auschwitz in 1942 and was responsible for the inmate compound of the concentration camp. He remained in that job until the end of the year and so, according to van Pelt, was present during the transformation of Auschwitz into an extermination camp. Arrested shortly after the end of the war, he claimed that during his time at the camp 3,000–3,500 prisoners died there. Initially he denied the existence of gas chambers. But later, in the summer of 1945, he admitted that gas chambers had been in operation in Auschwitz and that on many occasions they had been used for killing Jews. He stated that everyone was sworn to secrecy. (In a later statement he added that there was a *Reichsfuhrer-SS* order which banned written reports, counts and statistics of the activities). He described the initial gas chambers in Bunkers 1 and 2 at Birkenau, where, he said, each chamber accommodated 50–150 people. He gave a further account of the construction of crematorium 2 and crematorium 3 and their gas chambers which had a much larger capacity and began operating in April and May 1943 respectively.

7.33 Dr Ada Bimko, a Polish-Jewish physician, arrived at Auschwitz in August 1943 with 5,000 other Jews. According to her account, of these 4,500, including her close relatives, were sent straight to the crematoria. She later described to a British Military Tribunal the methods of selecting those who were to be gassed. She said that she had worked as a doctor in the hospital at the camp. She gave evidence that she was present at several selections of those who were to be exterminated. She stated that the condemned women were ordered to undress. She had not witnessed the victims enter the buildings. But she stated that she had seen one of the gas chambers when she was sent to recover hospital blankets used by those about to be killed. She described in some detail the chamber which had rows of sprays all over the ceiling but no drains.

Eye-witness evidence from inmates at Auschwitz

7.34 Over the years a large number of Jews who were, or at least claimed that they were, imprisoned at Auschwitz have given accounts of their experiences. The quality of their evidence is variable. Van Pelt explained that he placed greater reliance on those eye-witnesses who provided their accounts of what transpired at Auschwitz shortly after the war ended. Later accounts were vulnerable to the charge that the witness had become confused by the passage of time or had been influenced by what others had claimed. The witnesses upon whose accounts van Pelt was inclined to place reliance included the following.

7.35 Vrba, as already stated above escaped from Auschwitz and was one of the first to provide an account of the mass killing at the camp. On that account he is regarded by van Pelt as a significant witness. Vrba did not himself enter any of the gas chambers; he passed on what others had told him. But, as administrator of the sick barrack, he knew about the selection process. He described how those selected were loaded onto trucks and claimed that they were taken away to be gassed. He gave an account of the inauguration at Birkenau at the end of February 1943 of a new crematorium and gassing plant. He stated that there were four crematoria in operation. He described in some detail (albeit, as van Pelt accepted, at second hand) the layout of the interior.

7.36 *Sonderkommando* Salmen Gradowski kept a diary of his experiences at the camp which he buried in an aluminium can. Schlomo Dragon remembered where it was buried. Remarkably the can and its contents were found intact and dug up after the liberation of the camp. The can contained a notebook and a letter dated 6 September 1944. In the letter Gradowski explained that it was his aim to preserve a written account of what had happened at Auschwitz. He wrote that this task became even more important once the Nazis started to burn the bodies of those they had killed and to dispose of the ashes in the River Vistula. He said that he and fellow *Sonderkommandos* had scattered the teeth of the dead over a wide area so that they might be found by subsequent generations. Gradowski claimed that the Jewish nation had been destroyed in the camps. He recorded that he and fellow camp workers had planned a mutiny. (The uprising took place in October 1944. It failed and Gradowski was tortured and killed.) In his notebook Gradowski described his journey by train to the camp and the selection process on arrival. He gave an account of the living conditions for those deemed fit for work. That notebook did not contain descriptions of the work of the *Sonderkommandos*.

7.37 On 10 April 1945 Radio Luxembourg broadcast the account of an unnamed survivor of Auschwitz, who had subsequently been evacuated to Buchenwald. In the interview this witness stated that Auschwitz was an extermination camp which killed between 12,000 and 20,000 people a day. He described how the transports arrived, how the selection took place, and how those who were chosen to die were killed instantly and cremated.

7.38 Stanislaw Jankowksi gave evidence to the Polish Central Commission in 1946. He was the first *Sonderkommando* to testify before the Commission. He said that he worked in Crematorium 1 from November 1942 at which time it was only used sporadically for killing people. He described an occasion in November or December 1942 when a large number of inmates from Birkenau arrived under escort. He and the other *Sonderkommandos* were ordered to leave. When they returned they found only clothing. He was put to work carrying the corpses to the crematorium for burning. In July 1943 Jankowski was transferred to Birkenau and worked at Crematorium 5. He described how large number of Jews of various nationalities arrived at the camp. About half of them were selected for gassing, including the old and infirm and the pregnant and children. He stated that those who were to be gassed were not given camp numbers or registered at the camp. His evidence was that the killing reached its zenith with the Hungarian Jews in about July 1944 when, he claimed, 18,000 were being killed per day. Jankowski reckoned that Crematoria 2 and 3 had a daily incineration capacity of 2,500 corpses while Crematoria 4 and 5 could incinerate 1,500.

7.39 Schlomo Dragon, another *Sonderkommando*, gave evidence on 10 May 1945 to the Polish Central Commission. Dragon had worked at bunker 2 and crematoria 4 and 5. Van Pelt commented that, while Dragon was precise when he talked about what he has witnessed in person, he was less accurate when it came to estimating the number of people killed in Auschwitz, which he put at four million.

7.40 *Sonderkommando* Henry Tauber worked initially in crematorium 1 and later at crematoria 2 and 4. He also gave evidence to the Polish Central Commission. He gave a detailed account of the undressing rooms at the gas chamber, the signs which hung on the walls, the glass peep-hole in the door and how the doors were hermetically sealed. Further, he described the ventilation systems; how the floor of a gas chamber was to be washed and how the chamber in crematorium 2 was split into two in late 1943 by a dividing wall. He gave an exceedingly detailed account of the operation of crematoria, making it clear what he accepted on the basis of his own observations and what he accepted as hearsay. He described dragging gassed corpses from the gas chamber and loading them five at a time onto trucks which ran on rails to the furnaces where they were off-loaded. He described the three, two-muffle furnaces and said that each muffle would take five corpses. The incineration took up to one and a half hours. He explained that thin people burned more slowly than fat people. In summary his description of crematoria 2, both below and above ground corresponded very closely with the outline given in the blueprints. Van Pelt considered that Tauber's testimony is almost wholly corroborated by the German blueprints of the buildings and that it corroborates the accounts given by Jankowski and Dragon. Tauber estimated that the number of people who were gassed during his time at Auschwitz, between February 1943 and October 1944, was two million people from which figure he extrapolated that the total number gassed at Auschwitz amounted to four million.

7.41 Michael Kula was another former inmate of the camp who gave evidence to the Polish Commission. He had lived near Auschwitz before his incarceration. Kula gave evidence that, a year after his arrival at the camp in 1940, he observed the Nazis beginning to experiment with Zyklon-B. He observed that the corpses turned greenish after exposure to the gas. Kula worked in the metal workshop at the camp and forged many of the metal pieces required for the crematoria. He also took part in the construction of trucks for conveying corpses into the ovens. Kula testified that four wire mesh columns were made for the gas chambers in crematoria 2 and 3: these columns were described by Kula as 'structures of ever finer mesh', which contained a removable can within the innermost column which was used to extract, after the gassing, the Zyklon 'crystals' or pellets that had absorbed the hydrocyanide.

7.42 Marie Claude Vaillant-Couturier (to whom I have referred at section v.(xvii) above in connection with the Defendants' criticisms of Irving's historiography) gave evidence to the International Military Tribunal of the conditions in the women's camp at Birkenau, including the sterilization of women and the killing of babies of women who had arrived pregnant. She claimed that most of the Jewish women who had come from the same part of France as herself had been gassed immediately upon arrival at Auschwitz. Valliant-Couturier testified that the trains stopped close to the gas chamber; that the vast majority of the arriving Jews, including the old, mothers and children) would be selected for gassing; that they were made to undress and then taken to a room like a shower room into which gas capsules were thrown through an opening in the ceiling.

7.43 Severina Shmaglevskaya, a Polish inmate at Auschwitz, gave evidence she had seen many children brought to the camp. She had seen selections undertaken on some occasions by doctors and on others by SS men. She recalled that children were separated from their parents and taken off separately to the gas chambers. She stated that, at the time when the greatest number of Jews were being exterminated in the gas chambers, children were thrown alive into crematory ovens or ditches. She said that few of the children were registered, tattooed or counted. They were exterminated on arrival. As a consequence it was very difficult to know how many of the children were put to death.

7.44 Filip Muller, a *Sonderkommando*, gave an account in the 1970s of the process used to insert corpses into the ovens at crematorium 1. He described how trucks were used to transport the bodies to the ovens, how corpses were put into the ovens and the technical details involved in problems that arose during the process. Van Pelt pointed out that Muller's account accords with those of Jankowski, Tauber and Dragon. He considered that it is highly unlikely that Muller's memoirs were inspired by Tauber's testimony.

7.45 Janda Weiss, aged only fifteen years, was interviewed in 1945 by representatives of the Psychological Warfare Division of the Supreme Headquarters Allied Expeditionary Forces. She told them that she had been deported to Birkenau along with 1,500 Jews from Theresienstadt. She described how she was among the stronger ones who were selected to work in the camp. The rest of her family were taken off to be gassed. Weiss recalled her conversations with those who worked in the camps. She knew of the arrival of the Hungarian transports in 1944. She claimed that when transports arrived most of the Jews were selected to be gassed immediately. Having been told they were to have a shower, the victims undressed and went into the gas chamber. She recalled that when the room was full, small children were thrown into the chamber through the window. After the gassing *Sonderkommandos* pulled the corpses out took their rings off, cut off their hair, and took them to the ovens to cremate them.

7.46 Walter Bliss, a German Jew, was also interviewed. He too described the selection process which took place not only on arrival at the camp but also at regular intervals thereafter. He gave an account of a typical selection process: those selected for death were transferred to gassing barracks where they might be kept for up to two or three days often without food as they were going to die anyway. He claimed that 40% of the men in the camp and 60–70% of the women were murdered in January 1944.

Evidence from the Nuremberg trial

7.47 By an accord signed on the 8 August 1945 the Allies established the International Military Tribunal (at Nuremberg) to prosecute war criminals. Twenty two leaders of the Third Reich were charged. One of them was Kaltenbrunner, who was chief of the agency charged with carrying out the Final Solution. Others who gave evidence at Nuremberg have already been referred to above, including Vaillant-Couturier, Shmaglevskaya and Hoss. The Defendants rely in addition on the evidence of the following.

7.48 In January 1946 Dieter Wisliceny, who had been an aide to Eichmann, gave evidence in which he accepted his involvement in preparations for the transport to Auschwitz of some 50,000 Saloniki Jews who, he agreed, were destined for the 'so-called final solution'. He also gave evidence that he had been involved in the deportation of

450,000 Hungarian Jews to Auschwitz. In respect of the latter Wisliceny stated that they were all killed with the exception of those used for labour purposes.

7.49 SS-*Standartenfuhrer* Kurt Becher swore an affidavit which was submitted in March 1946 at Nuremberg. He described how people were exterminated by methods including gas at Majdanek. He deposed that, within days of an English newspaper report being received at Hitler's headquarters about gas chambers being used at Majdanek, Himmler ordered the cessation of gassing in Auschwitz and the dismantling of the extermination installations in the crematoria.

Evidence from the Eichmann trial

7.50 One of the witnesses at the trial of Eichmann was Hoss, to whom I have already made reference.

7.51 Another was Yehuda Bakon, an Israeli artist, who at Auschwitz had been employed to take papers to the crematoria for burning. Consequently he had entered the crematoria and had seen the gas chamber. In the summer of 1945 he drew illustrations of Auschwitz which he produced in the course of his evidence. The drawings depicted the inside of gas chambers, including the dummy shower heads and the mesh columns used to insert the Zyklon-B into the gas chamber. He also described how the gas chambers were ventilated after the gassings. Bakon's evidence included a description of how the corpses were put on to a lift which raised them up to the incinerators. Van Pelt relied on the evidence of Bakon that, when it was cold the head of the *Sonderkommando* would let them warm up in the gas chambers and undressing rooms when they were not in use. He argues that this evidence refutes Leuchter's contention that the temperature in the gas chambers was so low that there would have been condensed liquid hydrogen cyanide on the walls had it been used.

Evidence from other trials (Kremer; Mulka and others; Dejaco and Ertl)

7.52 Josef Kramer was a defendant in the Belsen trial of the SS personnel who operated Bergen-Belsen. He had also served as *Lagerfuhrer* of Birkenau during the time that Hungarians were being transported to Auschwitz. Like many camp personnel on trial Kramer had worked at

Auschwitz before being transferred to Belsen. At the trial he admitted to his involvement in the operation and use of gas chambers at Auschwitz. He stated that Hoss was in charge of the gas chambers and that he received his orders from Berlin. Mrs Rosina Kramer also testified on behalf of her husband. She states that everyone in Auschwitz knew about the gas chambers.

7.53 At Kramer's trial Bimko, the Polish-Jewish physician, gave the evidence to which I have already alluded.

7.54 Dr Charles Bendel, a Rumanian Jewish physician who had been living in Paris before he was deported to Auschwitz, gave evidence that he had been detailed to work as a *sonderkommando* and in that capacity observed the gas chambers and crematoria in action. He testified that on occasion the Nazis would burn corpses in pits because the ovens could not cope with the number of people who had been killed.

7.55 Defendants at the Belsen trial inlcluded Dr Fritz Klein, an ethnic German from Rumania, who was a member of the SS. As a physician he admitted having taken part in many of the selections of those who were to be gassed. He claimed that he was acting on orders which were always given verbally. Another defendant at the Belsen trial was Franz Hoessler, who had been *Lagerfuhrer* at Auschwitz. In his evidence he admitted that gas chambers operated there. He stated that the selection of prisoners who were to be killed was undertaken by the doctors in the camp. He testified that the camp was inspected once a year by Himmler, who had given the order for people to be gassed.

7.56 Mulka, a member of Hess's staff, and others stood trial at Frankfurt in 1963–5. Hans Stark, a former SS officer, gave evidence that he had been employed in the Auschwitz Political Department. He described the role of the Department in relation to executions by gassing. He admitted to participation in gassings including on occasion pouring the Zyklon-B in himself.

7.57 Walther Dejaco and Fritz Ertl were architects at Auschwitz. They were tried in Vienna in 1972. Ertl gave evidence that he had been employed at the Auschwitz Central Construction Office until 1943. He testified that new crematoria had been needed for 'special actions'. He confirmed that he knew the significance of that term. He said he had been told by Bischoff that no reference should be made to gassing.

Documentary evidence relating to the design and construction of the chambers

7.58 The Defendants assert that there exist contemporaneous documentary records which, on detailed examination, evidence the construction of gas chambers at Auschwitz. The most important Auschwitz archive that survived the war was that of the Central Construction Office at Auschwitz. The main archives of the camp *Kommandantur* had been destroyed by the Germans before they evacuated the camp in January 1945. The Construction Office was 300 yards away and through an oversight was left intact.

7.59 The first and most significant body of such evidence is the blueprint material, which consists of a series of architectural drawings which depict the adaptation of crematoria 2 and 3 and the construction of crematoria 4 and 5. None of these drawings refers overtly to any part of the buildings being designed or intended to serve as gas chambers whether for fumigation or extermination purposes. In particular the drawings for *Leichenkeller* (morgue) 1 in crematorium 2 make no provision for ducts or chimneys by means of which Zyklon-B pellets might be inserted through the roof. However, van Pelt sought to illustrate by means of detailed analyses of certain features of the drawings that it reasonable to infer that certain chambers were designed to function as gas chambers.

7.60 The principal feature identified by van Pelt is the redesign of the double door to the supposed gas chamber in crematorium 2. When in 1942 the drawings were executed for the adaptation of this crematorium, this door in common with others in the same building was designed to open inwards. Careful scrutiny of the drawings reveals, however, that the drawing of the inward-opening door has been scratched out. A fresh drawing dated 19 December 1942 was made by Jakob, the chief of the drawing office, who rarely undertook drawings himself. It provides for the door to the supposed gas chamber to open outwards. There is no apparent reason for this. To van Pelt the obvious explanation is that the chamber was to be used as a gas chamber. If the door opened inwards, it would be impossible to open it after the administration of the gas because of the crush of corpses against the inside or the door of those who struggled to get out when they realized what was happening to them.

7.61 The next feature identified by van Pelt relates to the entrance to crematorium 2 and the means of which access was gained to the morgue below. In its original design, the entrance was situated to one side of the building. Inside the entrance there was a slide down which corpses would be tipped to reach the level of the morgue. But the drawing shows that this design was changed in late 1942 so as to move the entrance to the crematorium to the street side of the building. At the same time a new stairway to the morgue was designed to replace the pre-existing slide. Van Pelt pointed out that the original design apparently contemplated that only corpses would need to be transported down to the morgue. The new design on the other hand is consistent with a wish to enable people transported to Auschwitz to proceed from the railway station through the new entrance, then to walk downstairs into what is alleged to have been the undressing room and thence into the supposed gas chamber. The stairway has been redesigned in such a way that it would be extremely awkward to carry corpses down to the morgue on stretchers. Van Pelt concludes that the object of the redesign of the stairway was to enable living people to walk downstairs rather than for corpses to be carried down.

7.62 The drawings further provide for the ventilation of the supposed gas chamber in crematorium 2. Van Pelt infers that the purpose of the system for extracting air was to extract poisonous air and so speed up the removal of the corpses to the incinerators.

7.63 Crematoria 4 and 5 were new buildings. The initial drawings are dated August 1942, not long after the visit paid to the camp by Himmler, which the Defendants say marks the inception of the accelerated extermination programme. According to van Pelt the design of these crematoria incorporated undressing rooms (although not so designated on the drawings) and morgues which were to serve as gas chambers. The drawings of the morgues make provision for several windows measuring 30 x 40cms. The size of these windows corresponds with the size of windows referred to elsewhere in construction documents as being required to be gas proof. The windows were to be above eye level. Van Pelt draws the inference that the purpose of these windows was to enable Zyklon-B pellets to be inserted through them into the building (a process which was observed by *Sonderkommando* Dragon, as mentioned above).

7.64 Van Pelt agreed that the drawings for crematoria 4 and 5 show a drainage system which appears to link up with the camp sewage system. He disagreed with Irving's suggestion that this would have been highly dangerous because large quantities of liquid cyanide would have found their way into the sewage system. Van Pelt claims that the gas would evaporate rather than turn into liquid.

7.65 In addition to the architectural drawings, there are other documents which, according to the Defendants, lend support to their contention that there were gas chambers at the camp which were used for genocidal purposes. I shall not itemize all the documents identified by the Defendants as belonging in this category. They include a patent application for multi-muffle ovens made by Topf. Although the patent application does not in fact relate to the ovens supplied to Auschwitz in 1942/3, it is said that the principle is the same. The two features of the application on which the Defendants focus are, firstly, the method of employing fat corpses to speed promote the rate at which corpses can be burned and, secondly, the claim that no fuel is required after the initial two day pre-heating period because of the amount of heat generated by the burning corpses. Van Pelt noted that both these features are reflected in the account given by Tauber of the way in which the corpses were incinerated.

7.66 Another allegedly incriminating document is the record of a meeting held on 19 August 1942 between members of the Auschwitz construction office and a representative of the engineers Topf to discuss the construction of four crematoria. The note of the meeting refers to the construction of triple oven incinerators near the 'Badenanstalten fur Sonderaktionen' ('bath-houses for special actions': the words are in quotations in the original).

7.67 In a different category is a report dated 16 December 1942 made by a corporal named Kinna, which made reference to an order that, in order to releive the camp, limited people, idiots, cripples and sick people must be removed from the same by liquidation. Kinna stated that the implementation of this order was difficult because the Poles, unlike the Jews, must die a natural death.

7.68 The Defendants rely on a letter dated 29 January 1943 from Bischoff, Chief of Central Construction Managemnet at the camp, to

SS *Brigadefuhrer* Kammler in which there is reference to a *Vergasungskammer* (gas chamber or cellar). There are also documents from February 1943 referring to the provision of gastight doors and windows. In a letter dated 31 March 1943 Bischoff presses for the delivery of a gastight door with a spyhole of 8mm glass, with a rubber seal and metal fitting. There is a timesheet of a construction worker which makes reference to fitting gastight windows to crematorium 4. Van Pelt pointed to a letter dated 6 March 1943 from Auschwitz to the Topf company which contemplated the use of hot air from the ventilators for the incinerators to pre-heat the *Leichenkeller* 1. Why, he asked, heat a morgue, which should be kept cool. Answering his own question, he claimed that Zyklon-B evaporates more quickly in high temperatures, so the killing process would be speeded up. (Irving answered that there is nothing sinister about heating the morgue: it was a requirement of good building practice in relation to civilian morgues.)

7.69 Finally under this head the Defendants rely on a letter dated 28 June 1943 from Bischoff to Kammler (the authenticity of which Irving challenges) setting figures for the incineration capacity of the five crematoria, according to which their total capacity is 4756 people in every 24 hours. The Defendants' case is that this capacity was at that time deemed to be necessary to burn the bodies of the Jews who were to be brought to Auschwitz to be gassed. Basing themselves on the evidence of *sonderkommandos* such as Tauber, the Defendants say further that the rate of incineration was broadly in line with the estimate in the letter of 28 June 1943. The Defendants suggest that the apparent urgency of the installation of the ovens, together with their huge capacity which, according to van Pelt, was far in excess of what could possibly have been required to cope with future typhus epidemics, reflects the policy adopted following Himmler's visit to the camp in July 1942.

Photographic evidence

7.70 In support of his contention that there were chimneys through which it is alleged that Zyklon-B would have been poured into morgue 1 at crematorium 2, van Pelt relied on a photograph taken by a camp official in February 1942. According to van Pelt in this photograph, when greatly enlarged, it is possible to detect smudges which he maintained represent the chimneys protruding through the morgue roof. Furthermore van Pelt remarked on the similarity in the alignment of the supposed chimneys in the photograph with the alignment of the chimneys in one of Olere's drawings. Van Pelt further relied on an aerial photograph which was taken in the summer of 1944 (to which I have referred earlier) on which, when greatly enlarged, spots are visible above the morgues of crematoria 2 and 3. He claims that these spots are the protruding chimneys, reduced in size because of the dirt laid onto the roof since the earlier photograph was taken. Irving gave reasons why he suspected that the 1944 photograph relied on by van Pelt had been tampered with.

7.71 Irving disputed van Pelt's interpretation of the photographs and suggested that tampering may have taken place. He produced a photograph showing the roof of morgue 1 in the background on which there is no sign of any protruding chimney. Van Pelt responded that this photograph (in which the construction of the roof of the crematorium can be seen to be incomplete) was probably taken in December 1942 at which date the chimneys would not have been installed. Van Pelt explained that the reason why no protruding chimneys are visible in another photograph produced by Irving is that it was taken after the Nazis had dismantled the gas chambers.

7.72 The Defendants also place reliance on a photograph taken at a time when Hungarian Jews were arriving at the camp in 1944. One such photograph depicts a column of women and children walking from the railway spur towards Auschwitz. Instead of proceeding into the camp through the entrance leading to the women and children's camp, the column can be seen to walking towards crematorium 2 (from which there is no access into the women and children's section).

Material evidence found at Auschwitz

7.73 The Leuchter report, which I have mentioned already and to which I will return in greater detail when I come to summarize the evidence relied on by Irving in connection with Auschwitz, claimed that forensic analysis revealed no trace of cyanide in the surviving ruins of the gas chambers at Auschwitz. Prompted by the publicity given to the Leuchter report, the director of the Auschwitz museum enlisted the expert assistance of Professor Markiewicz, Director of the Forensic Institute of Cracow, who arranged in February 1990 for further samples to be taken from Auschwitz for analysis.

7.74 Markiewicz decided that the so-called Prussian blue test was unreliable because its formation depended on the acidity of the environment which was particularly low in the alleged gas chambers. Markiewicz and his team therefore adopted microdiffusion techniques to test for cyanide samples from the crematoria, from the delousing chambers and a control sample taken from elsewhere within Auschwitz. The latter was tested because claims had been made that the cyanide traces in the gas chambers were explained by the fact that a single fumigation of the whole camp had taken place during the typhus epidemic. The control sample tested negative, refuting those claims. As to the tests on the crematoria and the delousing chambers, the conclusion arrived at by Markiewicz was that cyanide compounds are still to be found in all the facilities (that is, in both the delousing chambers and in the various supposed gas chambers) that, according to the source data, were in contact with cyanide. The concentration of cyanide compounds in the various samples varies greatly, even in the case of different samples taken from the same chamber or building. This indicated that the conditions producing the cyanide compounds varied locally. According to van Pelt, the Markiewicz report demonstrated positively that Zyklon-B had been introduced into the supposed gas chambers, albeit that the test results varied greatly. Van Pelt considered that the results for crematoria 4 and 5 were unreliable because they had been demolished at the end of the war with the result that it is difficult to know which brick came from where.

Conclusions to be drawn from the evidence, according to the Defendants' experts

7.75 The Defendants contend that the evidence, to any dispassionate mind, is overwhelming that the Nazis systematically murdered hundreds of thousands of Jews , mainly by the use of Zyklon-B pellets. The Defendants recognize that not all of the evidence which I have sought to summarize above is altogether reliable. This applies with particular force to the evidence of the eye-witnesses. It is also accepted by the Defendants that in certain respects the documentary evidence, including the photographic evidence, is capable of more than one interpretation. Nevertheless the Defendants argue that the different strands of evidence 'converge'. For example the eye-witness evidence is corroborated by the drawings and vice-versa. There is a striking similarity in the accounts of the eye-witnesses. The similarities in their recollections vastly outweigh the discrepancies. In the main, say the Defendants, their testimony is reliable. The documentary evidence is not overtly incriminating for the obvious reason that the Nazis wanted to keep the gas chambers secret. But it too lends support to there having been gas chambers in operation at the camp.

7.76 The overwhelming strength of the totality of the evidence may be the reason, suggest the Defendants, why in his cross-examination of van Pelt Irving chose to ignore most of it.

Irving's reasons for rejecting the evidence relied on by the Defendants as to the existence at Auschwitz of gas chambers for killing Jews

Irving as expert witness at the trial of Zundel

7.77 In his evidence Irving reiterated on a number of occasions that he is primarily a literary historian and that, at least until the present proceedings were commenced , he did not regard himself as an expert on the Holocaust. Accordingly until April 1988 he believed what he had been told about the killing of Jews in Auschwitz and the other death camps. The 1977 edition of *Hitler's War* contains several references to the gassing of Jews.

7.78 In April 1988 Irving went to Toronto in order to give expert evidence on behalf of Hans Zundel, a publisher, who was being prosecuted for infringing a Canadian law, since repealed, which made it a criminal offence to disseminate false information. Zundel had published a pamphlet entitled 'Did Six Million Really Die?' which questioned fundamental aspects of the Holocaust. Irving agreed to assist Zundel in his defence by giving evidence as an historian as to Hitler's role in the extermination of the Jews. He was not instructed to address the issue of gassing at Auschwitz or indeed at any other alleged death camp.

The impact of the Leuchter Report

7.79 Irving testified that on arrival in Toronto he was presented with a copy of a report compiled by Mr Fred Leuchter. It was what Irving read in Leuchter's report which convinced him that there is no truth in the claim that Jews met their death in gas chambers at Auschwitz. Irving made clear in his evidence that it was the Leuchter report and in particular the result of the chemical analysis of the samples taken from the fabric of the alleged gas chambers which had a profound impact on his thinking.

7.80 Leuchter had been retained by Zundel because he was a consultant retained by several penitentiaries to give advice about execution procedures including execution by means of the administration of gas. He had no formal professional qualifications. Zundel intended to use Leuchter's report to establish that no Jews, and certainly not six million Jews, died in gas chambers, so that he could not be said to have been spreading false information about the Holocaust. (As it turned out Leuchter did not give evidence at Zundel's trial)

7.81 In order to prepare his report, Leuchter visited Auschwitz in February 1988 to inspect the site. He removed 31 samples of brickwork and plaster from various crematoria and one control sample from a delousing chamber where cyanide was known to have been used and was visible in the form of blue staining. On his return to the US Leuchter had these samples analysed by a reputable laboratory in Massachussets. The object of the test was to discover whether the residual cyanide content of the samples was consistent with their having been exposed to high levels of cyanide over a prolonged period of time.

7.82 Chemical analysis of the control sample revealed a very heavy concentration of cyanide content, namely 1050mg/kg. By contrast the analysis of the other samples, taken from the alleged gas chambers, resulted in either negative findings or findings of very low concentration levels ranging from 1mg/g to 9 mg/kg. From this Leuchter concluded:

[this] supports the evidence that these facilities were not execution gas cham-

bers. The small quantities detected would indicate that some point these buildings were deloused with Zyklon-BV – as were all the buildings at these facilities. Additionally the areas of blue staining show a high iron content, indicating ferric-ferro-cyanide, no longer hydrogen cyanide.

One would have expected higher cyanide detection in the samples taken from the alleged gas chambers (because of the greater amount of gas allegedly used there) than that found in the control sample. Since the contrary is true, one must conclude that these facilities were not execution gas chambers, when coupled with all other evidence gained on inspection.

7.83 Apart from that conclusion, upon which Irving has focussed his attention, Leuchter in his report had a number of other observations to make. He expressed the opinion that crematoria 1, 2, 3, 4 and 5 have an extremely poor and dangerous design if they were to have served as execution gas chambers. There is no provision for gasketed doors, windows or vents; the structures are not coated with tar or other sealant to prevent leakage or absorption of gas. The adjacent crematories create the potential for an explosion. The exposed porous brick and mortar would accumulate any hydrogen cyanide and render the facilities dangerous to humans for several years.

7.84 Crematorium 1 is adjacent to the SS hospital and has floor drains connected to the main sewer of the camp, which, according to Leuchter, would have resulted in liquid cyanide being carried into every building at the facility. There were no exhaust systems to vent the gas after usage and no mechanism could be found for the Zyklon-B pellets to be introduced or evaporated. If indeed the Zyklon-B pellets were fed into the chamber through roof vents or windows, there were no means of ensuring the even distribution of the gas. The facilities are always damp and unheated, which conditions are unsuited to the use of Zyklon-B.

7.85 Leuchter considered the chambers to be too small physically to contain the number of occupants claimed. The doors open inwards, which would inhibit the removal of bodies. With the gas chambers fully packed with occupants, the hydrogen cyanide would not circulate within the room. If the gas did eventually fill the chamber, anyone feeding the pellets into the vents on the roof would die from exposure to the poisonous gas.

7.86 Of the crematoria Leuchter, having reviewed modern practices, calculated that their combined theoretical daily incineration capacity was 353.6 but that in practice the maximum number of corpses which could have been burned was 156. He thus arrived at the conclusion that over the period when the incinerators were being operated, the total number of cremations would have been 193,576 in theory but no more than 85,092 in practice.

7.87 Leuchter's evaluation of the crematory facilities produced, according to his report, conclusive evidence that contradicts the alleged volume of corpses having been cremated within the generally alleged time frame. His 'best engineering opinion' was that none of the facilities examined were ever utilized for the execution of human beings and that the crematories could not have supported the work load attributed to them.

7.88 Irving was convinced by the conclusion at which Leuchter arrived on the basis of the chemical analysis of the fabric of the supposed gas chambers. So convinced was he by Leuchter's reasoning, he decided to publish under his own imprint Focal Publications Limited, the text of the report with a foreword written by Irving. The Foreword accepts that there were methodological flaws in the report but it endorses Leuchter's findings, ending with the words 'Forensic chemistry is, I repeat, an exact science'.

7.89 It was put to Irving in cross-examination that the fallacy in the Leuchter report was his assumption that a far higher concentration of cyanide, in the region of 3,200 parts per million ('ppm'), would be required to kill people in the gas chambers than would be required for the purpose of delousing clothing. In truth, it was suggested to him, it is the other way round: high levels of cyanide are required for delousing purposes whereas in the region of 300 ppm will suffice for the purpose of killing human beings. Irving responded by saying that this criticism of the Leuchter report has to be 'taken on board' and that 'probably concessions have to be made at both ends of this scale'. Irving observed that the report had the desirable consequence of promoting public debate. He remained adamant that, whatever its flaws, the crucial conclusion of the Leuchter report, based on the chemical analysis, was correct. He argued that the chambers were freshly constructed out of concrete and so would have absorbed the hydrogen cyanide producing permanent chemical changes to the fabric of the walls and ceiling. Irving accepted that, if the concentration of cyanide required for delousing clothes is far higher than the level required to kill humans, one is more likely to find 40 years residual traces of the cyanide in the fabric of the delousing chamber than in the fabric of the supposed gas chambers. But he argued that one would still expect to find far more traces in the alleged gas chambers than those recorded in the Leuchter report.

Replication of Leuchter's findings

7.90 Irving contended that the results of the chemical test conducted on behalf of Leuchter had been replicated by amongst others Gelmar Rudolf, a chemist at the Max Planck Institute. Van Pelt knew little of his report but agreed that Rudolf's findings broadly corresponded with those of Leuchter. Irving produced a letter from the Institute for Historical Review which claimed that others had arrived at similar conclusions. He also claimed (and van Pelt accepted) that in about 1989 the Auschwitz authorities carried out tests which also found high cyanide traces in the delousing chambers and much lower quantities in crematoria 2 and 3. The results of these tests were not published. Subsequently further tests were conducted and the results were published in the so-called Markievicz report (the conclusions of which I have already summarized).

The absence of chimneys protruding through of morgue 1 of crematorium 2

7.91 As the trial progressed, it appeared that one of the main arguments advanced by Irving for denying the existence of homicidal gas chambers at Auschwitz, if not his main argument, is that the remains of the roof of morgue 1 at crematorium 2 show no sign of the chimneys which, according to the Defendants' case penetrated through the roof so as to enable Zyklon-B pellets to be tipped down into the morgue below. It will be recalled van Pelt claimed that crematorium 2 was the most lethal building of Auschwitz. In excess of 500,000 Jews lost their lives there, more than in any other place on the planet. It is the Defendants' case that the Zyklon-B pellets were fed into the chamber by means of wire mesh columns which ran upwards through the roof of the chamber with the chimney protruding above roof level. The roof was made of reinforced concrete about 18–20cm in thickness with reinforcing bars within the concrete. If the chimney passed through the roof, argued Irving, the roof would to this day have five holes in it where the chimneys passed through the roof.

7.92 It is common ground that the roof of *Leichenkeller* 1 was supported by seven concrete pillars. The Defendants allege that adjacent to four of these pillars there ran hollow ducts or chimneys made of heavy wire mesh which protruded through holes in the roof where the pellets were poured into them and ran down into the chamber below. These ducts were 70 square centimetres in size but tapered at the top where they passed through the roof. It is Irving's case that these ducts never existed. He made that assertion because, he said, there is no trace in what remains of the roof of any holes through it. Furthermore the chimneys do not appear in the blue prints for the construction of the crematoria. Part of the roof of *Leichenkeller* 1 is intact, although it has pancaked down on to the floor. Irving produced a photograph which appears to show no sign of any hole in the roof. Van Pelt conceded in one of his supplementary reports that there is no sign of the holes. It would be impossible for chimneys of the size described by Tauber and Kula to have disappeared. Irving contended that, if the holes exist, it would be a simple matter to uncover the roof so as to find out if they are there. But no one has attempted this task and he wondered why not.

7.93 As for such evidence as there is of the existence of the ducts, most of it comes from some of the eye-witnesses. But, claimed Irving, they give varying accounts of the manner in which the pellets were introduced into the gas chamber and most of them (including Bimko and Bendel) have turned out to be liars. Irving claimed to have destroyed the credibility of all of them in his cross-examination of van Pelt. Olere's drawings were probably influenced by what he was told by others and in any event he was a fantasist. The photograph taken in 1942 and relied on by van Pelt does not show the chimneys. The smudges on which van Pelt relies were probably barrels of tar parked on the roof during building operations. No such smudges were visible on aerial photographs taken in 1944.

7.94 At one stage in his evidence Irving appeared to concede that *Leichenkeller* 1 of crematorium 2 was a gas chamber but that it was used solely for delousing purposes. In the end, however, it was his position that he had not seen any evidence that there were any gas chambers at all there whether for delousing or extermination purposes. In his evidence he went so far as to say that, if anyone detected holes in the roof, he would abandon his libel action. As he graphically put it in his closing submission, Irving argued that '[the Defendants'] entire case on *Krema* 2 – the untruth that it was used as a factory of death, with SS guards tipping canisters of cyanide-soaked pellets into the building through those four (non-existent) holes – had caved in, as surely as has that roof'.

The reason for the alterations to crematorium 2: fumigation or alternatively air-raid shelter

7.95 One explanation put forward by Irving for the adaptation work to morgue 1 and crematorium 2 is that the chamber was being adapted to serve the purpose of fumigating clothes (and perhaps other objects). He relied on a document called an *Aufstellung* sent by Topf to the construction office at the camp in which reference is made *Entwesungsofen* (disinfestation ovens), which according to Irving proves that such was their true purpose. (Van Pelt countered that these ovens may well have been for disinfecting the clothing of the *Sonderkommando* or alternatively for a delousing chamber which is known to have been under construction in 1943 between crematoria 2 and 3. But he added that, if it was only clothing which was to be subjected to the gas treatment it was difficult to understand the need for a peephole to be fitted in the door).

7.96 Another thesis advanced by Irving is that the adaptation of crematorium 2 was undertaken in order to convert the building to an air raid shelter rather than to a gas chamber. He claimed that there was, at the time when the reconstruction work was undertaken, concern at Auschwitz about bombing raids. He claimed that this explains why the entrance to building was moved and why the staircase was altered to enable pedestrian access to *Leichenkeller* 1, which was to serve as the shelter.

7.97 Irving contended that it was standard practice at that time to fit gas tight doors on all air raid shelters in case of Allied poison gas attacks. Irving drew attention to the reference by an eye-witness named Hans Stark to the door of a chamber being *luftschutzer* which, as van Pelt accepted, signified proof against air raid. (Stark did, however, make that reference in the context of an account of 200 people being gassed). It was, according to Irving, also standard practice for the doors to have peep-holes (although he was uncertain why there should be a metal grill fitted protecting the inside of the peep-hole). Irving was scornful of the claim made by van Pelt that the doors to the chamber were redesigned to open outwards because of the difficulty of pushing the doors open if dead bodies were piled against the inside of the door. Irving claimed that it was standard practice at the time that air raid shelters should have doors which opened outwards. Van Pelt was, however, doubtful if the architectural drawing relied on by Irving to support his contention did indeed provide for doors which opened outwards.

The purpose of the supplies of Zyklon-B

7.98 It is common ground that quantities of Zyklon-B were delivered by truck from Dessau to Auschwitz. Irving contended that these deliveries were for the purpose of fumigating the camp and the clothes of the inmates. A large quantity of the cyanide was needed to combat the typhus outbreak in the summer of 1942. In reliance on figures provided by Mulka, an adjutant at Auschwitz with responsibility for the deliveries, as well as upon the quantity supplied to the camp at Oranienberg, Irving argues that the quantity of Zyklon-B delivered is consistent with it having been used for the purpose of fumigation and no other.

7.99 Irving pointed to a document recording permission being given for such a delivery which stated in terms that the purpose for which the Zyklon-B was required was to carry out fumigation. He relied also on an invoice which made reference to an *Entwesungsabteilung* (disinfestation department). Herr Tesch of the company which supplied Zyklon-B to the camp testified at his trial that the material was for disinfestation. If cyanide had been used in the alleged gas chambers on the scale claimed by the Defendants to kill Jews, there was, according to Irving, a real danger that the poison might have found its way into the water supply for the camp.

The logistical impossibility of extermination on the scale contended for by the Defendants

7.100 Irving produced an enlarged photograph depicting what he claimed to be the Auschwitz coke bunker. He argued that it is far too small to have been capable of accommodating the huge amount of coke which would have been needed for the incineration of thousands of bodies. (Van Pelt pointed out that each crematorium had its own coke storage bunker). Irving advanced the further related argument that it would have required 35kg of coke to incinerate a single body. He based that argument on evidence that at another camp at Gussen that was the weight of coke required. On that premise he contended that it was logistically impossible for sufficient coke to have been supplied and stored at Auschwitz to burn bodies at the rate envisaged in a letter of 28 June 1943 written by Bischoff, the Chief of the Central Construction Management at Auschwitz. Irving disputed the authenticity of that document for reasons which I set out at paragraph 7.105. Alternatively he contended that in any event it can be explained by the urgent need for capacity to incinerate the bodies of those who succumbed during the typhus epidemic which raged through Auschwitz in the summer of 1942.

7.101 Irving asserted that the only way of transporting corpses from the morgue up to the incinerators was by lift. He maintained that the lift was incapable of supplying the incinerators with bodies at rates which would have enabled the incinerators to burn the number of Jews claimed by the Defendants to have been gassed at the camp. In other words, the lift was a bottleneck which demonstrated the Defendants' figures for the numbers killed and incinerated to be flawed. In addition, since the incinerators would not have reduced the corpses to ash, Irving questioned how the bones and other unburned parts of so many bodies could have been disposed of.

Irving's investigation of the documentary evidence

7.102 The Leuchter report having acted as a catalyst, Irving testified that he spent some months in the period following its publication going round the archives with an open mind looking for evidence that Auschwitz was an extermination camp. Although that was the claim that he made in 1988, in his evidence he described the difficulties confronting him in regard to any such investigation. Auschwitz itself was still behind the Iron Curtain (although Irving agreed he made no attempt to gain access to the site). The Soviet archives (where most of the Auschwitz documents and in particular the construction documents had been consigned) remained closed to Westerners until 1990. So on his own account Irving's investigation was confined to the German Federal Archives (until he was finally banned from visiting Germany in late 1993), the national archives in Washington and libraries such as the Hoover library in California.

7.103 Hampered though he was in his attempt to investigate the issue, Irving relied strongly on the extreme paucity of the documentary evidence for the existence of genocidal gas chambers. He pointed out that there is no reference to the Russians having discovered gas chambers when they liberated the camp in January 1945. Irving relied further on the absence of any reference in the reports sent in cypher from Auschwitz to Berlin (which were intercepted and decoded at Bletchley and commented upon by Professor Himsley) to the death of any inmate in a gas chamber at the camp. Deaths from typhus and other causes, including shooting, are faithfully recorded but there is never any reference to killing by gas. Since the reports were secret, argued Irving, there would have been no need to omit deaths by gassing. Evans considered it to be unsurprising that there should have been no reference to the deaths in the gas chambers of registered inmates of the camp given the high level of secrecy which surrounded the policy of extermination by that method. As for those who were not registered as inmates, they would not have featured in the reports in any event.

7.104 Irving relied on the camp registers which have recently been released by the Russians. According to his argument, these registers demonstrate that the number of those registered as having been admitted to Auschwitz is wholly irreconcilable with the number of Jews said by the Defendants to have perished in the gas chambers there. The response of the Defendants to this argument is that there is clear evidence that the camp registers did not include those who were killed immediately on arrival at Auschwitz. In this connection the Defendants relied on the evidence to that effect of General Pohl, the economic director of the Nazi concentration camps, as well as upon the evidence of certain of the eye-witnesses (including for example Pery Broad) to which I have already made reference.

7.105 Those documents apart, Irving drew attention to the fact of the thousands of documents studied by historians over the years, hardly any have surfaced which lend real support for the case for the existence of the gas chambers being used for extermination purposes. Irving in his evidence at the Zundel trial dismissed as tendentious the translation of *Vergasungskeller* in Bischoff's letter of 29 January 1943 as 'gas chamber'. It signified no more than a room where gassing apparatus would be installed without the connotation that the gas would be used to kill human beings. The word *Vergasungskeller* would not be used by a German to refer to a gas chamber: he would use *Gasungskeller*. Similarly the *Vergasungsapparate* mentioned in Wetzel's letter of 25 October 1941 were required for fumigation and not genocidal purposes. Irving produced an invoice to the Auschwitz Construction office which refers to an *Entwesungsanlage* (disinfection chamber) in support of his contention that such a facility existed at the camp.

7.106 Irving dismissed several of the allegedly incriminating documents as unauthentic if not downright forgeries. One particular target for an attack of this kind was mounted upon Bischoff's estimate of the capacity of the incinerators in his letter of 28 June 1943 (to which I have already made reference). Irving relied, amongst other things, on the absence of a reference to Auschwitz in the heading of the letter; on the allegedly unusual, if not unique, way in which the reference is typed at the head of the letter; on the way the date is typed; on the initials of the secretary who typed the letter being the wrong initials for Bischoff's secretary; on the inaccurate designation of the rank of the addressee of the letter, General Kammler, which omitted the distinctive symbol used by the Nazis for members of the SS. Irving also pointed out that, at the date when the letter was written, one of the incinerators referred to in the letter had been taken out of commission and another was under repair, so that it would have been inappropriate and unlikely that Bischoff would have included them in his assessment of the overall incineration capacity of the camp.

7.107 Another argument advanced by Irving for doubting the genocidal use of gas chambers at Auschwitz was based upon an instruction circulated on 26 October 1943 by Pohl, chief of all concentration camps, to each camp commandant instructing him to implement measures to reduce the number of deaths amongst the inmates by the provision of better food and clothing and the like. Irving also produced a letter to doctors at the camps requiring them to make extra efforts to ensure the effectiveness of the labour force by improving their health and mortality. Irving also produced a table signed by Pohl which records a reduction in the level of mortality in camps generally from 10% in December 1942 to about 8% in January 1943 as a result of hygiene measures which had been taken. In the same vein Irving relied on the note of a conference in June 1942 presided over by Dannecker, Eichmann's subordinate, which made reference to orders issued by Himmler to increase the workforce at Auschwitz. Irving relied on the note as evidence that Auschwitz was essentially a work camp. But Longerich pointed out that Himmler had made provision that 10% of those deported did not need to be fit for work. Longerich inferred that they were to be killed on arrival. Irving contended that the 10% provision was for wives and children. Such documents are, Irving argued, wholly inconsistent with the Nazis having been engaged at the same time upon a programme of exterminating Jews in gas chambers at Auschwitz.

7.108 In the light of such research as he has been able to undertake since 1989, Irving deploys other arguments and contentions (many of them advanced in the course of his cross-examination of van Pelt) which he claims bear out Leuchter's conclusions and which afford further reasons for doubting the existence of killing by gas at Auschwitz.

Irving's response to the eye-witness evidence

7.109 As to the Defendants' reliance on the evidence of eye-witnesses, Irving asserted that, since as many as 6,000 have survived the camp, the proportion of witnesses confirming the existence of gas chambers is remarkably small. The vast majority have not claimed that there were gas chambers at the camp.

7.110 In any case Irving contended that generically the eye-witnesses, whilst they are not to be discounted altogether, are not reliable or credible. Some can be shown to be inaccurate in their claims (eg Dr Bimko) or inconsistent (eg Hoss). Others gave evidence through fear or in order to curry favour with their captors (eg Aumeier). The evidence of many of them was the result of 'cross-pollination' with the recollection of other supposed eye-witnesses or was influenced by their having been shown the blueprints for the alleged gas chambers (eg Tauber). The evidence of a number of such witnesses (eg Kramer) can be explained by the fact that they were describing chambers which were used for fumigation purposes rather then killing. Irving gives as a reason for doubting the reliability of Olere's sketches that he made the absurd claim to the historian Pressac that the SS made sausages in the crematoria. Another reason for doubting Olere's reliability, according to Irving, is that flame as well as smoke can be seen in one sketch emerging from the top of the main chimney. Van Pelt agreed that no flame would have been visible since the chimney was 90 feet tall. Irving suggested that Olere's drawings may have been based on post-war reports, adding the gratuitous comment that he appears to have taken a prurient interest in naked women.

7.111 Irving also relied on the figures for the numbers of deaths of inmates through illness or from overwork in support of an argument that the purpose, or at least the principal purpose, which the crematoria at Auschwitz served was to incinerate the corpses of those who had died in this way. So, Irving's argument proceeded, the eyewitness evidence of the *Sonderkommandos* and others of the operation of the crematoria and the stripping of gold from the mouths of the corpses can be explained on the basis that these were the corpses of those who had died from disease or overwork rather than those who had been murdered in the gas chambers.

7.112 For all these reasons, some positive and some negative but all pointing in the same direction, Irving concluded that his initial reaction to the Leuchter report was correct: the evidence does not bear out the claim that gas chambers were operated to liquidate hundreds of thousands of Jews. The evidence relied on by the Defendants is riddled with inconsistencies and remains unpersuasive. He accepted that the cellar at *Leichenkeller* 1 was used as a gassing cellar but only to fumigate 'objects or cadavers'. As to the use of gas to kill humans, the most he was prepared to concede was that there were gassings 'on some scale' at Auschwitz.

The Defendants' arguments in rebuttal

The Defendants' critique of the Leuchter Report

7.113 The Defendants are highly critical of Irving for having attached any credence to the Leuchter report. Van Pelt included in his report a detailed critique of Leuchter, his methodology and his conclusions. His criticisms echo those contained in a reasoned rebuttal sent to Irving late in 1989 by a Mr Colin Beer (which at that time Irving acknowledged had some force).

7.114 According to both van Pelt and Beer, the fundamental flaw in the report was Leuchter's assumption that the concentration of cyanide in the killing chambers would have needed to be greater than the concentration in the delousing chamber, that is, in the region of 3,200 ppm or higher. According to them that assumption is simply wrong. Moreover it demolished or at least undermined a number of the reasons advanced by Leuchter for denying the existence of the killing chambers. Basing himself on the high concentration of cyanide which he assumed would have been needed to gas humans, Leuchter had argued that the ventilation system of the chambers would have been wholly inadequate. But, say the Defendants, if the concentration required was much lower, it would follow that the ventilation requirements would be correspondingly reduced. Irving accepted that this was a logical conclusion. Similarly Leuchter's argument that the high concentration of cyanide required to kill humans would have created a high risk of toxic contamination of the sewers is invalidated if the concentration required was a fraction of that assumed by Leuchter. Irving again agreed that this is a logical conclusion. He also agrees that the need for elaborate safety precautions, also relied on by Leuchter, would be radically reduced.

7.115 The Defendants relied on the content of an interview of Dr Roth, the scientist at the Massachusetts laboratory which carried out the tests on Leuchter's samples. According to Dr Roth, cyanide produces a surface reaction which will penetrate no further than one tenth of the breadth of human hair. The samples with which he was provided by Leuchter ranged in size between a human thumb and a fist, so they had to be broken down with a hammer before analysis. Roth asserts that the resulting dilution of any cyanide traces effectively invalidates the test results.

7.116 Apart from what the Defendants regard as the fundamentally flawed assumption by Leuchter about the concentration of cyanide required for killing purposes, they identified numerous errors of fact in his report. He wrongly stated that there was no provision for gas-fitted (that is, sealed) doors and windows in the gas chambers. The walls of the *Leichenkeller* were, contrary to what Leuchter claimed, sealed with a coating of plaster. Leuchter wrongly assumed that there was a mains sewer. He wrongly stated that there was no exhaust or ventilation system and that the facilities were damp and unheated. He asserted unjustifiably that there would have been a risk of death to those inserting Zyklon-B pellets into the roof vents. Irving accepted the validity of most of these criticisms of the Leuchter report.

7.117 Basing himself on the arguments which I have rehearsed in abbreviated form, van Pelt, not mincing his words, dismissed the Leuchter report as 'scientific garbage'.

The Defendants' case as to the absence of signs of chimneys in the roof of Leichenkeller 1

7.118 The Defendants accept that the physical evidence remaining at the site of Auschwitz provides little evidence to support the claim that gas chambers were operated there for genocidal purposes. The explanation, according to the Defendants, is that, after the revelations in the Allied media concerning the gas chambers at the camp at Majdanek in late 1944, Himmler ordered the dismantling of the extermination installations in the crematoria at Auschwitz. In late 1944 the Nazis duly dynamited the crematoria and destroyed the camp archives (or so they intended: as has been observed above, documents from the Central Construction Office accidentally survived).

7.119 Van Pelt addressed in his evidence the argument that chimneys for inserting Zyklon-B pellets into *Leichenkeller* I cannot have existed because there is no trace of any holes in the roof of the chamber. He agreed that the blueprints for the design of the gas chamber in crematorium 2 did not provide for metal chimneys or ducts. They are not included in the drawings because, according to van Pelt, the drawings were prepared before the decision was taken to use *Leichenkeller* I as a gas chamber.

7.120 As to Irving's claim that the pancaked roof shows no sign of the chimneys, the Defendants point out that this is a new argument which Irving appears first to have lighted on in November 1998. Its relevance to the criticisms of Irving as an historian is therefore open to doubt. In response to Irving's claim van Pelt maintained, firstly, that the roof is in such a mess and most of it is so inaccessible that it is impossible to verify whether or not the holes existed. In any case he claimed that it is likely that, when the gas chambers were dismantled in 1944, the chimneys would have been removed and the holes cemented over so as to remove incriminating evidence. (Irving regards this as highly implausible since the Russians were by then poised on the eastern side of the Vistula.) Moreover, van Pelt repeated that there exists powerful evidence for the existence of chimneys, namely the photographic and eye-witness evidence (including Olere's drawings which I have summarized above).

The redesign of crematorium 2

7.121 The Defendants dismiss as nonsensical the claim that the reason for the redesign of crematorium was to facilitate the fumigation of 'objects and corpses'. Contemporaneous documents identified by the Defendants show that the new design incorporated a undressing room (*Auskleiderkeller*). Irving was unable to explain in cross-examination what need there would have been for an undressing room if the facility was to be used only for the fumigating of dead bodies and inanimate objects. Irving's theory is in any case untenable, argued van Pelt, because the redesign was clearly intended to enable live people to walk downstairs (see paragraph 7.61 above). Moreover, there would have been no need for a metal-protected, reinforced spy-hole if only corpses and metal objects were to be gassed (see paragraph 7.68 above).

7.122 Van Pelt rejected Irving's argument that the reconstruction work at crematorium 2 was carried out in order to convert it to use as an air raid shelter. In the first place he pointed out that crematorium 2 is some 1.5 miles away from the SS barracks, that is, too far away for members of the SS to reach in the event of a raid. The shelter would in any event have been too small to accommodate more than a fraction of the SS personnel and obviously wholly inadequate for the camp inmates (even if the Nazis had wanted to protect them). Van Pelt did not accept that, if the chamber was to become a shelter, it would have needed to have a gas-tight door with a peep-hole protected on the *inside* by a metal grill. He also disputed that, at the time of construction, there was any reason to fear air raids. However, Irving was able to produce a document dated 6 August 1942 setting out detailed guidelines as to the precautions against air raids to be taken in the military area of the General Government.

The quantity of Zyklon-B required

7.123 In relation to Irving's argument that the quantity of Zyklon-B delivered to the camp could be explained as being needed for fumigation purposes, van Pelt produced a supplementary report in which he noted that the amount of Zyklon-B delivered to Auschwitz vastly exceeded the quantity delivered to other camps. He made a detailed calculation, based on delivery documents and on stated assumptions about the frequency of fumigations, that of the total amount of Zyklon-B delivered to Auschwitz in 1943 (1,200 kilos) not more than 900 kilos would have been required for fumigation. That would leave unaccounted for 300 kilos, which van Pelt contended would have been more than enough to kill the 250,000 Jews estimated to have been gassed to death that year.

The Defendants' response to Irving's logistical argument

7.124 Van Pelt dismissed the suggestion made by Irving that if cyanide had been used to gas Jews in the chambers, there would have been a risk of the entire water supply at the camp becoming contaminated. The gas was evacuated from the chambers by means of the ventilation system through a chimney and not through the floor into a drain.

7.125 Likewise van Pelt rejected the argument that the quantity of coke delivered to Auschwitz was insufficient to fuel the incineration of the corpses in the numbers which the Defendants claim were killed at the camp. He challenged the premise of Irving's argument which was that as much as 35kg of coke would have been required for each body incinerated: basing himself on a contemporaneous calculation and assuming bodies were burned together at the rate contemplated in the Bischoff's letter of 28 June 1943, he maintained that the quantity of coke required per corpse would have been no more than 3.5kg.)

7.126 Van Pelt calculated that the capacity of the incinerators vastly exceeded what would have been required, even on a worst case scenario, to deal with deaths from typhus. He did not accept that the carrying capacity of the lift would have significantly limited that rate at which corpses could have been incinerated. As to the disposal of those parts of the bodies which were not reduced to ash in the ovens, van Pelt explained that the evidence is that the remains were pulverized by the Sonderkommandos and then buried in pits or dumped in the river Vistula.

The Defendants' response to Irving's argument in relation to the documentary evidence

7.127 The Defendants accept that there are few overt references to gas chambers at Auschwitz in contemporaneous documents but suggest that the absence is readily understandable. I have already alluded to the evidence of Ertl, the architect employed at the Auschwitz Central Construction Office, that he was told by Bischoff that no reference should be made to gassing and that such terms as 'special action' or 'special measure' should be used instead. The Defendants contend that it was standard procedure to disguise the existence of genocidal gas chambers either by the use of such innocuous terms or referring to their having a delousing function.

7.128 In answer to Irving's claim that documents exist which are irreconcilable with a programme of mass extermination at Auschwitz (for example urging that measures be taken to reduce the mortality rate), Longerich asserted that these documents have no bearing whatsoever on the treatment of those who were gassed on arrival at Auschwitz without becoming registered as inmates of the camps. The documents simply reflect a degree of caution in carrying out the policy of extermination by slave labour which had been proceeding in parallel with the gassing. The Nazis were becoming concerned at the rate at which the supply of labour was being reduced by death from typhus. Longerich further pointed out that the figures contained in the documents relied on by Irving were apt to mislead because they relate to both Jews and non-Jews: if the figures were confined to Jews, the picture would be very different.

7.129 But the Defendants contend that there are in the contemporaneous documents incriminating references. I have already made reference to some of them. Invited to comment on the catalogue of reasons given by Irving for denying the authenticity of Bischoff's letter of 28 June 1943 (see paragraph 7.106 above), van Pelt testified that the letter is in the Moscow archive. It first surfaced in the 1950s, that is, before any issue had been raised about the incineration capacity of the ovens, so that at the time there was no reason to have forged it. Van Pelt produced another version of the document which came from the Domburg archive. He suggested that no forger would have inserted the forged document into two different archives. Moreover, van Pelt would not accept that what Irving perceived to be oddities about the document suggesting it is a forgery were in truth anything of the kind. He assembled a clip of Auschwitz documents which display most of the odd features upon which Irving founded his argument that the letter is not genuine. He was unable, however, to produce another example of an error in the designation of the rank of an SS officer. In addition he agreed he had not come across another document which had the abbreviation 'Ne' for the name of the secretary who typed it. Van Pelt concludes that there was no standard format for documents at the camp. His overall conlusion was that he had no doubt about its authenticity.

7.130 In answer to Irving's reliance on the absence of references to deaths by gassing in either the decrypts or the camp 'death books', the Defendants contend (as already noted) that both relate to registered inmates at the camp and not to those who were gassed on arrival. There was moreover a natural concern to observe the greatest secrecy about the gassing operations.

viii. Justification: The Claim that Irving is a 'Holocaust Denier'

What is meant by the term 'Holocaust denier'

8.1 The threshold question is whether Irving has denied the Holocaust and, if so, in what terms and how comprehensively? Irving has at no time sought to controvert the following facts:

a   that the Nazis established concentration (as opposed to extermination) camps throughout their territories;

b   that from about June 1941 when the Nazis invaded the Soviet Union many thousands of Jews and others in the East were shot and killed by Nazi soldiers;

c   that from the end of 1941 onwards thousands of Jews were killed by gassing in the Reinhard death camps.

Irving did, however, challenge the proposition that there was a systematic programme, ordained at a high level, to exterminate European Jewry. He denied that there was mass killing of hundreds of thousands of Jews in gas chambers at Auschwitz.

8.2 That being in broad terms Irving's stance, it is necessary, in order to decide whether he is justifiably described by Lipstadt as a 'Holocaust denier' to define precisely what is meant by that term. There has been some debate between the parties as to its meaning. In ordinary usage the word 'holocaust' connotes complete destruction, especially of a large number of persons and usually by fire. Irving claimed that the term can be applied to the events of World War II as a whole. But I did not understand him to dispute that it is generally understood to have a narrower significance and that it is perceived to be specifically linked to the fate of Jews during the Third Reich (and not just during the war years).

8.3 Evans argued that the term is generally understood to denote 'the attempt by Nazi Germany, led by Hitler, to exterminate the Jewish population in Europe, which attempt succeeded to the extent of murdering between 5 and 6 million Jews in a variety of ways, including mass gassings in camps built for the purpose'. It follows that a 'Holocaust denier' is someone who, for one reason or another or for a combination of reasons, repudiates the notion that the above definition of the Holocaust is apt to describe what was sought to be done to the European Jews by the Nazis during World War II. Evans testified that a characteristic of Holocaust denial is that it involves a politically motivated falsification of history.

8.4 In the opinion of Evans, the views expressed by Holocaust deniers include the following:

i   that Jews were not killed in gas chambers or at least not on any significant scale;

ii that the Nazis had no policy and made no systematic attempt to exterminate European Jewry and that such deaths as did occur were the consequence of individual excesses unauthorized at senior level;

iii that the number of Jews murdered did not run into millions and that the true death toll was far lower;

iv that the Holocaust is largely or entirely a myth invented during the war by Allied propagandists and sustained after the war by Jews in order to obtain financial support for the newly-created state of Israel.

8.5 According to Evans, whilst the expression of those views is typical, Holocaust deniers do not necessarily subscribe to all of them and the views of some deniers may be more extreme than others. Irving made the point that it would be absurd to label a person a Holocaust denier merely because he or she questions the number of Jews killed under the Nazi regime.

The question whether the statements made by Irving qualify him as a 'Holocaust denier' in the above sense

The case for the Defendants

8.6 Evans considered that Irving's view of the Holocaust underwent a sea-change at or about the time he read and was converted by the Leuchter report on Auschwitz. Evans noted (and Irving accepted) that in the 1991 edition of *Hitler's War* most of the references to the extermination of the Jews, which had found a place in the 1977 edition, had been excised. In the 1991 edition the liquidation programme is referred to as 'a notion'.

8.7 The Defendants' case is that Irving is one of a small group of writers who can properly be described as Holocaust deniers. The group includes Paul Rassinier; Arthur Butz; Thies Christophersen; Wilhelm Staglich; Ernst Zundel and Robert Faurisson. (I shall have to return to a number of these individuals when I deal in Section x. below with the allegation that associates with right-wing extremists)

8.8 The way in which the Defendants seek to make good Lipstadt's allegation that Irving is a Holocaust denier (and a dangerous one at that) and that he fits well into the *galere* to which I have referred in paragraph 8.7 above, is by citing what Irving has said and written on the subject, principally from 1988 onwards. The Defendants contend that Irving stands condemned as a denier out of his own mouth. It is their case that on numerous occasions Irving has made statements which fall within each of Evans's categories which are listed at paragraph 8.4 above.

8.9 Amongst the assertions made by Irving which mark him out as a Holocaust denier, Evans noted in particular the following: his claim that the number who 'died' in Auschwitz, 'most of them from epidemics', was 100,000; his claim made expressly or by implication that the Jews had brought the Holocaust upon themselves; his assertion that the conduct of the Nazis in exterminating Jews could be excused by the fact that they or their families had suffered in the Allied bombing raids; the manner in which he dismissed the totality of the evidence of eye-witnesses from Auschwitz as unreliable because it is the product of mass hysteria; his claim, often repeated as will be seen, that the gas chambers at Auschwitz are a lie invented by British intelligence; his denunciation of the diary of Anne Frank as a forgery or as a novel like *Gone With the Wind*; his claim that the myth of the Holocaust is the product of a well-financed campaign by Jewry to legitimize the substantial payments made by Germany to the state of Israel since the war. This claim has been made by Irving on several occasions including the launch of the English edition of the Leuchter report. The Defendants contend that Irving qualifies as a Holocaust denier and that his denial flies in the face of the totality of the evidence.

Irving's denial that he is a Holocaust denier

8.10 In paragraph 6(i) of his Reply Irving answered the claim that he is a Holocaust denier in the following terms:

It is denied that the (Claimant) has denied the Holocaust; it is denied that the (Claimant) has denied that gas chambers were used by the Nazis as the principal means of carrying out that extermination; they may have used them on occasion on an experimental basis, which fact he does not deny.

Irving made clear that he is unaware of any authentic archival evidence that Jews were systematically exterminated in any of the camps identified by the Defendants in the particulars of justification. As has already appeared, Irving has substantially modified his position since appeared pleaded his statement of case.

8.11 Irving expressed his resentment of the passage in Evans's report which described his alleged links with the Holocaust deniers mentioned at paragraph 8.7 above. He dismissed that as guilt by association. Irving testified that there was no truth in Evans's assertion that his views about the Holocaust derive from Rassinier, described by Evans as one of the earliest and most important Holocaust deniers. Although he agreed he had contributed an Afterword to one of Rassinier's books, Irving maintained that he had not read that book or any other by Rassinier.

8.12 Irving asserted that, at least until he came to prepare for this case, he was not a Holocaust historian. He claimed that the topic bores him. He submitted that his comments about the Holocaust should be judged in the light of his lack of expertise. He did, however, agree that, when appearing as an expert witness in the Canadian prosecution of Zundel, he had answered questions about the Holocaust. He also accepted, moreover he had to agree that he had told an audience in Toronto in 1988 that he had been going round as many as forty archives relating to Auschwitz. He accepted he had said that he was writing a book about Auschwitz.

8.13 Irving complained that anyone who analyses or questions the evidence relating to the so-called Holocaust is automatically decried as a Holocaust denier. That, he claimed, is all that he has ever done. He tendered in evidence, as being a useful guide to what Holocaust denial should mean, a somewhat polemical paper by Barabara Kulaszka, who was one of the lawyers who represented Zundel at his trial in Canada in 1988.

8.14 Irving made the complaint that the passages relied on by the Defendants in support of their contention that he is a Holocaust denier omit the context, which often puts an entirely different complexion on what he said. Irving argued that he cannot be termed a Holocaust denier since he has always accepted that a very large number of Jews were shot and killed by the *Einsatzgruppen*. Merely to question the accuracy of their reports as to the numbers shot does not make him a Holocaust denier. Irving pointed out that on one occasion in July 1995 he put the number of deaths of Jews in the Holocaust as high as 4 million (although he claimed that most of these deaths were due to epidemics). He argued that he cannot therefore be described as a Holocaust denier. Irving cited his biography of Goering as further evidence that he is not a Holocaust denier. The index contains several references to the extermination of the Jews which, argued Irving, indicates that the topic is comprehensively dealt with.

The oral and written statements made by Irving which are relied on by the Defendants for their contention that he is a Holocaust denier and the evidence relied on by the Defendants for their assertion that Irving's denials are false

8.15 In order to evaluate the arguments which I have summarized above in relation to the issue whether Irving is correctly described as a Holocaust denier, it is necessary that I set out those extracts which the

Defendants have selected. But it is necessary also to consider whether and, if so, to what extent what Irving has said and written is consistent with or borne out by the available historical evidence. For, as the Defendants accept, there can be no valid criticism of Irving for denying that a particular event occurred unless it is shown that a competent and conscientious historian would appreciate that such a denial is to a greater or lesser extent contrary to the available historical evidence.

8.16 The categories of publications and statements which, according to the Defendants, establish Irving as a Holocaust denier are those relating to:

i   the existence of gas chambers at Auschwitz or elsewhere;
ii the existence of a systematic programme or policy of extermination of Jews;
iii the number of Jews killed and
iv the assertion that the gas chambers were a propaganda lie invented by the British.

The existence of gas chambers at Auschwitz or elsewhere

Claims made by Irving
8.17 The extracts relied on by the Defendants are as follows:

i) Christchurch, New Zealand – 26 March 1986
Irving's stated position as at 1986 before he read the Leuchter report.

Q: What is the proof about the gas chamber and how many Jews had been killed?
Irving: I don't want to get into that argument . . . it's really an unnecessary question. [P]refers to Dachau and the dismantled gas chamber.] . . . which were just an invention of the American army. That is the only gas chamber that was ever upon German soil. The gas chambers which we all know about supposed to have existed on Polish soil, I haven't investigated them, I don't intend to investigate them, I am too valuable for that (p. 40).

ii) Irving in evidence at the Zundel trial Toronto, 25 April 1988

Irving: I have carried out no investigation in-depth in equivalent depth of the Holocaust.

Q: But your mind changed?

Irving: My mind has now changed.

Q: You no longer believe it?

Irving: I have now begun to challenge that. I understand it is now a subject open to debate.

Q: But your belief changed even though you didn't do any research, is that what you are saying?

Irving: My belief has now changed because I understand that the whole of the Holocaust mythology is, after all, open to doubt and certainly in the course of what I have read in the last few days, in fact, in this trial, I am now becoming more and more hardened in this view.

Q: As a result of what you've read in the last few days? [That is, Leuchter]

Irving: Indeed.

iii) Irving's speech in Toronto – 13 August 1988

[on the Vrba/Wetzlar report] '. . . The report that was issued, is a report that may be familiar to some of you, allegedly written by two Slovak Jews who'd been in Auschwitz, for two years, they'd escaped – how is not related, they'd fled across the lines and been picked up by the Slovak resistance movement and the Slovak resistance movement had then obtained from them this very detailed report running to 25 or 30 pages of life at Auschwitz' (p. 13).

'. . . So it is very interesting to try and find out where the report came from. It's a report by two Slovak Jews and yet in the records of the War Refugee Board there are only two versions of it. One in English, translated from a version in German. There's no Slovak report there at all, in the Czechoslovakian language . . . (page 14) . . . And the interesting thing that occurred to me was that when this report came out published by the War Refugee Board in 1944, in November, five months after it came out of Europe, two newspapers immediately challenged its authenticity and refused to publish it. The New York Times and the Washington Post. Not just any two newspapers, but the two most prestigious newspapers in the United States. Initially refused to publish this report or to comment on it because it looked too phoney to them ... (page 15) ... A diabolical piece of propaganda issued by the Nazi Propaganda Ministry itself ... And the other hypothesis that I advance is even more insidious – that we British did it. We concocted that report ourselves. Through one of our exiled Governments in London, the Benes regime or the Slovaks. And this is, again, not just a wild hypothesis that I toss at you after just doing one month's work in the archives, this is in fact the result of work done by Paul Norris one of Zündel's men' (p. 15).

[on Marie Claude Vaillant-Couturier] '... And here Judge Biddle writes in brackets in his diary 'all this I doubt'. Why didn't he say it at the time for heaven's sake? But he just sat there with his face motionless, because he's an American Judge, but in his private diary he writes 'All this I doubt'. And so it goes on. The women being gassed, the children being torn apart, their legs being torn off by SS officers and a touching account of one baby, one child saying 'Mummy how can I walk now this man has torn my leg off'? [Laughter/ comments] I mean how can you accept this kind of thing' (p. 18).

iv) Letters

Letter from Irving to Zitelmann 21 May 1989: 'It is clear to me that no serious historian can now believe that Auschwitz, Treblinka, Majdanek were *Todesfabriken*. All the expert and scientific (forensic) evidence is to the contrary.'

Letter from Irving to Hugh Dykes MP 30 June 1989: '... if you persist in believing in gas chambers, you are on a loser'.

v) Leuchter Press Conference – 23 June 1989

'There was no equipment there for killing people en masse' (and hydrogen cyanide is wonderful for killing lice, but not so good for killing people, unless in colossal concentrations; the 'gas chambers' were 'routine designed crematoria') (p. 15).

'I'm quite happy to nail my colours to the mast ... and say that to the best of my knowledge, there is not one shower block in any of the concentration or slave labour camps that turns out to have been some kind of gas chamber ... My testimony is that the forensic evidence suggests that they [Jews] can't have been killed in gas chambers at Auschwitz ...' (p. 34).

'The eye witness testimonies of the survivors of Auschwitz first of all have been dismissed by eminent Jewish historians now as being largely worthless.' (p. 8)

(Irving was asked whether he accepted that there were death camps at Treblinka, Belzec, Sobibor and Chelmno.) 'Sadly, we're not in a position to carry out forensic tests on those sites' (p. 13).

Irving: 'Read the expertise which is in the Leuchter Report in your hands. The expertise on how difficult it is to kill someone by cyanide. More difficult than you and the Holocaust historians think' (p. 14).

'I'm prepared to accept that local Nazis tried bizarre methods of liquidating Jews, I'm quite prepared to accept that, and that they may have experimented using gas trucks because I've seen one or two documents in the archives implying that there was a rollover from the use of those methods of killing . . . the same people who created the euthanasia programme, and they may have tried to [unin] of killing Jews, but it's a very inefficient way of killing people. The Germans themselves had discovered this and there are much easier ways of killing people' (pp. 32–33).

(In answer to a question about Sobibor and Treblinka.)

'I think prima facie if they turned out to have been faked at Auschwitz then it's equally likely that they'd turn out to be fake at the other places behind the Iron Curtain too' (p. 35).

(Questioner points out there were no factories round Sobibor and Treblinka, they were entirely death camps.)

Irving: 'No, have you never heard of internment camps?'

Q: 'Yes, but 300,000 people don't get interned and die of natural causes in Treblinka as happened in summer 1943, I mean, it's not really plausible.'

Irving: 'Well, I'd like to see your evidence for it . . .'

vi) Dresden – 13 February 1990 (no tape or transcript, but see Irving's speech at 10th IHR Conference as reported in JHR)

'. . . the holocaust of Germans in Dresden really happened. That of the Jews in the gas chambers of Auschwitz is an invention. I am ashamed to be an Englishman.'

vii) Moers – 5th March 1990

'it is being shouted to the heavens that these things in Auschwitz and probably in Majdanek, Treblinka too, and the other extermination camps, so-called, in the East, are all only mock-ups' (p. 9).

'. . . there is one statement, one protocol about a man who maintained that there was a one-man gas chamber. Incidentally, she sees that, this man was, he had a very good imagination, he said, there is a one-man gas chamber. So that is, just big enough to gas one single victim. And it was transported around the countryside by two peasants, like a sedan chair. And of course, there are problems with it: how, if you please, do you get the victim to go into this one-man gas chamber? Quite clearly: if I'm a victim wandering, around the Polish countryside, and then suddenly I turn around and there's a one- man gas chamber behind me, I'm going to get suspicious. Well, it was disguised as a telephone box. That's what it says, in the witness statement. So it's a one-man gas chamber, disguised as a telephone box – well, I'm still suspicious. Here I am, I turn around, and suddenly there's a telephone box where there wasn't one before. How are you going to get me to climb into it? There is probably a telephone in it, which rings, and the man [*incomprehensible*] waves and says "It's for you". It's laughable, isn't it? It's well, you could describe it as a "free trip to the other side". But it's in the archives. We can all laugh about it, in this little intimate circle, but the other witness statements are equally ridiculous. So, the witness statements are a case for the psychiatrists' (p. 16).

viii) Latvian Hall, Toronto – 8 November 1990

'. . . more people died on the back seat of Senator Edward Kennedy's motor car at Chappaquiddick than died in the gas chamber at Auschwitz [applause]' (16).

ix) Calgary, Alberta – 29 September 1991

'. . . until 1988, I believed that there had been something like a Holocaust. I believed that millions of people had been killed in factories of death. I believed in the gas chamber. I believed in all the paraphernalia of the modern Holocaust. But 1988, when I came to Canada and gave evidence in the trial of Ernst Zündel, as an historian, I met people who knew differently and could prove to me that that story was just a legend. I changed my mind and I've now revised the Hitler book so that all reference to Auschwitz and the gas chamber and the factories of death have now been totally removed and eradicated' (p. 4).

'So they want to know who else have we invited, these journalists. And I said, "Well, I'll tell you another class of people we are inviting, we're inviting all the chemistry teachers at every public school in Britain." "Chemistry teachers?" they say. And I say, "Yes, there's no point inviting the history teachers or the politics teachers because they're blinkered and closed minded. They all know about the Holocaust because they've read about it and they've seen War and Remembrance with Robert Mitchum on television. They know it happened." But the chemistry teachers are coming to hear Fred Leuchter speak and they'll see the laboratory tests because we'll hand them out to them and the chemistry teachers will go back to their Masters' Common Rooms and they will tell the history teachers, and they'll be believed. So you can imagine that this is causing, this has really set the cat among the pigeons in Britain. And all the old stories are coming about, out again, about the eye-witnesses and all the vilification is starting again. And how do you explain the hundreds of thousands of eye-witnesses in Auschwitz? And I say, "Well, the existence of hundred of thousands of eye-witnesses from Auschwitz is in itself proof that there was no dedicated programme to kill them all." And anyway, as for eye-witnesses I'm inclined to go along with the Russian proverb, recently quoted by Julian Barnes, the novelist in a novel that he published called "Talking it Over". And he quotes the Russian proverb which is, "He lies like an eye-witness, he lies like an eye-witness" (pp. 13–14).

'And I'm in deep trouble for saying this around the world, that the eye-witnesses in Auschwitz who claim, like Eli Wiesel to have seen the gassings going on and the subsequent cremations, that they are liars . . . [page 14/15] . . . He's a liar. And so are the other eye-witnesses in Auschwitz who claim they saw gassings going on because there were no gas chambers in Auschwitz, as the forensic tests show. And I've got into a lot of trouble saying this. There's an arrest warrant out against me in Austria for using those very words. I said, in Austria, which is the criminal offence, when I was asked about the eye-witnesses, I said "Well, I've been waiting for somebody to ask me about the eye-witnesses, and to my mind the eye-witnesses to the gassings in Auschwitz are an interesting case for the psychiatrists." I'm not implying that they've got a mental problem, I'm implying that it's an interesting psychological phenomenon that people over a period of years begin kidding themselves that they have seen something. And the more they come to have taken part in a traumatic experience themselves, the more they are persuaded that they were right centre stage. They are the bride at every funeral and the corpse at every wedding, I think somebody once said' (pp. 14–15).

'And there are so many survivors of Auschwitz now, in fact, that I get very tasteless about all of this. I don't see any reason to be tasteful about Auschwitz. It's baloney, it's a legend. Once we admit the fact that it was a brutal slave labour camp and large numbers of people did die, as large numbers of innocent people died elsewhere in the War, why believe the rest of the baloney? I say quite tastelessly, in fact, that more women died on the back seat of Edward Kennedy's car at Chappaquiddick than ever died in a gas chamber in Auschwitz.[Laughter] Oh, you think that's tasteless, how about this? There are so many Auschwitz survivors going around, in fact the number increases as the years go past, which is biologically very odd to say the least. Because I'm going to form an Association of Auschwitz survivors, Survivors of the Holocaust and other liars, or the A-S-S-H-O-L-S. [Laughter] Gorbachev . . .'

x) Bayerische Hof, Milton, Ontario – 5 October 1991

'. . . you've got to be tasteless because these people deserve all our contempt' (p. 17).

xi) Clarendon Club, London – 15 November 1991

'The biggest lie of the lot, the "blood libel on the German people" as I call it, is the lie that the Germans had factories of death with gas chambers in which they liquidated millions of their opponents.' (p. 2)

xii) Chelsea Town Hall – 15 November 1991

'. . . Leuchter Report . . . shows quite clearly that according to chemical analysis, which is an exact science . . . And if these samples yielded no significant trace of cyanide whatsoever, then there has to be a scientific reason for it. . . . So Fred Leuchter is poison for the whole of the Holocaust legend' (p. 4).

'. . . after Fred Leuchter did his truly epoch-making investigation of the gas

chambers at Auschwitz, the forensic laboratory tests which yielded the extraordinary result which converted me, made me into a hard-core disbeliever, the
forensic laboratory tests which showed no significant trace whatsoever of
cyanide in rooms where apparently millions of people had been gassed with
cyanide . . .' (p. 6).

xiii) 11ᵗʰ IHR Conference – 11 October 1992

'. . . any historian can now confirm that nowhere in all the archives of the
world has yet been found one wartime document referring to a Führer's order
to destroy the Jews, or for that matter, one wartime document referring to gas
chambers or gassings . . . If there's no wartime document that says there was a
Führer order, if no wartime document talks of gas chambers, then there has to
be some explanation for that' (p. 21).

xiv) 'The Search for Truth in History – Banned!' – 1993 (Irving's video for Australia)

'Where did the Holocaust legend come from? You note I don't say Holocaust
lie because to say that it's a lie implies first of all you don't believe any of it,
and parts of it have to be believed. To say it's a lie also implies that it's a
malicious lie, that people know it's a lie and they've been spreading it knowingly
as a lie for the last 50 years. I call it a Holocaust legend because then it has
something like the quality of a religion almost. You believe things because
you've been told it by people who seem reliable . . . It's a long chain of gullible
people who over the last 50 years have been told it and have believed it because
they had no reason not to believe it, and this is why the Holocaust legend has
survived until now because nobody has come forward really with any kind of
credibility and has rattled at the foundations of that legend and said OK, prove
it' (p. 18).

'. . . The Holocaust legend is fizzling out. I said two years ago, it probably only
had two years left to survive. Probably I was wrong, it probably has about
another six months even now, but then it is finally dead. World wide it is
played out . . .' (p. 27).

'I think probably the most significant piece of evidence is what we British
ourselves did in the war, we actually broke the code of the SS and we began
reading in 1942 the coded top secret messages of the Commandant of Auschwitz

reporting back to Berlin . . . Nearly all the deaths in Auschwitz said Hinsley were from epidemics and disease and I quote Hinsley verbatim he said ''there is no reference in the intercepts to any gassing''. Remember these are the top secret signals written in the top secret code of the SS, so there can be no question of Höss writing something for the benefit of historians after the war' (p. 21).

'you can work out for yourselves, ladies and gentlemen, how many thousand tons of coke one needs for that. But we have the aerial photographs, where one can't see a single mound of coke. And not only that, but no railway, no railway siding leads to the crematorium, to bring theses masses of coke, these huge masses of coke, thousands of tons per day. No lorry convoys are to be seen, where the coke, under circumstances, might have been delivered by lorry' (p. 22).

'Now, I said that the eye witnesses are in fact a matter for psychological examination I think. Psychiatric examination even. . . .but I don't mean that in an offensive way. I wouldn't mind it if somebody said about me that some of my statements need to be psychiatrically analysed because the human being, the psyche, is a very complex instrument' (p. 22–3).

[an Auschwitz survivor] has probably been questioned by her friends and neighbours and relatives for the last 50 years about Auschwitz and she can't very well describe her everyday life as centring around the peeling of potatoes or some other menial task. She knows that the people who are questioning her about Auschwitz want to hear about the crematoria and the gas chambers and after a time she describes the crematoria and the gas chambers, because human pride demands that she may not have been in one of the other barracks, perhaps five miles away from the crematorium but right next door to it. It's a matter of human pride and we can't really begrudge these people for placing themselves and their recollections so close to the event, so close to the heart of the particular trauma. They're not dissimulating, they're not being consciously mendacious' (p. 23).

'The eye witness survivor testimony is very shaky. It's far too shaky on which to base the condemnation of an entire nation, namely the German nation, in my view, and I think probably any sober and independent Judge would probably back me up on that' (p. 24).

'The pictures have been analysed by independent aerial picture analysts. They found nothing. These are the scientific methods. We have truth on our side' (p. 27).

'The aerial photographs don't only show how we have right, truth on our side, but how the enemies have faked the pictures. Because you know the American or Canadian or South African plane which took these pictures [in] 1944 or 1945. [They] took not only the one picture, but a whole set of pictures, every five seconds a picture. One sees how the buildings, the people, the lorries etcetera, have moved in the five seconds. But one also sees how the one picture published fifteen years ago by the CIA at the behest of world Jewry, with the supposed holes in the roof of the gas chamber where the cyanide was poured in, with the supposed lines of people who queue to be gassed. If one looks at the surrounding pictures then one suddenly notices that on these surrounding pictures the holes are not present. And that the lines of people are not present. One sees conclusively that the CIA has faked these photos, retouched them to the benefit of world Jewry, who somehow wanted prove that the gas chambers had existed' (p. 28).

xv) Tampa Florida – 6 October 1995

'Eli Wiesel and the rest of them come up with these legends. The basic part of the legend is 65,000 of these people were being cremated every day . . . But by their greed they exposed themselves as liars. Because to cremate 65,000 bodies a day you are going to need 30 or 40 kilograms of coke for each cadaver. There is no way around that figure. It is a basic law of the rather macabre thermodynamics of the crematorium business that it takes 35 or 40 kilograms of coke or an equivalent amount of other fuels available to cremate a cadaver' (p. 11).

'I used to think that the world was full of a thousand survivors. I was wrong. It is full of hundreds of thousands of survivors of the Holocaust if not, in fact, millions by now. The numbers of survivors seems to grow these passing years, it defies all laws of natural deceased and all laws, now the number of survivors is growing. And I said isn't the existence of so many survivors in itself an indicator, something doesn't, it doesn't fit. If the Nazis had this dedicated programme to exterminate the Jews, how come so many of you have survived, were the Nazis sloppy or what? They let you out, they let you escape? It's a basic question' (p. 17).

' "But tell me one thing", and this is why I'm going to get tasteless with her, because you've got to get tasteless, "Mrs Altman, how much money have you made out of that tattoo since 1945? [Laughter] How much money have you coined for that bit of ink on your arm, which may indeed be real tattooed ink?" And I'll say this, "half a million dollars, three quarters of a million for you alone." It must be in that order of magnitude because think of the billions of dollars that have been sent that way, billions' (p. 17).

xvi) Errol Morris film rushes – 8 November 1998

'. . . that's what converted me, when I read that in the report, in the court room in Toronto, I became a hard core disbeliever. I thought, well, whatever the Nazis are doing to the Jews, they were not killing them on a conveyor belt system in gas chambers in Auschwitz, against which has to be said that I've read the manuscript memoirs of two commandants of Auschwitz . . . [Höss . . . and Almeyer (sic)] . . . and they both refer to people being gassed in Auschwitz, and this is a methodological problem for a historian then. You have to look at that and say: well, there's no trace of cyanide in the building, but you've got these confessions by these Germans. How do you explain that? That is where you enter a grey area; you don't know what the explanation is . . . I don't know what the answer is . . .' (p. 9/51 – 10/19).

Evidence of the truth/falsity of Irving's claims

8.18 I have set out in detail in sections vi. and vii. above the parties' arguments in relation to the evidence of the existence of gas chambers at the Reinhard death camps and at Auschwitz respectively. It is unnecessary for me to repeat those arguments here.

The existence of a systematic programme or policy for killing Jews

Claims made by Irving

8.19 The extracts relied on by the Defendants include the following:

i) ABC Radio 3LO – March 1986

'millions or hundreds of thousands liquidated in WW2 by Germans (or Latvians or Ukrainians) were victims of large number of nameless criminals into whose hands they fell on the Eastern front . . . acted on their own impulse, their own initiative within the general atmosphere of brutality' (p. 10–11).

ii) Toronto – 13 August 1988

'individual excesses and atrocities and pogroms in places like Minsk and Kiev and Riga' [were] 'crimes conducted for the most ordinary and repugnant motives of greed and thievery. Whatever happened, were the crimes of individual gangsters and criminals who deserved to be individually and separately punished (p. 23).

iii) 11th IHR Conference – 11 October 1992

'Now you probably know that I'm a Revisionist to a degree, but I'm not a Revisionist to the extent that I say that there were no murders of Jews. I think we have to accept that there were My Lai-type massacres where SS officers – the *Einsatzkommandos* – did machine-gun hundreds if not thousands of Jews into pits. On the Eastern Front, at Riga, at Minsk, and at other locations, this kind of thing did happen' (p. 21–22).

'Most of these SS officers – the gangsters that carried out the mass shootings – were, I think, acting from the meanest of motives. . . . [refers to Bruns.] And two days later the order comes back from Hitler, "These mass shootings have got to stop at once." So Hitler intervened to stop it. Which again fits in with my theory that Hitler was in the dark that this kind of mass crime was going on. I suspect that the SS officer concerned [Altemeyer] was only 23 or 24. That was the age of the gangs that were carrying out these kinds of crimes. Rather like [US Army] Lt. Calley in My Lai. I don't know why people do that kind of thing' (p. 24).

iv) 12th IHR Conference – September 1994

'Here I want to mention something that I'm always very adamant about. Although we revisionists say that gas chambers didn't exist, and that the "factories of death" didn't exist, there is no doubt in my mind that on the Eastern front large numbers of Jews were massacred by criminals with guns – SS men, Ukrainians, Lithuanians, whatever – to get rid of them. They were made to line up next to pits or ditches, and then shot. The eyewitness accounts I've seen of this are genuine and reliable' (p. 15–16).

v) Oakland, California – 10 September 1996

'The people who were pulling the triggers were on one level and the people who were taking the top level decisions were on the highest level and there wasn't necessarily perfect communication between them and anyway who cares because it's only the Jews and nobody liked them. This is the kind of atmosphere in which the decisions would have been taken' (p. 26).

Evidence of the truth/falsity of Irving's claims

The arguments of Irving and the Defendants in relation to this issue are also to be found in sections vi. and vii. of this judgment, so I do not repeat them here.

The numbers of Jews killed

Claims made by Irving

8.20 The extracts relied on by the Defendants include the following:

i) This Week interview – 9 November 1991

'25,000 innocent people executed by one means or another [in Auschwitz] but we killed that many people burning them alive in one night, not in three years, in a city like Pforzheim. We killed five times that number in Dresden in one night.'

ii) Moers – 9ᵗʰ March 1990

'One has to struggle with these problems as a historian in Germany. . . And that's the problem with Auschwitz. That is the problem which the county court judge in Remscheid hinted at correctly. It seemed quite unbelievable to him that an Englishman should discover the truth, where all the German historians allegedly did not discover this truth. But the explanation is perfectly simple: the Germans simply can't afford to do that, . . . Not murdered, not gassed – far more than half of the inmates of the concentration camp Auschwitz died of natural causes that means, of diseases, of epidemics, of typhus fever, of typhoid, of hunger, of cold or of being overworked or of various other natural causes, that's what far more than half of the Auschwitz inmates died of, that means perhaps 30,000 people at most were murdered at Auschwitz. That's bad enough, of course! That none of us want to approve of that in any way. 30,000 people in Auschwitz from beginning to end, that's about as many as we English killed in one night in Hamburg, burnt alive' (p. 12).

iii) 10ᵗʰ IHR Conference – 13ᵗʰ February 1990

'Let's be generous and say 40,000 may have been killed in Auschwitz over the three years – that's a bad figure! That's a grave crime, it's almost as many people as we British killed in Hamburg in one night' (p. 500).

iv) Victoria, British Columbia – 27ᵗʰ October 1990

'Let me draw up a comparison, seventy six thousand people killed in Auschwitz is a crime, there's no doubt at all, except they weren't killed in Auschwitz, they died in Auschwitz. The *Totenbucher* lists the reasons of the deaths in Auschwitz. Arno Meyer, the Professor in Princeton, a Jewish Professor in fact, who published a book called 'Why Did the Heavens not Darken?', he revealed in his book that of all the people who died in the concentration camps, including Auschwitz, by far the greatest part died of natural causes, whatever one could call 'natural causes' in wartime, I admit, natural causes in wartime are not what you or I would call natural causes today in Victoria. But they weren't executed, they weren't murdered, they weren't gassed. By far the greatest part of those who died in Auschwitz died of natural causes and I'm quoting Arno Meyer' (p. 9).

'Forty thousand people killed in Auschwitz in three years, bad enough. Undoubtedly a war crime, a war crime of the same order of magnitude as Hamburg, July, 1943 where we British killed forty thousand people in one night' (p. 13).

v) Latvian Hall, Toronto November 1990

'Ladies and gentlemen, fifty thousand people were killed in Auschwitz, were killed in Auschwitz from 1942 to 1944. That is a crime, as I said. Fifty thousand innocent people. It's about as many people who died in Auschwitz in those three years as we British killed in Hamburg in one night' [Applause] (p. 21).

vi) Latvian Hall, Toronto, November 1992

'To those of you who are new to my talks. Let me summarize the possible reasons why they are using these extraordinary techniques, these extra-governmental techniques to try and silence me. It is because I am probably the most credible voice in the entire revisionist campaign, or what I call the International Campaign for Real History . . . And my campaign is being met world-wide by these methods. 'Okay,' I say, 'a hundred thousand people did die in Auschwitz. . . . Around one hundred thousand dead in that brutal slave labour camp . . . How many were killed in Auschwitz? . . . how many had died.'

'Twenty-five thousand killed, if we take this grossly inflated figure to be on the safe side: That is a crime; there is no doubt. Killing twenty-five thousand in four years – 1941, 1942, 1943, and 1944 – that is a crime: there is no doubt.'

'Let me show you a picture of twenty-five thousand people being killed in twenty-five minutes. Here it is, in my book HITLER'S WAR, a vivid picture of twenty-five thousand people being killed in twenty-five minutes by us British [in February 1945] in Pforzheim, a little town where they make jewelry and watches in Baden, Germany. Twenty-five thousand people were being burned alive (p. 11).

vii) 'Search for Truth in History' (1993)

'25,000 people murdered in Auschwitz in three years. If we take that generous figure and I would say that 25,000 people murdered in Auschwitz in three years is still half the number of people that we murdered in Hamburg burning them alive in one night in 1943' (p. 25).

viii) Tampa, Florida: October 1995

'But if we were being liberal and generous and said that of the 100,000 deaths for which we have certificates and evidence, acceptable evidence. In Auschwitz, say that three quarters died a natural death, by natural I mean typhus, epidemics, starvation, exhaustion, worked to death, froze to death, can't really call it a natural death but it's not murder. If we say that three quarters died that kind of death then as many as one quarter were executed, you come to a figure of 25,000 people who were murdered in Auschwitz by the Nazis in the entire four years of that camps existence and I am going to show you a picture of not 25,000 people being murdered but of 40,000 people being murdered, not in four years but in the space of 20 minutes in Pforzheim. Not Dresden or Hiroshima or Tokyo but Pforzheim, a little town none of you have heard of. A little town in Germany in Badenburg where they make jewelry and watches. Here's a town photographed from the air by a friend of mine, a British Air Commodore with his Kodachrome film camera during the 20 minutes in which 40,000 are being burned alive. One person in four in that town was killed, burnt alive during that air raid, 10 days after the air raid on Dresden, and nobody has ever heard of it. 40,000 being burnt alive in 20 minutes compared with 25,000 people being murdered at the very outside in Auschwitz in the space of four years. It's a thought provoking comparison and the reason why I think it's proper to make this kind of comparison' (pp. 13–14).

ix) 'Cover Story' – 4 March 1997

Irving: Again, that's not what I say. I say there's no proof that six million did die, it's not quite the same thing. You may find it nit-picking.

Interviewer: So you're saying only 100,000 people died in Auschwitz.

Irving: I didn't say 'only'. You can't say 'only' 100,000 people died. If 100,000 innocent people died this is a crime, it's a war crime (p. 6).

The Defendants' evidence of the falsity of Irving's claims

8.21 A formidable obstacle in the way of arriving at an accurate number for those killed by gas is that no records were kept by the Nazis of the numbers put to death in the gas chambers or, if they were, none have survived. Records were kept, as I have mentioned earlier, of the number of deaths amongst those who were registered as inmates of the camp. But, for reasons which are perhaps obvious, none of those deaths is recorded as having been due to gassing.

8.22 The difficulty of arriving at an accurate estimate is compounded by the undoubted fact that many inmates died from disease and above all in the typhus epidemics which from time to time ravaged the camp. Whilst the Defendants do assert that these deaths are the result of deliberate genocidal policy on the part of the Nazis, they must of course be discounted in order to reach a correct estimate of the number of deaths in the gas chambers. Initial estimates, largely based on the capacity of the crematoria, ran as high as 4 million. As has been seen the camp commandant, Hoss, gave varying estimates, ranging from 3 million to 1.1 million. However, analysis of the numbers of Jews transported to Auschwitz produced a lower estimate of around 1 million. Research carried out more recently, notably by Raul Hilberg and by Dr Piper of the Auschwitz Museum, has concluded that the true figure for the number of deaths at Auschwitz is in the region of 1.1 million of which the vast majority perished in the gas chambers. This figure has, according to the evidence of van Pelt and Longerich, been endorsed by the majority of serious, professional historians concerned in this field. The only significant exception is Jean-Claude Pressac, a French chemist and amateur historian, whose study concluded that the overall number of deaths was 630–710,000, of which 470–550,000 were gassed on arrival at the camp.

8.23 Longerich estimated that between February 1942 and January 1945 between 900,000 and 1 million Jews died at Auschwitz. But he made clear that those figures included those who died otherwise than by being gassed, for example in epidemics. Deaths outside the gas chambers accounted for about 100,000 deaths, leaving 800,000 to 900,000 murders by gassing. Longerich made clear that he regarded all the deaths as genocidal since the conditions in the camp were deliberately prepared by the Nazis.

8.24 It is the contention of both van Pelt and Evans on behalf of the Defendants that Irving has consistently under-estimated the number of Jews killed in the Holocaust and more particularly at Auschwitz. The Defendants assert that the available evidence demonstrates that the number of Jews killed in the Holocaust, both at Auschwitz and more generally, far exceeds Irving's estimates (which themselves vary considerably). They contend that he has paid no proper regard to that evidence and that he has carried out no adequate research into the numbers killed.

Evidence relied on by Irving in support of his claims

8.25 Irving noted that shortly after the end of the war the Poles, who were in possession of all the records, claimed that altogether nearly 300,000 people of different nationalities died at Auschwitz. That figure gradually increased to four million, which was the number mentioned (until 1990) on the monument erected by the Communists in memory of the dead. The figure then came down again. As for the total number of those who died in the Holocaust, Irving claimed that the figure was said by Justice Jackson at Nuremberg to be a back of an envelope calculation. Other estimates were significantly lower. There are real doubts about the figures, concluded Irving. He said he did not want to 'play the numbers game'.

8.26 He nevertheless put to the Defendants' witnesses in cross-examination that figures for the total number of those killed at Auschwitz are to be found in the camp 'death books' and the cipher messages from Auschwitz to Berlin which were decrypted at Bletchley. I have already recorded the contention of the Defendants that these figures take account only of those who were registered at the camp and not those who were murdered in the gas chambers on arrival there. Irving also argued that the incineration capacity of the ovens meant that the number of those killed must have been far lower than Longerich claimed.

8.27 Irving relied on the contents of the Haganah report about the number of Jews who were transported at the end of the war from the displaced persons camps to Israel. This report explains, so Irving maintained, why many Jews could not be traced and so were erroneously thought to have lost their lives in the concentration camps when in truth they started new lives in Israel.

8.28 Irving also sought to justify his claim as to the number of Jews who were killed in the concentration camps by reference to what he said were the 450,000 Jews who had lodged claims for compensation arising out of the Holocaust. If that many survived, said Irving, the number of the dead must be far smaller than claimed. The Defendants did not accept Irving's figure for the number of claimants. In any event they pointed out that the claimants include the children and grandchildren of Holocaust victims for the return of property of which they were dispossessed many years ago and so cast no light on the number of those who lost their lives.

The assertion that the gas chambers were a propaganda lie invented by the British

Claims made by Irving

8.29 The extracts relied on by the Defendants are as follows:

i) Toronto – 13th August 1988

'And this is, again, not just a wild hypothesis that I toss at you after just doing one month's work in the archives, this is in fact the result of work done by Paul Norris one of Zündel's men . . . In the British archives Paul Norris found documents which he showed me in photostat, showing quite clearly that British intelligence deliberately masterminded the gas chamber lie. I am not saying it was the same gas chamber lie that they masterminded, but it was a gas chamber lie. 1942, 1943, 1944 the Joint Intelligence Committee deliberated with the Psychological Warfare Executive which they ran in London, the propaganda agency in London, . . . on ways of blackening the German name, on ways of enraging allied soldiers so that they would fight even harder. And one of the methods that they hit on in the Psychological Warfare Executive, it's there in the documents, to say let us say that the Germans are using gas chambers to get rid of hundreds of thousands of Jews and other minority groups in Germany. And the minutes go to and fro . . . In one memorandum, Victor Cavendish-

Bentinck, the Chairman of the Joint Intelligence Committee, writes a handwritten minute to this effect: "we have had a good run for our money with this gas chamber story we have been putting about, but don't we run the risk that eventually we are going to be found out and when we are found out the collapse of that lie is going to bring down the whole of our psychological warfare effort with it. So isn't it rather time now to let it drift off by itself and concentrate on other lines that we're running". "We had a good run for our money" he writes in 1944 and here we are 44 years later and that hare is still running, bigger and stronger than ever because nobody now dares to stand up and kill it. It has go out of control. The Auschwitz propaganda lie that was starting to run in 1944 is now out of control and it going to take he-men of the kind of stature of Ernst Zündel to kill that particular hare. [Applause]' (p. 15–16).

ii) P's foreword to the FPP publication of the Leuchter Report: May 1989

'. . . Too many hundreds of millions of honest, intelligent people have been duped by the well-financed and brilliantly successful postwar publicity campaign which followed on from the original ingenious plan of the British Psychological Warfare Executive (PWE) in 1942 to spread to the world the propaganda story that the Germans were using 'gas chambers' to kill millions of Jews and other 'undesirables'.

iii) Moers – 9th March 1990

'where did this myth come from? And for me as an Englishman, that is the most interesting question: who invented the myth of the gas chambers? Representatives of the victorious powers. We did it. The English. We invented the lie about the gas chambers, just as we invented the lie about the Belgian children with their hands hacked off in the first World War. The department the committee of the British PWE cabinet, Political Warfare Executive, psychological warfare . . .' (p. 17).

iv) Latvian Hall, Toronto – 8th November 1990

'How has this legend been propagated until now? Well, the legend was originally propagated, I think, by us British back in 1942. And I set out the reasons for believing this in my previous talk, 18 months ago. But since 1945, the legend has marched . And this is a great sad facet of war. In wartime, quite justifiably, the warring factions and powers decide to use propaganda, they lie about each other. They lie, massively . . . When the Victory Day comes, these Ministries of Lies are not replaced by Ministries of Truth. So the old propaganda continues to march on and nobody really has the job of stopping these lies from flooding out. Particularly when some people find they have a vested interest in keeping the lies spewing forth' (p. 12–13).

v) Chelsea Town Hall – 15th November 1991

'And if you ask where these legends come from, the trouble is that it comes in fact from us, the British, and we're very good liars. World War II showed this and the Falklands showed it, the Gulf War showed it, we're very good liars and in wartime we have ministers of propaganda whose job it is to lie and in fact we can show quite clearly how this particular lie started in our own Ministry of Propaganda, the Political Warfare Executive and you can go and get the records from the Public Records Office and you can see how we in September, October and November 1942 created the gas chamber lie as a weapon of war, perfectly justified. But the problem with all this is that after the war is over, the Government doesn't set up a Ministry of Truth whose job it is to go around with a bucket and mop cleaning-up all the lies that the Ministry of Information has been spreading and so the lies continue to soldier on. And if they're lies that are very profitable lies, as this particular lie is of course, and I'm not going to go into detail on that there, because then we're treading on very thin ice, but it has become a very profitable lie, a lie in fact on which the financial existence of the State of Israel depends, then the lie is not only soldiering on it becomes reinforced and bolstered in a quite extraordinary way' (p. 3).

The Defendants' evidence of the falsity of the claims made by Irving

8.30 The Defendants assert that Irving's claim that the existence of gas chambers was a lie invented by British intelligence can be shown to be false by reference to documents contained in the contemporaneous files of the British Foreign Office.

8.31 In August 1942 the Secretary of the World Jewish Congress based in Geneva received a report from an allegedly reliable source that in Hitler's head-quarters a plan was under discussion for the deportation and extermination by means including the use of prussic acid of all Jews in areas occupied or controlled by the Nazis. This information was relayed to London, where it was considered by Foreign Office officials. They also had reports of Jews being transported to the East. But they decided not to make use of the information.

8.32 The same Foreign Office file reveals that about a year later, in August 1943, further reports were received in London of deportation and extermination by means including systematic killing in gas chambers. These reports were more specific, referring to events in Bialystok and Lublin. Even so, the Foreign Office again decided, after discussion, not make use of the information.

8.33 On the basis of these documents the Defendants assert that the claim that Jews were being killed in gas chambers was invented by British Intelligence is unsustainable. The claim originated abroad. In any case, say the Defendants, the contemporaneous evidence shows that, whilst the British had doubts about the wisdom of using the information, they did not disbelieve it. There was no 'lie'. The Defendants argue that it is equally untrue that the reports of the extermination of Jews in gas chambers featured in propaganda put out by British Intelligence. The decision within the Foreign Office was to make no use of the reports. Moreover, say the Defendants, there is no reason to link British Intelligence with such reports of the gassing of Jews as did appear in the media at that time.

Irving's evidence of the truth of his claims

8.34 When asked in cross-examination whether it is his position that the existence of gas chambers was propaganda devised by British intelligence, Irving replied that British intelligence had repeatedly procured the broadcasting into Nazi Germany of information about the gas chambers at a time when they were not operating. He went on to claim that there is any amount of evidence that the gas chambers were invented by British propaganda.

8.35 Invited to accept that the source for the information about the gas chambers was a document sent to London by Riegner of the Geneva office of the World Jewish Congress in August 1942, Irving responded that British intelligence had been making claims about cyanide gas chambers before that document arrived. He did, however, accept that the message from Geneva was authentic. In any event, said Irving, it was clear from associated Foreign Office memoranda that the credibility of the claim in Regnier's message was doubted. Irving added that it has in any event been established that the person who Regnier claimed was the source of the information did not exist or at least was not a credible source. But the principal basis upon which Irving sought to justify his claim that the gas chambers were a mendacious invention by British propaganda was that about one year later, a senior Foreign Office official named Cavendish-Bentinck, commented on a report of Poles being put to death in gas chambers that he did not believe that there is any evidence that this was being done. Despite that, according to Irving British Intelligence put out through the BBC from late 1941 stories about the liquidation of Jews in the gas chambers. Irving was unable to produce transcripts of the broadcasts. He referred to diary entries by Mann and Ringelblum but agreed that he was unable to make the link between those entries referring to BBC broadcasts and British Intelligence.

8.36 Irving persisted in his claim that the gas chambers were a lie invented by British propaganda , 'if the word "invent" means anything at all'.

ix. Justification: The Allegation that Irving is an Anti-Semite and a Racist

Relevance of the allegation

9.1 No allegation of racism or of anti-semitism is levelled against Irving by Lipstadt in *Denying the Holocaust*. Nonetheless the Defendants maintained that they were entitled to adduce evidence in support of such allegations against Irving because, if true, they support the case that Irving has been guilty of deliberately falsifying the historical record for racist reasons of his own. The Defendants pose the question: what more would an anti-semite want to do than to manipulate and distort history in order to exculpate Hitler, the arch anti-semite? what more would an anti-semite want to do than to deny the existence of the Holocaust in which countless Jews perished. The Defendants, whilst not accepting that it is necessary for their plea of justification to succeed, attempt to make good the claim that Irving's alleged racism and anti-semitism (which is one aspect of racism) provide a motive for his falsification of the historical record.

9.2 Irving did not object to the admission of this body of evidence. Nor did he persist in any argument that it should be ignored.

9.3 The Defendants also accused Irving of misogyny. But that appears to me to have nothing to do with the issues which I have to decide.

The material relied on by the Defendants

9.4 As is clear from section viii. above Irving, in addition to writing history, regularly gives talks and interviews in the UK and elsewhere. For many years Irving has kept a detailed diary. Irving has, with some understandable reluctance, disclosed in this action a large number of diary entries. In this action the Defendants rely on a number of Irving's talks and interviews, as well as upon certain diary entries, as demonstrating by their tone and content that he is an anti-semite and a racist. They define anti-semitism to mean theory, action or practice directed against the Jews and racism as a belief in the superiority of a particular race leading to prejudice and antagonism towards people of other races, especially those in close proximity who might be felt as a threat to one's cultural and racial integrity or economic well-being.

9.5 The extracts relied on by the Defendants in support of their claim that Irving is anti-semitic are as follows (I set them out a greater length that I might otherwise have done, so as to avoid the risk of quoting out of context):

ix. Justification: Allegation Irving is Anti-Semite/Racist

i) Speech at Bayerische Hof, Milton, Ontario, 5 October 1991, (p. 15)

'And gradually the word is getting around Germany. Two years there from now too, the German historians will accept that we're right. They will accept that for fifty years they have believed a lie. And then there will come about a result, not only in Germany but around the world, which I deeply regret and abhor. There will be an immense tidal wave of anti-semitism. It is an inevitable result. And when people point an accusing finger at me and say, 'David Irving you are creating anti-semitism,' I have to say it is not the man who speaks the truth who creates the anti-semitism, it's the man who invented the lie of the legend in the first place.' [Applause]

ii) 'Cover Story' (Australian television) Sunday 4 March 1997, (p. 7)

PRESENTER: At times in your speech to these groups you speak at, you ask if the Jews have ever looked at themselves.

IRVING: Yes.

PRESENTER: To find a reason for the pogroms and the presentation and the extermination. In other words you're asking 'did they bring it on themselves?'

IRVING: Yes.

PRESENTER: Thereby excusing the Germans, the Nazis.

IRVING: Why. . . well, let us ask that simple question, why does it always happen to the Jews?

PRESENTER: But isn't that an ugly, racist sentiment?

IRVING: It is an ugly, of course it's an ugly, racist sentiment, of course it is, you're absolutely right but we can't just say therefore let's not discuss it, therefore let's not open that can of worms in case we find something inside there which we're not going to like looking at.

iii) Oakland, California, 10 September 1996, (pp. 14–15)

'And in Baton Rouge, Louisiana two years ago this half of the audience was entirely made up of Jewish hecklers who had decided to disrupt the meeting, not from outside but to come in, infiltrate the audience and as soon as I began speaking they began barracking and harassing much to the anger of the rest of the audience who wanted to hear what I had to say. And eventually I said to the ringleader, who came from North London, that anecdote, I know why I'm not liked. And I said to him 'you people aren't liked either. But you're not liked on a global scale, on a Millennium scale. You haven't been liked for thousands of years and you don't ask yourselves the question why. Maybe there's no answer, I don't know. You're not just disliked in the way that I'm disliked, that you get bad reviews in newspapers. You're disliked in the way that people put you into concentration camps and line you up at the edge of tank pits and machine gun you into them. You're victims of pogroms and you're harassed and hounded and made to move from country to country to country and you never ask yourselves 'Why us? Is it something we are doing. Is it a perception that people have of us that makes us unpopular?' I don't, I have to say at this point in the meeting that I don't know the answer and I cannot offer you an answer. But there must be some reason and if you want to prevent Holocausts, really this is the question that has to be answered, not just the question of what happened but why it happened. Why one nation can turn on its Jews or on its gypsies or on some other little faction who they can identify as a scapegoat and ruthlessly and inhumanely dispose of them. And there is something of the answer in Dr Goebbels' diaries.'

iv) Interview for 'This Week', 28 November 1991, (pp. 7–8)

INTERVIEWER: When one reads your speeches, one had the impression that Churchill was paid by the Jews, that the Jews dragged Britain into the war, that many of the Communist regimes have been dominated by Jews subsequently, and that a great deal of control over the world is exercised by Jews.

IRVING: Right, these are four separate facts, to each of which I would be willing to put my signature. They are four separate and unrelated facts. When you string them together like that, you might be entitled then to say: 'Question five, David Irving, are you therefore an antisemite?' This may well have been –

INTERVIEWER: No, this wasn't my question.

IRVING: But the answer is this, these are in fact four separate facts which happen to be true, in my considered opinion as a historian. And I think we can find the historical evidence for it.

v) Speech at the Bayerische Hof, Milton, Ontario, 5 October 1991, (p. 17, p. 18, p. 21)

'Or there is a one-man gas chamber. This causes a lot of hilarity, I can't help it, it may sound tasteless, but it is in the eye-witness account which nobody now quotes because of course they don't fit in with the streamline Robert Mitchum War and Remembrance version of Auschwitz. Well, there was the one-man gas chamber where you had the two German soldiers carrying a one man gas chamber around the Polish countryside looking for anybody who had escaped. Now there appear to be hundreds of thousands who've escaped but they were looking for individuals at that time. And all I can say is if I'm a, an Auschwitz inmate who is fortunate enough to have escaped which was undoubtedly a very brutal slave labour camp and I'm standing around in the countryside and suddenly a one-man gas chamber turns up next to me, I'm going to be queasy. I'm going to be a bit uneasy about this. So, how do they get me to step inside? Well, the answer is it's disguised as a telephone box, this one-man gas chamber. . .if I'm a, one man who's escaped from Auschwitz and, a harrowing experience, and I'm standing around in the Polish countryside and suddenly a telephone box appears where there wasn't one a few minutes ago and two German soldiers are standing around looking like nothing, nothing is going to get me inside that phone box. The eye-witnesses say that they got you to get inside by having the phone inside ringing. [Laughter]. Ludicrous. I'm reminded of the old Russian proverb which has recently been quoted again by Julian Barnes in a novel called Talking it Over. The old Russian proverb "He lied like an eye-witness." [Applause]' (pp. 17–18).

'Ridicule alone isn't enough, you've got to be tasteless about it. You've got to say things like more women died on the back seat of Edward Kennedy's car at Chappaquiddick than in the gas chambers at Auschwitz. [Applause] Now you think that's tasteless, what about this? I'm forming an association especially dedicated to all these liars, the ones who try and kid people that they were in these concentration camps, it's called the Auschwitz Survivors, Survivors of the Holocaust and other liars, A-S-S-H-O-L-E-S. Can't get more tasteless than that, but you've got to be tasteless because these people deserve our contempt' (p. 18).

'As he [Michael Milken] went to prison little tears rolled down his cheek and he pleaded not to be sent to prison and his beautiful, coiffured wife was aghast that her husband should be maltreated in this way. Thousands of people have suffered because of Michael Milken. But none of the newspapers dare be too harsh on him because of course his people have suffered so much this century, haven't they? [Laughter]

And that's what it is all about. The big lie is designed not only to distract attention from even bigger crimes than what the Nazis did, the big lie is designed to justify, both in arrears and in advance, the bigger crimes in the financial world and elsewhere that are being committed by the survivors of the Holocaust' (p. 21).

vi) 'The Search for Truth in History – Banned!' 1993, (15, pp. 26–27)

'So Mr Goldman, who is found in a camp somewhere in Bavaria is put aboard a truck with his family and shipped across to the Middle East to Palestine where he is given a new life and a new identity, an Israeli identity, with a Hebrew name. Mr Goldman has vanished and the Hebrew gentleman in the Middle East then starts drawing compensation because Mr Goldman has vanished. This is the irony which a lot of Germans are now beginning to worry about, and it has been going on for now for 50 years and you begin to suspect why the West German government for all these years has made it a criminal offence even to challenge and to question what has been going on. As the Chief Rabbi of Britain, Lord Jacobowitz, said it became 'big business' and it did no credit to the Jews as a whole because I know thousands of Jews, my publisher was a Jew, my Lawyer's a Jew, they are all perfectly ordinary, decent respectable people when you know them and those who you speak to thoroughly abhor what has been going on.'

vii) Speech in Tampa, Florida, 6 October 1995, (p. 16–19)

'When I get into Australia I know what is going to happen, the media will be there, they will trot out their own homebred survivors. Every town has a survivor. In Florida, I understand that every school now has its visiting survivor, who comes to inflict the nameless horrors on these eight-year-old toddlers, telling them what happened to them at the hands of the Germans. In Australia there are professional survivors, a woman called Mrs Altman who will roll up her sleeve and show the tattoo to prove that, yes, she was in Auschwitz. Of course already we sceptics have caused problems because when I spoke in Cincinnati, my host, his wife, she was a school teacher and she said you know

Mr Irving we've got a bit of a problem because we now have to teach the Holocaust – the same as you do in Florida – it is part of the school curriculum. You have to teach the Holocaust and last week we had a Holocaust survivor who came and lectured to the children, she was an old woman and she lectured to these eight year old children in my class and several other teachers came along to listen and one of the eight year old children, a girl piped up at the end of the lecture and said 'How did you survive then? How did you survive?' Out of the mouths of babes and sucklings come these questions and this woman, this survivor said, 'I managed to make a hole in the back of the gas chamber and escape'. [Laughing] And my friend said 'we teachers, we looked at each other and we didn't dare say anything. But the trouble is that the children believed it'. This is the basic problem. And that's how it's going to be with Mrs Altman. I was saying Mrs Altman, you have your tattoo this is an interesting thing to show everyone, but we have a basic problem here, you are a survivor. I used to think that the world was full of a thousand survivors. I was wrong. It is full of hundreds of thousands of survivors of the Holocaust if not, in fact, millions by now. The numbers of survivors seems to grow these passing years, it defies all laws of natural deceased and all laws, now the number of survivors is growing. And I said isn't the existence of so many survivors in itself an indicator, something doesn't, it doesn't fit. If the Nazis had this dedicated programme to exterminate the Jews, how come so many of you have survived, were the Nazis sloppy or what? They let you out, they let you escape?' It's a basic question. And she'll get very indignant and talk about her honour and her integrity and how she suffered and I'll say 'Mrs Altman, you have suffered undoubtedly, and I'm sure that life in a Nazi concentration camp, where you say you were, and I'm prepared to accept that, we have no reason to disbelieve you, was probably not very nice.' And life in Dresden probably wasn't very nice, and probably life in Pforzheim wasn't very nice. 'But tell me one thing', and this is why I'm going to get tasteless with her, because you've got to get tasteless, 'Mrs Altman, how much money have you made out of that tattoo since 1945? [Laughter] How much money have you coined for that bit of ink on your arm, which may indeed be real tattooed ink? And I'll say this, 'half a million dollars, three quarters of a million for you alone.' It must be in that order of magnitude because think of the billions of dollars that have been sent that way, billions. You American taxpayers are happily, indeed joyously, giving to the State of Israel 3 billion dollars a year, if not 4 by now. The German government is adding another 1 billion dollars a year in compensation. $5 billion go to be spent on people like Mrs Altman with their tattoo. Divide that up amongst all the survivors and it's a very sizeable annual income that they are getting. And I'll say – I'm in front of the television, 'Mrs Altman there must be a million Australians sitting there thinking to themselves 'why is it that they have got all the compensation and yet our troops who suffered in the Japanese camps and building the Burma railway and the people who died in the air raids cities and the rest of it didn't get one bent nickel by way of compensation?' How is it always these people who get compensation and not the others?' She won't have any answer for that I'm sure. And what these people don't understand, by way of conclusion, is that they are generating anti-semitism by their behaviour, and they can't understand it. They wonder where the anti-semitism comes from, and it comes from themselves, from their behaviour. We don't promote anti-semitism, we've got no reason whatsoever to promote anti-semitism. I find the whole Holocaust story utterly boring. It goes on and on and on and they keep on going on about the Holocaust because it's the only interesting thing that's happened to them in the last 3000 years. [Laughter]

We have no reason to promote anti-semitism, it's not in our interest one way or the other, but they are doing it. I don't know why. Whether it's because they want to be the centre of attention or what. To an audience in Louisiana, I spoke in Freeport, Louisiana about 6 months ago, and to my embarrassment half the audience turned out to be with the local Jewish community. They'd come along to cause trouble, the rest was normal, but half the audience was this Jewish community with their Jewish community leaders and they showed their true colours after I had begun to speak. And after they had interrupted and behaved in a thoroughly obnoxious manner, for about half an hour while the rest of the audience grew increasingly impatient with their behaviour. I interrupted the flow of my own lecture, and I said to their ringleader, who I recognized by his accent, which came from a particular suburb of London called Colindale or Cricklewood, we English can tell from their accent, from somebody's what class they are, what family they come from and also what particular suburb of London they come from. I said 'Do you come from Colindale or Cricklewood?' and he said 'Why do you say that?' and I said 'Well I can tell by the way you're shrieking at me, but do you mind if I say this, I am disliked, I know I'm disliked, I know I'm disliked because the Newspapers say I'm disliked. [. . .] And is it the historian's job to be liked? Obviously it isn't.

ix. Justification: Allegation Irving is Anti-Semite/Racist

An historian's job is to find out what happened and why. But I said to this man from Colindale, leader of the Jewish community in Louisiana, I said 'I'm disliked and I know why. I look in the mirror when I shave in the morning and I think 'You're disliked, you could alter it overnight, but you don't, it's your own fault, everything that's happening to you' You were disliked, you people. You have been disliked for 3000 years. You have been disliked so much that you have been hounded from country to country from pogrom to purge, from purge back to pogrom. And yet you never ask yourselves why you are disliked, that's the difference between you and me. It would never occur to you to look in the mirror and say 'why am I disliked, what is it the rest of humanity doesn't like about the Jewish people, to such an extent that they repeatedly put us through the grinder?' And he went berserk, he said, 'are you trying to say that we are responsible for Auschwitz, ourselves?' and I said, 'well the short answer is 'yes'. The short answer I have to say is yes'. I mean he really got my gander up. 'The short answer is yes, but that's the short answer obviously between your question and my answer, yes, there are several intervening stages but that is it. If you had behaved differently over the intervening 3000 years the Germans would have gone about their business and not have found it necessary to go around doing whatever they did to you. Nor would the Russians, nor the Ukrainians, nor the Lithuanians, Estonians, Latvians and all the other countries where you've had a rough time. So why haven't you ever asked yourself that question?' It's an interesting point, but they don't, they go round the other way and they make life unbearable for those who try to analyse whatever happened, whatever it was.'

viii) Speech at the Latvian Hall, Toronto, 8 November 1990, (p. 15)

[Following an exhortation to 'Sink the Auschwitz'] 'I should have warned you that I'm going to be very tasteless this evening, but it gets far more tasteless than this. [Laughter] Why should we be considerate about people who have lied to hundreds of millions of people for forty five years?'

ix) Speech at the Latvian Hall, Toronto, 8 November 1990, (pp. 17–18)

Suddenly a lot of people aren't claiming to be Auschwitz survivors any more. Elie Wiesel, for one, for example, he has always been uncertain whether it was Auschwitz he had been in, or Dachau, or Buchenwald. [Laughter]

Well, I say that, because there's a photograph, a photograph, in which he identifies himself as being a prisoner in a photograph of various prisoners in a bunk-house in a barracks in the concentration camp in Buchenwald, and he said, 'Yes, that's me'. But it turns out that photograph was in Auschwitz and he says, 'Ohh, yes, I meant Auschwitz.' I mean, what can we do about these people? And poor Mr Wiesel, I mean, it's terribly bad luck to be called 'Weasel' but that's no excuse [Laughter] I mean, these people do have a bad time, they had a very, very hard time and I do want to speak a few words of sympathy for them, like, I mean, like on Halloween's Night, for example, or say Saint Weisenthal's Night, as we call it in London. So they have had a very, very bad time and it's going to get tougher now that people are going to challenge them as to whether they really were in Auschwitz or not, because we now know exactly who was and who wasn't. And they have gone to immense troubles, ladies and gentlemen, even the ones who've got tattoo marks on their arms. Because the experts could look at the tattoo and say, 'Ohh, yes, One Hundred and Eighty One Thousand, Two Hundred and Nineteen, that means you entered Auschwitz in March 1943.' So, if you want to go and have a tattoo put on your arm, which a lot of them do, I'm afraid to say, and claim subsequently that you were in Auschwitz, you've go to make sure, 'A' that it fits in with the month you said you went to Auschwitz, and 'B' that it's not a number that anybody's used before. So there are actual, kind of, trainspotter guides of numbers that have been used already. And the whole of that hoax is now going to collapse because the Russians have released the index cards.'

x) Speech at the Bayerische Hof, Milton, Ontario, 5 October 1991, (p. 17)

'There's an arrest warrant because when I was in Austria I was tasteless enough to say, that to my mind as an historian and as a neutral observer, these eyewitness accounts are an interesting subject matter for psychiatry to have a look at. And I mean that seriously. People have to explain why people genuinely believe they experienced or had seen something years after the event simply when there's money involved and they can get a good compensation cash payment out of it.'

xi) 'Wiesenthalers Zap Jap "Crap"', Irving's Action Report, number 9, May 1995, (p. 11), (p. 51)

[A Japanese magazine published an article on the Holocaust under the title 'The Greatest Taboo of Postwar History: There Were No Nazi Gas Chambers'. Irving described that the magazine was ordered to close by the Japanese government when] 'the international Jewish community wagged its bejewelled finger'.

xii) Speech at Bow Town Hall, London, 29 May 1992, (p. 16)

'. . . and I never used to believe in the existence of an International Jewish Conspiracy and I am not even sure even now if there is an International Jewish Conspiracy all I know is that people are conspiring internationally against me, and they do turn out mostly to be [unintelligible]. [Applause].'

xiii) 'Will John Demjanjuk now Sue his Tormentors?', Irving's Action Report, number 9, May 1995, p. 10 (p. 50)

[On the acquittal of John Demjanjuk in June 1993] 'The world will not easily forget how . . . [he] was detained in custody by his enemies for two more weeks while they thumbed through their sweaty manuals looking for some way to crush him that they might have overlooked; nor how when they failed again, these Shylocks, cheated of their prey, frogmarched him to his plane home to freedom, still in handcuffs – like a convicted criminal.'

xiv) Videocassette 210, 'David Irving: "Ich komme wieder", ca. 1994', 26m 56s-26m 81s

[After the loss of his contract with the Sunday Times to serialize the Goebbels diaries he described a demonstration against him involving] 'The whole rabble, all the scum of humanity stand outside. The homosexuals, the gypsies, the lesbians, the Jews, the criminals, the communists, the left-wing extremists, the whole commune stands there and has to be held back behind steel barricades for two days.'

xv) Diary entry, 23 March 1996, (p. 54)

'I was toying with the idea of blaming the Publishers Weekly piece on Mad Jew Disease, but this might go too far. These people have no sense of humour whatsoever, these people. The slightest drop of rain falls on their butterfly-wings and they crumple into tears.'

xvi) 'Gold Rush! Diary', Irving's Action Report, number 11, 18 December 1996, p. 2 (p. 56)

'But we cannot help marvelling at the skill with which the world's media have trod the delicate path – reporting at length on these claims without seeming simultaneously to confirm every antisemite's distorted view of 'the Jews' as people who swiftly amass huge fortunes while residing in the countries of their choice and then furtively squirrel away their ill-gotten fortunes in secret numbered bank accounts in far-away countries to avoid taxation and the other lawful burdens imposed on their host peoples.'

xvii) 'Going for Gold: Opinion', Action Report, number 12, 15 August 1997, p. 2, (p. 57)

'What is remarkable is that this community have considered it worth taking such a long term risk [with their claims against Swiss banks], possibly even sowing the seeds of future Holocausts in the name of a short term gain in Gold: all the elements of antisemitic stereotype are there. The cosmopolitan, rootless, millionaire bereft of any local patriotism; flinging his (in popular perception, ill-gotten) gains out ahead as he escapes from the country where he has briefly rested; the demand for 'unclaimed' Gold regardless of whose it is – whether wedding-rings eased off the lifeless fingers of Hamburg or Dresden air raid casualties for identification purposes, and stored by the bucket-full in the Reichsbank vaults. . ., or dental fillings ripped out of the bodies of gas chamber victims by S.S. dentists somehow immune to the Zyklon fumes which had dispatched the others.'

xviii) 'A Radical's Diary', Action Report, number 14, July 1998, p. 3, (p. 61)

[A friend eating dinner with Irving explains that the] 'real estate deals he is doing at the expense of heavily mortgaged property owners. (Ouch.) I comment, "Sounds like you're out-jewing the Jews." He laughs, and agrees.'

xix) 'A Radical's Diary', Action Report, number 15, 20 July 1999, p. 20, (p. 65)

[Writing on a visit by a female friend who tells Irving about her partner, Irving wrote] '. . . who earns million-dollar bonuses each year as a broker, but, she laments, he does not have much time for her; she just gets talk about money. He squanders it like water, flies her everywhere first class, etc. (By this time I have guessed that he's Jewish.)'

xx) Diary entry, 10 June 1963, (p. 1)

'Arrived at office of Rubenstein-Nash. After delay, shown into office of Mr. Michael Rubenstein. Thick skinned these Jews are! Didn't bat an eyelid as he read out excerpts from my Carnival editorial, the "National Press owned by the Jews" the "Jews hating other races claiming to be the master race . . ."'

xxi) 'Revelations from the Goebbels Diaries' (JHR for Jan/Feb 1995), (p. 7)

[Writing about Dr. Berhard Weiss, the Berlin Deputy Police Chief, Irving wrote that he] '. . . looked so much like a Jewish caricature that his photographs didn't need to be re-touched by the Nazis. He was stereotypically Semitic in feature: short, with rounded ears and hook nose, and wearing spectacles.

In London I located Weiss' daughter, Hilda Baban-Weiss, and pleaded with her for a more attractive photo of her father, pointing out that the ones I have are not very flattering. I got total silence from the daughter, so I abandoned my quest. Unfortunately, when my biography of Dr. Goebbels comes out we're going to have to use these rather unattractive pictures.'

xxii) 'A Radical's Diary', Action Report, number 9, May 1995, p. 6, (p. 49)

[Commenting on a supposed 'Jewish-communist assault' on the Dresden cemetery and memorial to the occasion of the anniversary of the allied air raids. Irving dismissed suggestions that it might have been the work of right-wingers trying to blacken 'their opponents' because] 'framing your opponents is a trick used exclusively by our traditional enemy . . .'. 'I doubt they do it on central instructions. Actions like these seem to be embedded into their biological microchip before birth.'

xxiii) Clarendon Club speech, 19 September 1992, (pp. 3–4)

[After hiring him to help serialize the Goebbels' diaries, Irving claimed that Andrew Neil told him that he had never] 'come under such immense pressure from You Know Whom; from our traditional enemies' [including] 'the self-appointed, ugly, greasy, perverted representatives of that community in Britain'.

xxiv) Speech at the Bayerische Hof, Milton, Ontario, 5 October 1991, (p. 27)

'They [a British television company] telephoned me two days ago in Winnipeg to say "Mr Irving, we've been told by the British Minister of the Interior, the Home Office that they are going to ban Fred Leuchter setting foot in Britain at the request of the British Board of Deputies of Jews. And this is the way they work, they refuse to allow debate. They scurry and hide furtively, they're like the cockroaches who you don't see normally by light of day. They hide, they fear the truth, it bedazzles them, it blinds them, they can't stand that [unintelligible]. [Applause].'

xxv) Speech in Christchurch, New Zealand, 26 March 1986, (pp. 14–15)

'And I think, and I may be considered extremist for saying this, I think the Madagascar Solution would probably have been the most peaceful for the present world. The Jews would have been on an island about the size of Germany with a very temperate climate, interesting agriculture possibilities, far more suitable, I would have thought, than the desert they were finally settled in. And above all, like Australia, like New Zealand, like England, they would have had no neighbours, nobody who they could feel intimidated by and, of course, nobody who they in turn could intimidate. What a more peaceful place the world would be today of all days.'

xxvi) Speech in Tampa Florida, 6 October 1995, (p. 11)

'You know we have heard repeatedly how the eyewitnesses come forward like Elie Wiesel and say, Eli Weasel I don't know where they get these names from – every time they come up against you, these traditional enemies of the truth, they have a name like "Weasel" or in England the Director of the Board of Directors of British Jews, his name is Mark Whine, W H I N E or in New York it is something called "*Weasel Keir*" which means a nasty animal and I don't know. . . I think if my name was "Weasel Keir" I think I would change it two or three times, in case anybody asked me what my previous name was before I changed it. [Laughter].'

xxvii) Clarendon Club speech at Bow Town Hall, 29 May 1992, (p. 17)

I got back in Toronto at half past two on this November morning, and as I drove up [uninintelligible] Street in Toronto, which is the main artery of Toronto, I pulled up at the traffic lights and glaring at me from the car next to me in the traffic lights was Simon Wiesenthal himself, his face hideously contorted by rage. I got a real shock because he looked into me through my driver's window and there was Mr Wiesenthal, this hideous, leering, evil face glaring at me, then I realized it wasn't Simon Wiesenthal, it was a Halloween mask. [Applause]. Now those of you who have seen Mr Wiesenthal will know what I'm talking about. Mrs Wiesenthal who has seen Mr Wiesenthal many times of course, and she says to him at Halloween "Simon please keep the mask on, you look so much nicer with it on".'

xxviii) Interview with Errol Morris, 8 November 1998 (pp. 25–27, pp. 33–34)

IRVING: [. . .] But, if somebody says to the Jewish community, 'We think you're a liar,' suddenly the jail doors are swung open and people say 'This way! Come on! You've called them a liar.' And this I think does harm to the Jewish people in the long run, because the non-Jewish people will say, 'What is it about these people?' I am deeply concerned about this, and I've said this to people like Daniel Goldhagen, who I challenged to the debate at a meeting in New Orleans a few months ago. I said, 'You've written a book called 'Hitler's Willing Executioners'. You've talked to us this evening at great length about who pulled the trigger. But the question which would concern me, if I was a Jew, is not who pulled the trigger, but why? Why are we disliked? Is it something we are doing? I'm disliked. David Irving is disliked. I know that, because of the books I write. I could be instantly disliked by writing – I could become instantly liked by writing other books. You people are disliked on a global scale. You have been disliked for 3,000 years and yet you never seem to ask what is at the route of this dislike. You pretend that you're not disliked but you are disliked. No sooner do you arrive as a people in a new country then within 50 years you are already being disliked all over again. Now, what is it? And I don't know the answer to this. Is it built into our micro chip? When a people arrive who call themselves 'The Jews' you will dislike them; is there something in our micro chip? Is it in our micro chip that we don't like the way they look? Is it envy because they are more successful than us? I don't know the answer. But, if I was a Jew I would want to know what the reason is, why I'm being disliked. And not just disliked in a kind of nudge, nudge, wink, wink, he's not very nice kind of sort of way. But we are being disliked on a visceral, gut-wrenching, murderous level, that no sooner do we arrive then we are being massacred, and beaten, and brutalized and imprisoned, until we have to move on somewhere else. What's the reason?' I would want to know the answer to that, and nobody carries out an investigation about that.

INTERVIEWER: What would you say the reason is?

IRVING: Well, I'm just looking at this as an outsider. I come from Mars and I would say they're clever people. I'm a racist. I would say they're a clever race. I would say that as a race they are better at making money than I am. That's a racist remark, of course. But they appear to be better at making money than I am. If I was going to be crude, I would say not only are they better at making money, but they are greedy. I don't care about money. I don't give a hoot about money. As long as I've got enough money to pay the school fees and the grocer's bills, I don't mind. To me, money is not the most important thing. But the perception that the world has of the Jewish people is one of greed, and they contribute to that by their behaviour. They contribute to that, for example, in recent years by their behaviour over the Swiss gold business. It is a curious kind of vague clamour that has begun. We are not quite sure what the clamour is about. Is it about unclaimed bank accounts? Is it about gold that has been transferred from Nazi Germany to Switzerland? Is it about gold teeth and gold rings? Is it about insurance that they can't claim on? But suddenly the clamour is there. Fifty years after the War, an enormous clamour is being beaten up by the New York Jewish community, by Edgar Bronfman, for example, or by the Anti-Defamation League, and here it has to be said that the number of wise Jews – you'll notice I don't include them as the 'wise Jews' – the number of wise Jews, the English Jews, the Swiss Jews, for example, are expressing profound concern about the long term effects of this clamour. They're saying, 'This is just going to nourish the neo-Nazi stereotype of the Jew – grasping, gold hungry, greedy, inconsiderate, vengeful; all these anti-semitic stereotypes that the neo-Nazis have are just being nourished by this latest clamour about the Swiss gold''.'

'Well, they have been dining on Auschwitz. Auschwitz is a big tourist site now. They have millions of visitors every year. It's like Hitler's mountain-top retreat in Berchtesgaden. They have half a million visitors a year there too. They make money out of it. Auschwitz has become a major money-spinner, the Holocaust. I mean, it sounds distasteful to say it, but its true. There's big money in Auschwitz, and for somebody to come along who has a reputation and a legitimacy as a historian and say 'Hold it, fellahs. Make money if you want but you ought to know that it is a bit Disney-like.' The only answer is to shut him up, don't let him anywhere near the place. He's the last person we want here. We are all on to a very nice thing.'

9.6 The quotations which, according to the Defendants demonstrate Irving's racism are these (again I provide the context, where appropriate):

i) Interview for 'Cover Story' (Australian television) 4 March 1997 (pp. 6–7)

INTERVIEWER: Are you a racist?
IRVING: Well, are you using the word racist in a, in a, in a derogatory sense? This is it you see, you want to use the word in a derogatory sense. If we look for a different word, which has the same connotations as racist without the same flavor and say, am I a patriot, yes.
INTERVIEWER: They're not the same word at all.
IRVING: It is exactly the same word. I'm proud of being white and I'm proud of being British.
INTERVIEWER: You went to Britain to be white?
IRVING: Yes.

ii) Diary entry: September 17th 1994 (Saturday)

. . . Jessica is turning into a fine little lady. She sits very upright on an ordinary chair – her strong back muscles a product of our regular walks in my arms to the bank, etc., I am sure. On those walks we sing the Binkety-bankety-bonk Song. There are two other poems in which she stars: My name is Baby Jessica/

I've got a pretty dress-ica / But now it's in a mess-ica. And more scurrilously, when half-breed children are wheeled past:

I am a Baby Aryan
Not Jewish or Sectarian
I have no plans to marry-an
Ape or Rastafarian

Bente is suitably shocked.

iii) Clarendon Club speech, 19 September 1992, (pp. 10–11)

'For the last four weeks just for once I have gone away from London, where I have been sitting, down to Torquay, which is a white community. We saw perhaps one black man and one coloured family in the whole time I was down there. I am not anti-coloured, take it from me; nothing pleases me more than when I arrive at an airport, or a station, or a seaport, and I see a coloured family there – the black father, the black wife and the black children . . . When I see these families arriving at the airport I am happy (and when I see them leaving at London airport I am happy. [Cheers and Laughter]. But if there is one thing that gets up my nose, I must admit, it is this – the way. . .the thing is when I am down in Torquay and I switch on my television and I see one of them reading our news to us. It is our news and they're reading it to me. (If I was a chauvinist I would even say I object even to seeing women reading our news to us.) ['Hear, hear', and Laughter]

Because basically international news is a serious thing and I yearn for the old days of Lord Reith, when the news reader on the BBC, which was the only channel in those times, wore a dinner jacket and bow tie and rose to the occasion [. . .]For the time being, for a transitional period I'd be prepared to accept that the BBC should have a dinner-jacketed gentleman reading the important news to us, following by a lady reading all the less important news, followed by Trevor Macdonald giving us all the latest news about the muggings and the drug busts – [rest lost in loud Laughter and Applause].'

iv) Interview for the Holmes Show (New Zealand television) 4 June 1993, (pp. 3– 4)

Interviewer: . . . you were quoted on, Mr Irving, you were quoted on radio in Australia yesterday saying it makes you queasy seeing black men playing cricket for England. Can you explain to us what you mean by that?

Irving: Well I think probably if you spoke to a lot of English people they'd, they'd find the same thing but not many of them are prepared to say it in public. You see there's so much intimidation in our so-called liberal free democratic society that, that people are forced to live an almost schizophrenic existence. They make statements in public which they consider to be safe but privately at the back of their heads they think differently and I say what I think. And, I'm queasy when I see, now you see I was born in England in 1938 and people will know what I'm saying now, 1938 England was a different country from the way England is now and I'm unhappy to see what we have done to England. We've abdicated, we've committed a kind of international hari kari, we've inflicted great misery on ourselves with coloured immigration and we've inflicted, let's be frank, we've inflicted misery on the coloured immigrants as well. It's a kind of 20th century slave trade. I don't like it and I'm queasy about it and I'm frank enough to say it and no-one's going to prevent me from speaking my mind about it.'

v) Focal Point, 8 March 1982, (p. 7)

[Setting out a speech he would have made at the Oxford Union had he not been prevented by a 'campaign of slanders and smear'] '. . . the compulsory repatriation of Blacks from this country is never likely to command an over-whelming majority of votes. True, as both public polls and our postbag show, British citizens as a whole are in favour, but they will hesitate to vote for any policy which may attract the opprobrium of the rest of the world, or drag Britain's name in the mud. Why not therefore adopt a Benevolent Repatriation policy [. . .] if the introduction of a compulsory repatriation programme is likely to meet with delay, then let us start first with a Benevolent Repatriation scheme as outlined in FP, Dec. 20. The one does not preclude the other.'

vi) Speech at Bow Town Hall, 29 May 1992, (p. 3)

'. . . and the journalist has said "Mr Irving, we read in today's newspapers that you told the ABC radio that you feel queasy about the immigration disaster that's happened to Britain. Is that your opinion?" And I said "well yes, I have to admit to being born in England in 1938, which was a totally different England, I feel queasy when I look and see what has happened to our country and nobody has stood up and objected to it" and he says "well what do you think about black people on the Australian, on the British cricket team then? How do you feel about that then, the black cricketers?" So I said "that makes me even more queasy . . ." and so he says "right", and I say "no, hang on, it makes me feel queasy but I would like to think we've got white cricketers who are as good as the black ones" and he couldn't climb out of that you see. And then he says "so what you're advocating then is a kind of race hatred." So I said "before I answer your questions, would you tell me what you believe in, as a journalist, an Australian journalist. Do you believe in mixing up all god's races into one super, kind of mixed up race. Are you in favour of racial inter-marriage and racial mixing and he said 'well I believe in multiculturalism', of course that's the buzzword, it will come here sooner or later.'

vii) Diary entry, 10 November, 1987 (p. 19)

'God works in mysterious ways, but here, we agree, he appears to be working [unreadable word] towards a Final Solution, which may cruelly wipe out not only Blacks and homosexuals but a large part of the drug addicts and sexually promiscuous and indiscriminate heterosexual population as well . . . "The only weapon against AIDS," I suggest, "is an aspirin: clenched firmly between the knees at all times." '

viii) From Mr Irving's web-site: From a speech to the Clarendon Club, 1990 'We Have Lost Our Sense of Destiny' – David Irving

'. . . THUS WE FOLLOW this tangled thread. At the end of the war, in 1945, the British empire was at its greatest ever extent in history. Our armies straddled the globe. We were beginning to get back the territories we had lost in the Far East through Churchill's foolish military and naval strategy. And suddenly the empire went. Groping around in the darkness, we look for the Guilty Men.

Partly I think we must blame sins of omission. If we look back from where Britain is now, with just a handful of people of true English, Irish, Scots and Welsh stock – apprehensive, furtively meeting in dinners like this, exchanging our own shared sensations and sorrows – then we can see where some of the worst errors have been made. In 1958, for example we find Lord Hailsham saying at a Cabinet meeting: "I don't think this Coloured Immigration is going to be much of a problem in Britain. We only have 100,000 of these immigrants so far, and I don't think the numbers are likely to grow much beyond that! So on chance I am against having any restrictions imposed." Traitor No. 1 to the British cause. (I should like to think there is somebody, somewhere, doing what Gilbert and Sullivan would have had the Mikado do: which is, making up a "little list" of names of people . . .) Even if we all pull together, jointly and severally for the next ten, twenty or thirty years, and manage to put the clock back, say, half an hour of its time, the really Guilty People will have passed on, commemorated only by the bronze plaques and the statues and the memorials scattered around our capital. We can go around and efface those monuments; but it is going to be a damn sight harder to put Britain back where it was. I don't think Mrs. Thatcher or her like are going to be the people to do it. Even less do I think the Socialist Party are going to be the people to do it. Nothing makes me shudder more than two or three months, working on a new manuscript, and I arrive back at Heathrow Airport – where of course, my passport is checked by a Pakistani immigration officer (Laughter). Isn't that a humiliation for us English? (Applause) – and I go outside the Terminal building and there is the Evening Standard placard saying "Kinnock in Fresh Wedgwood Benn Row". This I think is about the lowest point in one's human emotions: "Kinnock in Fresh Wedgwood Benn Row." Britain's destiny, in the hands of people whose minds are so small that they could pass effortlessly through the eye of a needle. (Applause).'

9.7 The Defendants allege that in the extracts quoted at paragraph 9.5 above Irving variously blames the Jews for the existence of anti-semitism; seeks to pin the responsibility for their misfortunes (including the Holocaust) on the Jews themselves; mocks the Holocaust survivors and accuses them of seeking to make money out of their experiences and the tattoos on their arms; characterizes Jews individually and generically in offensive and insulting terms; portray Jews as greedy, conspiratorial and 'traditional enemies of the truth'. Evans regarded Irving's claim of the existence of an international Jewish conspiracy to be a central element of one of the most extreme forms of anti-semitism.

Irving's denial that he is anti-semitic or a racist

9.8 Irving firmly denied the charge that he is an anti-semite or a racist, adding that the Court should in any case concentrate on his historical writings rather than on his speeches and entries in his private diary. Irving pointed out that he has disclosed millions of words from his diaries to the Defendants, who have made tendentious and unrepresentative use of them in order to vilify him as anti-semitic and racist.

Anti-semitism

9.9 In regard to his attitude towards Jews, Irving asserted that there is no reason why the Jews should be immune from criticism, but that is not to be equated with anti-semitism. It is not anti-semitic to make a statement hostile to Jews if the statement is justified.

9.10 In the course of the trial I acceded to a request by Irving to listen to a video, about one hour in length, of a speech delivered by him fluently and without notes to an audience in Tampa, Florida in October 1995. (The text of part of that speech is set out at (vii) in paragraph 9.5 above).The purpose, as I understood, was that in that speech Irving deployed his argument as to the reason for the existence of anti-semitism. He said that, if the argument is properly understood, it demonstrates that he is not anti-semitic. I hope I do not over-simplify the argument if I summarize it in this way: Jews have been hated for 3000 years. They are hated wherever they go. Instead of pointing the finger at those who are anti-semtic, they should ask themselves why they are anti-semitic; why do they persistently attract an anti-semitic reaction. The answer is that they provoke the anti-semitism by their own actions. Irving cited examples, including claims for huge compensation from the Germans for the Holocaust and dishonesty on the part of Jewish financiers. The Jews have brought the anti-semitism on themselves by their own conduct and attitudes. Irving argued that in this speech he was explaining anti-semitism and not justifying it. That was what he claimed he meant when he answered in the affirmative the question asked of him at the meeting in Tampa: 'Are you trying to suggest that [the Jews] are responsible for Auschwitz [themselves]?'

9.11 Irving agreed that he had criticized individual Jews, including on several occasions survivors of the Holocaust or those claiming to be survivors. But, he explained, the criticism was not anti-semitic. Thus the rhetorical question which Irving asked Mrs Altman, the woman with an Auschwitz tattoo on her arm, how much money have you made out of that tattoo since 1945, was indeed a criticism of Mrs Altman but there was nothing anti-semitic about it.

9.12 When asked by Mr Rampton in cross-examination what was the origin of the anecdote included in his speech in Milton, Ontario 1991 about the portable telephone box supposedly used to gas Jewish escapees from Auschwitz, Irving replied that it derived from an account by an Auschwitz survivor. He was, however, unable to recall who the witness was or when he heard about it. He accepted that the claim that the Jews were lured to enter the box by the telephone bell ringing was an 'embellishment'. Irving explained that he wanted to capture the attention of his audience. He justified his use of this 'ludicrous' story by saying that it illustrates the problem with eye-witness evidence about the death camps, namely that such witnesses convince themselves of the truth of manifestly incredible events. He was unable to explain why the audience found the story so funny. He repudiated the suggestion that he was feeding the anti-semitism of his audience instead of discussing the eye-witness evidence as a serious historian would do. Irving argued that he was not talking about Jews in that part of his speech.

9.13 Irving defended his comment in the same speech that more people died in the back seat of Edward Kennedy's car at Chappaquiddick than died in the gas chambers at Auschwitz. He claimed that in his speech he had in fact referred to the gas chambers of Auschwitz 'which are shown to the tourists', that is, the gas chambers which were reconstructed after the war. He claimed he always added those words. Irving explained that the applause from the audience had drowned those last words of the sentence. But, when the video was played, it was apparent, as Irving had to accept, that he had not added the words 'which are shown to the tourists'. Irving had to accept also that he has on other occasions, for example at Moers in Germany in 1990, claimed that the extermination camps not only at Auschwitz but also elsewhere are 'dummies'.

9.14 Irving agreed that on occasion he has been provoked into making insulting remarks about Jews. His remark, set out at (xiv) in paragraph 9.5 above, in which he made reference to the sum of humanities including homosexuals, gypsies, homosexuals and Jews, was made in circumstances of extreme pressure when his home was being besieged by rioters who, according to Irving, included members of all those groups. He was describing, literally, those whom he could see on the other side of the barricades. Similarly his adverse characterization of Simon Wiesenthal was not because he is a Jew but because he is ugly.

9.15 Irving explained that the object of his reference to the 'Association of spurious survivors of Auschwitz' was to mock the so-called eye-witnesses who tell lies about what happened to them. His reference to their needing psychiatric treatment while admittedly tasteless was of drawing attention to the problem that these witnesses are deluding themselves about their experiences. Irving claimed that the reference was greeted by renewed applause from the audience because he is a good speaker and not because the audience was composed of like minded anti-semites and neo-Nazis.

9.16 Irving denied he adopts or promotes a stereotype of the ugly, greedy Jew. Rather he employs that stereotype to explore how it came into existence and to give a warning to Jews against taking actions that may reinforce it. When asked about his statement, that the perception the world has of the Jewish people is one of greed to which they contribute by their behaviour, Irving replied that he was investigating the reasons why people become anti-semitic. He was just putting himself into the skin of an anti-semite. Irving defended his derogatory references to the physical appearance and names of a number of Jews as making fun of them.

9.17 As I have already recorded in section iii. above, Irving believes that self-appointed leaders of the Jewish community are persecuting him by suppressing his freedom of speech and seeking to abrogate his right to travel around the world. They are amongst 'the traditional enemies of the truth'. That being so, Irving argued that he has every right to criticize them for doing so without attracting the label of anti-semitism. Irving defends his reference to members of the Board of Deputies of British Jews as 'cockroaches' because he regards them as being responsible for an attempt to destroy his professional career and family by persuading his American publisher not to publish his books. When challenged to produce his evidence for that accusation, Irving produced the minute of a meeting (which post-dated his reference to 'cockroaches') in which the representatives of the Board who were present agreed not to take any action.

Racism

9.18 Denying the accusation that he is a racist, Irving said that he has in the past employed several members of the ethnic minorities. He produced photographs to prove it.

9.19 Irving explained that the ditty which he composed for his daughter, set out at (ii) in paragraph 9.6 above was his angry response to an article which had appeared in a magazine, which had put a sneering and offensive caption beneath a photograph of himself and his daughter. It was not intended to be racist. He said the same of the entry in his diary which refers to God moving in a mysterious way towards a Final Solution wiping all the blacks, homosexuals and others in Africa through an AIDS epidemic, which is at (vii) in paragraph 9.6 above. Irving explained that he is a religious man and was musing about the strange way in which God works. He was not approving the spread of AIDS.

9.20 Irving stated that he does condemn as traitors those politicians who condoned the immigration into this country on a large scale of black people in the 1950s and 60s. He admits to chauvinism. He was joking when he told members of the Clarendon Club that he was glad to see coloured families arrive at London airport and glad to see them go. This was part of a standard speech which he gives for debating purposes. He denies that he is anti-coloured or a racist. He argued that it was not racist for him to say that it got up his nose to see 'one of them' reading the news on television or to suggest that black news-readers should be confined to the less important news about muggings and drug busts. (The extract is set out at (iii) in paragraph 9.6 above). He hankers after the days when the BBC news was read by a man wearing a dinner jacket.

9.21 Irving defended his comment that he felt 'queasy' about black people playing sports for England as an expression of his 'patriotic' private thoughts on the topic. When he said that it was 'humiliating' to have his passport checked by a Pakistani, he was not making a racist remark. What he meant was that an Englishman would be better at controlling immigration than someone born out of this country. Irving's comments are at (iv) and (viii) in paragraph 9.6 above.

x. Justification: The Claim that Irving Associates with Right-Wing Extremists

Introductory

10.1 It is common knowledge that there exist within this country, as well as in Europe, the United States and elsewhere, a variety of right-wing groups and organizations. Of course some stand further to the right in the political spectrum than others. The groups themselves differ in their structure: some are formally constituted and readily identifiable; others are loose-knit and hard to pin down. By virtue of their policies and chosen political methods, including on occasion the use of violence, some of these groups may be characterized as right-wing extremists.

10.2 The same is true of the individuals who make up these groups and organizations. Some are neo-Nazis, dedicated to overthrowing by violent means democratic systems of government and replacing them with the machinery of nationalist totalitarianism. Others are less extreme: they may themselves be non-violent and oppose the stirring up of violence by rabble-rousing public speeches and demonstrations.

The political objectives of some of these individuals may be limited to the adoption of right-wing policies on such issues as immigration, housing and social policy within the framework of existing democratic structures. Others subscribe to doctrines of racial supremacy, ethnic purification and national expansion and policies which advance the allocation of resources on racial lines.

10.3 The question is whether and, if so, to what extent Irving associates or has associated himself with such groups and individuals. The question arises for two reasons. The first is that Lipstadt in *Denying the Holocaust* links Irving to various extremist organizations (though the Defendants do not, as I have already noted, seek to justify the existence of the links mentioned by Lipstadt). The second reason is that, according to the Defendants, the existence of an association between Irving and right-wing extremist groups or individuals supports their case that the reason for his falsification of the historical record is that he is himself a right-wing ideologue.

Case for the Defendants

10.4 The case for the Defendants is that Irving has regular and close relationships with right-wing extremists in various parts of the world. In support of this case they rely on the expert evidence of Funke and upon the written evidence of Ms Rebecca Guttman as to Irving's alleged relationship with an extremist American organization.

10.5 In his report and in his oral evidence Funke gave evidence of Irving's alleged association with right-wing extremists and neo-Nazis in Germany. He explained how right-wing extremism emerged in Germany. There were, he asserted, three stages: the first was in the late 1940s and resulted in the ban of the Socialist Reich Party ('SRP') in 1952. The second was in the late 1960s and centred on the German National Democratic Party ('NPD') and, after its 1969 election defeat, on Dr Gerhard Frey's German People's Union ('DVU'). The third started in the late 1980s and has involved the DVU and various groups of militant neo-Nazi activists. Amongst the latter he cited in particular the *Nationale Offensive* or National Offensive ('NO'), the *Nationale Liste* or National List ('NL') and the *Althans Vertriebsbewege und Offentlichkeitsarbeit* ('AVO').

10.6 Basing himself on a painstaking study of Irving's diaries, video and audio material and reports from the Office for the Protection of the Constitution, ('OPC'), Funke described the association which he alleged existed between various extremists in Germany. He gave an account how in 1993 Irving came to be banned from entering Germany following action being taken against him at the instigation of the OPC.

10.7 But the Defendants ultimately rested their case for saying that Irving associates with right-wing extremists upon a limited number of groups and individuals which they identified. According to the Defendants, they share the characteristic that they promote Holocaust denial, anti-semitism and racism. Some of them engage in or advocate the use of violence. I shall list them, summarizing in each case where, according to the Defendants, they stand in the political spectrum and what is the nature of Irving's alleged association with them.

10.8 Gerhard Frey/ DVU:

Frey is the leader of the DVU and, it is alleged, a leading right-wing extremist who plays down the crimes of the Nazi period. He helped to organize the meeting at Passau for the DVU on 16 February 1991. He can be seen in a video made by Irving of a meeting at Passau. Irving has corresponded with Frey and spoken regularly at DVU meetings. Frey has also offered Irving advice on the contents of his speeches.

10.9 Gunther Deckert/NPD:

Deckert joined the NPD in 1966. The NPD is a right-wing party which is alleged to have become more radical under Deckert's leadership. He became deputy chairman and head of its youth wing in the 1970s. Deckert has been convicted of incitement to racial hatred and defamation of the memory of the dead. The Defendants claim that the NPD have organized many of Irving's speeches in Germany.

10.10 Ewald Althans:

Althans has had connections with many groups on the extreme right. In particular he was the organizer of the AVO from 1986 until its closure in 1992. The AVO has a programme which is anti-semitic. It has also been associated with revisionists such as Zundel and has contacts with neo-Nazis. Althans has been convicted of incitement to racial hatred and defaming the memory of the dead. According to Funke, Althans was much inluenced by Remer. He can be seen in the video of a meeting at Munich on 21 April 1990 and in a video of the Leuchter Congress in Munich on 23 March 1991. According to the Defendants, Althans has organized many of Irving's speaking engagements in Germany. He also organized a dinner on the anniversary of Hitler's birthday which Irving attended. The relationship between the two men deteriorated in the early 1990s.

10.11 Karl Philipp:

Philipp was an active member of the NPD in the 1970s and 1980s. He has been fined for incitement of the people and defamation. He has written for a number of neo-Nazi newspapers. He has worked with Ahmed Rami. He can be seen in the video of the meeting at Munich on 21 April 1990, which was attended by Irving. Irving met him in 1989. According to the Defendants, Philip subsequently arranged speaking tours for him. He was involved in the production of Irving's video *Ich Komme Wieder*.

10.12 Christian and Ursula Worch:

The Worchs founded the Akionsfront Nationale Sozialisten ('ANS'). After it was banned, Christian Worch became a member and later one of the leaders of the *Gesinnungsgemeinshaft der neuen Front* ('GdNF'). From 1993 he was deputy chairman of the NL. He has a conviction for contravening the ban on the ANS. He can be seen in videos of a meeting at Hagenau on the 12 November 1989; the meeting at Munich on 21 April 1990; the Leuchter Congress in Munich on 23 March 1991 and the meeting at Halle on 9 November 1991. All these meetings were attended by Irving. According to Funke, he has organized speaking engagements for Irving on behalf of the NL; they have spoken together in public and they correspond regularly. Ursula Worch is active in the same groups as her husband.

10.13 Thies Christophersen:

Christophersen was an *SS-Sonderfuhrer* in a plant nursery near Auschwitz. In 1973 he published *Die Auschwitz-Luge* or The Auschwitz Lie. He has sought the re-legalization of the Nazi party. In 1988 he appeared at the trial of Ernst Zundel in Toronto. In his evidence Funke contended that he was responsible for organizing the meeting at Hagenau on 12 November 1989. At this meeting were Faurisson and Zundel among others.

10.14 Michael Swierczek/National Offensive:

Swierczek has been a member of ANS. In 1990 he founded the NO, which was banned in December 1992. In 1995 he was convicted for attempts to revive the ANS/NA. According to Funke, he is one of the more important functionaries in the militant neo-Nazi scene. He has also been involved with the GdNF. Irving spoke at an NO meeting in 1992 where he was introduced by Worch.

10.15 Wilhelm Staglich:

Staglich was stationed at Auschwitz before 1945. In 1972 he was a member of the NPD. Having been disciplined for his connection with a right-wing extremist newspaper, he retired from his job as a judge in 1975. He published a book *The Auschwitz Myth. Legends and Reality?* In 1987 his doctorate from the University of Gottingen was removed. He has been a member of the Editorial Advisory Committee of the IHR's *Journal of Historical Review*. He has had contacts with Althans and Christophersen. He died in the middle of the 1990s. He can be seen in the videos of the Hagenau meeting on the 12 November 1989, the meeting at Munich on 21 April 1990 and the Leuchter Congress in Munich on 23 March 1991. Irving appeared alongside Staglich at the 5 IHR Conference in September 1983.

10.16 Ahmed Rami:

Rami is a Swede. According to Funke, he is an anti-semite who speaks frequently about the so-called 'Zionist Mafia'. He is alleged to be a close ally of Faurisson. He and Irving both spoke at the Leuchter Congress in Munich in March 1991 and at the 11 IHR Conference in 1992.

10.17 Pedro Varela:

According to Funke, he is a revisionist and neo-Nazi who now lives in Spain. He can be seem in the video of the Leuchter Congress in Munich on 23 March 1991. He organized a speaking tour of Spain for Irving in 1989 and had been in contact with him before that.

10.18 Ernst Zundel:

Zundel is a leading revisionist. His company is alleged to be one of the biggest producers of neo-Nazi and racist material in the world. He is the author of *The Hitler We Loved and Why*. In his evidence Funke described him as a kind of pupil of Remer. He can be seen in the video of the Hagenau meeting on the 12 November 1989. Irving appeared at his first trial in Canada in 1986. Zundel and Irving subsequently corresponded regularly. Irving appeared also at Zundel's second trial in 1988.

10.19 Otto Ernst Remer:

Remer was formerly a Commander of the Berlin Watch Regiment 'Gross Deutschland', which helped to crush the revolt against Hitler on 20 July 1944. He co-founded the SRP which was banned in 1952. In the 1980s he founded the neo-Nazi German Freedom Movement. In the 1990s he was convicted for incitement to racial hatred. Funke alleges that he has extensive contacts with strands of right-wing extremism in Germany and abroad. He can be seen in the video of the meeting at Munich on 21 April 1990. Irving has interviewed Remer and written favourably about him regularly in his *Action Reports*.

10.20 Ingrid Weckert:

Weckert is a leader of the GdNF group 'Action Protection of Life', which uses ecological and biological ideas to promote a form of racial purity for Aryans. Irving has been in contact with her since 1979. She has been convicted for inciting racial hatred.

10.21 Thomas Dienel:

Dienel was the state chairman of the NPD in Thuringen. He helped to organize the rally in Halle on 9 November 1991. He also led the Thuringen neo-Nazi DNP founded in 1992. In 1992 he was convicted of incitement of the people and defaming the memory of the dead. He can be seen in the video of the meeting at Halle on 9 November 1991. He was one of the organizers of that meeting; he spoke on the same platform as Irving and Christian Worch.

10.22 Gottfried Kussel:

Kussel has been a member of the NSDAP/AO since 1977. According to Funke, he is a leading activist in the German and Austrian neo-Nazi scenes. He has been sentenced in Austria for National Socialist activity. In his evidence Funke stated that he has worked closely with Christian and Ursula Worch and with Althans. He has been one of the leading figures in the GdNF. He can be seen in the video of the meeting at Halle on 9 November 1991 which he had helped to organize.

10.23 The Institute of Historical Review ('IHR') (including Mark Weber, Tom Marcellus and Greg Raven):

The IHR was founded in the US in 1979. It is alleged to be an organization which is well-known for its denial of the Holocaust. It organizes annual 'Revisionist' conferences. It produces the *Journal of Historical Review* ('JHR'). Irving first appeared at its conference in 1980 and has subsequently participated in five further conferences. In 1991 Irving is alleged to have organized a meeting between Weber of the IHR and Weckert of the DVU in Germany. Irving's works are promoted in IHR literature. The IHR is involved in arranging some of Irving's speaking tours in the United States.

10.24 National Alliance:

the National Alliance is a large neo-Nazi organization in the US led by William Pierce. It is right-wing, racist and anti-Semitic. In his answers to pre-trial requests by the Defendants for information Irving stated:

I have no association with the body known to the Defendants as the National Alliance as such or whatsoever. I cannot rule out that members of that organization . . . have attended functions at which I spoke. . . . I do not agree that I have spoken at any National Alliance meetings. It might be that on occasions a gentleman who was a member of the National Alliance offered to organize a lecture for me. In other words, he undertook to find a suitable room. But I then circulated 'my' entire local mailing list to provide an audience. No doubt he brought his friends as well . . .

It is the case for the Defendants that those answers are false. They contend that Irving has spoken at three National Alliance meetings, one of which was recorded on video and which shows Irving speaking with an Alliance banner visible on a wall to one side of him. They rely further on Irving's correspondence and diary entries as showing that he received an invitation on headed National Alliance notepaper to speak at a meeting arranged by that organization. One of Irving's diary entries records that the meeting which he was to address that evening was 'also organized by the National Alliance'. The Defendants also produced a National Alliance bulletin which reports one of Irving's talks at a meeting of a branch of the organization. They rely in addition on the recording of the talk he gave in Tampa, Florida in 1996 in which Irving is welcomed by the chairman 'on behalf of the National Alliance'. National Alliance literature, which is on sale at the meetings arranged by the organization, reveals that membership is limited to 'non-Jewish

Whites', who support the goals of the organization which include building a new White world, the advancement of the Aryan race and the restoration of White living space.

10.25 Robert Faurisson:

Faurisson is a former French literature teacher who has argued that Anne Frank's diary is a forgery; that the gas chambers and the genocide of the Jews are lies and that there is a Jewish conspiracy to exploit the Holocaust in order to obtain money for Israel. He gave evidence at the first Zundel trial in 1986. He has been found guilty of distorting history and incitement to racial hatred in France. Faurisson has attended and spoken at IHR conferences; he is a member of the editorial board of its journal. Faurisson can be seen in the video for the Hagenau meeting on the 12 November 1989. Irving has on several occasions spoken on the same platform as Faurisson. He also spoke in 1991 at the Clarendon Club meeting organized by Irving. The two men have corresponded regularly.

Irving's response

10.26 Irving agrees that he did from time to time, prior to being prohibited from entering Germany, address both the NPD and the DVU. They were organizations which were under Germany's strict laws both legal and constitutional; they were not extremist. Irving was critical of what he regards as the repressive laws in place in Germany which have the effect of stifling freedom of expression. Irving said that he had disclosed in the action transcripts of his addresses: there was nothing extremist in what he said. He had not spoken of Holocaust denial or engaged in anti-semitism at any of these meetings. Irving agreed that Deckert of the NPD is a friend with whom he is in regular contact. But there has been nothing extremist or anti-semitic in the correspondence which they have exchanged.

10.27 In regard to the list of alleged extremists compiled by Funke, Irving described them as an 'ugly ragbag of neo-Nazi extremists'. He claimed that most of the names were completely unknown to him. He pointed out that the Defendants and their team of experts and lawyers have spent many man-hours trawling through his diaries and other papers looking for mention of them. For the most part the trawl has been unsuccessful. Irving also mounted the argument that it would not be in the least reprehensible for him to associate with somebody holding extremist views. It would be objectionable to associate with extremists only if they were violent.

10.28 Irving sees this part of the Defendants' plea of justification as an attempt at 'guilt by association', comparable with the worst excesses of the McCarthy era in the US. As an illustration of what he regarded as an attempt by the Defendants to smear him, Irving cited Funke's claim that a man named simply as 'Thomas' in his diary was in fact Thomas Dienel. But Irving said he never learned Thomas's last name and has not, to his knowledge, ever encountered Dienel. In the same way, the Defendants had introduced into the evidence Michael Kuhnen. But, said Irving, he had explicitly said he would not attend any function at which he was present and had never had anything to do with him.

10.29 Of the individuals identified by the Defendants, Irving submitted that 'shorn of their commercial packaging, they do not amount to very much'. Althans was accepted by Irving to be an extremist, although that had not been apparent when they first met. Irving regretted his acqaintance with him. As to Philip, Irving agreed that he is a friend and a revisionist. His position in relation to Zundel was similar: he agreed that he is a revisionist holding right-wing political views but considers him to be a respectable man who is 'free of any conviction'. He holds no brief for Zundel's particular views and 'wild horses would not make him read some of his books'. He described his relationship with Christophersen as 'tenuous'. Irving admitted to an association with Varela and Weckert. Despite the evidence of meetings which they attended together and the correspondence exchanged between them, Irving was reluctant to admit any association between them. As to Staglich, Irving testified that he did not speak to him at the Hagenau dinner to commemorate Hitler's birthday but did have breakfast with him the following morning. Irving denies any association with Rami or Kussel (although he agreed that he has shared a platform with both of them on one occasion). His only contact with Remer (who he accepted is 'an unreconstructed Nazi') was to interview him for a book He had no recollection of Swierczek and categorically denied any association with Dienel.

10.30 Irving acknowledged that he is friendly with both the Worches but not intimately so. It was Ursula Worch who invited him to speak at the rally at Halle. Irving was at pains to refute the Defendants' claim that the video of that meeting revealed him to be associating with well-known extremists in an environment where Nazi slogans, salutes and uniforms were much in evidence. In the first place, asserted Irving, the video has been edited and re-edited so as to make it appear compromizing. In any case he spoke briefly at the meeting, taking no part in the procession beforehand and leaving promptly after he had spoken. He can be seen shaking his head in disapproval at the Nazi slogans. He paid little attention to the others on the platform. There was nothing about Holocaust denial in his speech.

10.31 In relation to the IHR, Irving said that it included elements which are 'cracked anti-semites'. But he said that its officials nearly all held academic qualifications. Irving claimed that he had tried to introduce to the IHR what he called 'mainline historians'. He said he had never been an official of the IHR. He agreed that he has on several occasions spoken at their meetings (though he put it that he had done so no more than 'occasionally'). He spoke on historical events, some of them uncomfortable for his audience. There was nothing extremist in what he said. It was not his decision to include reports of those speeches in the IHR Newsletter. He accepted that he regards the IHR as an ally but claimed that his association with them is minimal.

10.32 Irving claimed that he had no knowledge of the neo-Nazi nature of the National Alliance. He had not seen or read the literature put out by the organization. He had no interest in it. Although his diary records his having 'set up the room' for one of his talks, he had not noticed that the literature of the Association was on sale at the meetings at which he spoke. He asserted that his denial in the pre-trial answers to the Defendants' request for information of any association with the National Alliance was true. He had not noticed the National Alliance banner which can be seen in the video of his talk in Tampa, Florida in 1996. He corresponded with Gliebe (who is a prominent member of the Alliance) because he is a personal friend. The headed National Alliance notepaper used by Gliebe meant nothing to him. The three meetings at which he spoke were not National Alliance meetings. He agreed that an entry in his diary refers to meetings being organized by the National Alliance but claimed that he had not the slightest notion who those people were. He also agreed that his diary makes reference to a Nazi-style introduction at one of the meetings at which he spoke and to Nazi-looking crackpots being present but explained that he had no control over who was present.

xi. Justification: The Bombing of Dresden

Introduction

11.1 As I have already pointed out, *Denying the Holocaust* contains no reference to the bombing of Dresden. As explained in paragraph 4.4 above, the evidence is nevertheless admissible in support of the plea of justification. Before addressing the way in which the Defendants seek to place reliance on this topic, I shall summarize the events in question.

11.2 Early in 1945 Soviet forces were advancing on Germany from the East driving back not only the German military but also a large number of refugees. It was against that background that the Allies embarked on a policy of carrying out bombing raids upon German cities, amongst which the principal targets were Berlin, Leipzig and Dresden. Of these cities Dresden was at that time the least industrialized. It was an historic city in which were contained many of Germany's finest old buildings and cultural treasures. There were industries (including armament factories) there too but the city's main function was as an administrative, transportation and communication centre.

11.3 On two successive nights, 13 and 14 February 1945, British bombers carried out massive bombing raids on Dresden. The ostensible purpose of the raids was to disrupt military industrial production. However, the target of the raids was not the industrial sector but rather the historic centre of the city, consisting for the most part of timbered residential buildings. The consequences of the raids were on any view horrific. The effect on industrial capacity was modest and the disruption of transportation limited. But the damage in terms of loss of life and destruction of property was catastrophic: a very substantial number were killed, consisting almost exclusively of civilian residents and refugees, and some 15 square kilometres of the heart of the city were razed to the ground.

11.4 One of Irving's most widely read books is an account of these events, entitled *Apocalypse 1945: The Destruction of Dresden*, first published in 1963 under the title *The Destruction of Dresden*. He has also made frequent reference to the bombing of Dresden in his speeches (some of which are mentioned in section viii. above).

The Defendants' criticisms of Irving's account of the bombing

11.5 The Defendants rely on Irving's *Dresden* as a further illustration of the manner in which he distorts and twists historical facts in order to make them conform to his own political ideology. In particular the Defendants allege that Irving has relied on forged evidence; that he has attached credence to unreliable evidence; that he has twisted reliable evidence and falsified statistics; that he has suppressed or ignored reliable evidence and that he has misrepresented the facts as they appear from the available evidence. I shall set out the parties' arguments in relation to each of these allegations. But, since one of the major criticisms levelled at Irving by the Defendants relates to his claim as to the number of those killed in the raids, I shall first set out what his claims have been.

Numbers killed – Irving's claims
11.6 The estimates placed by Irving in succeeding editions of *Dresden* and in his speeches on the number of fatalities due to the bombing of Dresden are as follows:

i   in the 1966 edition of *The Destruction of Dresden* Irving contended that 135,000 were estimated authoritatively to have been killed and further contended that the documentation suggested a figure between 100,00 and 250,000;

ii in the 1971 edition the figure for those killed was placed at more than 100,000;

iii in 1989 when launching the 'Leuchter Report' in Britain Irving informed journalists present that between 100,000 and 250,000 were killed;

iv in 1992 Irving told the Institute of Historical Review that 100,000 people were killed in twelve hours by the British and the Americans;

v in 1993 in a video made for the Australian public Irving contended that over 130,000 died;

vi in the 1995 edition of *The Destruction of Dresden* the attack was estimated to have killed 50,000 and 100,000 inhabitants;

vii in 1996 in *Goebbels: The Mastermind of the Third Reich* Irving noted that between 60,000 and 100,000 people had been killed in the raids on Dresden.

11.7 Other such claims made by Irving include the following:

i in a speech in South Africa in 1986 Irving stated that 100,000 people were killed in one night in Dresden;

ii in Ontario in 1991 he told an audience that over 100,000 people were killed in one night in February 1945;

iii in a television documentary screened on 28 November 1991 Irving said that 25,000 people may have been executed in Auschwitz but five times that number were killed in Dresden in one night, and

iv at the launch of the 'Leuchter Report' in 1989 Irving stated that there were 1,000,000 refugees in Dresden of whom 'hundreds of thousands' were killed.

11.8 In his Reply in the present action Irving asserted an intention to prove at trial that estimates of casualties in Dresden have indeed ranged between 35,000 and 250,000. At trial he testified that the best margins for figures which he would accept were between 60,000 and 100,000. Irving contended that earlier estimates had been inflated by the communist government of East Germany (in which Dresden was situated) for essentially political reasons. He denied that he had been responsible for some of the claims made on the dustjacket of the paperback editions of *The Destruction of Dresden*.

The Defendants' claim that Irving relied on forged evidence

The case for the Defendants

11.9 The main plank of the Defendants' case against Irving in relation to his book about Dresden is the way in which he used forged evidence, namely *Tagesbefehl* (Order of the Day) no. 47 ('TB47'). This document was dated 22 March 1945 and attributed to a Colonel Grosse. It purported to quote a brief extract from a statement made earlier by the Police President of Dresden. It put the number of dead at 202,040 and expressed the expectation of a final figure of 250,000. TB47 features in the 1966 and 1967 editions of Irving's book and is reproduced in both as an appendix.

11.10 Irving had previously in 1963 denounced TB47 as spurious and as an ingenious piece of propaganda. In the 1963 edition of *Dresden* Irving had referred to Goebbels having deliberately started a rumour about the death toll in Dresden 'wildly exceeding any figure within the realms of possibility'. He also referred in that edition to the leaking of what he described as a 'spurious' order of 23 March 1945 which gave a figure for deaths of 202,040 and an estimate of more than 250,000 for the final total. TB47 had already been denounced as 'false and fraudulently invented and publicized' in a book by Professor Seydewitz.

11.11 But Irving subsequently changed his mind about the authenticity of TB47 when he was provided with a copy of it. In the 1966 edition of *Dresden* Irving was coy about naming his source. The indirect source was a resident of Dresden named Dr Funfack, who according to Irving had received the document through official channels. Dr Funfack showed the document to a Dresden photographer, Walter Hahn, who made a copy of it. Irving visited Hahn in November 1964 and saw the copy of the so-called TB47 and asked for a copy of that copy. Hahn's wife obliged and typed out a copy for Irving. Walter Lange, the Dresden City archivist was also at the Hahns' that day and he told Irving that the document was a patent forgery. Irving's copy was not authenticated by any official stamp.

11.12 The Defendants contend that, in these circumstances, Irving should not have made any use of TB47 or the figures contained in it. Yet, despite the lack of verification and despite the doubts which he himself expressed about the figures at the time, Irving began to circulate information about TB47, claiming that he was in no doubt as to the authenticity of the document, adding that it remained to be established if the figure for casualties was equally genuine.

11.13 Whatever may have been his reservations about the figure, Irving on 28 November 1964 wrote to his German publisher that the information in TB47 was 'sensational'. On 6 December 1964 he wrote to the Provost of Coventry Cathedral in connection with a forthcoming exhibition enclosing a copy of his copy of TB47:

To drive home the impact of the exhibition I also suggest that you have the text of the Police President's report on the Dresden raids (attached) printed in large type; I think that its nonchalance and the casualties it mentions have a shattering impact . . . I am myself in no doubt as to the authenticity of the document, having obtained it from the Dresden Deputy Chief Medical Officer responsible for disposing of the victims.

11.14 When the German edition of *The Destruction of Dresden* was reviewed in December 1964, Funfack was named in the press as the author of the new casualty figures. This prompted the latter to write to Irving on 16 January 1965 to say that he had not been the Dresden Deputy Chief Medical officer; that he had only ever heard the numbers third hand and that he had not been involved in any official capacity. He also pointed out that he was only given a copy of TB47. In the same letter Funfack told Irving that General Mehnert, the city commander, had spoken of 140,000 deaths and that Professor Fetscher, head of civilian air defence, had spoken of 180,000. Mehnert and Fetscher had both since died but Funfack told Irving that an International Red Cross delegation had visited the city and that the head of that delegation would know best. Funfack suggested that Irving contact the Red Cross. However, the Red Cross informed Irving that, whilst a delegate of theirs named Kleinert had been in the area at the time, no information concerning the numbers killed in the raids had been gathered by him. His reports had not even referred to the air raids.

11.15 Despite Funfack's expressed inability to authenticate TB47, Irving continued to promote TB47 in the German press. Irving had received the letter from Funfack in late January 1965 at the latest. Yet in February 1965 he wrote a draft article for the *Sunday Telegraph* which persisted in the claim that he had received TB47 from Dr Funfack, who Irving continued to describe as Deputy Chief Medical Officer, Dresden District, and as such responsible for the cremation and disposal of the victims.

11.16 On 19 March 1965 Irving wrote to his Italian publishers that his then figure of 135,000 for the death toll was 'probably too low'. He told them that he had obtained copy of an official police report which gave a final figure for the death toll of between 202,040 and 250,000. He asked that, if the Italian edition had not gone to press, this new fact and document be inserted. He added that it was going into the German and East German editions.

11.17 The Defendants contend that the use made by Irving of the purported TB47, as described at paragraphs 11.13, 15 and 16 was unconscionable. The Defendants contend that, in the light of Funfack's denials, it was worse than irresponsible for Irving to promote the new figures without revealing Funfack's denials. Irving was making use of a document which he knew might well have been forged. He was well aware that the Nazis themselves had used similar figures and versions of TB47 when promoting the numbers of dead in Dresden to the foreign neutral press and to Germans for domestic propaganda purposes.

11.18 Evans claimed that there were internal reasons why Irving should have been suspicious about the supposed TB47. Apart from the lack of official stamps or signature, the text of TB47 is indicative of a clumsy forgery. It opens with the words 'In order to be able to counter wild rumours' and closes 'As the rumours exceed the reality, open use can be made of the actual figures'. But the rumours themselves never pointed to more than 200,000, so quoting 202,040 could do little to counter the wild rumours. Furthermore, Evans noted that comparable raids on other German cities had led to casualties representing between 1% and 3.3% of their populations. In Dresden 250,000 dead would have meant 20–30% of the population. How, asked Evans, would it have been possible to have removed 200,000 bodies within a month.

Moreover the claim in TB47 that 68,650 were incinerated in the *Altmarkt* defies belief, according to Evans, since it would have taken weeks and many gallons of gasoline to burn so many corpses in the available space.

11.19 In February 1965 Theo Miller, who had been a member of the Dresden clearing staff in 1945, wrote two letters to Irving in which he gave a detailed account of the system whereby commanders of the rescue units reported the number of corpses found and the numbers were entered in a book kept by him. He continued:

Soon after the attack we heard in (sic) the radio Joseph Goebbels reporting on the attack on Dresden. He spoke of 300,000 deads (sic). In your book you mention the figure of 135,000. My records at the Clearing Staff showed 30,000 corpses. If you assume that amount of deads (sic) completely burnt etc would reach 20%, the total figure of victims will not exceed 36,000. Still this figure – two full divisions – is terrible enough'.

Miller's second letter went into even greater detail and reiterated the figure of 30,000 which he said that he remembered well.

11.20 The Defendants say that this was apparently credible evidence from a witness who on the face of it was ideally placed to know the true facts. They contend that no conscientious seeker after the truth could honestly have ignored this evidence. Irving never mentioned Miller or his testimony.

11.21 Irving went on 10 July 1965 to interview the widow of Colonel Grosse, the purported author of TB47. She showed some letters her husband had written in 1945. Irving later claimed that their style and expression resembled that of TB47 (which was typewritten). He did not, however, spell out what the similarities were. Subsequently Irving claimed that Frau Grosse remembered her husband saying that the final toll of the dead would be 250,000. In the 1966 Corgi edition of his book Irving wrote that she had said that her husband spoke of the final total as having been 250,000.

11.22 The 1966 Corgi edition of *Dresden* continued to rely on TB47 and the doument was quoted in an appendix. Irving included in this the claim that Kleiner, the leader of the Red Cross delegation, had been informed in the presence of witnesses by Mehnert that the death toll was 140,000. In the 1995 edition Irving went further and claimed that the report of the representative of the Red Cross might well have contained other information than about the number of prisoners among the casualties. Whilst it is true that Funfack had told Irving of Mehnert's figure of 140,000 (which figure Mehnert had stressed was not based on any documents he had seen), there is, according to Evans, no evidence that the figure of 140,000 was ever supplied to the Red Cross. The Defendants contend that no honest-minded objective historian would rely on a story told to him at third hand by a source (Funfack) who himself had no reliable evidence on the number killed. Moreover the Red Cross had no connection with the figure given by Mehnert. The Defendants allege that the reference to the Red Cross in the 1966 edition was designed by Irving to give spurious credibility to what Mehnert is claimed to have said about the number of deaths.

11.23 In 1965 the document on which TB47 was based surfaced. It was the Final Report issued by the Dresden police on 15 March 1945. It bore the initials of a Dresden police officer named Jurk, whose daughter-in-law gave it to an historian named Weidauer. It was signed by Thierig, who had been a colonel in the Dresden police force at the material time. It recorded the number of deaths up to 10 March 1945 as 18,375.

11.24 In May 1966 another document came to light which confirmed the authenticity of the Final report. It was a Situation Report No 1404 of the Berlin Chief of Police dated 22 March 1945 (the same day as TB47). It recorded the same data as the Final Report, giving the current death toll as 18,375 and predicting a final toll of 25,000. Another Situation Report No. 1414 also made by the Berlin Chief of Police and dated 3 April 1945 put the figure for the number of killed recovered persons at 22,096. Evans argued that, in the light of these documents, Irving should have abandoned all reliance on TB47. He noted that Irving affected to take the matter seriously and announced his intention to publicize the new evidence. Evans claimed that when Irving did finally reveal the existence of the 'Final Report', through *The Times* and *Sunday Telegraph* in June and July 1966, it was too little and too late.

11.25 Moreover Irving began publicly to cast doubt on the veracity of statistics in the Final Report, suggesting that the circumstances in which the data contained in it was collected meant that the final figures could not be relied upon. Evans made the point that, if the ability to count 18,375 in the 'Final Report' could not be relied upon, as Irving contends, how then could the figure of 202,040 in TB47 be trusted. When asked in the summer of 1966 by his Italian publishers if he wanted the text of his letter to *The Times* reproduced in the forthcoming new Italian edition, Irving replied that he did not and added 'despite what I wrote to *The Times* I do no think that too much importance can be attached to the figures given in the new German document'.

11.26 Despite Irving's professed intention to publicize the 'Final Report', the figure given for the number of dead in the 1967 Corgi edition of *The Destruction of Dresden* was revised from 135,000 down to 100,000 but no lower. The German edition of the same year gave the same prominence to TB47 as it had enjoyed in the 1966 Corgi edition and gave 135,000 as the 'most probable' figure. The 1977 edition of *Hitler's War* made the following reference to the raid: 'The night's death toll in Dresden was estimated at a quarter of a million'. The Defendants maintain that, on the evidence which had then become available including the discrediting of TB47, no honest historian would have put forward a figure for the death toll in excess of 35,000.

11.27 The Defendants contend that in 1977 TB47 was conclusively proved to have been a forgery. The historian Bergander obtained a copy of the original of TB47 from a reservist, Werner Ehlich, who had had the original document in his hands and, in his capacity as a member of the Dresden police force, had made one typed and one hand-written copy of it. Ehlich's copy of TB47 put the total number of deaths at 20,204 and the expected dead at 25,000. Evans surmized that the fake TB47 came into existence when someone doctored the genuine document by adding a 'o' at the end of each number. Evans expressed the opinion that the version of TB47 on which Irving had relied for so long was beyond question a forgery.

11.28 But Irving continued, perversely and unforgivably say the Defendants, to make claims for a higher number of casualties. For instance in *Goering* Irving claimed that the death toll would rise to 100,000. At the press conference held in June 1989 to introduce the Leuchter report, he said that anything between 100,000 and 250,000 had been killed. In an interview with *This Week* on 28 November 1991 Irving referred to 25,000 having been killed at Auschwitz, adding that 'we killed five times that number in Dresden in one night'. Other speeches in Canada and in the US in 1991 and 1992 included similar claims. The 1995 edition of *Destruction of Dresden* gave a figure of between 50,000 and 100,000.

Irving's case as to the death toll and his use of TB47

11.29 By way of general answer to the criticism of manner in which he has made exaggerated claims as to the number of those killed in the bombing, Irving submits that at all times (a) he has set and published the proper upper and lower limits for the estimates that he gave, giving a range of figures which necessarily decreased over the years as the state of information improved and (b) that he had an adequate basis for the figures which he provided in his works.

11.30 Irving emphasized that he had not been responsible for the claims as to the number of casualties made on the dustjacket of the sub-licensed Corgi edition of *Dresden*. He agreed that in the 1977 and 1991 editions of the book he wrote that the death toll was estimated at a quarter of a million. There were estimates as high as that. One such estimate derived from a West German government publication. Irving referred also to a US Air Force document dated 19 July 1945 which gave an estimate of 250,000 for the number of casualties in Dresden but had to accept that there was no indication where the informants identified in the document (who were Nazi medical officers) had got their information from.

11.31 Irving accepted that he had been aware that during the war Goebbels had sought to make use for propaganda purposes of the raid on Dresden and that to that end he had put into circulation a forged document giving a figure for deaths of 202,040. He mentioned this in the first edition of Destruction of Dresden published in 1963 as well as in a letter to his publisher in the same year.

11.32 Irving agreed that in 1964 he was provided with a copy of TB47 by Hahn in the circumstances I have described. It was because of its provenance that Irving did not immediately dismiss it as a forgery on the ground that the figures contained in it were the same as those contained in Goebbels's propaganda forgery. When he first saw TB47,

Irving believed that his indirect source for the document, Dr Funfack, had been the Deputy Chief Medical Officer who had been responsible for disposing of the corpses of the victims. He agreed that in January 1965 he received a letter from Dr Funfack in which the doctor denied having been Deputy Chief Medical Officer or having been involved with the disposal of corpses. But Irving testified that he did not believe what Funfack said. He produced a photograph depicting piles of corpses in which he claimed that Funfack can be seen in the background wearing Nazi uniform. The reason, according to Irving, for Funfack's false denial is that he, living in Communist East Germany, was terrified to admit that he had been a senior medical officer in a Nazi city during the war. Irving claimed that he had been informed that Funfack had indeed been Deputy Chief Medical Officer but he did not vouchsafe who provided that information. Irving agreed that he had never revealed the fact that Funfack had denied knowledge of TB47.

11.33 When Irving first saw the figures in TB47, his reaction was that, if true, they were sensational. However, Irving accepted that from the first there was grave doubt about the figures contained it and that there was concern that the figures for deaths (202,000) and expected deaths (250,000) might be forged. Asked about letters he wrote soon after coming into possession of TB47, Irving agreed that he had expressed himself as entirely satisfied as to the authenticity of the document, despite his reservations about the figures for deaths contained in it. He did, however point out that in his letter to Irving of 19 January 1965 Funfack wrote that in February 1945 General Mehnert, City Kommandant of Dresden, had mentioned to him a figure of 140,000 dead and that Professor Fetscher of the Civil Defence Organization had spoken of 180,000 dead. Even so, he agreed that the figures in the purported TB47 called for proper enquiries and for further investigations to be made. Irving duly wrote to the German Federal Archive enquiring about the document and sought information as to the whereabouts of its author, Colonel Grosse.

11.34 In relation to his letter to the Provost of Coventry urging him to display TB47 because of the impact the figure for deaths would achieve, Irving pointed out that TB47 mentions not only casualties but also damage to property. He conceded that the figures had not been substantiated but added that a figure for deaths of 35,000 would have been equally shocking. Irving said that the higher figure of over 200,000 deaths appeared to him to be in line with the number of deaths in Hiroshima and other major air-raid disasters. Irving saw nothing improper in the use of TB47 made in his letter to the Provost.

11.35 Irving claimed to have gone to great lengths to follow up the suggestion made in Funfack's letter to Irving of 16 January 1965 that the Red Cross might be able to provide him with information. He agreed that in the event the Red Cross had been unable to provide any information. He denied that in the 1966 Corgi edition of *Destruction of Dresden* the assertion that Kleiner of the Red Cross had been informed by General Mehnert that the death toll was 140,000 was an invention by him. But he was unable to be specific as to where the information came from.

11.36 Irving acknowledged that in February 1965 he had received a letter from Theo Miller, formerly of the Dresden clearing staff. He conceded that there was no reason to doubt Miller's good faith but claimed (despite the fact that Miller's figure of 30,000 is very close to the figure in the genuine TB47) that he may have been fantasizing. He agreed that he had made no mention of Miller's evidence. But he rejected the suggestion that he had been guilty of applying double standards in placing reliance on third-hand hearsay accounts provided by Funfack and ignoring first-hand evidence from someone directly involved in dealing with the bodies of those killed in the raid. Irving explained that it is part of the skill of an historian to select and reject evidence according to his assessment of its reliability. Irving indignantly denied the suggestion that he had deliberately suppressed the evidence of Miller.

11.37 Irving confirmed that he had tracked down the widow of Colonel Grosse, the author of TB47. He said that Frau Grosse remembered her husband having spoken of a figure of about 202,000 deaths.

11.38 Irving received a copy of Situation Report 1404, which estimated the final death toll at 25,000, in May 1966 (see paragraph 11.24 above). Irving says that he was advised at that time by his London publisher to keep quiet about the new figures. But he emphasized that he promptly made the new figures public in his letter to *The Times*, in which he made clear his acceptance of the fact that the figures in the copy of TB47 on which he had relied had been forged. He circulated 500 copies of his letter. He suggested that this was a highly unusual step for an historian to take. Most historians would wait and publish the new information in their next book. He argued that his conduct demonstrates that he has not sought to obfuscate the true number killed in the bombing. Asked to explain why, having done that, he had written to his Italian publisher that he did not think too much importance should be attached to Situation Report 1404, Irving replied that he had in mind the estimates reportedly made by Mehnert and Fetscher; death tolls in other comparable disasters and the view expressed in letters to him by Dresden civilians that the upper limit was 250,000 deaths. Irving added that the author of the report, being the man in charge of civil defence, had a motive for understating the number of casualties.

11.39 Irving testified that he was unaware of the genuine TB47, discovered by Bergander, until it was put to him in cross-examination. He accepted, however, that the figures contained in it (deaths 20,000, expected ultimate death toll 25,000) are correct since they tally with the report of the Dresden Police Chief and the Situation Report 1404. Despite this concession Irving argued that the true figure for the number of deaths is between 60,000 and 100,000. He maintained that, at the date of TB47 and the two reports, the corpses in the cellars of the city's houses had not been cleared. He agreed, however, that research indicates that only 1,800 bodies were recovered from beneath the ruined buildings in Dresden. Irving suggested that many would have been burnt literally to ashes. He pointed out that the city was at the time crowded with refugees fleeing from the Russians advancing from the east. It is impossible to know how many refugees there were or what has become of them. Irving would not accept the suggestion put to him that the maximum total figure is 35,000.

11.40 When asked why, after authentic reports had come to light all giving figures for deaths in the region of 30,000 he had repeatedly mentioned, on the occasions I have already itemized in paragraph 11.6 and 11.7 above, vastly higher figures, Irving explained that the top bracket was based on many letters he had received over the years. It is, said Irving, a matter of paying your money and taking your choice. As to the reference in *Hitler's War* (1991 edition) to a death toll of a quarter of a million, Irving explained that this was the estimate which had been given to Hitler. The lowest figures became available to him in 1997 when he received the book which Friedrich Reichert had published in 1994. Unfortunately this information was received after the most recent edition of Dresden had gone to press.

The claim that Irving attached credence to unreliable evidence

The case for the Defendants

11.41 This part of the Defendants' case has been largely summarized already in paragraphs 11.9 to 11.40. As examples of the credence given by Irving to unreliable sources, the Defendants cite his reliance on the forged TB 47; his reliance on evidence from unidentified individuals as to the number of deaths (see paragraph 11.38); his speculation about the number of refugees in the city that night (see paragraph 11.39 above); his reliance on the figure given to him by *Frau Grosse* (see paragraph 11.37 above) and his reliance on the figures provided by Mehnert and Fetscher (see paragraph 11.33 above).

11.42 Another instance where Irving is alleged by the Defendants to have given credence to unreliable testimony is the evidence of Hans Voigt. He was the sole source for Irving's claim that 135,000 people died. Voigt worked for the Saxon Ministry of the Interior in a central bureau of missing persons. His job was to collect the records of the dead and of those still buried in the ruins. His department was responsible for arriving at a final estimate of the death toll. Using four different systems for filing different data, Voigt's department was apparently able to identify some 40,000 of the dead. Irving took this figure as the absolute minimum for those killed. He adopted Voigt's estimate of 135,000 for the total number of those killed. This figure was confirmed to Irving by Voigt. According to Irving, Voigt told him that the estimate of 35,000 made by the Russians had been arrived at by striking off the first digit from the figure of 135,000.

11.43 Evans criticized Irving for giving any weight to so unreliable a source. Voigt's estimate is not corroborated by anyone else; nor is it supported by any documentary evidence. There is no corroborative evidence for Voigt's theory that the Russians struck off the first digit from the figure of 135,000. Walter Weidauer, the author of *Inferno Dresden*, disputed Voigt's claim that the death register records between 80,000 and 90,000 deaths. The register is still in Dresden Town Hall. Deaths by reason of the bombing are recorded on numbered cards. The highest card number for an unidentified body was 31,102. This number tallies with the number given in the so-called street books where deaths were recorded by reference to the streets and houses where the dead were found. Evans alleged that no objective historian would rely, still less adopt, the evidence of such a source as Voigt.

Irving's response

11.44 I have summarized Irving's response at paragraphs 11.8 and 11.29 to 40 above.

The allegation that Irving has bent reliable evidence and falsified statistics

The case for the Defendants

11.45 The first example provided by Evans of Irving's alleged falsification of statistics and misuse of figures is his attribution to the Federal Ministry of Statistics of a figure of between 120,000 and 150,000 (and later 500,000) deaths. The source for these figures was Dr Sperling of that Ministry. But in reality Dr Sperling concluded that the most probable figure was 60,000.

11.46 As evidence that Irving bends reliable sources, Evans cited a letter that Irving wrote to *Suddeutsche Zeitung* which claimed that the police chief who wrote the Final Report had a reason to minimize his losses as he was charged with air-raid protection.

Irving's response

11.47 In relation to Sperling's estimate of the number of those killed, Irving pointed out that Sperling had given the figures of 120,000 and 150,000 in a letter which he produced. Irving explained that Sperling's 'best estimate' of 60,000 was arrived at because he wanted to play down the figures. Irving adhered to his suggestion that the police chief was likely, by virtue of his office, to have minimized the number of casualties.

The allegation that Irving suppressed or failed to take account of reliable evidence

The case for the defendants

11.48 The Defendants rely on the suppression by Irving of the evidence of Miller, which is referred to at paragraph 11.36 above. It was, say the Defendants, perverse and unwarranted for Irving to have preferred the uncorroborated hearsay evidence of Mehnert to the credible, first-hand testimony of Miller.

11.49 The Defendants also criticize Irving for his treatment of the two reports which are referred to in paragraph 11.23 and 24 above. Irving made clear on several occasions at the time when he received copies of these reports that he regarded them 'with extreme caution' and that he remained 'a little suspicious' of the new figures. He told his Italian publishers not to attach too much importance to them. According to the Defendants, there was no justification whatever for such caution in the face of the hard evidence of the two reports.

11.50 Thirdly, the Defendants allege that Irving is perverse when he sticks to his estimate of 60,000 to 100,000 when Reichert (definitively, according to Evans) fixes the figure at 25,000 (see paragraph 11.40 above)

Irving's response

11.51 The only explanation offered by Irving for his disregard of the testimony of Miller was that he had been fantasizing. It was, however, not made clear by Irving on what evidence he based this assertion.

11.52 Irving gave as his reasons for being cautious about the two reports that the figure given in them conflicted with the figures quoted by Mehnert and Fetscher; these conflicted also with the figures for those killed in comparable disasters in other cities and with estimates given by Dresden civilians. The Chief of Police had every reason to minimize the figure.

11.53 I have already spelled out at paragraphs 1.39 and 40 the reasons given by Irving for his adherence to figures greater than Reichert's 25,000.

The allegation that Irving has misrepresented evidence

The case for the Defendants

11.54 The prime instance cited by the Defendants is the persistent misrepresentation by Irving of the evidence (referred to above) as to the number of those killed in the bombing of Dresden. They rely also on his misrepresentation of the evidence of Dr Sperling as to the number killed (see paragraph 11.45 above). Finally they rely on what the Defendants assert to be not merely misrepresentation of the evidence but an invention on the part of Irving, namely his claim that the figures of 140,000 and 180,000 had been supplied at the time to Kleinert of the Red Cross (see paragraph 11.39 above).

Irving's response

11.55 I have already summarized Irving' answers to these criticisms (see in particular paragraphs 11.56 and 11.45.

xii. Justification: Irving's Conduct in Relation to the Goebbels Diaries in the Moscow Archive

Introduction

12.1 In 1992 Irving was told by Elke Frohlich, the widow of Professor Broszat, who edited fragments of the diaries of Goebbels, of the existence in Moscow of the long lost diaries themselves. They were, she said, in the form of microfiches recorded on hundreds of glass plates. She suggested to Irving that he might be able to buy the plates, since they were not listed on the archive inventories. She advised Irving to raise the necessary money. She gave him the name of the director of the archive. Irving approached him at the end of May 1992.

12.2 On 26 May 1992 Irving contacted the *Sunday Times*, whose editor at that time was Andrew Neil, with a view to making an agreement about the diaries. Neil expressed serious misgivings about their authenticity. (He had good reason for his caution, since the *Sunday Times* had recently had the misfortune to publish Hitler's diaries which turned out to be forgeries). Neil, however, agreed to provide the finance needed for a preliminary visit to Moscow by Irving. He travelled there on 6 June 1992. He was introduced by a *Sunday Times* journalist based in Moscow, Peter Millar, to Vladimir Taraso, the Head of the Department of International Contacts at Rosarchiv. Irving, having inspected the diaries, was satisfied of their genuineness. On his return to London, Irving entered into an agreement with the *Sunday Times* whereby the newspaper would pay him £75,000 in return for his translation of parts of the diaries. Irving returned to Moscow on 28 June 1992 and remained there working on the diaries until 4 July. The diaries were stored on 1,600 glass plates, each glass plate holding about 45 pages of diary.

12.3 In *Denying the Holocaust*, Lipstadt wrote in a footnote:

The Russian archives granted Irving permission to copy two microfiche plates, each of which held about forty-five pages of the diaries. Irving immediately violated his agreement, took many plates, transported them abroad, and had them copied without archival permission. There is serious concern in archival circles that he may have significantly damaged the plates when he did so, rendering them of limited use to subsequent researchers.

Irving complains that in that passage Lipstadt accused him of violating an agreement with the Russian archives in that he took and copied many plates without permission causing significant damage them and rendering them of limited use to subsequent researchers. Readers would infer that he is a person unfit to be allowed access to archival collections.

The claim that Irving broke an agreement with the Moscow archive and risked damage to the glass plates

The allegation as formulated in the Defendants' statements of case

12.4 In their original statement of case the Defendants alleged no more than that there were grounds to suspect that Irving had removed certain microfiches of Goebbels' diaries from the Moscow archive without permission. Subsequently, in their *Summary of Case*, the Defendants revised their case to allege that Irving broke an agreement he had made with the Moscow archive by (without permission) removing from the archive glass plates on which the diaries were recorded; having copies made of those plates and transporting two plates to London, where they were subjected to forensic tests. The Defendants allege that Irving's conduct gave rise to a significant risk that the plates might have been damaged, rendering them of limited use to subsequent researchers. They maintain that Irving's conduct was unbecoming of a reputable historian.

12.5 In the outline of their Statement of Case the Defendants alleged that, in the course of his first visit to Moscow on the 10 and/or 11 June, Irving, acting without permission and without the knowledge of Tarasov (or any other Rosarchiv official) took three glass microfiche plates, including what he considered to be two of the most important plates, and gave them to Peter Millar so that they could be passed to the *Sunday Times* Moscow photographer to make enlarged prints. The Defendants allege that Irving had prints made and then had the plates forensically tested in London. The tests were completed by 2 July 1992, at which time the plates were returned to Moscow by another journalist. The tests which had been carried out in England risked damaging the fragile plates, according to the Defendants.

12.6 The Defendants alleged further that on 19 June 1992 Irving had requested permission from Tarasov to take plates out of the archive for a short period in order to carry out tests. Tarasov gave permission for two plates to be taken out of the archive. According to the Defendants' case, he was unaware that any plates had been removed earlier. When he returned to the Moscow archive in late June, Irving took more glass plates and gave them to the *Sunday Times* photographer to make prints.

12.7 The gravamen of the case stated by the Defendants is that Irving abused the trust placed in him by Tarasov and violated his agreement with him. They allege also that, by covertly removing the glass plates and handing them over to a journalist for testing to be carried out abroad, Irving was guilty of a further serious breach of trust which gave rise to a significant risk that the plates might suffer damage.

The evidence relied on by the Defendants for the allegation of breach of an agreement

12.8 Although the Defendants had served written statements accompanied by notices under the Civil Evidence Act, in the result they called no evidence on this part of their plea of justification. They relied on the evidence given by and on behalf of Irving to establish their case.

12.9 In relation to the first issue, namely whether Irving violated an agreement with the Moscow archive, the Defendants' case, elicited from Irving and Millar in cross-examination, can be summarized as follows: Irving was keen to gain access to the diaries because (apart from the money and the kudos) he wanted the material for his biography of Goebbels. It is clear from his diary that on his first visit to Moscow Tarasov, on behalf of the archive, gave him access to the material, to read it and perhaps to copy some pages.

12.10 Irving's diary entry for the following day, 10 June 1992, records that he 'illicitly borrowed the fiche we had found covering the weeks before the war broke out and took it out of the archives at lunch for copying'. Irving recorded that he tucked the envelope with the glass plates into a hiding place before re-entering the archive. At the end of the afternoon, Irving took them to the *Sunday Times* photographer, who printed copies to be shown to Neil in London. The plates were returned to the archive the following morning. The Defendants allege that this amounted to a breach of the agreement Irving had made with Tarasov.

12.11 On 11 June 1992, again according to Irving's diary, he removed by the same means two further plates from the archive. These plates were taken by Irving to Munich where they were left in a safe (whilst Irving travelled to Rome). On his return he took them to London, where they were tested at Pilkington's laboratories. They were taken back to Moscow by a *Sunday Times* journalist on 2 July 1992 and replaced in the archive on the following day. This, according to the Defendants, constituted a further breach of agreement. Irving conceded that an historian would normally require the agreement of an archive before removing material. Irving had no such agreement. The most that Tarasov had originally agreed was that Irving could read the plates and perhaps copy them. On the second visit Tarasov agreed that Irving might remove two plates but that was in order to copy them. Millar, the *Sunday Times* journalist who accompanied Irving, acknowledged in evidence that Irving knew that he should not be taking the plates out of the archive and expressed his disapproval to Irving because doing so might jeopardize the chances of continuing access to the plates. Irving agreed that had not obtained permission to take the plates back to England.

The evidence relied on by the Defendants for the risk of damage to the plates

12.12 The risk of damage arose, according to the Defendants, in three ways. Firstly, when during Irving's first visit the plates were removed from the archive, there was risk to the plates when they were left in a hiding place. According to the evidence, the plates were left on waste ground for the whole afternoon. There was a risk of someone taking them or of damage if it rained.

12.13 The plates were exposed to further risk by reason of their being handled and, on the second visit, by their being taken via Munich to London and back. Even allowing that Irving took great care of them the plates were at one time or another in the hands of three *Sunday Times* employees.

12.14 The third way in which the plates were put at significant risk arose out of the testing of the plates in London. A small fragment was cut off one plate. Irving was not on hand when the testing was carried out and so was not in a position to ensure that the plates came to no harm.

Irving's case that there was no breach of agreement

12.15 According to Irving, the glass plates on which the diaries were recorded had been neglected by the Russians. They were in bad condition. Material from the archive was being sold by the Russians. Irving's major concern was to gain access to the diaries before the Germans. If the Germans were to gain access first, Irving was concerned that the diaries would vanish for a considerable period.

12.16 Irving stressed (and Millar confirmed) that there was no agreement with the Russians. On 9 June 1992 Millar spoke to Tarasov, who telephoned the curator of the archive, Bondarev and told him to permit Irving to have access to the plates and to work on them. The arrangement was a verbal one. Millar testified that there was no restriction on access.

12.17 On the first occasion when plates were removed from the archive, Irving agreed that he did not seek permission to do so. He did not tell the Russians what he was intending to do. His concern was to copy the plates before the archive was 'sealed', that is, before he lost access to the plates by reason of some action by his German competitors. Irving gave evidence that he had felt that the situation required desperate remedies. He agreed in cross-examination that he acted 'illicitly' and felt ashamed about his conduct. Millar disapproved of what he was doing because he (Millar) feared that future access to the diaries might be jeopardized. But there were no means of copying the diaries in the archive. Irving acknowledged that it could have been understood that the plates should not be taken out of the archive. But he felt he was providing a valuable service in making sure that the contents of the diaries would be available to historians. He disagreed that there was any breach of agreement on his part. It was 'neither here nor there' to the archivist if he removed the plates.

12.18 On the second occasion when he removed plates from the archive, Irving did so in order to have the plates tested, as his contract with the *Sunday Times* required him to do. On this occasion he did seek and obtain permission from the Russians to remove the plates. But he did not tell them of his intention to take them out of the country for testing. Again Irving accepted in cross-examination that he had acted 'illicitly'. But he said that he assumed he had permission to 'borrow' the plates. Irving denied any breach of agreement.

Irving's denial that the plates were put at risk of damage

12.19 In relation to the first occasion on which he removed plates from the archive, Irving testified that he took them out of the archive at lunchtime. He said that the plates were carefully packaged in plastic and cardboard. He hid them during the afternoon on waste ground about 100 yards from the Institute. Apart from that, there was no risk of damage to the plates. The plates were returned the next morning, after they had been copied.

12.20 On the second occasion when plates were removed, Irving denied that at any stage there was any risk of damage to them. At all times when the plates were *en route* they were safely packed. He took them to Munich, where he left them in a safe whilst he travelled to Rome and back. Irving claimed that they were safer there than they had been in the archive. He then took them to England. The testing did not involve any risk of damage. The plates were returned to the archive after three weeks.

xiii. Findings on Justification

Scheme of this section of the judgment

13.1 The charges levelled at Irving's historiography appear to me to lie at the heart of what Lipstadt wrote about him in *Denying the Holocaust*. I propose therefore to consider first whether the Defendants have made good their claim that, in what he has written and said about the Third Reich, Irving has falsified and misrepresented the historical evidence.

13.2 There are several aspects to this. The falsification and misrepresentation alleged by the Defendants relate to (a) the specific individual criticisms of Irving's historiography which are addressed in section v. above; (b) his portrayal of Hitler, which is dealt with at section vi.; (c) his claims in relation to Auschwitz covered in section vii. and, finally, (d) the bombing of Dresden which is dealt with in section xi.

13.3 The question which I shall have to decide is whether the Defendants have discharged the burden of establishing the substantial truth of their claim that Irving has falsified the historical record. In this connection I should repeat the caveat expressed at the beginning of this judgment: the issue with which I am concerned is Irving's treatment of the available evidence. It is no part of my function to attempt to make findings as to what actually happened during the Nazi regime. The distinction may be a fine one but it is important to bear it in mind.

13.4 If the charge of misrepresentation and falsification of the historical evidence is substantially made out, there remains the question whether it was deliberate. Irving rightly stresses that the Defendants have accused him of deliberately perverting the evidence. For their part the Defendants recognize that it is incumbent on them to establish, according to the appropriate standard of proof, that the misrepresentation and falsification were motivated by Irving's ideological beliefs or prejudices. In this context, I shall consider the submission made by Irving that he has been guilty, at worst, of making errors in his handling of the historical record. As I will explain in assess Irving's motivation, I will also take into account the evidence of the public statements by Irving in which he allegedly denied the Holocaust; the evidence upon the basis of which the Defendants accuse him of anti-semitism and racism and the evidence of his alleged association with right-wing extremists.

13.5 That leaves the questions which arise out of Irving's visits to the Moscow archive in 1992 to inspect the Goebbels's diaries, namely whether he broke an agreement with the Russians by removing glass plates from the archive and whether he put the plates at risk of damage.

13.6 Finally, depending on my decisions on the issues to which I have already referred, it may be necessary to consider the relevance, if any, to my finding on the defence of justification of the imputations in *Denying the Holocaust* which the Defendants have either failed or not sought to justify. I shall also determine, if the need arises, whether the Defendants are entitled to pray in aid the provision of section 5 of the Defamation Act.

The allegation that Irving has falsified and misrepresented the historical evidence

Irving the historian

13.7 My assessment is that, as a military historian, Irving has much to commend him. For his works of military history Irving has undertaken thorough and painstaking research into the archives. He has discovered and disclosed to historians and others many documents which, but for his efforts, might have remained unnoticed for years. It was plain from the way in which he conducted his case and dealt with a sustained and penetrating cross-examination that his knowledge of World War II is unparalleled. His mastery of the detail of the historical documents is remarkable. He is beyond question able and intelligent. He was invariably quick to spot the significance of documents which he had not previously seen. Moreover he writes his military history in a clear and vivid style. I accept the favourable assessment by Professor Watt and Sir John Keegan of the calibre of Irving's military history (mentioned in paragraph 3.4 above) and reject as too sweeping the negative assessment of Evans (quoted in paragraph 3.5).

13.8 But the questions to which this action has given rise do not relate to the quality of Irving's military history but rather to the manner in which he has written about the attitude adopted by Hitler towards the Jews and in particular his responsibility for the fate which befell them under the Nazi regime.

The specific historiographical criticisms of Irving

13.9 As appears from section v above, the Defendants have selected nineteen instances where they contend that Irving has in one way or another distorted the evidence. Having considered the arguments, which I have summarized at some length, I have come to the conclusion that the criticisms advanced by the Defendants are almost invariably well-founded. For whatever reason (and I shall consider later the question of Irving's motivation), I am satisfied that in most of the instances cited by the Defendants Irving has significantly misrepresented what the evidence, objectively examined, reveals.

13.10 Whilst it is by no means a conclusive consideration, it is right that I should bear in mind that the criticisms which the Defendants make of Irving's historiography are supported by the evidence of historians of the greatest distinction. They are set out (along with many other similar criticisms that the Defendants have not pressed in the submissions made in these proceedings) in the meticulous written report of Evans, who is himself an historian of high standing. In the course of his prolonged cross-examination, Evans justified each and every one of the criticisms on which the Defendants have chosen to rely. In several instances his criticisms were supported by the Defendants' other experts, van Pelt, Browning and Longerich. I am satisfied that each of them is outstanding in his field. I take note of the fact that the expert witnesses who were summoned by Irving to give evidence on his behalf did not in their evidence dispute the validity of the points made by Evans; nor did they seek to support or justify Irving's portrayal of Hitler.

13.11 Whilst I take account of the standing of the witnesses who have spoken to the criticisms of Irving as an historian, I must arrive at my own assessment of the evidence relating to the nineteen instances relied on by the Defendants. In doing so, I have well in mind that many of the documents which I will need to analyse were chosen by Irving himself because they demonstrate, according to him, that Hitler was a friend of the Jews. Having set out the arguments at length in section v above, I am able to express my conclusions more succinctly than would otherwise have been the case. Whilst I will not attempt to address every argument that has been mounted, I will indicate in each case the reasons why I have concluded that Irving has misrepresented the evidence.

Hitler's trial in 1924 (paragraphs 5.17–28 above)

13.12 I am satisfied that in *Goering* and to a lesser extent in *Hitler's War*, Irving misrepresents Hitler's role in the *putsch*. The evidence does not support the claim that Hitler was seeking to maintain order. Irving embroiders the incident when the ex-Army lieutenant is disciplined in such a way as to present Hitler as having behaved responsibly. But the evidence of Hitler's role in the *putsch* suggests otherwise. Irving ought to have appreciated that Hofmann's allegiance to Hitler rendered his testimony untrustworthy.

Crime statistics for Berlin in 1932 (paragraphs 5.29–36 above)

13.13 In my judgment it is a valid criticism of Irving that he chose to cite, without qualification, the claim made by Daluege, a committed Nazi, that in 1930 a strikingly large proportion of the offences of fraud were committed by Jews. Daluege's enthusiastic membership of the Nazi party together with his activities on the Eastern front during the war should have led Irving to doubt any pronouncement of his affecting the Jews. Whilst I am sympathetic to Irving's handicap in being unable now to obtain access to documents in the German archives, I am not persuaded that there exist documents which justify Irving in quoting without any reservation the claim made by Daluege.

The events of Kristallnacht (paragraphs 5.37–72 above)

13.14 It was, I believe, common ground between the parties that Kristallnacht marked a vital stage in the evolution of the Nazis' attitude towards and treatment of the Jews. It was the first occasion on which there was mass destruction of Jewish property and wholesale violence directed at Jews across the whole of Germany. As an historian of the Nazi regime, it was therefore important for Irving to analyse with care the evidence how that violence came about and what role was played by Hitler.

13.15 Readers of the account in *Goebbels* of the events of 9 and 10 November 1938 were given by Irving to understand that Hitler bore no responsibility for the starting of the pogrom and that, once he learned of it, he reacted angrily and thereafter intervened to call a halt to the violence. I accept the evidence of Evans and Longerich that this picture seriously misrepresents the available contemporaneous evidence.

13.16 Irving's endeavour to cast sole blame for the pogrom onto Goebbels is at odds with the documentary evidence. Goebbels' diary entry for 9 November, the telegram sent by Muller at 23.55 that night and the message despatched by Bohmcker all suggest that Hitler knew and approved of the anti-Jewish demonstrations. Given the significance of the events of Kristallnacht, an objective historian would in my view dismiss the notion that Hitler was kept in ignorance until a relatively late stage. Yet Irving pays little attention to the evidence which implicates Hitler. He gives a misleading and partial account of Goebbels' diary entry. I cannot accept Irving's explanation for his omission to refer to Muller's telegram and Bohmcker's message, namely that they add little, for both lend support to the thesis that Hitler knew and approved of the violence. Irving also omits to refer to the statement contained in the report of the internal party enquiry into the events of Kristallnacht that Goebbels had claimed in his speech at the Old Town Hall that Hitler had been told of the burning of Jewish shops and synagogues and had decided that such spontaneous actions should continue.

13.17 Irving's account of Hitler's reaction upon hearing (for the first time, according to Irving) of the violence is heavily dependent on what Irving was told by Hitler's adjutants many years after the event. Whilst Irving is to be commended for his diligence in tracing and interviewing these witnesses, there is in my judgment force in the Defendants' contention that Irving is unduly uncritical in his use of their evidence especially when it runs counter to the evidence of contemporaneous documents. I do not suggest that Irving should have discounted altogether the evidence he obtained from Bruckner, Schaub, von Below, Hederich and Futkammer. But in my view he ought to have approached their accounts with considerable scepticism and rejected them where they conflict with the evidence of the contemporaneous documents both before and after 1am on 10 November. That documentary evidence is, as Irving should have appreciated, inconsistent with the notion that Hitler was angry when he first heard of the destruction of Jewish property which was in progress. To write, as Irving did, that Hitler was 'totally unaware of what Goebbels had done' is in my view to pervert the evidence.

13.18 In my judgment the account given by Irving of the interventions by Nazi leaders during the night of 9/10 November distorts the evidence. Irving's interpretation at p. 276 of *Goebbels* and in his evidence in these proceedings of the telex sent by Heydrich at 1.20am on 10 November is misconceived. The terms of the telex demonstrate, in my view, that Heydrich was not seeking to protect Jewish property but rather was authorizing the continuation of the destruction save in certain narrowly defined circumstances. Similarly I accept the evidence of Evans that the telex sent by Hess at 2.56am on 10 November (which, it is agreed, emanated from Hitler) was not a general instruction to 'halt the madness' but rather to stop acts of arson against Jewish shops and the like, so permitting other acts of destruction to continue and Jewish homes and synagogues to be set on fire. Furthermore Irving should at the very least have doubted the claim by Wiedemann that Goebbels spent much of the night making telephone calls to stop the most violent excesses. The claim that during that night Hitler did everything he could to prevent violence against the Jews and their property is in my judgment based upon misrepresentation, misconstruction and omission of the documentary evidence.

The aftermath of Kristallnacht (paragraphs 5.73–89 above)

13.19 Notwithstanding Irving's argument, I am unable to detect any evidence that Goebbels felt apprehensive when he went to see Hitler on the morning of 10 November. It is in my judgment inconsistent with the evidence of what Hitler had ordered in the course of the previous night. Goebbels' diary entry about his meeting with Hitler at the Osteria is clear evidence of Hitler's approval of the pogrom. Irving very properly quotes the entry but immediately follows the quotation with the categorical assertion that Goebbels was making a false claim in his diary about Hitler's approval. I do not accept that the available evidence justifies Irving's dismissal of this diary entry by Goebbels.

13.20 I accept the evidence given by Evans that Irving's account of the investigation into the events of Kristallnacht and such disciplinary action as was taken thereafter fails lamentably to reveal to his readers how much of a whitewash it was. I have summarized in paragraphs 5.79 and 5.80 above the evidence of the cursory investigation and the derisorily inadequate disciplinary action taken. Irving, in Goebbels, ignores these deficiencies.

The expulsion of Jews from Berlin in 1941 (paragraphs 5.90–110 above)

13.21 The Defendants advance two criticisms of Irving's treatment of Himmler's note of his conversation with Heydrich on 30 November 1941. In my view both criticisms are justified. The first is that Irving was wrong in his claim that the instruction *Keine liquidierung* (no liquidation) was intended to apply to Jews generally. Irving acknowledged that the inclusion in Himmler's note of the words '*aus Berlin*' is clear evidence that the instruction relates solely to Jews being deported from Berlin and not to Jews from elsewhere. After some prevarication during the trial, Irving also accepted that he was mistaken when he read *Judentransport* (in the singular) as referring to Jewish transports (in the plural). The second criticism (which is more important for the purpose of this case) is that Irving is in error when he claims that the instruction not to liquidate the Jews on that transport emanated from Hitler. There is no evidence that Hitler 'summoned' Himmler to his headquarters and 'obliged' him to telephone to Heydrich an order that Jews were not to be liquidated.

13.22 Whilst I accept that an historian is entitled to speculate, he must spell out clearly to the reader when he is speculating rather than reciting established facts. In *Hitler's War* (1977 edition) Irving presents Himmler's note as 'incontrovertible evidence' that Hitler issued a general order prohibiting the liquidation of Jews. The evidence from Wisliceny and Greiser, which is not mentioned by Irving, supports the view that Hitler was complicit in the deportation and killing of Jews in 1941. I do not accept Irving's argument that the evidence of the summoning of Jeckeln to Berlin and the reference in Himmler's diary for 4 December 1941 to 'guidelines' amount to evidence from which it is reasonable to infer that there was a general prohibition in force at this time against the killing of all European Jews.

13.23 In regard to Himmler's log for 1 December 1941, his manuscript is difficult to decipher. Irving claimed that that was the reason why he misread '*haben*' as '*Juden*'. Be that as it may, Irving accepted that he misrepresented this document. I do not accept that the error is immaterial: if it ordained that Jews were to remain where they were, out of harm's way, it would have given protection to a very large number of Jews whose lives were in jeopardy if they were moved elsewhere. But, as Irving accepts, that was not what Himmler was ordering.

The shooting of the Jews in Riga (paragraphs 5.111–122)

13.24 An objective historian is obliged to be even-handed in his approach to historical evidence: he cannot pick and choose without adequate reason. I consider that there is justification for the Defendants' complaint that Irving was not even-handed in his treatment in *Hitler's War* of the account given by General Bruns of the shooting of thousands of Jews in Riga. Irving appears readily to accept that part of Bruns's account which refers to Altemeyer bringing him an order which prohibited mass shootings from taking place in the future. On the other hand Irving takes no account of the fact that, according to Bruns, it was only shootings 'on that scale' which were not to take place in future. (A total of 5,000 Jews were shot in Riga on 30 November 1941). Nor does Irving mention that the order apparently stated that the shootings were to be carried out 'more discreetly'. In other words the shooting was to continue. Moreover Irving ignores Bruns's earlier reference to Altemeyer telling him of an order that the Berlin Jews were to be shot in accordance with Hitler's orders. My conclusion is that in these respects Irving has perverted the sense of Bruns's account. I was unpersuaded by the explanation offered by Irving for his treatment of this evidence.

13.25 There is a related criticism made by the Defendants in relation to the Riga shooting, namely that Irving suppressed the evidence of the widow of Schultz-Dubois about Hitler's reaction to a protest about the shooting. I am not satisfied that this criticism is made out. In the first place I am not persuaded by the evidence that at the material time Irving was aware of the account of Frau Schultz-Dubois: he testified that he had not read the relevant passage in Professor Fleming's book. In the second place, I take the view that the nature of the evidence was such that Irving was entitled to discount it: it was at least third-hand and emanated from Admiral Canaris who was anti-Nazi and no friend of Hitler.

Hitler's views on the Jewish question (paragraphs 5.123–150 above)

13.26 Irving's submissions on this topic appear to me to have a distinct air of unreality about them. It is common ground between the parties that, until the latter part of 1941, the solution to the Jewish question which Hitler preferred was their mass deportation. On the Defendants' case, however, from the end of 1941 onwards the policy of which Hitler knew and approved was the extermination of Jews in huge numbers. Irving on the other hand argued that Hitler continued to be the Jews' friend at least until October 1943. The unreality of Irving's stance, as I see it, derives from his persistence in that claim, despite his acceptance in the course of this trial that the evidence shows that Hitler knew about and approved of the wholesale shooting of Jews in the East and, later, was complicit in the gassing of hundreds of thousands of Jews in the Reinhard and other death camps.

13.27 The evidence is incontrovertible (and Irving does not seek to dispute it) that Hitler was rabidly anti-semitic from the earliest days. He spoke, in his famous speech of 30 January 1939 and on other occasions, in the most sinister and menacing terms of the fate which awaited the Jews: they were a bacillus which had to be destroyed. The Defendants do not suggest that in the 1930s Hitler should be understood to have been speaking in genocidal terms. But, according to the Defendants, the position changed from late 1941 onwards. I was unconvinced by the strenuous efforts made by Irving to refute the sinister interpretation placed by the Defendants on Hitler's pronouncements on the Jewish question from late 1941 onwards.

13.28 I do not propose to make individual findings about the Defendants' criticisms of Irving's treatment of those statements by Hitler. I have summarized them and the parties' respective contentions about them in paragraphs 5.125–136 above. Much of the argument revolved around questions of translation. I did not derive much assistance from the debate as to how words such as *ausrotten, vernichten, abschaffen, umsiedeln* and *abtransportieren* are to be translated. I believe that Irving accepted the argument of the Defendants' experts that the Nazis often resorted to euphemism and camouflage when discussing the radical solutions to the Jewish question. For that and other reasons it was agreed on all sides that all depends on the context.

13.29 In my view consideration of the context requires an objective historian to take into account such matters as Hitler's history of anti-semitism; the importance in the Nazi ideology of achieving racial purity; the attacks on Jews and their property before the outbreak of war; the policy of deporting Jews and the systematic programme, approved by Hitler, of shooting Jews in the East. So considered, I am satisfied that most, if not all, of the pronouncements by Hitler which are relied on by the Defendants do bear the sinister connotation which they put on them. To take but one example, when Frank said on 16 December 1941 that he had been told in Berlin 'liquidate [the Jews] yourselves', I am satisfied that the evidence strongly supports the conclusion that he was reporting what Hitler had said to the *Gauleiter* on 12 December and that Hitler had indeed given instructions for the liquidation of the Jews. That after all is what the evidence suggests happened on an ever-increasing scale in the following months. Irving's claim that Frank was telling his audience what he had told the authorities in Berlin (and not the other way round) appears to me to be wholly untenable.

13.30 As I have recorded at paragraphs 5.137–8 above, Irving produced another 'chain of documents' in support of his contention that the attitude of Hitler to the Jewish question was sympathetic and protective. I accept that on occasion, particularly in the early years, Hitler did intervene on behalf of Jews (usually individuals or identified groups). I accept also (as I have already said) that until 1941 Hitler favoured deporting the Jews. But I note that few documents in this chain come after the autumn of 1941. Those that do are at best equivocal. It appears to me to be perverse to interpret Himmler's compromizing letter to Berger of 28 July 1942 as referring to deportation. Objective consideration of that document suggests strongly that the responsibility with which Himmler said he had been entrusted by Hitler was the implementation of the policy of exterminating the Jews. I accept the conclusion of Evans that the chain of documents does little to justify or excuse Irving's portrayal of Hitler's views on the Jewish question.

13.31 It is my conclusion that the Defendants are justified in their assertion that Irving has seriously misrepresented Hitler's views on the Jewish question. He has done so in some instances by misinterpreting and mistranslating documents and in other instances by omitting documents or parts of them. In the result the picture which he provides to readers of *Hitler and his attitude towards the Jews* is at odds with the evidence.

*The timing of the 'final solution' to the Jewish question: the
Schlegelberger note*

13.32 In my opinion Irving's treatment of the Schlegelberger note and
the importance which he attaches to it shed important light on the
quality of his historiography.

13.33 It is to be borne in mind that the note is undated and unsigned.
It is hearsay in the sense that its author is recording what Lammers
claims to have been told by Hitler. It is an *Abschrift* (copy) rather than
an original document. It has a number of unsatisfactory features, which
might give rise to doubts about its authenticity. There is no clear
evidence of the context in which the note came into existence. Yet
Irving has seized upon the note and regards it, to quote his own words,
as a 'high-level diamond document'. According to Irving, the note
demonstrates that it was Hitler's wish that the entire Jewish question
be postponed until the end of the war. It is therefore the linchpin of
his argument that Hitler was the Jews' friend. The question is whether
that is a conclusion to which an objective historian might sensibly
come, taking due account of the surrounding circumstances.

13.34 I shall not devote time to discussing the question whether the
document dates from 1941 (in which case it would be a wholly
unremarkable document since it was at that time Hitler's view that the
Jews should in due course be deported) or from 1942, since Evans was
disposed to accept, at least for the sake of argument, that the latter date
may well be the correct one.

13.35 On the assumption that the note is a 1942 document, I consider
that, in the light of all the surrounding circumstances and in the light
of subsequent events, it is (to put it no higher) very doubtful if the
Schlegelberger note is evidence of a wish on the part of Hitler to
postpone the Jewish question until after the war, that is, to take no
offensive action against them of any kind until after the cessation of
hostilities. I do not believe that Irving was able to provide a satisfactory
answer to the Defendants' question: why should Hitler have decided
suddenly in March 1942 to call a halt to a process which had been
going on with his authority on a massive scale for at least six months.
I am persuaded that, for the reasons advanced by Evans, it is at least
equally likely that the note is concerned with the complex problems

thrown up by the question how to treat half-Jews (*mischlinge*). It is noteworthy that the evidence suggests that at the Wannsee conference in January 1942 (where Heydrich claimed to be speaking with the authority of Hitler) a programme for the extermination of Jews had been discussed and in broad terms agreed upon. The delegates were, however, unable to resolve the thorny question of the *mischlinge*. That issue caused concern within the Ministry of Justice (where both Lammers and Schlegelberger worked). A resumed session of the Wannsee conference was arranged for 6 March 1942, when the question of the *mischlinge* was again discussed. There is no support in the documentary evidence for Irving's contention that there was on this occasion general discussion of the Jewish question. No solution having been agreed, the balance of the evidence in my view suggests that it was decided to refer the issue of the *mischlinge* to Hitler for his decision. If that be right, the note simply records what Hitler decided on that limited question. If the Defendants' explanation of the note is correct (and I have held that it is at least as likely an explanation as that put forward by Irving), the note does not possess the significance which Irving attaches to it.

13.36 I do not regard the arguments advanced by Irving, which I have set out at paragraphs 5.165–7, as being without merit: they are worthy of consideration. But I do consider the Defendants' criticism to be well-founded that Irving presents the Schlegelberger note as decisive and incontrovertible evidence (see *Hitler's War* at p. 464) when, as he should have appreciated, there are powerful reasons for doubting that it has the significance which he attaches to it. Irving's perception of the importance of the note appears to take no account of the mass murder of the Jews which took place soon afterwards.

Goebbels' diary entry for 27 March 1942 (paragraphs 5.170–186 above)

13.37 I have concluded without hesitation that the manner in which Irving deals in *Hitler's War* (both editions) with Goebbels' diary entry of 27 March 1942 is misleading and unsupported by the circumstantial evidence. A comparison between the language of the diary (see paragraph 5.174 above) and the account provided by Irving to his readers (see paragraph 5.173) reveals stark discrepancies.

13.38 I recognize that Irving is justified in his claim that Goebbels was often mendacious in his diary entries. So the entries have to be scrutinized in the light of surrounding circumstances. But I do not accept that the evidence of the circumstances as they existed in March 1942 lends support to Irving's claim that Goebbels concealed from Hitler the reality of what was happening in the death camps. I do not consider that Irving was able to point to evidence which controverted the contention of the Defendants that by March 1942 the 'radical solution' favoured by Hitler was extermination and not deportation. It follows that I accept the submission that the way in which Irving deals with this diary is tendentious and unjustified.

Himmler minute of 22 September 1942 (paragraphs 5.187–198 above)

13.39 I consider that the interpretation of Himmler's terse note is problematic. I recognize that there are pointers (including for example the reference to Globocnik) which might be said to render this an incriminating document. But there is force in Irving's argument that the internal evidence consisting in the language used in the note (*auswanderung* or emigration) is consistent with the discussion between Himmler and Hitler having been about resettlement and not extermination.

13.40 That said, I accept the validity of the criticism that there was no warrant for the claim made by Irving that at that meeting Himmler pulled the wool over Hitler's eyes. In my judgment, that claim ignores the circumstantial evidence as to the state of Hitler's knowledge by September 1942 of the use of gas chambers to kill Jews. It also runs counter to the evidence of the nature of the relationship between Hitler and Himmler, who does not appear to have been a man likely to have practised a deception of this kind on his *Fuhrer*. I therefore accept the contention of the Defendants that Irving's treatment of this minute is unjustifiably favourable to Hitler.

Himmler's note for his meeting with Hitler on 10 December 1942 (paragraphs 5.194–198 above)

13.41 This is another document where much of the argument turned on a question of translation namely whether *abschaffen* was to be translated as 'to remove' or 'to liquidate'. I do not criticize Irving for opting for the former. However, I accept the Defendants' argument that the reference in the note to keeping the well-to-do French Jews 'healthy and alive' should have alerted an objective historian to the sinister significance of the note in regard to the fate awaiting the other French Jews. To that extent I accept the criticism of Irving for the way he has dealt with this note in *Hitler's War*.

Hitler's meetings with Antonescu and Horthy in April 1943 (paragraphs 5.199–214 above)

13.42 I regard the issue raised by the criticisms of Irving's accounts of these meetings as important in assessing Irving's historiography. It appears to me to be significant that there exist minutes of both meetings taken by officials who (as I believe Irving accepted) had no reason to obfuscate the effect of what was said.

13.43 I am satisfied that the Defendants' criticisms of Irving's treatment of the evidence relating to the meeting with Antonescu and, more particularly, with Horthy have substance. In assessing the evidence it appears to me that an objective historian would take into consideration, firstly, Hitler's apparent objective in meeting the two leaders: it was to enable the Nazis to get their hands on the Romanian and Hungarian Jews respectively. Such an historian would ponder whether the language of the minutes can be said to be consistent with a desire on the part of the Nazis to secure the deportation of the Jews and nothing more. He would also have in mind the subsequent history of the Romanian and Hungarian Jews.

13.44 It does not appear to me that, in relation to these meetings, Irving approached the evidence in an objective manner. His account of the meeting with Antonescu was partial and on that account misleading. In relation to the meeting with Horthy, Irving failed to heed what appears to me to be powerful evidence that on the second day, 17 April, both Hitler and Ribbentrop spoke in uncompromising and unequivocal terms about their genocidal intentions in regard to the Hungarian Jews.

Irving was constrained to accept that the pretext which he put forward for the meeting with Horthy (the Warsaw ghetto uprising which happened afterwards) was false, as was his explanation for the harsh attitude evinced by Hitler at the meeting (recent Allied bombing raids). I was not persuaded that Irving had any satisfactory explanation for his transposition from 16 to 17 April of Hitler's comforting remark, made on 16 April, that there was no need for the murder or elimination of the Hungarian Jews. In my judgment Irving materially perverts the evidence of what passed between the Nazis and Horthy on 17 April.

The deportation and murder of the Roman Jews in October 1943 (paragraphs 5.215–221 above)

13.45 I do not accept that an objective analysis of the available evidence supports Irving's claim that the effect of Hitler's intervention was to prevent Himmler's murderous plans for the Jews being brought into effect. It appears to me that it was specious for Irving to argue, as he did, that Hitler's intervention was for the benefit of the Roman Jews, when the result of that intervention was that the Roman Jews were sent to the notorious concentration camp at Mauthausen where they were at the mercy of the SS. I also take the view that it was a culpable omission on Irving's part not to inform his readers that these Jews were ultimately murdered.

Himmler's speeches of 6 October 1943 and 5 and 24 May 1944 (paragaphs 5.222–230 above)

13.46 It is a common ground that in these three speeches Himmler was speaking, with remarkable frankness, about the murder of the Jews. The question is whether Irving dealt in an objective and fair manner with the evidence which those speeches afford as to Hitler's knowledge of and complicity in the murder of the Jews. I am satisfied that he did not. Two of the speeches provide powerful evidence that Hitler ordered that the extermination of the Jews should take place. Yet in the 1977 edition of *Hitler's War* Irving suggests that the existence of a Hitler order was an invention on the part of Himmler. It does not appear to me that the evidence supports that suggestion. I consider that Irving's deduction that the transcript of the speech of 5 May was either altered after

Himmler delivered the speech or sanitized before it was shown to Hitler is fanciful. The absence of any mention of that speech in the 1991 edition of *Hitler's War* was in my judgment another culpable omission.

Hitler's speech on 26 May 1944 (paragraph 5.235–239 above)
13.47 Irving quoted the material part of this speech in full in *Hitler's War*. I do not accept the Defendants' argument that his prefatory comment amounts to misrepresenting or twisting Hitler's words. The reader can judge for himself.

Ribbentrop's testimony from his cell at Nuremberg (paragraphs 5.235–239 above)
13.48 I accept that historians are bound by the constraints of space to edit quotations. But there is an obligation on them not to give the reader a distorted impression by selective quotation. In my view Irving fails to observe this duty when in the 1977 edition of *Hitler's War* he quotes Ribbentrop's belief that Hitler did not order the destruction of the Jews but fails to quote his immediately following comment that he at least knew about it.

Marie Vaillant-Couturier (paragraphs 5.240–244 above)
13.49 I have no hesitation in concluding that the Defendants' criticism of Irving in relation to the evidence of Vaillant-Couturier is justified. The evidence appears to me to be plain that the Judge's note 'This I doubt' referred and referred only to her supposition (for it was no more than that) that other camps (of which she would have had no direct knowledge) had systems for selecting inmates as prostitutes for SS officers. There is no reason to suppose that the Judge had any reservations about Vaillant-Couturier's vivid, detailed and credible evidence about the womens' camp at Auschwitz. Irving's claim that Judge Biddle thought she was 'a bloody liar' is a travesty of the evidence.

Kurt Aumeier (paragraphs 5.245–249 above)
13.50 I find myself unconvinced by Irving's argument that Aumeier is an unreliable witness. I prefer the contention of van Pelt and Evans for the Defendants that he is an important and credible witness as to the

gassing procedures in place at Auschwitz. As deputy commander at the camp, he was in a position to know. Whilst there are clearly errors in his account, for the most part his recollections are convincing. It was of course legitimate for Irving to suggest that his account was the result of brutal pressure being brought to bear by his British captors, if he had evidence for such a suggestion. But it was not clear to me what evidence Irving was relying on. I further accept that Irving minimized the significance of Aumeier's evidence (even if he did not suppress it altogether) when he confined reference to it to a footnote in *Nuremberg*.

Findings in relation to the instances of Irving's historiography cited by the Defendants

13.51 For the reasons which I have given, I find that in most of the instances which they cite the Defendants' criticisms are justified. In those instances it is my conclusion that, judged objectively, Irving treated the historical evidence in a manner which fell far short of the standard to be expected of a conscientious historian. Irving in those respects misrepresented and distorted the evidence which was available to him.

Evidence of Hitler's attitude towards the Jews and the extent, if any, of his knowledge of and responsibility for the evolving policy of extermination

13.52 Some of the findings which I have already made in relation to the Defendants' specific criticisms of Irving's historiography bear upon the broader questions of Hitler's attitude towards the Jews and his involvement, if any, in the ethnic cleansing of the Jews. I will not repeat those findings in this section of the judgment. Although the questions with which I am in this part of the judgement concerned are broad ones, they narrowed and crystallized in the course of the trial. As will be apparent from section vi. above, the Defendants focused their attention upon Irving's treatment of the evidence relating to the following topics: Hitler's anti-semitism; the scale of the so-called executions of Jews in the East; the alleged use of gas chambers at the Operation

Reinhard camps to kill Jews and evidence relating to the question of Hitler's knowledge of and authority for the extermination of Jews by shooting and by gassing. In relation to all of these issues save the first, Irving's stance appeared to me to alter in the course of the trial.

Hitler's anti-semitism (paragraphs 6.3–9 above)

13.53 Irving having accepted that Hitler was profoundly anti-semitic until he came to power, the question is whether, as Irving claimed, he lost interest in anti-semitism from about 1933 onwards because it was no longer politically advantageous for him.

13.54 In his comprehensive and scholarly report, Longerich analysed the evidence of Hitler's anti-semitism both before and after 1933. He examined in particular Hitler's public pronouncements on the Jewish question. I have already set out in this judgment many of those statements. Ignoring for the moment the question whether Hitler was advocating the deportation of the Jews or their extermination, the argument appears to me hopeless that after 1933 Hitler lost interest in anti-semitism or that he ceased to be anti-semitic when he came to power. Despite his increasing preoccupation with other matters, Hitler reverted time and again to the topic of the Jews and what was to be done with them. He continued to speak of them in terms which were both vitriolic and menacing. For the reasons which I have already expressed in the earlier paragraphs of this section of the judgment, I am satisfied on the evidence of his public statements that Hitler's anti-semitism continued unabated after 1933.

13.55 But account must also be taken not only of what Hitler said but also of what he did or authorized to be done or at least knew was being done in relation to the Jews. In the following paragraphs of this judgment I will summarize what appears to me to be the evidence of Hitler's involvement in the successive programmes of shooting, deporting and gassing Jews in large numbers. This evidence (which is in large part accepted by Irving) would in my view convince a dispassionate historian of Hitler's persistent anti-semitism. Even if (which I do not accept) the evidence supported the proposition that Hitler's policy towards the Jews remained throughout that they should be deported, it cannot in my view sensibly be argued that uprooting

Jewish men, women and children from their homes and dumping them in often appalling conditions many miles away to the East was other than anti-semitic. I therefore reject as being contrary to the evidence Irving's claim that Hitler ceased to be anti-semitic from 1933 onwards.

The scale and systematic nature of the shooting of Jews by the Einsatzgruppen (paragraphs 6.10–59 above)

13.56 I can deal quite briefly with the extensive evidence relied on by the parties in relation to this topic. The reason I can take that course is that Irving, as the case progressed, appeared to accept much of what Longerich and Browning said in their reports and in their oral evidence. In particular Irving agreed that the evidence, principally in the form of reports by the Einsatzgruppen, appears to establish that between 500,000 and 1,500,000 people (including a large proportion of Jews) were shot by those groups and by the auxiliary Wehrmacht units seconded to assist them. My understanding is that the Defendants suggest that the true figure was higher than this. But I do not see that, in the context of this case, any useful purpose would be served by my attempting to assess whether the evidence supports a higher figure.

13.57 Irving further accepted that the evidence indicates that the programme of shooting Jews in the East was systematic, in the sense that it originated in Berlin and was organized and co-ordinated from there. Furthermore Irving conceded that the evidence bears out the contention of the Defendants that Hitler sanctioned the killings. Irving testified that, if he had given audiences the impression by what he said in Australia in 1986 that the killings on the Eastern front had taken place without the knowledge and approval of Hitler and his cronies, he had been wrong to do so. His evidence was that 'certainly Hitler sanctioned the killing of the Jews on the Eastern front'. The evidence which prompted Irving to make these concessions consisted in the regular reports made by the Einsatzgruppen to Berlin; the preparation by the RHSA in Berlin of Ereignismeldungen (event announcements) and a report numbered 51 dated 29 December 1942 which recorded the 'execution' of 363,112 Jews and which (as Irving accepted) was probably shown to Hitler. The Defendants also relied on the so-called Muller order of 1

August 1941 to which I shall have to return later. It appears to me that these concessions by Irving were rightly made. Apart form the existence of the evidence to which I have just referred the vast manpower required to carry out the programme at a critical stage in the war would surely have required the approval of Hitler.

13.58 It inexorably follows that Irving was misrepresenting the historical evidence when he told audiences in Australia, Canada and the US (as he accepted he did) that the shooting of Jews in the East was arbitrary, unauthorized and undertaken by individual groups or commanders.

The deportation of the Jews (paragraphs 6.60–67 above)

13.59 As I have already indicated, there is little dispute between the parties that the policy of deportation emerged and evolved along the lines described in the report of Longerich. I have already rejected Irving's argument that the evidence, whether in the form of the Schlegelberger note or otherwise, supports his contention that in early 1942 Hitler decided that the entire Jewish question should be postponed until after the war. In any event Irving does not dispute that the deportation of the European Jews continued apace in the months and years after the Wannsee conference. The real issue is whether their deportation was a prelude to their extermination and, if so, on what scale such extermination took place.

The scale on which Jews were gassed to death at camps including the Reinhard Camps but excluding Auschwitz (paragraphs 6.73–144 above)

13.60 There is no dispute that the use by the Nazis of gas to kill human beings had its origins in the euthanasia programme. When that ended, the gas vans were diverted to the Eastern territories where (as Irving accepts) they were used to kill healthy Jews in substantial numbers. Again there is some argument as to the numbers killed in the gas vans: Irving was reluctant to commit himself to an estimate of the number killed but he accepted that it ran into thousands. In the circumstances I do not intend to explore any further the evidence as to the number of those killed in vans.

13.61 Although strictly the camps at Chelmno and Semlin did not form part of Operation Reinhard, which was confined to the area of the General Government, I shall for convenience refer collectively to those two camps and to the camps at Belzec, Sobibor and Treblinka as 'the Reinhard Camps'. In relation to the Reinhard camps there are two issues: the first is how many Jews were gassed to death at these camps. The second is whether Hitler knew or approved of the extermination of Jews at these camps. (I will deal separately with the evidence about Auschwitz.)

13.62 Addressing first the issue of the scale of the killings by gas at the Reinhard camps, it was Longerich's opinion that the policy of exterminating Jews by the use of gas was an extension or development of the programme of shooting Jews which had commenced in the late autumn of 1941. As has been seen, Irving conceded that Jews were shot in enormous numbers over the ensuing months. In paragraphs 6.75 to 6.105 above I have endeavoured to trace and summarize the evidence on which the Defendants rely in support of their case that the gassing which took place at the Reinhard Camps was on a truly genocidal scale. The evidence can be categorized as documentary (although most of the Reinhard documents were destroyed), demographic and the accounts of eye-witnesses. On the basis of this evidence both Browning and Longerich conclude that many hundreds of thousands died in the gas chambers at the Reinhard camps.

13.63 I have summarized at paragraphs 6.106–8 above some of the arguments deployed by Irving for saying that the killing at the Reinhard camps was on nothing like the scale contended by the Defendants. But, as pointed out at paragraph 6.109–110, Irving did ultimately accept that the camps at Chelmno, Treblinka, and Sobibor were Nazi killing centres. He claimed, disingenuously in my opinion, that he made this concession so as to progress the trial and thereby to enable the issue regarding Auschwitz to be examined in greater detail. Be that as it may, I understood Irving to accept that hundreds of thousands of Jews were killed at the Reinhard camps to which I have referred. I readily acknowledge that he disputed the estimates put on the number gassed to death by Longerich and Browning. But, given the huge number of deaths accepted by Irving, little appears to me to turn on the disparity in their respective estimates.

Evidence of Hitler's knowledge of and/or complicity in the extermination of Jews in the gas chambers at the Reinhard camps (paragraphs 6.81–95 and 6.114–144)

13.64 I turn to the issue regarding Hitler's knowledge of and complicity in the gassing programme at the Reinhard camps. In my view that issue has to be examined in the light of three propositions, each of which I understood to be accepted by Irving. The first is that, from about November 1941, the Nazis had been engaged in carrying out a programme, which Hitler knew about and authorized, of killing by shooting many hundreds of thousands of Jews and others, initially in Russia and later spreading to towns in the Warthegau (the area of Poland incorporated into the Reich), the General Government (the remainder of Poland) and Serbia. The second is that hundreds of thousands of Jews were killed in the death camps set up under Operation Reinhard. The third is that, as Irving explicitly accepted, Hitler cannot have remained in ignorance of the extermination programme after October 1943. In the light of those propositions it is legitimate to formulate the question in this way: does the evidence establish or suggest that, whilst he approved of the genocidal policy of shooting Jews in the East, Hitler did not approve or sanction the genocidal use of the gas chambers at the Reinhard camps over the months from December 1941 until October 1943, and was also kept in ignorance that gassing on that scale was taking place?

13.65 I have used the phrase 'kept in ignorance' in the preceding paragraph because it is part of the positive case advanced by Irving that the genocidal use of the gas chambers at the Reinhard camps was planned and implemented by Heydrich and overseen by Himmler. Does the evidence support Irving's contention that Hitler was kept in ignorance of the manner in which Heydrich and Himmler were setting about solving the Jewish question?

13.66 At paragraphs 6.81 to 6.105 above I have examined some of the documents on which the Defendants rely as evidence of Hitler's involvement in the extermination at the Reinhard camps, starting with the meeting between Hitler, Himmler and Heydrich on 25 October 1941 and culminating in the letter written in 1977 by Hitler's former personal secretary. Against those documents must be set Irving's comment, which I accept is accurate, that there is no reference to be found to a *Hitler Befehl* (Hitler order) authorizing the extermination of Jews by gassing at the Reinhard Camps. But, given the secrecy which surrounded the operation of the gas chambers, I would not have expected to have found such a document. For the same reason I consider that Irving's argument as to Hitler's ignorance derives little assistance from the fact that he is able to point to a number of documents where Hitler can be found still talking of the Madagascar plan or deportation to some other destination. The need for secrecy required the use of camouflage language when the fate of Jews was under public discussion.

13.67 My conclusion on this issue is that the evidence discloses substantial, even if not wholly irrefutable, reasons for concluding not only that Hitler was aware of the gassing in the Reinhard Camps but also that he was consulted and approved the extermination. My reasons for arriving at this conclusion are, firstly, that if (as Irving accepts) Hitler knew and approved the programme of shooting Jews, it is reasonable to suppose that he would have been consulted about and approved a policy to exterminate them by another means, namely by the use of gas. I consider that there are a number of documents which suggest that Hitler knew and approved the implementation of the new policy: for example the protocol of the Wannsee conference, at which the extermination programme was discussed, records Heydrich in his opening remarks that he was speaking with the authority of Hitler. But the main reason for my conclusion is that it appears to me to be unreal to suppose that Himmler would not have obtained the authority of Hitler for the gassing programme (and even more unlikely that he would have concealed it from his Fuhrer). Himmler's *Dienstkalendar* provides clear evidence of the regularity of the meetings between Hitler and Himmler and of their having discussed the Jewish question at the time when Himmler was actively supervizing the setting up and operation of the gas chambers in the Reinhard Camps. I therefore accept the evidence of Longerich and Browning which I have summarized at paragraph 6.105 above.

Auschwitz

Identifying the issue

13.68 When the trial started, it appeared from Irving's written statement of case that he was adhering to the position often adopted in his speeches about Auschwitz, namely that no gas chambers were commissioned or operated at the camp and that in consequence no Jew lost his or her life in gas chambers there.

13.69 As I have already observed in paragraph 7.11 above, in the course of the trial Irving modified his position: he accepted that there was at least one gas chamber (or 'cellar') at Auschwitz, albeit used solely or mainly for the fumigation of clothing. He also accepted that gassing of Jews had taken place at the camp 'on some scale'. He did not indicate on what scale. Irving firmly denied the claim advanced by van Pelt that 500,000 Jews were killed in morgue 1 of crematorium 2. The case for the Defendants on the other hand was, as I have said, that almost one million Jews were put to death in the gas chambers of Auschwitz.

13.70 In these circumstances the central question which, as it appears to me, falls to be determined is whether or not the evidence supports the Defendants' contention that the number of deaths ran into hundreds of thousands or whether Irving is right when he claims that the killing by gas was on a modest scale.

The scale of the killing of Jews in the gas chambers

13.71 I have to confess that, in common I suspect with most other people, I had supposed that the evidence of mass extermination of Jews in the gas chambers at Auschwitz was compelling. I have, however, set aside this preconception when assessing the evidence adduced by the parties in these proceedings.

The 'convergence' of evidence

13.72 The case for the Defendants, summarized above, is that there exists what van Pelt described as a 'convergence' of evidence which is to the ordinary, dispassionate mind overwhelming that hundreds of thousands of Jews were systematically gassed to death at Auschwitz, mainly by the use of hydrogen cyanide pellets called Zyklon-B. I have set out at paragraphs 7.15 to 7.74 above the individual elements which make up that convergence of evidence. I have done so at some length (although not at such length as did van Pelt in his report) because it appears to me to be important to keep well in mind the diversity of the categories and the extent to which those categories are mutually corroborative.

13.73 I recognize the force of many of Irving's comments upon some of those categories. He is right to point out that the contemporaneous documents, such as drawings, plans, correspondence with contractors and the like, yield little clear evidence of the existence of gas chambers designed to kill humans. Such isolated references to the use of gas as are to be found amongst these documents can be explained by the need to fumigate clothes so as to reduce the incidence of diseases such as typhus. The quantities of Zyklon-B delivered to the camp may arguably be explained by the need to fumigate clothes and other objects. It is also correct that one of the most compromising documents, namely Muller's letter of 28 June 1943 setting out the number of cadavers capable of being burnt in the incinerators, has a number of curious features which raise the possibility that it is not authentic. In addition, the photographic evidence for the existence of chimneys protruding through the roof of morgue 1 at crematorium 2 is, I accept, hard to interpret.

13.74 Similarly Irving had some valid comments to make about the various accounts given by survivors of the camp and by camp officials. Some of those accounts were given in evidence at the post-war trials. The possibility exists that some of these witnesses invented some or even all of the experiences which they describe. Irving suggested the possibility of cross-pollination, by which he meant the possibility that witnesses may have repeated and even embellished the (invented) accounts of other witnesses with the consequence that a corpus of false testimony is built up. Irving pointed out that parts of some of the accounts of some of the witnesses are obviously wrong or (like some of Olere's drawings) clearly exaggerated. He suggested various motives why witnesses might have given false accounts, such as greed and resentment (in the case of survivors) and fear and the wish to ingratiate themselves with their captors (in the case of camp officials). Van Pelt accepted that these possibilities exist. I agree.

The documentary evidence

13.75 Vulnerable though the individual categories of evidence may be to criticisms of the kind mentioned in the preceding paragraphs, it appears to me that the cumulative effect of the documentary evidence for the genocidal operation of gas chambers at Auschwitz is considerable.

13.76 The nature of the redesign in 1942 of crematorium 2 appears to me, for the reasons summarized in paragraph 7.59 to 7.63 above, to constitute powerful evidence that the morgue was to be used to gas live human beings who had been able to walk downstairs. Few and far between though they may be, documents do exist for which it is difficult to find an innocent explanation. I have in mind for example the minute of the meeting of 19 August 1942 (paragraph 7.66 above), which refers to *Badenanstalten fur Sonderaktionen* ('bath-houses for special actions') and the so-called Kinna report (paragraph 7.67 above). As to Bischoff's letter about the incineration capacity of the ovens (see paragraphs 7.69 and 7.106 above), it does not seem to me that, despite its unusual features, a dispassionate historian would dismiss it out of hand, as did Irving, as a forgery. Van Pelt believed it to be genuine. He pointed out that there are two copies in different archives (in Domburg and in Moscow, where it has been since 1945). It was used at the trial of Hoss in 1948.If it had been forged before 1948, it would have been unlikely that the capacity would have been given as 4,756 corpses per day since that is a lower figure than the figures published by the Russians and the Poles at the end of the war. I accept the reasoning of van Pelt. If the Bischoff document is authentic, it is further cogent evidence of genocidal gassing because the capacity to which Bischoff refers cannot have been needed to incinerate those who succumbed to disease. Finally, there is the scientific evidence gathered by the Polish Central Commission in 1945–7 (paragraph 7.2 above) and the evidence of the Markiewicz report (see paragraphs 7.73 to 7.74 above).

The eye-witness evidence

13.77 Whilst I acknowledge that the reliability of the eye-witness evidence is variable, what is to me striking about that category of evidence is the similarity of the accounts and the extent to which they are consistent with the documentary evidence. The account of, for example, Tauber, is so clear and detailed that, in my judgment, no objective historian would dismiss it as invention unless there were powerful reasons for doing so. Tauber's account is corroborated by and corroborative of the accounts given by others such as Jankowski and Dragon. Their descriptions marry up with Olere's drawings. The evidence of other eye-witnesses, such as Hoss and Broad, would in my view appear credible to a dispassionate student of Auschwitz. There is no evidence of cross-pollination having occurred. It is in the circumstances an unlikely explanation for the broad similarity of the accounts in this category.

13.78 My conclusion is that the various categories of evidence do 'converge' in the manner suggested by the Defendants. I accept their contention which I have summarized in paragraph 7.75 above. My overall assessment of the totality of the evidence that Jews were killed in large numbers in the gas chambers at Auschwitz is that it would require exceedingly powerful reasons to reject it. Irving has argued that such reasons do exist.

The Leuchter report

13.79 The reason why Irving initially denied the existence of gas chambers at Auschwitz was, as has been seen, the Leuchter report. I have summarized in some detail the findings made by Leuchter at paragraphs 7.82 to 7.89 above. I will not repeat myself. I have also set out at paragraphs 7.104 to 7.108 above the reasons why van Pelt on behalf of the Defendants dismissed the Leuchter report as flawed and unreliable. Those reasons were put to Irving in cross-examination. It is a fair summary of his evidence to say that he accepted the validity of most of them. He agreed that the Leuchter report was fundamentally flawed. In regard to the chemical analysis, Irving was unable to controvert the evidence of Dr Roth (summarized at paragraph 7.106 above) that, because the cyanide would have penetrated the brickwork and plaster to a depth of no more than one tenth of the breadth of a human hair, any cyanide present in the relatively large samples taken by Leuchter (which had to be pulverized before analysis) would have been so diluted that the results on which Leuchter relied had effectively no validity. What is more significant is that Leuchter assumed, wrongly as Irving agreed, that a greater concentration of cyanide would have been required to kill humans than was required to fumigate clothing. In fact the concentration required to kill humans is 22 times less than is required for fumigation purposes. As indicated in paragraph 7.105 above, and as Irving was constrained to accept, Leuchter's false assumption vitiated his conclusion. Irving conceded the existence of many other factual errors in the Leuchter report.

13.80 In the light of the evidence of van Pelt and Irving's answers in cross-examination, I do not consider that an objective historian would have regarded the Leuchter report as a sufficient reason for dismissing, or even doubting, the convergence of evidence on which the Defendants rely for the presence of homicidal gas chambers at Auschwitz. I have not overlooked the fact that Irving claimed that Leuchter's findings have been replicated, notably in a report by Germar Rudolf. That report was produced at the trial but it is impossible for me to assess its evidential value.

Holes in the roof of morgue 1 at crematorium 2?

13.81 The strength of the criticisms of the Leuchter report may explain why, as the trial progressed, the emphasis of Irving's case on Auschwitz appeared to shift from the absence of cyanide in the brick and plaster to the roof of morgue 1 at crematorium 2. As I have explained in paragraphs 7.91 to 7.93 above, Irving argues that there is no evidence of the presence of the chimneys or ducts by means of which, on the Defendants' case, Zyklon-B pellets were poured down from the roof of morgue 1 into the gas chamber below (where the Defendants claim most of the deaths occurred). In particular Irving relied on a photograph of part of the collapsed roof which displayed no evidence of the apertures through which the chimneys would have protruded.

13.82 As the Defendants point out, this argument has some curious features. Firstly, Irving embraced it relatively recently in late 1998 (so that it cannot have been the basis for his denials before that date of the existence of gas chambers at Auschwitz). Secondly, Irving appeared at one stage to accept that there was a gas chamber in morgue 1 at crematorium 2, albeit one that was used for fumigation and not for killing. In that case it would seem that ducts or some other form of aperture would have been required to introduce the pellets into the chamber, since the morgue had no windows and a single gas-tight door. Thirdly, the argument is confined to morgue 1 at crematorium 2. Although Irving spent hardly any time in his cross-examination of van Pelt on the evidence that gassing took place elsewhere at Auschwitz, it is the Defendants' case that gassing took place in other gas chambers, notably at crematorium 3.

13.83 Despite those curious features, Irving's argument deserves to be taken seriously. I have summarized the Defendants' response to it at paragraphs 7.109 to 7.111 above. In the end, the task for an historian is to weigh the evidence of the absence of signs of holes in the roof of the morgue against the opposing evidence that there were chimneys running through the roof. In my view van Pelt is right in his opinion that it is after so many years difficult to verify whether or not holes at one time existed in a roof which collapsed as long ago as 1944. It is unclear how much of the roof can be seen in the photograph on which Irving relies. The roof is in a bad state, so that it is hard to tell if there were holes in it. There is a possibility that the holes were backfilled. There is the evidence of eye-witnesses who observed or at least described pellets being poured down through the roof of the morgue. Olere's drawing depicts clearly the chimneys running up towards the roof of the gas chamber. Their appearance in his drawing corresponds with the description of them by Tauber and others. Photographs taken in 1942 (or 1943) and 1944, whilst difficult to interpret, are consistent with the presence of protruding chimneys. In these circumstances, I consider that an objective historian, taking account of all the evidence, would conclude that the apparent absence of evidence of holes in the roof of morgue at crematorium 2 falls far short of being a good reason for rejecting the cumulative effect of the evidence on which the Defendants rely.

Gas chambers for fumigation purposes or to serve as air raid shelters

13.84 I have no doubt that Irving is right that there was throughout a need to have fumigation facilities at the camp. There is documentary evidence of concern about the effect on the labour supply of prevailing mortality levels. As van Pelt accepted, ovens would have been required to cremate the large number who succumbed to disease. But in my judgment there is ample evidence which would have convinced an objective commentator that there were also gas chambers which were put to use to kill humans. In the first place there is the eye-witness evidence to which I have referred. Secondly, there is the evidence of van Pelt that the redesign of crematorium 2 in late 1942 was intended to cater for live human beings to walk down to an undressing room before being led into the chamber and to do away with the corpse-slide previously used to convey dead bodies downstairs. Thirdly, there is evidence that a camp doctor asked in January 1943 for the provision of an undressing-room, which would have been unnecessary if the crematorium were intended for corpses. Finally there is the evidence of the letter dated 31 March 1943 in which Bischoff requisitions, as a matter of urgency, a gas-tight door with a spy-hole of extra thickness. It is difficult to see why a spy-hole would be necessary in the door of a chamber used only for fumigating corpses or other objects. For these reasons I do not accept that an objective historian would be persuaded that the gas chambers served only the purposes of fumigation. The evidence points firmly in the direction of a homicidal use of the chambers as well.

13.85 I turn to Irving's alternative argument that the redesign work carried out in early 1943 was to convert crematorium 2 (and crematorium 3) for use as an air-raid shelter. I accept his claim that there was at the time some concern about Allied air-raids in the region. I am prepared to assume in Irving's favour that it was standard practice to equip shelters with gas-tight doors opening outwards and equipped with a peephole (although probably not with a metal grille on the inside). Nevertheless there appear to me to be cogent pragmatic reasons for a historian to conclude that the evidence does not support the air-raid shelter argument.

13.86 If the redesign was to convert the buildings to air raid shelters, there would have been no reason why the drawings and associated documents should not say so. But there is no hint in the documents that such was the intention. The question arises for whose benefit such shelters would have been built. It appears to me to be unlikely that the Nazis would be concerned to shelter the camp inmates. In any case the shelters would have been too small to accommodate more than a fraction of them. But the shelters would not have been suitable for SS personnel either, since the SS barracks were about one and a half miles away. So I cannot accept that this argument comes anywhere near displacing the conclusion to be drawn from the convergent evidence relied on by the Defendants for their contention as to the object of the redesign work.

'Death books'; decrypts and coke consumption

13.87 Irving advanced a number of subsidiary arguments. I can deal with them briefly because they did not impress me. I do not consider that they would have impressed a dispassionate historian either.

13.88 Irving relied on the fact that the camp registers or 'death books' released by the Russians record deaths at Auschwitz, but make no mention of any deaths by gassing. The short answer to this point is that, according to the unchallenged evidence of a large number of witnesses, the books record only the deaths of those who were formally registered as inmates of the camp. The Jews who were selected on arrival to die were taken straight to the gas chambers without being registered. One would not therefore expect to find mention of the cause of death of those Jews in the death books.

13.89 Reports were sent regularly from the camp to Berlin in cypher. They were intercepted and decoded at Bletchley Park. Although these reports often gave the cause of death, they did not mention gassing. In my judgment there are two reasons why little significance is to be attached to this: the first is that there was a strict rule of secrecy about the gassing and the second is that, like the death books, these reports related to registered inmates only.

13.90 Irving argued that the quantity of coke required to burn one body would have been 35kg. He contended that the amount of coke which is recorded as having been delivered to Auschwitz is nothing like enough to kill the number of Jews who the Defendants say lost their lives in the gas chambers. But I accept that the evidence of van Pelt, which was based on contemporaneous documents (see paragraph 7.125 above), that, if the incinerators were operated continuously and many corpses were burnt together so themselves providing fuel, no more than 3.5kg of coke would have been required per corpse.

Conclusion

13.91 Having considered the various arguments advanced by Irving to assail the effect of the convergent evidence relied on by the Defendants, it is my conclusion that no objective, fair-minded historian would have serious cause to doubt that there were gas chambers at Auschwitz and that they were operated on a substantial scale to kill hundreds of thousands of Jews.

Whether Irving is a 'Holocaust denier'

13.92 I accept the evidence of Evans, which was not challenged by Irving, that what characterizes a 'Holocaust denier', in the sense in which that term is used by Lipstadt in *Denying the Holocaust*, is that he or she holds or expresses some or all of the views which I have listed in paragraph 8.5 above.

Irving's statements about the Holocaust

13.93 In paragraphs 8.16 to 8.36 above I have quoted passages from a selection of Irving's statements about the Holocaust. (It is a selection only: the Defendants adduced in evidence many more statements.) I have divided the statements into groups which broadly correspond with the criteria included within Evans's definition of a Holocaust denier. The principal category consists of statements made by Irving denying the existence of gas chambers at Auschwitz or elsewhere. But there are also statements by him denying the existence of a broader policy to exterminate Jews. There are statements too about the number of Jews killed at Auschwitz and in the Holocaust. Finally there are claims by him that the gas chambers were a lie invented by British intelligence.

13.94 In addressing the question whether Irving is justifiably described as Holocaust denier, I make allowance for the fact that, when addressing live audiences as opposed to writing history books, Irving needed to hold the attention of his audience by expressing himself in a vivid and colourful style. I agree that it is necessary to take care to ensure that Irving is not quoted out of context. I accept that merely to question aspects of the Holocaust does not make a person a Holocaust denier. I recognize also that Irving came relatively late to the issue of the Holocaust: he claimed to have paid little attention to it before 1989.

13.95 Even so, it appears to me to be incontrovertible that Irving qualifies as a Holocaust denier. Not only has he denied the existence of gas chambers at Auschwitz and asserted that no Jew was gassed there, he has done so on frequent occasions and sometimes in the most offensive terms. By way of examples, I cite his story of the Jew climbing into a mobile telephone box-cum-gas chamber; his claim that more people died in the back of Kennedy's car at Chappaquiddick than died in the gas chambers at Auschwitz; his dismissal of the eye-witnesses en masse as liars or as suffering from a mental problem; his reference to an Association of Auschwitz Survivors and Other Liars or 'ASSHOLS' and the question he asked of Mrs Altman how much money she had made from her tattoo. I reject as being untrue the claim made by Irving in his evidence that in his denial of the existence of any gas chambers at Auschwitz, he was referring solely to the gas chamber constructed by the Poles after the war for the benefit of visitors to the site or, as Irving put it, as a 'tourist attraction'. In this connection I refer to paragraph 9.13 above. Even if Irving had referred to gas chamber in the singular, it would not have been apparent that he was speaking of the reconstructed gas chamber at the camp.

13.96 Irving has also made broader claims which tend to minimize the Holocaust. For example he has claimed that the Jews in the East were shot by individual gangsters and criminals and that there was no direction or policy in place for mass extermination to be carried out. I do, however, accept that Irving expressed himself in more measured language on this topic than in the case of the gas chambers. But he has also minimized the number of those killed by means other than gas at Auschwitz and elsewhere. Having grossly underestimated the number who lost their lives in the camps, Irving is prone to claim that a greater number than that were killed in Allied bombing raids on Dresden and elsewhere. He has, moreover, repeatedly claimed that the British Psychological War Executive ingeniously invented the lie that the Nazis were killing Jews in gas chambers in order to use it as propaganda.

Whether Irving's denials are borne out by the evidence

13.97 It is part of the Defendants' case on justification that the statements made by Irving which are apostrophized by the Defendants as Holocaust denials are false in the sense that they are unsupported by the evidence. I have summarized in paragraphs 8.16 to 8.36 the reasons why the Defendants so contend.

13.98 I have already made findings that the evidence supports the following propositions: that the shooting of the Jews in the East was systematic and directed from Berlin with the knowledge and approval of Hitler; that there were gas chambers at several of the Operation Reinhard camps and that (as Irving during the trial admitted) hundreds of thousands of Jews were killed in them and that there were gas chambers at Auschwitz, where hundreds of thousands more Jews were gassed to death. It follows that it is my conclusion that Irving's denials of these propositions were contrary to the evidence.

13.99 There remains only the question whether the evidence supports Irving's claim that the gas chambers were a propaganda lie invented by British Intelligence. I have recited the rival contentions of the parties in paragraphs 8.31 to 8.36 above. There are three questions: firstly, did the British invent the notion that Jews were being killed by the Nazis in gas chambers; secondly, even if the British did not invent the story, did they disbelieve it and, thirdly, was use made of the story for propaganda purposes. As to the first question, Irving was unable to present any evidence that the British invented the story. It was provided to the Foreign Office by the secretary to the World Jewish Council, who in turn had received it from a source in Berlin. As to whether the British disbelieved the story, the only evidence to which Irving was able to point was the note made by Cavendish-Bentinck that there was no evidence to support the claim. That appears to me to be far cry from disbelieving the story. As to whether British Intelligence made propaganda use of the story, the evidence produced by Irving extended no further than second-hand accounts of BBC broadcasts about the gassing. There was no indication that British intelligence played any part in these broadcasts. In my judgment the evidence does not support the claim made by Irving.

Whether Irving is an anti-semite and a racist

13.100 I have set out at some length at paragraph 9.5 above the statements made by Irving which the Defendants maintain demonstrate his anti-semitism and at paragraph 9.6 above the statements which the Defendants allege manifest racism. I hope and believe that none of the quotations has been taken out of context. I appreciate the point made by Irving that these statements are a selection from the many millions of words spoken and written by him through which the Defendants have trawled for the purpose of this litigation.

Anti-semitism

13.101 It appears to me to be undeniable that most, if not all, of the statements set out in paragraph 9.5 reveal clear evidence that, in the absence of any excuse or suitable explanation for what he said or wrote, Irving is anti-semitic. His words are directed against Jews, either individually or collectively, in the sense that they are by turns hostile, critical, offensive and derisory in their references to semitic people, their characteristics and appearances. A few examples will suffice: Irving has made claims that the Jews deserve to be disliked; that they brought the Holocaust on themselves; that Jewish financiers are crooked; that Jews generate anti-semitism by their greed and mendacity; that it is bad luck for Mr Wiesel to be called 'Weasel'; that Jews are amongst the scum of humanity; that Jews scurry and hide furtively, unable to stand the light of day; that Simon Wiesenthal has a hideous, leering evil face; and so on.

13.102 In the preceding paragraph I did introduce the caveat that the evidence of Irving's anti-semitism is clear in the absence of any excuse or sensible explanation for his words. It is possible to envisage circumstances in which words, which on their face are anti-semitic, turn out on analysis to be susceptible of innocent explanation. Irving did advance a number of reasons why he claims it is unreasonable to regard him as an anti-semite. I have summarized them at paragraphs 9.9 to 9.17 above.

13.103 The principal explanation or justification offered by Irving for his comments about Jews is that he is seeking to explain to Jews why anti-semitism exists and not himself adopting the anti-semitism. But I do not think that this was the message that Irving was seeking to convey to his audiences and it was certainly not the sense in which his remarks were understood. Irving advances a similar justification of his characterization of the Jewish stereotype as an attempt to warn Jews not to enhance by their conduct the negative public perception of them. If this were Irving's objective, I do not believe that he would have used such offensive language. If (as Irving claims) his remark about Wiesenthal was a joke, it was an anti-semitic joke.

13.104 I have more sympathy for Irving's argument that Jews are not immune from his criticism. He said that he was simply expressing legitimate criticisms of them. Irving gave as an example what he claimed was his justified criticism of the Jews for suppressing his freedom of expression. Another legitimate ground of criticism might be the manner in which Jews in certain parts of the world appear to exploit the Holocaust. I agree that Jews are as open to criticism as anyone else. But it appears to me that Irving has repeatedly crossed the divide between legitimate criticism and prejudiced vilification of the Jewish race and people. I can well understand too that, because of his perceived views, Irving and his family have from time to time been subjected to extreme pressure, for example when his flat house was besieged by rioters in 1994 (see paragraph 9.14 above). In the heat of the moment ill-considered remarks are often made. But it is in just such circumstances that racial prejudice manifests itself. In my view that is what occurred in 1994.

13.105 The inference which in my judgment is clearly to be drawn from what Irving has said and written is that he is anti-semitic.

Racism

13.106 I have concluded that the allegation that Irving is a racist is also established for broadly analogous reasons. This is unsurprising for anti-semitism is a form of racism. It appears to me that the sample quotations set out in paragraph 9.6 above provide ample evidence of racism. The ditty composed by Irving for his daughter is undeniably racist in putting into her mouth the words 'I am a Baby Aryan . . . I have no plans to marry an Ape or Rastafarian'. Similarly, Irving's reference to 'one of them' reading the television news strikes me as evidence of racism of a more insidious kind. The same applies to Irving's proclaimed queasiness on seeing black men playing cricket for England. The manner in which Irving speaks of the AIDS epidemic wiping out blacks, homosexuals, drug addicts and others has in my view a distinctly racist flavour. Irving's statements about coloured immigration are also racist in their overtones even if less overtly so.

13.107 I cannot accept that the various explanations put forward by Irving for what he said and wrote deprive his words of their racist quality. It is possible to employ members of ethnic minorities and yet hold racist views. I do not accept that the statements relied on by the Defendants can be defended as expressions of patriotic sentiments. I reject Irving's explanations, set out at paragraphs 9.19 and 9.21 above, of his comments about the spread of AIDS in Africa and about the feeling of humiliation he experienced when his passport was checked at Heathrow by a Pakistani.

13.108 I accept that Irving is not obsessed with race. He has certainly not condoned or excused racist violence or thuggery. But he has on many occasions spoken in terms which are plainly racist. Racism is to be condemned even if it is confined, as in Irving's case, to expressions of the kind which I have mentioned.

Irving's alleged association with right-wing extremists

13.109 I am conscious of the complaint made by Irving that in this part of their case the Defendants are seeking to prove him guilty by association. In assessing whether there is an ideological motivation underlying what he has written about the Nazis and the Jews, I shall therefore concentrate on what he has himself written and said on the subject. Although Irving invited me to discount what he has said and written down in his many talks in Europe and elsewhere and to concentrate on his historical works, it appears to me that to do so would be artificial and even potentially misleading.

13.110 It does, however, appear to me that some legitimate light is or may be cast on Irving's motivation by an examination of those groups and individuals with whom he associates. It cannot of course be held against Irving that on occasion by happenstance he has found himself at the same meeting, or even on the same platform, as some acknowledged extremist. It is a question of the degree of association.

13.111 Funke in his report made reference to a bewildering array of organizations and individuals. He devoted many pages to a close analysis of the links and relationships between political bodies and the overlap in their policies. But Irving's association with many of those organizations is tenuous to say the least. I am satisfied that Irving has had no significant association with a great many of them. The same applies to the individuals named by Funke. For instance I accept that he has not consciously encountered Thomas Dienel or Michael Kuhnen. I am not persuaded by the evidence that Irving was aware that Dienel was at the meeting at Halle on 9 November 1991.

Right-wing political organizations

13.112 Irving accepted that he has from time to time addressed the German National Democratic Party and the German Peoples' Union. I recognize that these organizations are not banned as being unconstitutional but I accept the evidence of Funke that they and their members are on the extreme right of the political spectrum. There would be many who would refuse any invitation to address meetings of such groups. Irving must be aware of the political complexion of these organizations. His willingness to speak at their meetings is, to put it at its lowest, indicative of a tolerance on his part of right-wing extremism. But I accept that, when he has spoken at their meetings, Irving has not expressed himself in extremist or anti-semitic terms.

13.113 Some time was spent during the evidence viewing a video of a meeting in Halle on 9 November 1991, which was attended by Irving at the invitation of Ursula Worch (see paragraph 10.12 above). Irving complains that the film has been edited and re-edited so as to present him in a prejudicial light. I do not accept that the effect of the editing materially distorts the nature of the meeting. Irving can be seen watching assorted groups, many of them in uniform, march towards the meeting place. Irving is shown on the platform when he was introduced to the crowd. He then addressed the meeting. There is nothing objectionable in what he is recorded as having said. He can be seen shaking his head in disapproval when Nazi slogans such as 'Sieg Heil' are chanted. He spoke in the early afternoon and claimed in his evidence that he left soon afterwards. His diary, however, records him as having left at 5pm. I believe that he remained at the meeting for longer than he was prepared to admit. The significance of the video of the Halle meeting, in my judgment, is that it evidences Irving's willingness to participate in a meeting at which a motley collection of militant neo-Nazis were also present.

13.114 The evidence supports the claim that Irving has associated with several extreme right-wing organizations in the US. He has a close and longstanding relationship with the Institute of Historical Review (see paragraph 10.23 above). It is an avowedly revisionist organization whose membership undoubtedly includes many from the extreme right wing. Irving agreed that the membership of the IHR includes 'cracked anti-semites'. The evidence indicates that Irving is also associated with the National Alliance. I accept the Defendants' case as set out in paragraph 10.24 above. In my view Irving cannot fail to have become aware that the National Alliance is a neo-Nazi and anti-semitic organization. The regularity of Irving's contacts with the National Alliance and its officers confirms Irving's sympathetic attitude towards an organization whose tenets would be abhorrent to most people.

Right-wing individuals

13.115 I am satisfied that Irving has associated to a significant extent with the following individuals: Frey, Deckert, Althans, Philip, the Worches, Christophersen, Staglich, Rami, Varela, Zundel, Remer, Weckert and Faurisson. They are described in paragraphs 10.8 to 10.25

above. They are all right-wing extremists. I have no doubt that most, if not all of them, are neo-Nazis who deny the Holocaust and who are racist and anti-semitic. I also have no doubt that Irving was aware of their political views. His association with such individuals indicates in my judgement that Irving shares many of their political beliefs.

Irving's accounts of the bombing of Dresden

13.116 The immediate question is whether the Defendants have justified their criticisms of Irving's account, principally in *The Destruction of Dresden*, of the circumstances and consequences of the Allied bombing raid on Dresden on the nights of 13 and 14 February 1945. The principal allegation is that Irving relied on forged evidence. But the Defendants also accuse him of misrepresentation, falsification, suppression of the evidence and twisting the facts for his own purposes (see paragraph 11.5 above).

Irving's reliance on the forged Tagesbefehl No. 47

13.117 The forged evidence on which Irving is said to have relied is *Tagesbefehl* (Order of the day) No 47 ('TB47'). The majority of the Defendants' criticisms relate to or are connected with the way in which Irving dealt with this document.

13.118 I have set out in detail in paragraphs 11.9 to 11.40 above the history of the forged TB47 and the parties' respective arguments about Irving's reliance on it. In my judgment there are serious criticisms to be made of Irving's use of this document. In the first place Irving knew all along that there were powerful reasons for doubting the genuineness of the purported TB47. It had been denounced by Seydewitz as fraudulent. Indeed Irving himself was aware that Goebbels had been seeking to take propagandist advantage of the raid by making exaggerated claims as to the number of deaths. Irving in 1963 described the so-called TB47 as 'spurious' (although I accept that at that date he had not seen a copy). When he did receive a copy, he was warned by Lange, the Dresden archivist, that it was a patent forgery. I accept the evidence of Evans, which I have summarized at paragraph 11.18 above, that there were features within the document itself which cast doubt on its *bona fides*. Irving therefore had every reason to be suspicious about the claim that the death toll might ultimately be 250,000.

13.119 Yet when in 1964 Irving received a copy of TB47 from Funfack via Hahn, he appears to have been eager to accept the document as a true copy and the figures claimed in it as accurate. I am not persuaded that there is any valid explanation for Irving's change of heart about the genuineness of the document. Indeed in a memorandum written shortly after he obtained his copy of TB47 Irving expressed distinct reservations about its authenticity and the accuracy of the figures contained in it. In these circumstances it was in my view incumbent of Irving, as a responsible historian, to treat the document with extreme caution. He should have verified the *provenance* of the document with Funfack and with anyone else in a position to assist. In the meantime he should not have made use of so suspect a document.

13.120 There is no evidence that Irving sought Funfack's comments about the document. He did nothing to dispel the doubts he had previously entertained about it. In these circumstances it was in my judgment reprehensible for Irving to write to the Provost of Coventry Cathedral enclosing a copy of the supposed TB47 and expressing himself to be in no doubt as to its authenticity. It was equally reprehensible of Irving to write in similar terms to his German publisher.

13.121 Irving's conduct thereafter is even less defensible. As I have described in paragraph 11.14 above, he was told by Funfack that he was in no position to vouch for TB47. I accept that Irving was also told by Funfack of the estimates of 180,000 and 140,00 put on the number of casualties by Mehnert and Fetscher respectively. But that information (which was never verified) did little to remove the suspicion surrounding TB47. I do not accept Irving's explanation that he disbelieved what Funfack told him because he was living in a regime which was still Communist and was fearful of the consequences of being linked to the Nazi regime. Nor can I accept that the recollection of *Frau* Grosse of the estimate her husband had put on the number of casualties should have weighed significantly with Irving in assessing the reliablity of the figures in TB47.

13.122 Irving made reference to the fake TB47 as a genuine document in the Italian edition of *Dresden* in terms which suggested that it was a genuine document. Doubts about the authenticity of the document were subsequently increased yet further by Miller's letters to Irving to which I have referred at paragraph 11.19. Irving's disregard of that apparently credible evidence was, in my view, a further grave lapse on his part. His explanation that he considered that Miller was 'fantasizing' when he gave a figure of 30,000 deaths strikes me as absurd. There was nothing in what Miller wrote to suggest to an objective commentator that Miller was other than a credible and reliable witness. (In the event the figure in the genuine TB47 turned out to be 25,000 which was close to Miller's figure.) The subsequent publication of TB47 in an appendix to the 1966 Corgi edition of *Dresden* without the expression of any reservations about its genuineness or the figures contained in it was in my view another grave lapse on Irving's part.

13.123 The Final Report and Situation Report No 1404, to which I have referred in paragraphs 11.23 and 11.24 above, would have been regarded by any dispassionate historian as conclusive proof that the purported copy of TB47 was a fake and that there was good reason to suppose that the death toll was in the region of 25,000. This was the figure accepted by Reichert in his book on the bombing, which is regarded by Evans as authoritative. I accept that Irving is entitled to credit for having taken the unusual step of writing to *The Times* about the new casualty figure. But that does not in my judgment excuse the doubts he continued to cast upon the accuracy of the new figure, still less does it excuse the grossly inflated claims as to the number of casualties which Irving continued to make in a subsequent edition of *Dresden* and in the speeches detailed in paragraphs 11.6 and 11.7 above.

13.124 When asked what was the supporting evidence for these inflated claims, Irving relied on the estimates for the number of casualties made by Mehnert and Fetscher and on the recollection of Frau Grosse, which I have mentioned. He also testified that his claims had been based on estimates as high as 250,000 which he had received from a great many individuals. Irving neither identified the individuals nor disclosed the letters. He prayed in aid also the fact that there were in Dresden at the time an unquantified number of refugees fleeing before the advancing Russian army. Finally he relied on the estimate of Hans Voigt, summarized in paragraph 11.52 above, that 135,000 had been killed. But, as stated in paragraph 13.126 below, none of this material casts significant doubt on the accumulation of evidence that the true death toll was within the bracket of 25–30,000.

Whether Irving has attached credence to unreliable evidence and/or failed to take account of reliable evidence

13.125 The unreliable evidence upon which, according to the Defendants, Irving was unjustified in relying is set out in the preceding paragraph. Historical evidence cannot of course be compartmentalized into reliable and unreliable evidence. It is part of the skill of an historian to evaluate the degree of individual items of evidence, seeking to adopt a consistent approach throughout.

13.126 It appears to me that the evidence which I have summarized in paragraph 13.124 affords a very slender basis for the claims which Irving has made for the numbers killed in the raids. The evidence of Mehnert, Fetscher and Frau Grosse was secondhand and unverified. In the absence of any indication on what they were based, I do not consider that Irving should have given any credence to estimates in letters from unidentified individuals. His speculation about the number of refugees does little to cast doubt on the reliability of the figures quoted in the official reports. Voigt's evidence was uncorroborated and unlikely to be correct in the light of the number of deaths recorded on the official cards. In my view, Irving should not have quoted numbers based on this evidence. Irving should have taken far greater account of the doubts about the genuineness of TB47; of the cogent and credible evidence of Miller and above all of the figures contained in the Final Report and in Situation Report No 1404. Having done so, Irving should have discounted altogether the unsatisfactory evidence collected in paragraph 13.124 above. In my judgment the estimates of 100,000 and more deaths which Irving continued to put about in the 1990s lacked any evidential basis and were such as no responsible historian would have made.

Whether Irving has bent or falsified or misrepresented evidence

13.127 I am not persuaded that the criticism of Irving for the way in which he presented the statistical evidence of Dr Sperling is justified. I accept the explanation given by Irving why he chose to rely on his higher figure, namely that the estimate which he gave unofficially in a letter was the most reliable one. In the light of Irving's assertion that he had seen evidence which established that Mehnert had informed Kleiner that his estimate of the number of deaths was 40,000, I am not prepared to accept the Defendants' contention that this was an invention on Irving's part. The other criticisms of Irving under this head have already been addressed in the earlier paragraphs of this section of the judgment.

Irving's conduct in relation to the Goebbels diaries in the Moscow archive

13.128 I do not consider that the issues as to Irving's conduct in relation to the Goebbels diaries in the Moscow archive have any bearing whatsoever on the central issue of Irving's conduct as an historian. But Irving complains of Lipstadt's account of his conduct and the Defendants seek to justify those criticisms. I shall therefore deal with this discrete issue now.

13.129 The two questions raised by this part of the plea of justification are, firstly, whether Irving broke (or, to use Lipstadt's word, 'violated') an agreement with the Moscow archive in regard to his use of the glass plates on which the Goebbels diaries were inscribed and, secondly, whether by the manner in which he handled the plates Irving placed them at risk of damage.

The alleged breach of agreement

13.130 There were two occasions on which Irving removed plates from the archive: the first was on 10 June 1992, when he wanted to make copies of the plates; the second was on the following day when he removed two more plates in order to take them to London for testing. The two occasions need to be considered separately.

13.131 In relation to the first occasion, as I have summarized in paragraphs 12.9 and 12.17 above, there was a conversation between Millar and Tarasov, who telephoned Bondarev to tell him to grant Irving access to the diaries. Irving stressed (and Millar confirmed) that there was no agreement as such with the Russians. I accept that there was nothing more than a single conversation between Millar and Tarasov. But it is possible to infer an agreement from that conversation and from the parties' subsequent conduct. In my view it is right to do so.

13.132 Was there an implied term of that inferred agreement that Irving should not remove the plates from the archive? This question falls to be answered by reference to the circumstances as they existed in Moscow at the time. According to Irving, the archive was in a state of chaos. The Russians were willing to sell archive material if the price was right. There were no copying facilities in the archive. Irving testified that it was neither here nor there to the archivist if he removed the plates. I bear in mind that Irving acknowledged that he removed the plates 'illicitly'. But he denied breaching any agreement and I took him to mean that the removal was illicit in the sense that in normal circumstances an historian would not remove material from an archive. In these somewhat unusual circumstances I am not persuaded that Irving broke an agreement when he removed the plates overnight to have them copied.

13.133 The second occasion when plates were removed was rather different in the sense that Irving sought and obtained permission to remove the plates from the archive. The breach of agreement, according to the Defendants, arises out of the fact that, having removed the plates from the archive, Irving then took them to England to have them tested prior to their return to the archive. Was this a breach of the arrangement? Irving did not tell the Russians of his intentions. But there is no evidence that the Russians showed interest or concern what would happen to the plates whilst they were out of the archive. I have no doubt that it was throughout Irving's intention to return the plates. I am not satisfied that a breach of an implied term of the arrangement has been established by the Defendants.

The alleged risk of damage to the plates

13.134 It is clear to me that, according to what Lipstadt wrote in *Denying the Holocaust* and the Summary of the Defendants' case, her allegation was that the risk of damage arose on the occasion of the second removal of plates from the archive. According to Lipstadt, it was the transport of the plates to England and the testing which took place there, followed by the return journey to Moscow, which gave rise to the risk of damage. It was this which caused 'serious concern in archival circles' about significant damage to the plates. I do not consider that the evidence bears out the allegation that any real risk of significant damage did arise. According to the unchallenged evidence of Irving, the plates were at all times securely packaged. When they were in possession of others, I see no reason to suppose that they were at risk. Showing one plate at a meeting in Munich does not appear to me to give rise to a risk of damage. When Irving left the plates in Munich, whilst he made an excursion to Rome, they were left in the hotel safe. In England the tests were carried out in reputable laboratories belonging to Kodak and Pilkington. I am satisfied that the physical interference was minimal and caused no risk to the integrity of the plates. The emulsion of the plates was not tested. Irving may well be right in his comment that the plates were safer whilst in his custody than they were in the archive. Accordingly I do not accept that the allegation of risk of damage to the plates is made out in relation to their removal from the archive to be taken to England for testing.

13.135 But the Defendants advanced an argument that, on the occasion of the first removal on 10 June, the plates were put at risk when they were left during the afternoon hidden behind a wall on some waste ground a short distance from the archive. I am satisfied that the plates were carefully wrapped in cardboard and plastic thereby eliminating the risk of physical damage. So the only risk which might be said to arise was if someone came across the plates by chance and removed them. Bearing in mind how far this is removed from the risk of which Lipstadt wrote and the unlikelihood of a passer-by showing interest in a package consisting of a couple of pieces of glass, I am not prepared to find that the allegation of risk to the plates is proved.

Assessment of Irving as an historian

The issue as to Irving's motivation

13.136 After that brief digression to Moscow, I return to the central issue of Irving's historiography. As I have already held, the passages in *Denying the Holocaust* of which Irving complains include as an important part of their defamatory sting the meaning that he has *deliberately* falsified and distorted the historical evidence because he is an apologist for and a partisan of Hitler and on that account is intent on exonerating him.

13.137 Irving considers, rightly, that this is a grave imputation because it reflects on his integrity as an historian. It is an imputation which the Defendants have sought to justify. Because of the seriousness of the charge, the standard of proof required is, in accordance with the approach which I have outlined in paragraph 4.10 above, commensurately higher. It goes without saying that it is an issue which requires anxious consideration.

13.138 It is necessary to define clearly what is the issue which must be decided. In the earlier parts of this section of the judgement, I have made findings adverse to Irving in relation to his historiography and in relation to his account of Hitler's attitude towards the Jews including in particular Hitler's complicity in the policy of exterminating them. I have further made findings, also adverse to Irving, in relation to his claims about Auschwitz and in relation to his account of the bombing of Dresden. Irving sought to defend what he has written and said as being a fair and accurate account of the historical evidence available to him. In the respects already set out in detail in this judgement, I have in the main found against him. But the Defendants must, as they accept, go further if they are to succeed in their plea of justification: they must establish that the misrepresentation by Irving of the historical record was deliberate in the sense that Irving was motivated by a desire borne of his own ideological beliefs to present Hitler in a favourable light. Irving's case is that, if (which he denied but which I have found) he has misrepresented the evidence, such misrepresentation was innocent in the sense that it arose through simple mistake or misapprehension. He denied the charge of deliberate falsification or perversion of the evidence. The issue which I must decide is whether the Defendants have proved that denial to be false.

The relevant considerations

13.139 Issues as to a person's motivation have to be decided by reference not only to the direct evidence of the person concerned (in this case Irving) but also by reference to the surrounding circumstances from which inferences as to his motivation may be drawn. In the present case such circumstances include the nature and extent of the misrepresentations of the evidence together with Irving's explanation or excuse for them. But in my judgment it is relevant to take into account also such matters as Irving's conduct and attitudes outwith the immediate context of his work as a professional historian, including the evidence of his political or ideological beliefs as derived from his speeches, his diaries and his associates. I also consider that it is material to have regard to the manner in which he has conducted these proceedings. These are all matters from which inferences may legitimately be drawn as to Irving's motivation.

The convergence of the historiographical misrepresentations

13.140 Historians are human: they make mistakes, misread and misconstrue documents and overlook material evidence. I have found that, in numerous respects, Irving has misstated historical evidence; adopted positions which run counter to the weight of the evidence; given credence to unreliable evidence and disregarded or dismissed credible evidence. It appears to me that an analysis of those instances may shed light on the question whether Irving's misrepresentation of the historical evidence was deliberate.

13.141 I have found that most of the Defendants' historiographical criticisms of Irving set out in section v. of this judgement are justified. In the vast majority of those instances the effect of what Irving has written has been to portray Hitler in a favourable light and to divert blame from him onto others. I have held that this is unjustified by the evidence. Examples include Irving's portrayal of Hitler's conduct and attitude towards the events of *Kristallnacht* and the importance attached by Irving to Hitler's attitude towards the Jewish question as he claims is evidenced by the Schlegelberger note. I have seen no instance where Irving has misinterpreted the evidence or misstated the facts in a manner which is detrimental to Hitler. Irving appears to take every opportunity to exculpate Hitler. The same is true of the broader criticism made by the Defendants' of Irving's unwarrantedly favourable depiction of Hitler in regard to his attitude towards the Jews, which criticism I have found in section vi. above to be justified. Irving sought in his writings to distance Hitler from the programme of shooting Jews in the East and from the later genocide in the death camps in a manner which the evidence did not warrant. Irving has argued, unjustifiably as I have found, that the evidence indicates that Hitler was unaware of any programme for the extermination of Jews at Auschwitz. In his account of the bombing of Dresden Irving (as I have found in section xi.above) persistently exaggerates the number of casualties, so enabling him to make comparisons between the number of civilians killed in Allied bombing raids with the number of Jews killed in the camps.

13.142 In my opinion there is force in the opinion expressed by Evans that all Irving's historiographical 'errors' converge, in the sense that they all tend to exonerate Hitler and to reflect Irving's partisanship for the Nazi leader. If indeed they were genuine errors or mistakes, one would not expect to find this consistency. I accept the Defendants' contention that this convergence is a cogent reason for supposing that the evidence has been deliberately slanted by Irving.

The nature of some of Irving's errors

13.143 As I have already indicated it is material to take account of the nature or quality of what Irving claims to have been mistakes or misapprehensions on his part. Certain of Irving's misrepresentations of the historical evidence might appear to be simple mistakes on his part, for instance the misreading of *haben* as *Juden* in Himmler's telephone log for 1 December 1941. But there are other occasions where Irving's treatment of the historical evidence is so perverse and egregious that it is difficult to accept that it is inadvertence on his part. Examples include Irving's rejection of the evidence for the existence of gas chambers at Auschwitz; his claim that Hitler lost interest in anti-semitism on coming to power; his account of Hitler's meeting with Horthy in April 1943;

his wholesale dismissal of the testimony of Marie Vaillant-Couturier and his continued reliance on the forged *Tagesbefehl* No. 47 which purportedly gave the number of casualties in Dresden. I have referred in the course of this judgment to other instances where Irving's account flies in the face of the available evidence.

13.144 Mistakes and misconceptions such as these appear to me by their nature unlikely to have been innocent. They are more consistent with a willingness on Irving's part knowingly to misrepresent or manipulate or put a 'spin' on the evidence so as to make it conform with his own preconceptions. In my judgment the nature of these misstatements and misjudgments by Irving is a further pointer towards the conclusion that he has deliberately skewed the evidence to bring it into line with his political beliefs.

Irving's explanations for his errors

13.145 In the course of his cross-examination Irving was asked on numerous occasions to provide explanations for what he had written or said. Thus he was asked why he had omitted to make reference to apparently significant events; why he had relied on sources whose reliability there was good reason to doubt; what was the source of evidence for particular assertions. It seems to me that one way of testing whether Irving's errors were the product of innocent mistakes on his part is to look at his explanations.

13.146 In his answers Irving offered various explanations for his omission of apparently significant evidence. He gave as the reason why he did not refer to the evidence of Hofmann when dealing with the trial of Hitler in 1924 that it was too long to be included. But the records of Hofmann's testimony ran to no more than five pages. He sought to excuse his omission to include in his account of the shooting of Berlin Jews in Riga the claim made by Bruns that there had been a Hitler order by saying that it 'would bore the pants off an audience'. Asked to explain why he omitted to refer in the 1991 edition of *Hitler's War* to the sinister fate awaiting the 600,000 French Jews who were not well-to-do and so not to kept healthy and alive, Irving answered that the 1991 edition was an abridged version and the omission had to be made for editorial reasons. His explanation for not informing his readers of the reasons for supposing that the Schlegelberger note may have been concerned with the problem of the mischlinge was that he was writing a book which had to be kept within the confines of a single volume. Irving gave a similar explanation for his suppression (as the Defendants claim that it was) of material parts of Goebbels' diary entry of 27 March 1942. Irving excused his inability to answer certain questions about Auschwitz (for example about cremations there and his reason for not having visited Auschwitz) by saying that he is not an expert on Auschwitz. Irving blamed his editor for the retention of his mistranslation of *haben zu bleiben* as 'Jews are to stay' after he had been informed of his error. When he was asked to identify the eye-witness who told him about the telephone box-cum-gas chamber story, Irving replied that he could not recall but that he had read about it or seen it some ten years ago. Earlier in this judgment I have cited other examples of Irving's explanations for his lapses.

13.147 I recognize that it is not always easy for Irving to cast his mind back over the years so as to explain why and how his mistakes were made. In my view, however, in many instances, including those set out in the preceding paragraph, the explanations which he offered were unconvincing. The absence of credible explanations lends further support to the Defendants' argument that Irving's misrepresentation of the historical record was not inadvertent.

Irving's readiness to challenge the authenticity of inconvenient documents and the credibility of apparently credible witnesses

13.148 I accept that it is necessary for historians, not least historians of the Nazi era, to be on their guard against documents which are forged or otherwise unauthentic. But it appeared to me that in the course of these proceedings Irving challenged the authenticity of certain documents, not because there was any substantial reason for doubting their genuineness but because they did not fit in with his thesis.

13.149 The prime example of this is Irving's dismissal of Bischoff's letter of 28 June 1943 dealing with the incineration capacity of the ovens at Auschwitz (to which I have referred at paragraph 7.106 and 7.120).As already stated at paragraph 13.76 I agree with the assessment of van Pelt that there is little reason to doubt the authenticity of this document. Yet Irving argued strenuously that it should be dismissed as a forgery. In my judgment he did so because it does not conform to his ideological agenda. Similarly Irving devoted much time to challenging the authenticity of Muller's instruction to furnish Hitler with reports of the shooting. I believe that he did so because this was for him an inconvenient document and not because there were real doubts about it genuineness. (Irving ultimately accepted its *bona fides*). There were other occasions when Irving sought to cast doubt on the authenticity of documents relied on by the Defendants (for example the Anne Frank diaries and the report of the gassing of 97,000 Jews at Chelmno referred to at paragraph 6.71 above). In neither case did Irving's doubts appear to me to have any real substance. His attitude to these documents was in stark contrast to his treatment of other documents which were more obviously open to question. One example is Irving's unquestioning acceptance of the Schlegelberger memorandum despite the uncertainty of its provenance. Another is his reliance on *Tagesbefehl* No. 47 in the teeth of mounting evidence that it was a forgery. In my judgment there is force in the Defendants' contention that Irving on occasion applies double standards to the documentary evidence, accepting documents which fit in with his thesis and rejecting those which do not.

13.150 As I have already observed in the course of dealing with the historiographical criticism of Irving, there is a comparable lack of even-handedness when it comes to Irving's treatment of eye-witnesses. He takes a highly sceptical approach towards the evidence of the survivors and camp officials at Auschwitz and elsewhere who confirm the genocidal operation of gas chambers at the camp (Tauber, Olere, Wisliceny, Hoss and Miller). But in relation to other witnesses (such as Hitler's adjutants, Christa Schroder and Voigt), where there is greater reason for caution about their testimony, Irving appears to adopt it uncritically. I accept that Irving had interviewed personally many of the witnesses in the latter category and so could form his own assessment. Even so, the contrast in approach is remarkable.

13.151 The double standards which Irving adopts to some of the documents and to some of the witnesses appears to me to be further evidence that Irving is seeking to manipulate the evidence rather than approaching it as a dispassionate, if sometimes mistaken, historian.

Irving's concessions

13.152 It was a striking feature of the case that in the course of it Irving made, or appeared to make, concessions about major issues. In doing so he resiled from the stance adopted by him in relation to those issues before trial. Such concessions were made by Irving in relation to the shooting of Jews in the East; the use of gas vans at Chelmno and in Yugoslavia; the gassing of Jews at the Action Reinhard camps; the existence and genocidal use of gas chambers at Auschwitz and the Leuchter report.

13.153 Thus the Defendants contend that, having previously asserted that the shooting of Jews in the East was generally unauthorized and carried out by small bands of criminals with Hitler's partial knowledge but without any order from him, Irving accepted at trial that perhaps as many as 1.5 million Jews were killed on the authority of Heydrich and on a systematic basis. He conceded also that Hitler not only knew of the shooting of the Jews in the East but also sanctioned their murder. He agreed that Hitler had taken the initiative in ridding the Altreich of Jews. Irving's concessions on these issues were in stark contrast to his case as it stood before trial.

13.154 At a later stage in the trial, however, Irving retracted, as least in part, the concessions he had made. He partially withdrew his acceptance of Hitler's responsibility for the shooting. In a written submission Irving argued that the treatment of deported Jews suggested a lack of system and co-ordination and that there was no clear and unambiguous evidence of Hitler's awareness of the mass murder in the East of European Jews. Irving claimed that he had adopted the position before trial that the killing of the Jews in the East had been largely systematic and much of it had been carried out under orders. He claimed that there was no significant shift of position on his part. But it appears to me that Irving did shift his ground in a significant way in the course of the trial, especially in regard to Hitler's authorization of the killing.

13.155 In regard to the use of gas vans, Irving was prepared before trial to accept no more than that there had been an 'alleged liquidation' of 152,000 Jews at Chelmno and that gas vans had been used on an experimental basis and on a very limited scale. At trial he accepted that there had been a systematic use of gas vans at the camp; that in one relatively short period 97,000 Jews had been murdered there and that he had been wrong to say that the use of the vans was experimental. He also accepted that the Nazis used gas vans to kill Jews in Yugoslavia instead of shooting them. Irving's explanation for these changes in his case was that he was making admissions in order to deal with the issues expeditiously.

13.156 In relation to the Reinhard camps, having claimed before the trial that there were no gas chambers at Treblinka, Sobibor or Belzec, Irving accepted at trial that he could not challenge the accepted figures for the numbers of Jews killed at those camps which were 700–950,000, 200,000 and 550,000 respectively. He again later explained his concessions as having been made 'formally' in order to speed the trial along, adding later that he had seen no documentary evidence to support the figures for those killed. I have already given my reaction to that response.

13.157 I have earlier summarized the manner in which Irving altered his position in relation to the number of Jews killed there by gas but also to the existence of homicidal gas chambers at Auschwitz. On both these issues there was in my view a radical shift of ground. Irving says that he has always accepted that many Jews were killed at Auschwitz. So he has, but not by gassing.

13.158 I have also described Irving's concessions in relation to the Leuchter report: see paragraph 7.89. Irving had previously expressed the view that the conclusions of the report were irrefutable. At trial, as has been seen, he agreed without any great protest that the vast majority of Leuchter's findings were wrong and the report was fundamentally flawed.

13.159 What is the significance of these alterations in Irving's stance in relation to the issue with which I am at present concerned, namely Irving's motivation? It seems to me that the Defendants are justified in their contention that Irving's readiness to resile from positions he had adopted in what he has written and said about important aspects of the Holocaust demonstrates his willingness to make assertions about the Nazi era which, as he must appreciate, are irreconcilable with the available evidence. I also consider that there is force in the Defendants' contention that Irving's retraction of some of his concessions, made when he was confronted with the evidence relied on by the Defendants, manifests a determination to adhere to his preferred version of history, even if the evidence does not support it.

Extraneous circumstances: Irving's denials of the Holocaust, his racism, anti-semitism and association with right-wing extremists

13.160 I pointed out in paragraph 13.139 above that there may be circumstances extraneous to Irving's practice of his profession as an historian from which it may be the legitimate to draw inferences as to whether his misrepresentation of the historical evidence has been deliberate. If the evidence supports the view that Irving is a dispassionate objective student and chronicler of the Nazi era, that would militate powerfully against the conclusion that he is working to an agenda of his own. Conversely, if the extraneous evidence indicates that Irving holds views which are pro-Nazi and anti-semitic and that he is an active protagonist and supporter of extreme right-wing policies, that would support the inference that he perverts the historical evidence so as to make it conform with his ideological beliefs.

13.161 I have already set out in section viii. above my conclusion that Irving displays all the characteristics of a Holocaust denier. He repeatedly makes assertions about the Holocaust which are offensive to Jews in their terms and unsupported by or contrary to the historical record. I have also given at section ix. above the reasons for my findings that Irving is an anti-semite and a racist. As I have found in section x above, Irving associates regularly with extremist and neo-Nazi organizations and individuals. The conclusion which I draw from the evidence is that Irving is sympathetic towards and on occasion promotes the views held by those individuals and organizations.

13.162 It is not difficult to discern a pattern to the activities and attitudes to which I have alluded in the preceding paragraph. Over the past fifteen years or so, Irving appears to have become more active politically than was previously the case. He speaks regularly at political or quasi-political meetings in Germany, the United States, Canada and the New World. The content of his speeches and interviews often displays a distinctly pro-Nazi and anti-Jewish bias. He makes surprising and often unfounded assertions about the Nazi regime which tend to exonerate the Nazis for the appalling atrocities which they inflicted on the Jews. He is content to mix with neo-fascists and appears to share many of their racist and anti-semitic prejudices. The picture of Irving which emerges from the evidence of his extra-curricular activities reveals him to be a right-wing pro-Nazi polemicist. In my view the Defendants have established that Irving has a political agenda. It is one which, it is legitimate to infer, disposes him, where he deems it necessary, to manipulate the historical record in order to make it conform with his political beliefs.

Finding as to Irving's motivation

13.163 Having reviewed what appear to me to be the relevant considerations, I return to the issue which I defined in paragraph 13.138 above. I find myself unable to accept Irving's contention that his falsification of the historical record is the product of innocent error or misinterpretation or incompetence on his part. When account is taken of all the considerations set out in paragraphs 13.140 to 13.161 above, it appears to me that the correct and inevitable inference must be that for the most part the falsification of the historical record was deliberate and that Irving was motivated by a desire to present events in a manner consistent with his own ideological beliefs even if that involved distortion and manipulation of historical evidence.

Finding in relation to the defence of justification

The test

13.164 I have already set out at paragraphs 4.7 to 4.9 above the test which is to be applied when deciding the fate of the plea of justification, namely whether the Defendants have established to the appropriate standard that the imputations published about Irving are, in the meanings which I have found them to bear, *substantially* justified. As I have pointed out, the Defendants are entitled, if and to the extent that may be necessary, to take advantage of the provisions of section 5 of the Defamation Act 1952.

*The anti-Zionist conference, the Moscow archive and section 5 of the
Defamation Act 1952*

13.165 My overall finding in relation to the plea of justification is that
the Defendants have proved the substantial truth of the imputations,
most of which relate to Irving's conduct as an historian, with which I
have dealt in paragraphs 13.7 to 13.127 above. My finding is that the
defamatory meanings set out in paragraph 2.15 above at (i), (ii), (iii)
and the first part of (iv) are substantially justified.

13.166 But there are certain defamatory imputations which I have found
to be defamatory of Irving but which have not been proved to be true.
The Defendants made no attempt to prove the truth of Lipstadt's claim
that Irving was scheduled to speak at an anti-Zionist conference in
Sweden in 1992, which was also to be attended by various representatives of terrorist organizations such as Hezbollah and Hamas. Nor did
they seek to justify Lipstadt's claim that Irving has a self-portrait by
Hitler hanging over his desk. Furthermore the Defendants have, as I
have held, failed in their attempt to justify the defamatory imputations
made against Irving in relation to the Goebbels diaries in the Moscow
archive. The question which I have to ask myself is whether the
consequence of the Defendants' failure to prove the truth of these
matters is that the defence of justification fails in its entirety.

13.167 The answer to that question requires me to decide whether (I
am paraphrasing section 5 of the Defamation Act 1952) the failure on
the part of the Defendants to prove the truth of those charges materially
injures the reputation of Irving, in view of the fact that the other
defamatory charges made against him have been proved to be justified.
The charges which I have found to be substantially true include the
charges that Irving has for his own ideological reasons persistently and
deliberately misrepresented and manipulated historical evidence; that
for the same reasons he has portrayed Hitler in an unwarrantedly
favourable light, principally in relation to his attitude towards and
responsibility for the treatment of the Jews; that he is an active Holocaust
denier; that he is anti-semitic and racist and that he associates with
right-wing extremists who promote neo-Nazism. In my judgment the
charges against Irving which have been proved to be true are of
sufficient gravity for it be clear that the failure to prove the truth of the

matters set out in paragraph 13.165 above does not have any material effect on Irving's reputation.

13.168 In the result therefore the defence of justification succeeds.

xiv. Verdict

14.1 It follows that there must be judgment for the Defendants.